Beginning C# 2008

From Novice to Professional

D1517834

Christian Gross

Apress®

Beginning C# 2008: From Novice to Professional

Copyright © 2007 by Christian Gross

ISBN-13 (pbk): 978-1-59059-869-6

ISBN-10 (pbk): 1-59059-869-5

eISBN-13: 978-1-4302-0417-6

Printed and bound in the United States of America 9 8 7 6 5 4 3 2

Lead Editor: Ewan Buckingham
Technical Reviewer: Christian Kenyeres
Editorial Board: Steve Anglin, Ewan Buckingham, Tony Campbell, Gary Cornell, Jonathan Gennick, Jason Gilmore, Kevin Goff, Jonathan Hassell, Matthew Moodie, Joseph Ottinger, Jeffrey Pepper, Ben Renow-Clarke, Dominic Shakeshaft, Matt Wade, Tom Welsh
Project Manager: Sofia Marchant
Copy Editor: Marilyn Smith
Associate Production Director: Kari Brooks-Copony
Production Editor: Kelly Winquist
Compositor: Kinetic Publishing Services
Proofreader: Nancy Riddiough
Indexer: Broccoli Information Management
Artist: Kinetic Publishing Services
Cover Designer: Kurt Krames
Manufacturing Director: Tom Debolski

Distributed to the book trade worldwide by Springer-Verlag New York, Inc., 233 Spring Street, 6th Floor, New York, NY 10013. Phone 1-800-SPRINGER, fax 201-348-4505, e-mail orders-ny@springer-sbm.com, or visit http://www.springeronline.com.

For information on translations, please contact Apress directly at 2855 Telegraph Avenue, Suite 600, Berkeley, CA 94705. Phone 510-549-5930, fax 510-549-5939, e-mail info@apress.com, or visit http://www.apress.com.

The source code for this book is available to readers at http://www.apress.com.

Some food for thought when writing software:

"A common mistake that people make when trying to design something completely foolproof is to underestimate the ingenuity of complete fools."

"The major difference between a thing that might go wrong and a thing that cannot possibly go wrong is that when a thing that cannot possibly go wrong goes wrong it usually turns out to be impossible to get at or repair."

—Douglas Adams, Mostly Harmless

Contents at a Glance

Contents

About the Author

Many people say that by looking at a person's dog, you can tell what the person is like. Well, the picture is of my dog Louys, an English bulldog. And yes, my English bulldog and I have many common characteristics.

But what about the biography of the author, **CHRISTIAN GROSS**? It's pretty simple: I'm a guy who has spent oodles of time strapped to a chair debugging and taking apart code. In fact, I really enjoy this business we call software development. I have loved it ever since I learned how to peek and poke my first bytes. I have written various books, including *Ajax and REST Recipes: A Problem-Solution Approach, Foundations of Object-Oriented Programming Using .NET 2.0 Patterns*, and *A Programmer's Introduction to Windows DNA*, all available from Apress.

These days, I enjoy coding and experimenting with .NET, as it is a fascinating environment. .NET makes me feel like a kid opening a present on Christmas morning. You had an idea what the gift was, but you were not completely sure. And with .NET, there is no relative giving you socks or a sweater. It's excitement all the way!

About the Technical Reviewer

CHRISTIAN KENYERES, principal architect for Collaborative Consulting, is a visionary technology professional with more than 15 years of extensive information technology experience. He has served numerous high-profile clients as an enterprise architect and boasts a broad range of technical and business knowledge.

Prior to joining Collaborative, Christian performed consulting for various companies such as Compaq, EMC, Fidelity Investments, Liberty Mutual Insurance, and John Hancock. He holds B.S. and M.S. degrees in Computer Science from the University of Massachusetts and Boston University, respectively.

Introduction

The first computer programming book I read was entitled *Programming Windows 3.0* by Charles Petzold. This was around the time when Microsoft Windows 3.0 (circa 1992) once and for all showed the industry that Microsoft was a company with a future. Writing code for Windows back then was complicated by many things: lack of documentation, 16-bit architecture, and the necessity of buying a compiler separate from the software development kit (SDK). Charles's book tied everything together and solved the problem of how to write a program for Windows.

Now the problems are quite the opposite: we have too much documentation, we have 64-bit architectures, and everything including the kitchen sink is thrown into a development environment. Now we need to figure out what we actually need. We have too many options—too many ways to solve the same problem. What I am trying to do with this book is the same thing that Charles did for me when I first started out, and that was to help me figure out what I needed to write code.

This book is about explaining the C# programming language in the context of solving problems. C# has become a sophisticated programming language that can achieve many goals, but you are left wondering what techniques to use when. This book is here to answer your questions.

This book is not a reference to all of the features of the C# programming language. I don't explain the esoteric C# features. I stick to the C# programming features that you will use day in and day out. That does not mean that you will be missing certain C# programming language constructs, because I have covered all of the major features.

To get the full benefit of this book, I suggest that you do the exercises at the end of the chapters. The answers are available on the Apress web site (`http://www.apress.com`), and you can cheat and not do the exercises, but I advise against that.

If you are a beginning programmer who has no clue about C#, and you read this book and do the exercises, I am almost entirely sure that you will be a solid and knowledgeable C# programmer by the end of the book. If that sounds like a big promise, well, yes it is. The chapter text is intended to get you acquainted with the C# programming language and how to apply its features. The exercises are intended to make sure you actually understand the C# programming language and its features.

The chapter exercises are challenging. They cannot be solved within a few minutes. In fact, when I did all of the exercises, it took me five working-hour days to do all of them!

If you have any questions, such as, "So what was he trying to get at with that exercise?" I am available on Skype with the user ID christianhgross. Please don't just ring me. First chat using text, and if necessary, we can have a voice conversation. Also, you can send e-mail to me at `christianhgross@gmail.com`.

Thanks and good luck.

■ ■ ■

CHAPTER 1

Ready, Steady, Go!

This book is about the C# programming language first and foremost. It is about becoming a proficient C# programmer. Reading this book from cover to cover will not make you a superstar, but it will make you a programmer who understands what needs to be done when writing robust, stable, and maintainable C# applications.

In this chapter, you'll get started by acquiring the tools you need to develop C# applications and taking those tools for a test spin. Along the way, you'll create a couple C# applications.

Downloading and Installing the Tools

Getting started with C# 3.0, you're probably really excited about writing some code that does something. It's like getting your driver's license and wanting to drive a car without even thinking about where you want to drive. You just want to drive. The great part of .NET is that you can start writing some code after you have installed either the .NET software development kit (.NET SDK) or a Visual Studio integrated development environment (IDE). Downloading and installing the right environment is critical to taking your first step toward an enjoyable coding experience.

■**Note** Software version numbers, product descriptions, and technologies can be confusing. Having used Microsoft technologies for over a decade, I can say that naming a technology or product has never been Microsoft's strong point. The technologies have (for the most part) been great, but product classification and identification have not been so great. Thus, this book covers the C# 3.0 programming language that is used to write applications for the .NET Framework. With C# 3.0, the .NET 3.0 and 3.5 Frameworks are used. .NET 3.0 gives you all of the essentials, and .NET 3.5 gives you the extras.

For the examples in this book, you'll be using Visual C# 2008 Express Edition, because it's freely available and has everything you need to get started with C# 3.0. The other Express Edition IDEs available from Microsoft are tailored to different languages (Visual Basic and C++) or, in the case of Visual Web Developer Express, specific functionality that is too restrictive for our purposes.

Microsoft also offers full versions of the Visual Studio IDE, such as the Standard, Professional, and Team editions. Each of these editions has different features and different price tags. See the Microsoft Visual Studio web site (http://msdn2.microsoft.com/en-us/vstudio/default.aspx) for more information. If you already have Visual Studio 2008 Professional, you can use that for the examples in this book. That edition can do everything that Visual C# Express can do, and in fact, has many more options.

▓Note I personally use Visual Studio Standard or Professional in combination with other tools such as X-develop and JustCode! from Omnicore (http://www.omnicore.com), TestDriven.NET (http://www.testdriven.net/), and NUnit (http://www.nunit.org). The Visual Studio products are very good, but others are available. Being a good developer means knowing which tools work best for you.

Installing and downloading Visual C# Express from the Microsoft web site involves the transfer of large files. If you do not have a broadband connection, I suggest that you install the IDE from a CD instead.

Downloading Visual C# Express

The following is the procedure for downloading Visual C# Express from the Microsoft web site. By the time you are reading this book, the procedure may be a bit different, but it will be similar enough that you'll be able to find and download the IDE package.

1. Go to http://msdn.microsoft.com/vstudio/express/.

2. Select the Visual Studio 2008 Express Editions link.

3. Select Windows Development (because for the scope of this book, that is what you'll be doing).

4. Click the Visual Studio Express Download link.

5. You'll see a list of Visual Studio Express editions, as shown in Figure 1-1. Click Visual C# 2008 Express Edition.

Figure 1-1. *Selecting Visual C# 2008 Express Edition*

6. A dialog box appears, asking where you want to store the downloaded file. The file that you are downloading is a small bootstrap file, which you'll use to begin the actual installation of the Visual C# Express IDE. Choose to save the file on the desktop.

These steps can be carried out very quickly, probably within a few minutes. Do not mistake this procedure for downloading the complete Visual C# Express application, because that's not what happened. The installation procedure will download the vast majority of the IDE.

Installing Visual C# Express

After you've downloaded the setup file, you can start the Visual C# Express installation. During this process, all the pieces of the IDE—about 300MB—are downloaded and installed. Follow these steps:

1. On your desktop, double-click the vcssetup.exe file. Wait while the setup program loads all the required components.

2. Click Next on the initial setup screen.

3. A series of dialog boxes will appear. Select the defaults and click Next to continue through the setup program. In the final dialog box, click Install.

4. After all the elements have been downloaded and installed, you may need to restart your computer.

After Visual C# Express is installed, you can start it by selecting it from the Start menu.

Choosing the Application Type

With Visual C# Express running, you're ready to write your first .NET application. However, first you need to make a choice: what type of application will you write? Broadly speaking, in .NET, you can develop three main types of programs:

- A *console application* is designed to run at the command line with no user interface.

- A *Windows application* is designed to run on a user's desktop and has a user interface.

- A *class library* holds reusable functionality that can be used by console and Windows applications. It cannot be run by itself.

So that you know what each type of program is about, in this chapter, you will code all three. They are all variations of the Hello, World example, which displays the text "hello, world" on the screen. Hello, World programs have been used for decades to demonstrate what a programming language can do.

Creating Projects and Solutions

Regardless of which program type you are going to code, when using the Visual Studio line of products, you will create projects and solutions:

- A *project* is a classification used to describe a type of .NET application.

- A *solution* is a classification used to describe multiple .NET applications that most likely relate to each other.

Imagine building a car. A project could be the steering wheel, engine, or car body. Putting all of the car projects together creates a complete solution called the car.

A solution contains projects. For the examples in this chapter, our solution will contain three projects representing each of the three different program types.

When using Visual C# Express, creating a project implies creating a solution, because creating an empty solution without a project does not make sense. It's like building a car with no parts. When I say "project" or "application" in this book, from a workspace organization perspective, it means the same thing. *Solution* is an explicit reference to one or more projects or applications.

Our plan of action in terms of projects and solutions in this chapter is as follows:

- Create the .NET solution by creating the Windows application called Example1 (creating this application also creates a solution).

- Add to the created solution a console application called Example2.

- Add to the created solution a class library project called Example3.

Creating the Windows Application

We'll dive right in and start with the Windows application. With Visual C# Express running, follow these steps to create the Windows application:

1. Select File ➤ New Project from the menu.

2. Select the Windows Application icon. This represents a project style based on a predefined template called Windows Application,

3. Change the default name to Example1.

4. Click OK.

These steps create a new project and solution at the same time: the Example1 solution and Example1 project. Visual C# Express will display a complete project and solution, as shown in Figure 1-2.

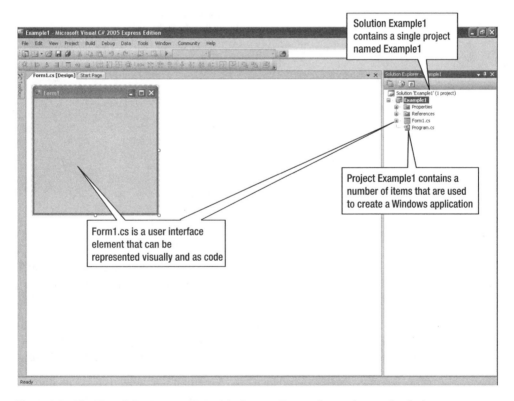

Figure 1-2. *The Visual C# Express IDE with the new Example1 project and solution*

Viewing the Source Code

When you create a new application, Visual C# Express automatically generates some source code for it. Double-click Program.cs in the Solution Explorer to see the generated code. The source code shown in Figure 1-3 will appear in the area to the left of the Solution Explorer.

■**Note** To shift between the user interface and generated code, right-click Form1.cs in the Solution Explorer. A submenu appears with the options View Code (to see the code) or View Designer (to see the user interface).

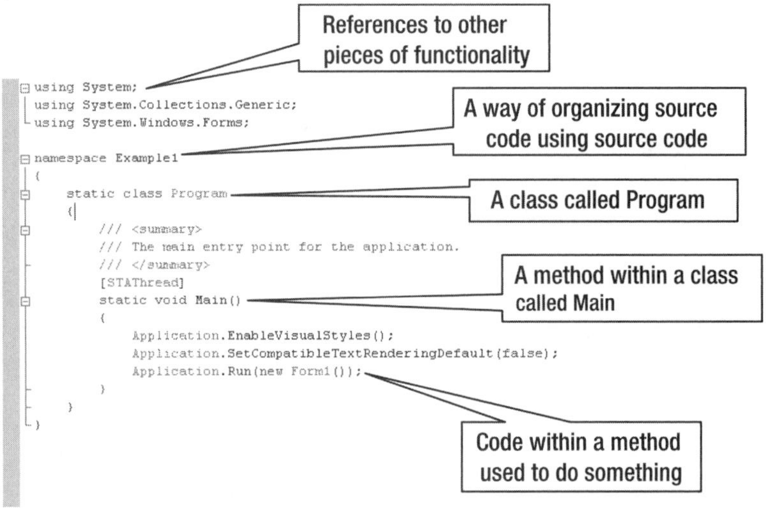

Figure 1-3. *Source code pieces in a C# file*

The elements labeled in Figure 1-3 represent the essence of the C# source code that you'll be writing. You'll learn about them throughout this book. For now, the main elements to note are as follows:

Class: An organizational unit that groups related code together. This grouping is much more specific than a solution or a project. To use the car analogy again, if a project is a car engine, then a class can be the carburetor. In other words, projects are made up of multiple classes.

Method: A set of instructions that carry out a task. A method is analogous to a function in many other languages. The Main() method runs when an application starts; therefore, it contains the code you want to use at the beginning of any program.

Renaming the Solution

Visual C# Express named both the solution and project Example1 automatically, which isn't ideal. Fortunately, it's easy to rename the solution. Follow these steps:

1. Right-click the solution name in the Solution Explorer and select Rename from the context menu.

2. The solution name will become editable. Change it to `ThreeExamples`.

3. Press Enter to apply the change.

You can use this same technique to rename projects or any other items shown in the Solution Explorer.

Saving the Solution

After you've renamed the solution, it's good practice to save your changes. To save the project, follow these steps:

1. Highlight the solution name in the Solution Explorer.

2. Select File ➤ Save ThreeExamples.sln.

3. Notice that Visual C# Express wants to save the solution using the old `Example1` name, not the new solution name (`ThreeExamples`). To save the new solution name to the hard disk, you need to yet again change `Example1` to `ThreeExamples`. Note the path of where Visual C# Express saves your projects, as you will need to know it from time to time.

4. Click the Save button.

When the solution and project are successfully saved, you'll see the message "Item(s) Saved" in the status bar in the lower-left corner of the window.

In the future, whenever you want to save the solution and project, you can use the keyboard shortcut: Ctrl+S.

■Note If you have not saved your changes and choose to exit Visual C# Express, you will be asked if you want to save or discard the solution and project.

To open a solution you have previously saved, you can choose File ➤ Open Project at any time and navigate to the solution file. You can also select the solution from the Recent Projects window when you first start Visual C# Express. The Recent Projects window is always available on the Start Page tab of the main Visual C# Express window as well.

Running the Windows Application

The source code generated by Visual C# Express is a basic application that contains an empty window with no functionality. The source code gives you a starting point where you can add more source code, debug the source code, and run the application.

To run the application, select Debug ➤ Start Without Debugging. Alternatively, use the keyboard shortcut Ctrl+F5. You'll see a window representing the `Example1` application. You can exit the application by clicking the window's close button. Figure 1-4 illustrates the process.

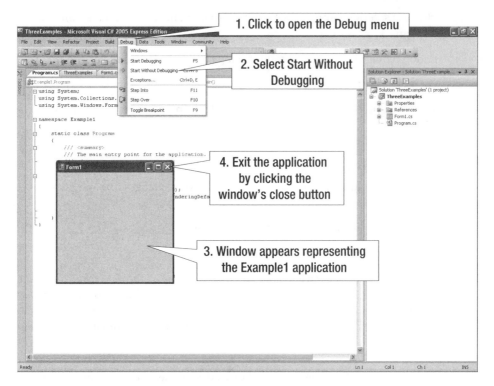

Figure 1-4. *Running an application*

Running the application enables you to see what it does. When you run an application though the IDE, it is identical to a user clicking to start the application from the desktop. In this example, Example1 displays an empty window without any controls or functionality. The source code's functionality is to display an empty window when started and provide a button to end the application.

You have not written a single line of code, yet you have created an application and something actually happened, and all because Visual C# generates some boilerplate C# code that works straight out of the box.

You have created an application, seen its source code, and run it. You did all of this in the context of a comfortable, do-it-all-for-you development environment called Visual C# Express. Visual C# Express is both a good thing and a bad thing. Visual C# Express is good because it hides the messy details, but it is bad because the messy details are hidden. Imagine being a car mechanic. It is good that car manufacturers produce dashboards that have little lights that go on when something is wrong. But it would be bad if the mechanic had to rely on the little lights to fix problems in a car.

Making the Windows Application Say Hello

The Windows application does nothing other than appear with a blank window that you can close. To make the application do something, you need to add user interface elements or add some code. Adding code without adding user interface elements will make the program do something, but it's not as exciting. So, we'll add a button that, when clicked, will display "hello, world" in a text box.

First, you need to add the Button control to the form. Double-click Form1.cs in the Solution Explorer to display a blank form. Then click the Toolbox tab to access the controls. Click Button, and then click the form to place the button on the form. These steps are illustrated in Figure 1-5.

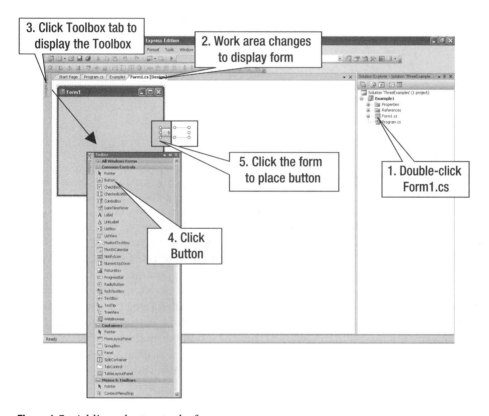

Figure 1-5. *Adding a button to the form*

Next, add a TextBox control using the same basic procedure. Finally, align the button and text box as shown in Figure 1-6. To move a control, use the handles that appear when you highlight the control. Visual C# Express will align the edge of a control to nearby edges as you drag it, so that you can align controls accurately.

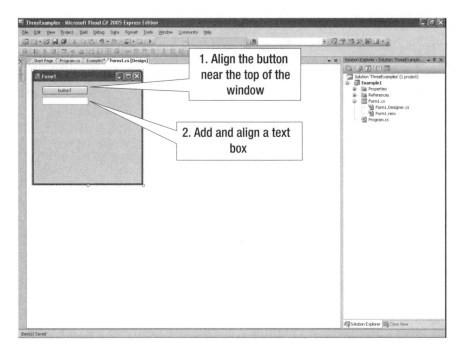

Figure 1-6. *Aligned button and text box*

If you now executed Example1 by pressing Ctrl+F5, you would see a window with a button and a text box. You can click the button and add or delete text from the text box. But whatever you do has no effect, because neither control has been associated with any code.

To make the application do something, you need to think in terms of *events*. For example, if you have a garage with an automatic door opener, you would expect that pressing the remote control button would open the garage door when it's closed and close the door when it's open. The automatic garage door manufacturer associated the event of pushing the remote control button with the action of either opening or closing the garage door. In Example1, we'll associate the clicking of the button with the action of showing text in the text box.

Select the button on the form and double-click it. The work area changes to source code, with the cursor in the button_Click function. Add this source code to function:

```
TextBox1.text = "hello, world";
```

Figure 1-7 illustrates the procedure for associating an event with an action.

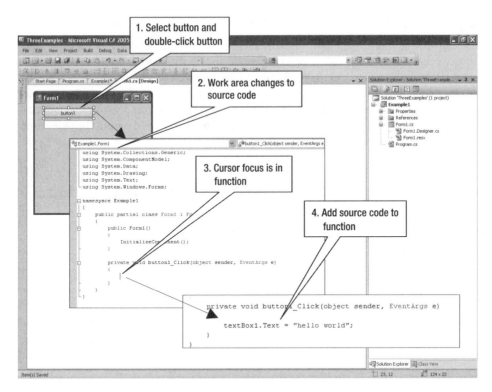

Figure 1-7. *Associating the button click event with the action of adding text to the text box*

Note that `textBox1` is the name of the text box you added to the form. This name is gener-ated by Visual C# Express, just as it generated a default name for the button. You can change the default names (through each control's Properties window), but we've left the default for this example.

Adding an action to an event is very simple when following the instructions shown in Figure 1-7. The simplicity is due to Visual C# Express, and not because the event or action is simple. Visual C# Express makes the assumption that when you double-click a control, you want to modify the *default event* of the control, and as such, automatically generates the code in step 3 of Figure 1-7. In the case of a button, the default event is the click event; that is, the event that corresponds to a user clicking the button. The assumption of the click event being the default event for a button is logical. Other controls have different default events. For exam-ple, double-clicking a TextBox control will generate the code for the text-changed event.

Run the application by pressing Ctrl+F5, and then click the button. The text box fills with the text "hello, world." Congratulations, you've just finished your first C# application!

You have associated an event with an action: the button click with the text display. Associ-ating events with actions is the basis of all Windows applications.

Adding Comments to the Application

Now that you have a working program, it would be good to document what it does, right there in the source code. Then if you come back to the application in the future, you won't be puzzled by your previous work. In fact, you may not even be the person who maintains your code, so leaving comments in the code to help explain it is definitely good practice. Even if you know you will be maintaining the code forever, treat your future self as a stranger. You may be surprised how long it takes to decipher code you have written when revisited months or years later.

To add a single-line comment, use the following syntax:

```
// A single-line comment
```

Anything after the // is ignored by the compiler and is not included in the final application. Let's document our Windows application:

```
// When the user clicks the button, we display text in the text box
private void button1_Click(object sender, EventArgs e)
{
    textBox1.Text = "hello, world";
}
```

It's always worth leaving simple comments like this as you go, because it helps greatly when working out an application's logic. However, what if we want to leave longer comments, such as a more detailed comment describing a whole class? The answer is the multiline comment:

```
/* The first line of a multiline comment.
 * The second line.
 * The third line.
 */
```

This time, the /* starts the comment and the */ ends it; anything in between is ignored by the compiler as before. Note that the asterisks before the second and third lines are added by Visual C# Express as extra dressing, but are not a requirement of a multiline comment.

Let's write a multiline comment for our Windows application:

```
namespace Example1
{
    /* This is the example simple form for Chapter 1,
     * which displays text when the user clicks the button.
     * It is a first look at event-driven programming.
     */

    public partial class Form1 : Form
    {
        public Form1()
        {
            InitializeComponent();
        }
```

```
        // When the user clicks the button, we
        // display text in the text box
        private void button1_Click(object sender, EventArgs e)
        {
            textBox1.Text = "hello, world";
        }
    }
}
```

There are other variations of comments that Visual C# Express can hook into to provide more information in its graphical user interface (GUI). You'll learn about these in Chapter 10.

Navigating the User Controls of the Solution

When you are writing your code, your most important form of navigation is the Solution Explorer. The Solution Explorer is the tree control that contains the references to your solutions and projects. Consider the Solution Explorer as your developer dashboard, which you can use to fine-tune how your .NET application is assembled and executed.

I suggest that you take a moment to click around the Solution Explorer. Try some right-clicks on various elements. The context-sensitive click is a fast way of fine-tuning particular aspects of your solution and project. However, when clicking, please do not click OK in any dialog box; for now, click Cancel so that any changes you may have made are not saved.

To the left of the Solution Explorer is your work area. The work area is where you write your code or edit your user interface. The work area will display only a single piece of information, which could be some code, a user interface, or a project. As you saw earlier, when you double-click Program.cs in the Solution Explorer, the work area displays the code related to the Program.cs file.

Program.cs is a plain-vanilla source code file from Example1. Plain-vanilla source code files are source code files that have no special representation in Visual C# Express and simply contain source code. Program.cs contains source code to initialize the application and looks like this:

```
using System;
using System.Collections.Generic;
using System.Linq;
using System.Windows.Forms;

namespace Example1
{
    static class Program
    {
        /// <summary>
        /// The main entry point for the application.
        /// </summary>
        [STAThread]
        static void Main()
        {
            Application.EnableVisualStyles();
```

```
            Application.SetCompatibleTextRenderingDefault(false);
            Application.Run(new Form1());
        }
    }
}
```

Plain-vanilla source code files contain the logic that makes your application do something useful. The advantage of plain-vanilla source code files is that they provide a complete view of your application's logic. A typical application will contain many plain-vanilla source code files.

The Solution Explorer also shows specialized groupings, which are specific items that Visual C# Express recognizes and organizes. A specialized grouping contains a number of files that rely on each other and implement a specific piece of functionality. Form1 is an example of a specialized grouping that manages the layout of the user interface, elements of the user interface, and your custom code. The individual file pieces of Form1 are illustrated in Figure 1-8.

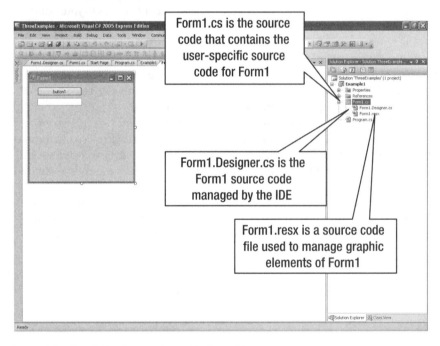

Figure 1-8. *Specialized grouping with three files*

In Figure 1-8, the Solution Explorer contains a top-level item called Form1.cs, which is a source code file that contains the user-defined pieces of Form1. Form1 can be represented in one of two ways in the work area: graphically and textually (source code). For the most part, you will be editing Form1.cs using source code and graphical means, and will let Visual C# Express handle the Form1.Designer.cs, and Form1.resx files.

The Form1 specialized grouping exists to make the organization of the code that represents the user interface of Form1 easier to manage for you and the IDE. It does not mean that you cannot edit the Form1.Designer.cs and Form1.resx files. If you double-click Form1.Designer.cs, you will see source code, which you can modify. However, be forewarned that if you mess up the source code in that file, Visual C# Express might stop functioning properly when editing Form1.

Knowing that the specialized grouping called Form1 should be taken as a whole, you might wonder where the definition of textBox1 came from. The answer is that textBox1 is defined and assigned in one of the IDE-generated source code files. Figure 1-9 illustrates what the generated source code file does with textBox1.

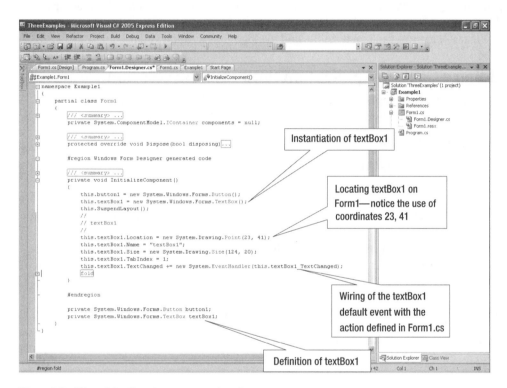

Figure 1-9. *Visual C# Express-generated code*

Notice that everything—definition, wiring of events to actions, and placement of the controls—is managed by Visual C# Express. For example, if you were to change the placement of textBox1 by altering the location coordinates, Visual C# Express would read and process the change. However, if you were to make larger changes that Visual C# Express could not process, you would corrupt the user interface.

Now that you have an idea of how the IDE works, let's continue with our examples. Next up is the console application.

Creating the Console Application

A console application is a text-based application. This means that rather than displaying a GUI, it uses a command-line interface.

The console has a very long history because the console was the first way to interact with a computer. Consoles are not very user-friendly and become very tedious for any complex operations, yet some people claim that a console is all you need. (See http://en.wikipedia.org/wiki/Command_line_interface for more information about the console.)

Writing to the console works only if the currently running application has a console. To open the console in Windows, select Start ➤ Accessories ➤ Command Prompt. Alternatively, select Start ➤ Run and type cmd in the dialog box.

Visual C# Express can create, build, and manage console applications.

Adding a Console Application Project to the Solution

We will now create an application that outputs the text "hello, world" to the console. Follow these steps to add the new project to the ThreeExamples solution:

1. Right-click the solution name, ThreeExamples, in the Solution Explorer.

2. Select Add ➤ New Project.

3. Select Console Application and change the name to Example2.

The Solution Explorer changes to show the additional project, and the work area displays the source code in the new Program.cs.

Notice the simplicity of the console application. It contains a single plain-vanilla source code file, called Program.cs. Console applications typically do not have any specialized groupings and do not have any events.

Making the Console Application Say Hello

To make the console application do something, you need to add some source code to the Main() method, as follows:

```
namespace Example2
{
    class Program
    {
        static void Main(string[] args)
        {
            Console.WriteLine("hello, world");
        }
    }
}
```

The bolded line writes the text "hello, world" to the console.

If you tried to run the console application by pressing Ctrl+F5, you would instead cause the Windows application Example1 to run. Let's change that next.

Setting the Startup Project

To execute the console application, you need to set the console application as the *startup project*. Did you notice how the Example1 project is in bold type in the Solution Explorer? That means Example1 is the startup project. Whenever you run or debug an application, the startup project is executed or debugged.

To switch the startup project to Example2, right-click the Example2 project and select Set As Startup Project. Example2 will now be bolded, meaning it is the startup project of the ThreeExamples solution.

Running the Console Project

With Example2 set as the startup project, you can now press Ctrl+F5 to run the console application. The output is as follows:

```
hello, world
Press any key to continue
```

Executing the console application does not generate a window, as did the Windows application. Instead, a command prompt is started with Example2 as the application to execute. Executing that application generates the text "hello, world." You can also see that you can press any key to close the command prompt window. Visual C# Express automatically generated the code to show this output and execute this action.

In general, the console application is limited, but it's an easy way to run specific tasks. Now let's move on to the next example.

Creating the Class Library

The third example is not a .NET application; rather, it is a shareable piece of functionality, typically called a *class library*. Windows applications and console applications are programs that you can execute from a command prompt or Windows Explorer. A class library cannot be executed by the user, but needs to be accessed by a Windows application or console application. It is a convenient place to put code that can be used by more than one application.

Adding a Class Library Project to the Solution

We will now create a class library for the Windows application and console application to share. Follow these steps to add the new project to the ThreeExamples solution:

1. Right-click the solution name, ThreeExamples, in the Solution Explorer.

2. Select Add ➤ New Project.

3. Select Class Library and change the name to Example3.

The resulting solution project should look like Figure 1-10.

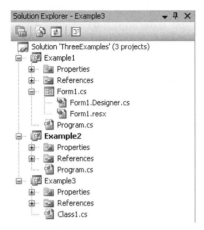

Figure 1-10. *Updated solution structure that contains three projects*

The added Example3 project has a single file called Class1.cs, which is a plain-vanilla source code file.

Moving Functionality

Now we will move the code used to say "hello, world" from Example2 to Example3. Add the code to Class1.cs as follows (the bolded code):

```
using System;
using System.Collections.Generic;
using System.Text;

namespace Example3
{
    public class Class1
    {
        public static void HelloWorld()
        {
            Console.WriteLine("hello, world");
        }
    }
}
```

The modified code contains a method called HelloWorld(). When called, this method will output the text "hello, world." As mentioned earlier in the chapter, a method is a set of instructions that carry out a task. Methods are discussed in more detail in Chapter 2.

In order for applications to actually share the code that's in a class library, you must make the projects aware of each other's existence. You do that through references.

Defining References

To make one project aware of definitions in another project, you need to define a *reference*. The idea behind a reference is to indicate that a project knows about another piece of functionality.

Note The project only knows about the functionality that has been declared as being public. Public functionality, or what C# programmers call *public scope*, is when you declare a type with the `public` keyword. You will learn about public and other scopes throughout this book.

To make `Example2` aware of the functionality in `Class1`, you need to set a physical reference, as follows:

1. Click and expand the References node under `Example2`. Notice that three references already exist. When you typed `Console.WriteLine()` in `Class1.cs`, you were using functionality from the `System` reference.

2. Right-click References and select Add Reference.

3. Click the Projects tab.

4. Select `Example3`, and then click OK. `Example3` will be added to `Example2`'s references.

Once the reference has been assigned, `Example2` can call the functionality in `Example3`.

Note In `Class1.cs`, the first three lines begin with the keyword `using`. The keyword `using` tells Visual C# Express you want to use the functionality defined in the reference after the `using` keyword. This is a shortcut, which we didn't use in this example so that you could see another way of using a reference.

Calling Class Library Functionality

Now we need to change `Example2` so that it calls the function in `Example3`. Modify the `Program.cs` file in `Example2` as follows:

```
using System;
using System.Collections.Generic;
using System.Text;

namespace Example2
{
    class Program
    {
        static void Main(string[] args)
        {
            Console.WriteLine("hello, world");
```

```
                Example3.Class1.HelloWorld();
            }
        }
}
```

Run `Example2` by pressing Ctrl+F5. A command prompt window should appear and generate the "hello, world" text twice. The first "hello, world" is generated by the code `Console.WriteLine()`. Calling the function `Example3.Class1.HelloWorld()` generates the second "hello, world."

USING REFERENCE SHORTHAND

`Example3.Class1.HelloWorld()` is the longhand way to use a reference. If we were to use longhand for the `Console.WriteLine()` call, we would write `System.Console.WriteLine()`, because the `Console.WriteLine()` method is defined in the `System` reference. However, we have used the `using System` line, so we don't need to do it this way.

To use shorthand for the `Example3` call, we would include a new `using` line at the beginning of `Program.cs` in `Example2` and change the call to `Class1`'s `HelloWorld()` method:

```
using System;
using System.Collections.Generic;
using System.Text;
using Example3;

namespace Example2
{
    class Program
    {
        static void Main(string[] args)
        {
            Console.WriteLine("hello, world");
            Class1.HelloWorld();
        }
    }
}
```

But shorthand like this has a downside. What if we had many references, each containing a class called `Class1`? In this case, Visual C# Express wouldn't know which `Class1` to use without the help of longhand. Granted, you are not likely to name multiple classes `Class1`, but even sensible names can be duplicated in a collection of references. And if you are using someone else's code as a reference, the possibility of duplicate names becomes higher.

Using Variables and Constants

One of the core concepts in a C# program is to use variables. Think of a variable as a block of memory where you can store data for later use. This allows you to pass data around within your program very easily.

In our Example3 project, it would make life easier if we could define the message to display at the beginning of the method. That way, if we decide to change the message, we can get at it much more easily. As it stands, if we were to add more code before the Console.WriteLine() call, we would need to scroll through the text to find the message to change. A variable is perfect for this, as we can define some data (the message to print), and then use it later in our program.

```
namespace Example3
{
    public class Class1
    {
        public static void HelloWorld()
        {
            // The message to display, held in a variable
            string message = "hello, world";
            Console.WriteLine(message);
        }

    }
}
```

Here, we've defined a variable called message of type string (a string is a length of text). We can then refer to the message variable later when we want to place its contents into the code. In the example, we place its contents into the Console.WriteLine() call, which works as before. This time, however, we have set the message to display in a separate statement.

This is very useful for us, but there is more to variables than this. They have something that is called *scope*. The message variable has method-level scope, which means it is available only in the method in which it is defined. Consider this code:

```
        public static void HelloWorld()
        {
            // The message to display
            string message = "hello, world";
            Console.WriteLine(message);
        }

        public static void DisplayMessageText()
        {
            Console.WriteLine("The message text is: ");
            Console.WriteLine(message);
        }
```

The DisplayMessageText() method prints two lines of text to tell us what the message text should be. However, this doesn't compile, because the compiler knows that the variable message is not available to the DisplayMessageText() method because of its method-level scope.

To fix this, we need to give message class-level scope by moving it to the beginning of the class definition (as it is used by methods marked static. it must also be static):

```
public class Class1
{
    // The message to display
    static string message = "hello, world";

    public static void HelloWorld()
    {
        Console.WriteLine(message);
    }


    public static void DisplayMessageText()
    {
        Console.WriteLine("The message text is: ");
        Console.WriteLine(message);
    }
}
```

Now the variable message is shared by all the methods of Class1. You'll learn much more about method-level and class-level scopes, as well as the public and static keywords, throughout this book.

Sharing a variable among methods of a class can be useful, but it's sometimes not wise to do this. That's because methods can change variables as they carry out their tasks, which can produce unpredictable results further down the line. We can lock the value by using a *constant* instead of a variable. The const keyword denotes the constant:

```
// The message to display
const string MESSAGE = "hello, world";

public static void HelloWorld()
{
    Console.WriteLine(MESSAGE);
}

public static void DisplayMessageText()
{
    Console.WriteLine("The message text is: ");
    Console.WriteLine(MESSAGE);
}
```

Constant names should always be all uppercase. The contents of a constant cannot be changed at any point. The following would not compile, for instance.

```csharp
// The message to display
const string MESSAGE = "hello, world";

public static void HelloWorld()
{
    MESSAGE = "goodbye, world";
    Console.WriteLine(MESSAGE);
}
```

Now that you've worked through this chapter's examples, let's talk a bit about how your C# code in Visual C# Express actually turns into a program that can run on an operating system like Windows.

Understanding How the .NET Framework Works

When you write C# source code, you are creating instructions for the program to follow. The instructions are defined using the C# programming language, which is useful for you, but not useful for the computer. The computer does not understand pieces of text; it understands ones and zeros. To feed instructions to the computer, developers have created a higher-level instruction mechanism that converts your instructions into something that the computer can understand. The conversion utility is called a *compiler*.

The twist with .NET, in contrast to traditional programming languages such as C++ and C, is that the compiler generates a binary-based intermediate language called Common Intermediate Language (CIL). The .NET Framework then converts the CIL into the binary instructions required by the computer's processor.

You might think converting the source code into an intermediate language is inefficient, but it is a good approach. Let's use an analogy. There are dogs that learn quickly and those that take a while to learn. For example, German shepherds tend to learn quickly and don't require much repetition of lessons. On the other hand, bullmastiffs need quite a bit of patience, as they tend to be stubborn. Now imagine being a trainer who has created instructions on how to teach things specifically geared towards the bullmastiff. If those same instructions are used on the German shepherd, you end up boring the German shepherd and possibly failing to teach the German shepherd what you wanted him to learn.

The problem with the instructions is that they are specifically tuned for a single dog. If you want to teach both dogs, you need two sets of instructions. To solve this problem, the instructions should be general, with added interpretation notes saying things like, "If dog is stubborn, repeat."

Converting this into computer-speak, the two sets of instructions are for two different processors or processors used in specific situations. For example, there are server computers and client computers. Each type of computer has different requirements. A server computer needs to process data as quickly as possible, whereas a client computer needs to show data on the screen as quickly as possible. There are compilers for each context, but to have the developer create multiple distributions with different compiler(s) or setting(s) is inefficient. The solution is to create a set of instructions that are general, but have associated interpretation notes. The .NET Framework then applies these instructions using the interpretation notes.

The .NET Framework compiles to instructions (CIL) that are then converted into processor-specific instructions using notes embedded in the .NET Framework. The .NET architecture is illustrated in Figure 1-11.

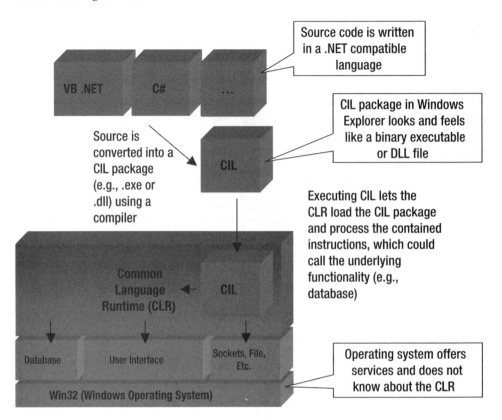

Figure 1-11. *.NET architecture*

In Figure 1-11, Visual C# Express is responsible for converting the C# source code into a CIL package. The converted CIL package is a binary file that when executed requires a common language runtime (CLR). Without a CLR installed on your computer, you cannot run the CIL package. When you installed Visual C# Express, you installed the CLR in the background as a separate package. Visual C# Express is an application that allows you to develop for the CLR, but it also uses the CLR.

The CLR has the ability to transform your instructions in the CIL package into something that the operating system and processor can understand. If you look at the syntax of .NET-compatible languages, such as Visual Basic, C#, or Eiffel.NET, you will see that they are not similar. Yet the CLR can process the CIL package generated by one of those languages because a .NET compiler, regardless of programming language, generates a set of instructions common to the CLR.

When using the .NET Framework, you are writing for the CLR, and everything you do must be understood by the CLR. Generally speaking, this is not a problem if you are writing code in C#. The following are some advantages of writing code targeted to the CLR:

Memory and garbage collection: Programs use resources such as memory, files, and so on. In traditional programming languages, such as C and C++, you are expected to open and close a file, and allocate and free memory. With .NET, you don't need to worry about closing files or freeing memory. The CLR knows when a file or memory is not in use and will automatically close the file or free the memory.

Note Some programmers may think that the CLR promotes sloppy programming behavior, as you don't need to clean up after yourself. However, practice has shown that for any complex application, you will waste time and resources figuring out where memory has not been freed.

Custom optimization: Some programs need to process large amounts of data, such as that from a database, or display a complex user interface. The performance focus for each is on a different piece of code. The CLR has the ability to optimize the CIL package and decide how to run it as quickly and efficiently as possible.

Common Type System (CTS): A string in Visual Basic is a string in C#. This ensures that when a CIL package generated by C# talks to a CIL package generated by Visual Basic, there will be no data type misrepresentations.

Safe code: When writing programs that interact with files or memory, there is a possibility that a program error can cause security problems. Hackers will make use of that security error to run their own programs and potentially cause financial disaster. The CLR cannot stop application-defined errors, but can stop and rein in a program that generates an error due to incorrect file or memory access.

The benefit of the CLR is allowing developers to focus on application-related problems, because they do not need to worry about infrastructure-related problems. With the CLR, you focus on the application code that reads and processes the content of a file. Without the CLR, you would need to also come up with the code that uses the content in the file and the code that is responsible for opening, reading, and closing the file.

The Important Stuff to Remember

This chapter got you started working with C# in an IDE. Here are the key points to remember:

- There are three major types of C# programs: Windows applications, console applications, and class libraries.

- A Windows application has a user interface and behaves like other Windows applications (such as Notepad and Calculator). For Windows applications, you associate events with actions.

- A console application is simpler than a Windows application and has no events. It is used to process data. Console applications generate and accept data from the command line.

- You will want to use an IDE to manage your development cycle of coding, debugging, and application execution.

- Among other things, IDEs manage the organization of your source code using projects and solutions.

- In an IDE, keyboard shortcuts make it easier for you to perform operations that you will do repeatedly. For example, in Visual C# Express, use Ctrl+S to save your work and Ctrl+F5 to run your application without debugging.

- In Visual C# Express projects, there are plain-vanilla files and specialized groupings. When dealing with specialized groupings, make sure that you understand how the groupings function and modify only those files that you are meant to modify.

Some Things for You to Do

The following are some questions related to what you've learned in this chapter. Answering them will help you to get started developing your projects in the IDE.

■**Note** The answers/solutions to the questions/exercises included at the end of each chapter are available with this book's downloadable code, found in the Source Code/Download section of the Apress web site (http://www.apress.com). Additionally, you can send me an e-mail message at christianhgross@gmail.com.

---

1. In an IDE, solutions and projects are used to classify related pieces of functionality. The analogy I used talked about cars and car pieces. Would you ever create a solution that contained unrelated pieces of functionality? For example, would you create an airplane solution that contained car pieces?

2. Projects are based on templates created by Microsoft. Can you think of a situation where you would create your own template and add it to Visual C# Express?

3. In the Solution Explorer, each item in the tree control represents a single item (such as a file, user interface control, and so on). If you were to double-click a .cs file, you would be manipulating a C# file that would contain C# code. Should a single C# file reference a single C# class or namespace? And if not, how would you organize your C# code with respect to C# files?

4. You have learned about how a .NET application generates an executable file. Let's say that you take the generated application and execute it on another Windows computer. Will the generated application run? Let's say that you take the executable file to a Macintosh OS X or Linux computer: will the application run? Why will it run or not run?

5. You are not happy with the naming of the element textBox1, and want to rename it to txtOutput. How do you go about renaming textBox1?

6. Example3 has embedded logic that assumes the caller of the method is a console application. Is it good to assume a specific application type or logic of the caller in a library? If yes, why? If no, why not?

■■■

CHAPTER 2

Learning About .NET Number and Value Types

In the previous chapter, you learned how to use Visual C# Express, and what .NET is in terms of the CIL and CLR. In this chapter, we are going to roll up our sleeves and begin writing real C# code, specifically a calculator.

A calculator is an ideal example to start with, because it allows you to focus on the application without having to deal with all of the nasty details that are normally associated with programs. In a programming language like C#, adding two numbers is trivial. What is not trivial is how to put the operation of adding two numbers into a program.

This chapter focuses on the mechanics of writing a program in C#—taking an idea and converting it into a C# program that can execute your intentions. You'll learn how to organize your development and implement a C# class library, as well as how the .NET CLR manages number types.

Focusing and Organizing Your Development

When you develop software, you will split your work into two main tasks: organizing and implementing. Organizing your development involves figuring out what features and libraries you are going to define, how many people are going to be developing the features, and so on.

Organizing your development is one of the most important tasks when writing code, and it is also typically the most confusing for new developers. Professional developers seem to organize their work instinctively, but it only appears that way because they have done it so many times that the process has become automatic.

When developers are tasked with creating a program, they are asked to write software that implements a set of features. Features could include calculating daily interest payments, automatically generating letters indicating the acceptance or rejection of a loan, and so on. A feature always relates to performing some task that is determined by some process. You could say that feature implementation is the direct implementation of a task.

When defining the features, two major steps are involved:

- Gain an understanding of the features. You can't implement something that you don't understand. To be able to write the source code for a feature, you need to know the whys and whats of a feature.

- Describe the features using structured design methods. Simply organizing your thoughts may be enough if you are the only person working on a program; however, more often than not, you will be part of a team. You need to use a structured design method so that you and your team members can communicate the thoughts related to program development.

One common structured design method is the Unified Modeling Language (UML). UML is used to organize the features into units that correspond to programming language constructs, such as classes. Think of UML as a software developer-specific lingo used to describe the various aspects of a programming environment at a higher level of abstraction. UML allows you to get an overall understanding of the architecture without having to read the source code. Think of UML as the structured doodle on the napkin of software programming.

Along with UML, there are other ways of structuring your development process. For example, another technique is called agile software development. The idea with agile software development is to use a whiteboard and develop your own structured communication mechanism.

The choice of UML, agile software development, or another structured design method is up to you and your team members. But you will need to organize your thoughts and have a structured communication technique. If you don't, your software will be late, buggy, too expensive, or incomplete. It is not an understatement to say that organization is half the battle.

In this chapter, I am going to give you a taste of a simplified structured development technique, so that you at least have an idea of how structured development works.

Organizing the Calculator

To begin this chapter's example, get a piece of paper and a pen or pencil, or you can use a tablet PC for writing, if you have one. Next, in the center of the paper (or virtual paper), draw a circle and in it write the word *Calculator*. Now stop and think about what a calculator means with respect to the software that you will be writing. Write those ideas on the paper surrounding the circle. My thoughts are shown in Figure 2-1.

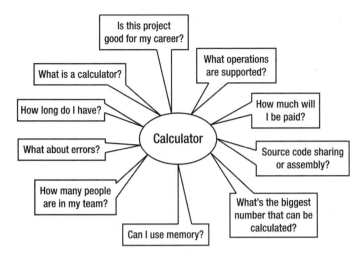

Figure 2-1. *Brainstorming what the calculator application represents*

Your thoughts and my thoughts may or may not be the same, but what our results will have in common is a hodgepodge of ideas everywhere. Figure 2-1 illustrates that one of the biggest problems software developers face is lack of focus and organization. It is not that developers can't focus or organize, but that developers are bombarded by information, and it is a Herculean task to keep track of, let alone organize, all of that information. But software projects that are successful must remain focused and organized. Therefore, the next step is to focus and organize your thoughts, which results in something like Figure 2-2.

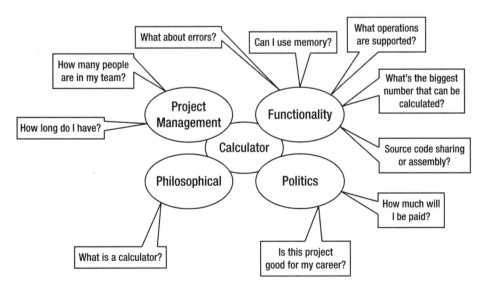

Figure 2-2. *Focused and organized brainstorming*

In Figure 2-2, the ideas are organized by classification. As this is book is about a programming language, the only relevant ideas are those related to source code functionality. Roughly speaking, in the source code category, each thought corresponds to a feature to implement.

Focusing the Calculator

To implement a feature, you need source code, which means a file, project, and other programming techniques. Before you can implement the features, you need to figure out how the source code will be organized. There are two levels of organization:

- *File level*: At the file level, you are organizing what kinds of projects and solutions you will be creating.

- *Source code level*: At the source code level, you are organizing the namespaces, class names, and other identifiers that are referenced throughout the source code.

Implementing a calculator at the file level starts with a decision about which of the three kinds of projects the calculator should be. As discussed in Chapter 1, you have three choices: Windows application, console application, or class library.

If the calculator were a Windows application, it could look like Figure 2-3.

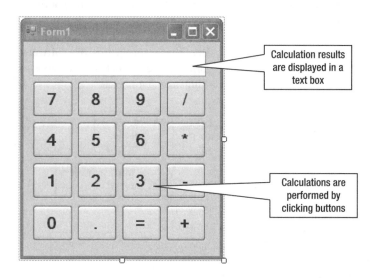

Figure 2-3. *A calculator implemented as a Windows application*

A calculator implemented as a Windows application allows users to perform calculations by clicking the appropriate buttons. To add two numbers, the user would click the appropriate buttons to key in the first number, then an operation, then the second number, with a final step of the clicking the equal sign button. The equal sign is a signal to the calculator application to process the data that has been entered and generate a result. The text box would display the results.

The second choice is to implement a calculator using a console application, where the numbers are entered as text, as illustrated in Figure 2-4.

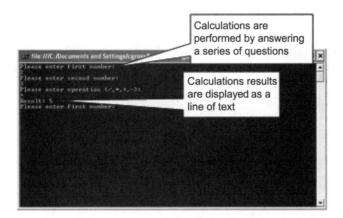

Figure 2-4. *A calculator implemented as a console application*

As a console application, the calculator does not expect users to click buttons; rather, they press the appropriate keyboard keys to enter the appropriate number at the appropriate time with the appropriate operation. Typically, an Enter key will serve as an equal sign button and perform a calculation, which is output to the console. Once one calculation has completed, the cycle starts again.

The user interaction between the two types of applications is dramatically different, and implies two different programs, even though they implement the same features. The focus is not on creating a particular program type, but on the overall programming structure.

If you had to choose between a Windows or console application for the calculator, you would choose the Windows application because it looks better and is easier to use. In the focused thoughts of Figure 2-2, ease of use was not defined as a feature. Should the user interface type have been a feature? Normally yes, but for the scope of this chapter, no.

Let's step back and think about this abstractly. You are a programmer and have been charged with the task of implementing the calculator for both user interfaces. Again, thinking abstractly, would you implement all the functionality twice, or would you try to think about which parts of the calculator could be reused for both user interfaces? Most likely, your answer will be that you want to reuse parts of the calculator so that you have less work. But you also want to reuse parts so that you can avoid additional maintenance and program extension problems.

So, for software development, you need to think of the software as pieces that are assembled into a program. Some pieces can be reused, and other pieces cannot be reused. Therefore, think of the calculator application as two pieces: the user interface and the piece that performs calculations based on data delivered by the user interface. From an organizational perspective, or in developer lingo, from an architectural perspective, the calculator pieces would be arranged as shown in Figure 2-5.

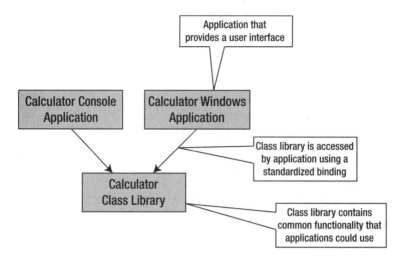

Figure 2-5. *Arrangement of calculator pieces*

The individual pieces in Figure 2-5 are called *components*. (Some individuals might even call the pieces *modules*, but I personally prefer the term *components*.) The components are arranged from the lower-level functionality at the bottom of the picture to the higher-level functionality near the top of the picture.

Each component fulfills a particular task, and the higher-level components use those tasks implemented at a lower level. The idea is that each level is responsible for certain functionality, and other levels do not duplicate efforts by reimplementing certain functionality. The higher-level functionality does have a lower-level dependency, but the lower level does not have a higher-level dependency.

Applications are realized using either top-down or bottom-up architecture. A top-down methodology means creating the higher-level components and then implementing the lower-level components when needed. In contrast, a bottom-up methodology means creating the bottom components first.

A bottom-up approach is useful when you know clearly which features need to be implemented. A top-down approach is better when you have a rough idea of what features need to be implemented, but don't want to stray too far from the goal of the application. The focus of this chapter is to develop the Calculator class library, shown at the bottom of Figure 2-5, thus we will take the bottom-up approach in this chapter.

Implementing the Class Library

The creation of a class library is a form of file organization. The next step is to create some source code for the class library. The source code is implemented in two steps:

- Define the class and methods.

- Implement the methods.

One of the biggest problems when learning a new language is understanding what the language can and cannot do. You can't write source code that the language does not understand. So it is extremely important to know the programming language, because it determines how your thoughts will be structured.

You will write two types of source code: source code that organizes and source code that does something. Organizational source code is like a filing system with folders. Source code that does something is like a folder with stuff in it. When you are creating the filing system, you don't care about the contents of the folder. And when you fill the folder, you generally don't care about the filing system.

Classes, namespaces, and methods are all concepts used to organize source code. A method is filled with source code and does something like add numbers or create a textual string.

One of the most common things that you will do when filling a method with source code is reference other pieces of organized source code. Think of referencing as putting a sticky note in a folder with the text, "Please also look in folder B."

Following is a piece of source code that is 100% organizational and does nothing.

```
namespace MyMainTypes {
    static class AType {
        public static void DoSomething() { }
    }
}
namespace MyOtherMainTypes {
    static class AnotherType {
        public static void DoSomething() { }
    }
}
```

The source code has three levels of organization. A namespace (MyMainTypes and MyOtherMainTypes in the example) encapsulates types like classes (AType and AnotherType in the example). Classes encapsulate methods (DoSomething in the example) or properties. Within a namespace, all types must be unique. You can have two types with the same identifier in different namespaces. Within a type, you cannot have identical identifiers with identical parameters. (This will be clearer as you learn more about C# in the upcoming chapters.)

Following is the same organizational code with some source code added to do something (shown in boldface).

```
namespace MyMainTypes {
    static class AType {
        public static void DoSomething() { }
    }
}
namespace MyOtherMainTypes {
    static class AnotherType {
        public static void DoSomething() {
            MyMainTypes.AType.DoSomething();
        }
    }
}
```

In the bolded code, there is a reference to another namespace, type, and method with a pair of parentheses. This is called making a method call on a static class and static method. This says that the implementation of the method is the calling of another method.

Notice how the other method is referenced using both namespace and type identifiers. This is how all types and methods are always referenced. A namespace identifier is only necessary if the type (for example, class) is not defined in the current namespace.

If you have namespaces with long names, this referencing can get tedious. As an alternative, you can add a using statement to reference the namespace, similar to the following.

```
using MyMainTypes;
namespace MyOtherMainTypes {
    static class AnotherType {
        public static void DoSomething() {
            AType.DoSomething();
        }
    }
}
```

The using statement says that if the code references any types that are not defined locally, look in this namespace (MyMainTypes in the example) to find the type. Note that if you use using two namespaces that have identically named types, then referencing that type will result in a compiler failure, because it won't know which type to reference.

This covers the absolute basics of writing some code, and we are ready to write some code to do something.

Writing the Add() Method

We'll write the code to add two numbers. To begin, create a new project in Visual C#:

1. Open Visual C# (if Visual C# is open, choose File ➤ Close Solution to ensure you have a clean slate).

2. Click File ➤ New Project or choose Create: Project.

3. Choose Class Library, name it Calculator, and click OK.

4. Rename Class1.cs to Calculator.cs.

5. Save the solution.

We can now write the Add() method. Add the bolded code to the Calculator.cs file.

```
using System;
using System.Collections.Generic;
using System.Text;

namespace Calculator
{
    public class Calculator
    {
    }
```

```
public class Operations
{
    public static int Add(int number1, int number2)
    {
        return number1 + number2;
    }
}
}
```

Figure 2-6 breaks down the various parts of the Add() method so you can see what it all means.

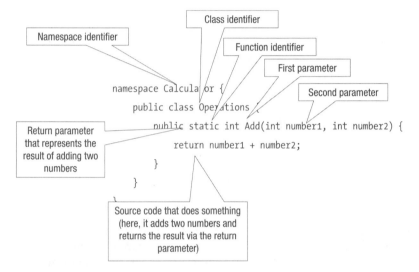

Figure 2-6. *Dissecting the addition operation*

In the code, parameters are used to specify the input data. Each parameter represents one of the numbers to be added.

In the declaration of Add(), the return parameter is the identifier int, which is the integer data type. Methods and parameters must be associated with a type, as C# is a type-safe programming language. *Type-safe* means that when you write code, you know what you are manipulating.

Suppose that you are writing code and are confronted with the numbers 1, 1.0, and "1.0". To you, these three numbers are identical. But in the context of the source code, they are not identical. The 1 is an integer, the 1.0 is a double, and the "1.0" is a string. When you want to add, subtract, or otherwise manipulate pieces of data, they should be the same types; otherwise, you might run into consistency errors. Type-safe programming languages help avoid such problems. The .NET number types are discussed in more detail in the "Understanding the CLR Numeric Types" section later in this chapter.

The declaration of Add() says that we need to pass in two integer-based numeric values, and the method returns an integer-based numeric value. The combination of parameters and a return type is a *method signature*. The method signature becomes important when another piece of code calls the Add() method. The other piece of code must use the same types as the declaration. Figure 2-7 shows a piece of code that calls the Add() method, which we'll do from another application in the next section.

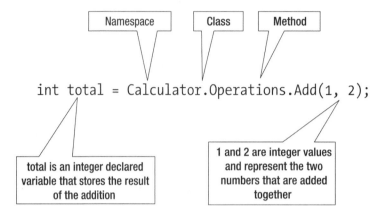

Figure 2-7. *The Add() method is called by referencing the namespace and class containing the method. A period is used to separate the identifiers.*

The caller must do two things:

- Reference the correct combination of namespace, class, and method identifiers.

- Pass the correct types for the method signature.

In the example, the addition of 1 and 2 results in 3, and therefore the variable total should contain the value of 3 (the equal sign assigns the value returned from the method to the variable on its left). I say "should contain the value," because when writing code, you are not always sure. Sometimes the code you write will be wrong because you overlooked something or forgot to reference something.

Look at the calling code, and ask yourself if you are guaranteed that calling Add() with 1 and 2 will result in 3. The answer is that, as a caller, you cannot be 100% sure that the total variable will contain 3. Just because a box has the label "Dishes" does not necessarily mean that dishes are in the box. You think you know the contents, but you cannot be 100% sure until you open the box. Likewise, in code, you need to look at how the Add() method is implemented to be sure of the contents of the total variable.

In a production coding session, looking at the implementation code to verify it is doing what you expect is not a feasible solution, because that would take too much time and be completely unreliable. The only real solution is to write test code.

Writing Code to Test the Add() Method

Test code is caller code that passes parameters with targeted values and expects a targeted answer. If the caller does not get the targeted answer, then the implementation of the tested method is wrong. Figure 2-8 shows sample caller code that tests the Add() operation (we'll add this to a project next).

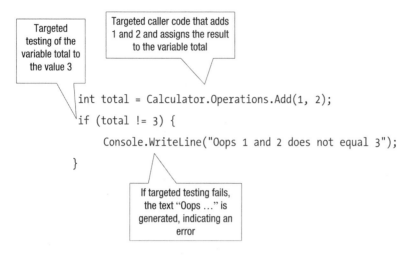

Targeted testing of the variable total to the value 3

Targeted caller code that adds 1 and 2 and assigns the result to the variable total

```
int total = Calculator.Operations.Add(1, 2);
if (total != 3) {
        Console.WriteLine("Oops 1 and 2 does not equal 3");
}
```

If targeted testing fails, the text "Oops …" is generated, indicating an error

Figure 2-8. *Testing the Add() method*

The calling code of the test bears an uncanny resemblance to the code you saw in the previous section. The difference is that the test code uses targeted variables and values, whereas the other code could contain any variables and values. Another requirement of test code is to verify the answers returned by the method with targeted responses. The if statement is used to check whether the value of the variable total is equal to 3.

When writing test code, the way the Add() method is used must be the same way the console or Windows application uses the method. Otherwise, it would be like testing a winter tire in the middle of the Sahara—fun to do but irrelevant.

The verification code in the test is a bit special. Do you or don't you verify the answer in the production? The answer is maybe. When you write verification code in a testing scenario, you are writing a 100% verification. When you write verification code in a production scenario, you are testing generally. For example, you might test for reasonableness of the data or whether the data exists.

Another question related to testing has to do with the timing of tests. Do you create the tests before or after implementing the Add() method? To get a clear understanding of the problem, imagine the development of a tire. Do you define the tests for the tire before or after the tire has been developed? Most likely, the answer is before, during, and after development. This is an important consideration when developing software. Tests are written before, during, and after implementation, as follows:

- You develop tests before implementing the Add() method to get an idea of what name-spaces, classes, and methods you will be defining. The definition of the different items gives the developer an idea of how the items will be used.

- You develop tests during the implementation of the Add() method to verify that your source code implementation is on the right track.

- You develop tests after the implementation of the Add() method as an exhaustive meas-ure to make sure you've dotted the i's and crossed the t's in the implementation.

Adding a Test Project to Your Solution

When writing test routines, you will need to organize the source code, and that means figuring out to which project the tests are added. For the calculator application, you could place the test routines within the Calculator class library. However, doing that is not the proper approach due to distribution of the class library and correct testing context. Remember that the test rou-tines must be identical to how the code will be used. Thus, the appropriate place for the test routines is in their own application.

The ideal approach is to create another application that represents the tests. Figure 2-5 illustrated how a Windows and console application could use the Calculator class library. Figure 2-9 adds the testing console application that also uses the class library.

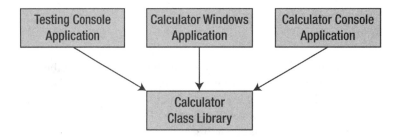

Figure 2-9. *Adding the testing console application, an application with limited functionality used to exercise the exposed functionality of the Calculator class library*

The testing console application is like the console application created in Chapter 1, and it references the Calculator class library. Both projects should be part of the Calculator solution.

Go ahead and add the TestCalculator project to the Calculator solution. Remember to add a reference to the Calculator class library (right-click References and choose Add Reference ➤ Project ➤ Calculator). Remember to set TestCalculator as the startup project for debugging purposes. Figure 2-10 shows the TestCalculator and Calculator projects in Solution Explorer.

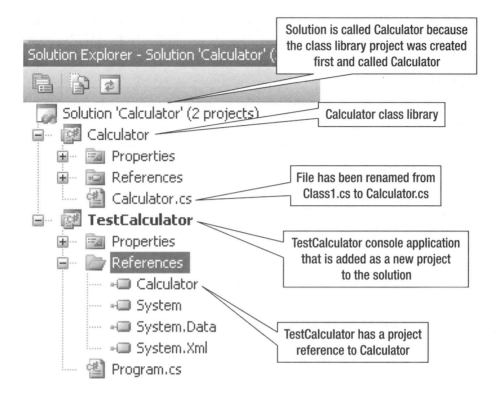

Figure 2-10. *Solution Explorer showing the testing console application and Calculator class library*

Testing Simple Addition

Add the boldfaced code to Program.cs in the testing console project to verify the addition of 1 and 2:

```
namespace TestCalculator {

    class Program {
        public static void TestSimpleAddition() {
            int total = Calculator.Operations.Add(1,2);
            if (total !=3) {
                Console.WriteLine ("Oops 1 and 2 does not equal 3");
            }
        }
        static void Main(string[] args){
            TestSimpleAddition();
        }
    }
}
```

Press Ctrl+F5 to test the calculation. When executed, the testing console application calls the test method `TestSimpleAddition()`, which calls and verifies the functionality of the Calculator class library.

■Note Recall that the `Main()` method is where a project begins its operation. To make an application do something, you must add code to its `Main()` method.

To see that the test also fails, change the `Add()` method as follows:

```
public static int Add(int number1, int number2)
{
  return number1 * number2;
}
```

Now rerun the program, and you'll see the failure message.

THE DEVELOPMENT CYCLE

So far in this chapter, we've dealt with three pieces of code:

- The code segment that implements the `Add()` method is a component that performs the calculation operation.

- The code that represents a caller, which could be either the Windows application or the console application, is considered production code.

- The code that contains the production code with some verification routines represents testing code. The testing code is important because, if the component implementation is altered, you need to rerun only the testing code to make sure everything works as it should.

These three pieces of code have demonstrated a complete development cycle.

Testing the Addition of Two Very Large Numbers

The code and projects have been organized, but we're missing some tests. The current test adds two simple numbers. Another test could be to add two really big numbers, such as 2 billion and 2 billion.

The code to test the addition of two really big numbers is shown in Figure 2-11. Add this to `Program.cs` in the `TestCalculator` project.

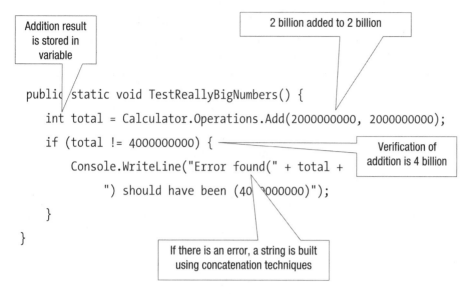

Figure 2-11. *Testing the addition of two large numbers*

The test to add two very large numbers is identical to the test to add two simple numbers, except for the numbers themselves. The error message is handled a bit differently than in the previous code, in that it is built using concatenation techniques. In the example, a string is concatenated with an integer with a string. C# will automatically convert the integer into a string.

Often, you will write tests where the only real difference is the data itself, not the ramifications of the data. Do you thinking of adding two very large numbers (such as 2 billion plus 2 billion) and two smaller numbers (such as 2 plus 2) as different? No, because to humans, the major difference between 2 billion and 2 is a bunch of zeros; the result is either 4 billion or 4, which seems very trivial. Yet with respect to a computer, 4 billion is very different from 4, as you'll soon see.

Before you run the test, you need to add a call to it in the Main() method:

```
static void Main(string[] args)
{
  TestSimpleAddition();
  TestReallyBigNumbers();
}
```

Now run the very large number test. You will see the following output:

```
Error found(-294967296) should have been (4869586958695)
```

The generated output indicates that an error occurred and that adding 2 billion to 2 billion results in a value of -294967296, which makes no sense whatsoever. What happened? The problem has to do with the type of number (int) used to declare the Add() method.

Understanding Problems with Numeric Numbers

What you understand as numbers and what the computer understands as numbers are two completely different things. As a child, you learn to count starting at 1 and ending at 100, which you thought was a gargantuan number. As you grew up, you learned about zero and numbers less than zero. Later, you advanced to studying fractions and decimal values.

Throughout all of this learning about numbers, you considered the number 1 and the number 1.5 to be the same kind of thing—that is, numbers. Yet to the computer, they are not the same type of values.

The reason numbers are different to computers has to do with computer efficiency and how the computer stores numbers. For those who have learned the decimal system with place-holders, you start counting at 0, continue to 9, and then the next number is a decimal increment called 10. The decimal system is originally accredited to the Babylonians, but they used a decimal system that was sexagesimal (60 unique identifiers versus our decimal 10 unique identifiers). The computer has a similar counting scheme, except it is binary with only two unique identifiers: 1 and 0. Computers have two unique identifiers because they signify two unique states: on and off. At the heart of a computer is a transistor that has the ability to distinguish between on and off; there are no "sort of" on and "sort of" off states.

Figure 2-12 shows an example of how a computer would count to 7 using the binary system.

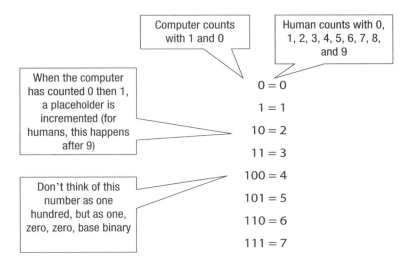

Figure 2-12. *How a computer counts to 7*

In theory, you could count until you die. You have that ability because you are human and have no limits on how high you can count. A computer does have limits, such as random-access memory (RAM), hard disk, and so on. Specific numeric data types on a computer also have limits on how high they can count. For example, the integer (int) data type that we have been using can count to only a specific number and can store only whole numbers.

Think of the different numeric data types as odometers. Most car odometers have upper limits of 1 million miles/kilometers. Imagine adding 900,000 and 200,000 using an odometer. The result would be 100,000, and not the 1.1 million that you expected. This is exactly the problem that we encountered when adding 2 billion and 2 billion.

The bad part of an odometer is that you don't know when the odometer has been wrapped around. You could end up with a car whose odometer read 100,000 miles/kilometers, but actually had driven 1.1 million. Luckily, .NET knows when the number type has been wrapped around. The technical jargon for this situation is *overflow* or *underflow*. Overflow is when the odometer wraps over in the positive direction (900,000 to 1.1 million), and underflow is when the odometer wraps around in the negative direction (0 to –100,000). Detection of either situation is activated as a project property. Follow these steps to activate overflow/underflow detection for the Calculator class library:

1. Right-click the Calculator project in the Calculator solution and select Properties.

2. Click Build, and then click Advanced.

3. Check "Check for arithmetic overflow/underflow" to test for overflow/underflow situations.

4. Click OK to finish.

Rerun the test console application, and you will get an exception indicating that an overflow has occurred (choose to continue not debug):

```
Unhandled Exception: System.OverflowException: Arithmetic operation resulted in
an overflow.
```

You can find out where the error is by running the application in debug mode. Press F5, and you should see something similar to Figure 2-13. To stop debugging, press Shift+F5.

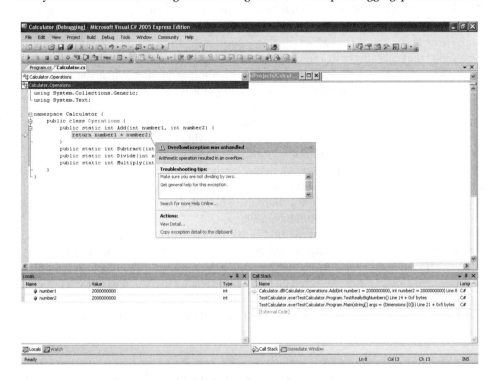

Figure 2-13. *Visual C# Express highlighting the overflow error*

Having an overflow situation is a problem, and the fact that .NET can catch it is a good thing. But at the end of the day, our preferred solution is to be able to add 2 billion plus 2 billion. After all, Bill Gates would probably prefer having 4 billion in his bank account instead of the calculated minus value or an error indicating that the bank cannot accept his 4 billion.

Understanding Numeric and Value Data Types

A *data type* is a way of describing a piece of data using a metadescription. For example, if you have a double type, you know you will have a double number. Many data types are available: int, long, short, single, double, string, enum, struct, and so on. You can even define your own data types. Data types are the heart of the CLR and a type-safe programming environment.

Understanding Value and Reference Types

The CLR supports two ways of representing data: value and reference. The major difference between a value and reference type is how the information associated with the type is stored. The problem with value and reference types is that they are a technical invention and can be confusing.

When the CLR runs an application, a thread is executing the Common Language Infrastructure (CLI). Think of a thread as you wandering around a mall buying things. You are an individual and can buy things independently of other people. The store will have many people looking around and buying different things. Likewise, a computer has many threads doing many different independent things. When you look around in a store, you might bump into people and cause them to drop things. While the CLR tries to avoid such problems, if you try hard enough in your code, you can cause other threads to "drop" things.

When it executes, a thread has a local memory pool called a *stack*, which is akin to you carrying a wallet that contains cash and credit cards. You carry the wallet with you from store to store, like a thread carries a stack when calling one method to another. When you enter the store and want to purchase something, you have two major ways of paying for the item: with cash or by using a credit/debit card. However, with a credit/debit card, you can't pay immediately. You need a machine that calls a server to verify that your piece of plastic has enough money to pay for the item. Paying with cash is much faster than paying with a credit card, because you don't need to talk to a remote computer.

Now suppose you and your spouse want to pay for the item. You could use the same credit card account, but you have unique credit cards. But you cannot do the same thing with cash. If you have a $10 bill, your spouse cannot share the $10 with you. Your spouse would need a second $10 bill, and together you would have $20.

The cash and credit card payment methods are analogous to value and reference types. Cash is a value type, and the credit card is a reference type. When the CLR executes, the code dragged from one method call to another method call is the stack that contains a number of value type variables. Value types are stored directly on the stack like cash. Reference types are stored as pointers to memory on the stack, just like a credit/debit card points to cash somewhere else. The reference pointer points to a piece of memory called the *heap*. These concepts are illustrated in Figure 2-14.

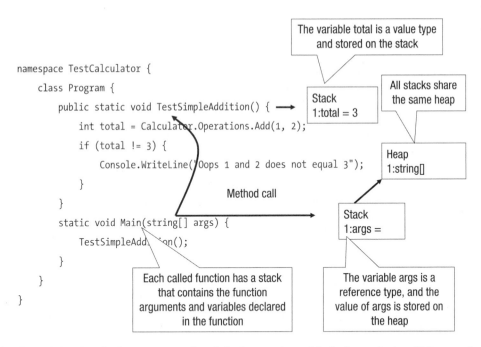

Figure 2-14. *Stacks that are created and the interaction with the heap during CLR execution*

With value types, when one value type is assigned to another, the contents are copied. If you modify one of the copies, the original will not be altered. In contrast, when you change the value of a reference type, the values of all the pointers to that reference type change. Going back to the credit card and cash example, if you have $10 and so does your spouse, then when you spend $8, it does not affect the $10 that your spouse has, as befits the value type model. However, if you and your spouse have $10 available with your credit card and you spend $8, only $2 remain, as you would expect with a reference type.

There are times when you use value types and times when you use reference types, just as there are times when you pay for things using cash and times when you use a credit card. Typically though, you use credit cards when you want to pay for expensive things, because you don't want to carry around large amounts of cash. This applies to value and reference types, in that you don't want to keep large footprint value types on the stack.

By knowing the difference between the stack and heap, you automatically know the difference between a value type and a reference type, as they are directly related. Value types are generally stored on the stack, and the contents of reference types are always stored on the heap.

Understanding the CLR Numeric Types

The CLR has two major types of numbers: whole numbers and fractional numbers. Both of these number types are value-based data types, as explained in the previous section. The Add() method used the type int, which is a whole number-based value type. As you saw, whole numbers have upper limits, which are set by the space available.

Consider the following number:

123456

This number takes six spaces of room. For illustrative purposes, imagine that the page you are reading allows only six spaces of room for numerals. Based on that information, the largest number that can be written on this page is 999,999, and the smallest is 0. In a similar manner, specific number types force the CLR to impose restrictions on how many spaces can be used to represent a number. Each space is a 1 or a 0, allowing the CLR to represent numbers in binary notation.

Computers may use binary notations, but humans work better with decimals, so to calculate the largest possible number a data type can store, you use 2 to the power of the number of spaces and then subtract 1. In the case of the int type, there are 32 spaces. Before we calculate the biggest number int can store, though, we need to consider negative numbers. The upper limit of int isn't actually 4,294,967,295 (the result of $2^{32} - 1$), because int also stores negative numbers. In other words, it can save a negative whole number, such as –2.

The computer uses a trick in that the first space of the number is reserved for the sign (plus or minus) of the number. In the case of int, that means there are only 31 spaces for numbers, so the largest number that can be represented is 2,147,483,647, and the smallest is –2,147,483,648. Going back to our addition example, this fact means that when the result of our addition is 4 billion, which in binary requires 32 spaces, int does not have the space to store it.

The .NET environment has the numeric data types listed in Table 2-1, which have varying sizes and storage capabilities. The following terminology is used to describe numeric data types:

- A *bit* is a space of storage, and 8 bits make a *byte*.

- *Integers* are whole numbers.

- *Floating-point* types are fractional numbers.

- *Signed* means one space in the number is reserved for the plus or negative sign.

Table 2-1. *.NET Numeric Data Types*

Type	Description
byte	Unsigned 8-bit integer; the smallest value is 0, and the largest value is 255
sbyte	Signed 8-bit integer; the smallest value is –128, and the largest value is 127
ushort	Unsigned 16-bit integer; the smallest value is 0, and the largest value is 65535
short	Signed 16-bit integer; the smallest value is –32768, and the largest value is 32767
uint	Unsigned 32-bit integer; the smallest value is 0, and the largest value is 4294967295
int	Signed 32-bit integer; the smallest value is –2147483648, and the largest value is 2147483647
ulong	Unsigned 64-bit integer; the smallest value is 0, and the largest value is 18446744073709551615
long	Signed 64-bit integer; the smallest value is –9223372036854775808, and the largest value is 9223372036854775807

Type	Description
float	32-bit floating-point number; the smallest value is $1.5 \times 10-45$, and the largest value is 3.4×1038, with a precision of 7 digits
double	64-bit floating-point number; the smallest value is $5.0 \times 10-324$, and the largest value is 1.7×10308, with 15 to 16 digits of precision
decimal	Special 128-bit data type; the smallest value is $1.0 \times 10-28$, and the largest value is 1.0×1028, with at least 28 significant digits of precision[a]

[a] *The* decimal *type is often used for financial data because sometimes a calculation will result in one penny less than the correct result (for example, 14.9999, instead of 15.00) due to rounding errors.*

With so many variations of number types available, you may be wondering which ones to use and when. The quick answer is that it depends on your needs. When performing scientific calculations, you probably need to use a double or float. If you are calculating mortgages, you probably need to use a decimal. And if you are performing set calculations, you probably should use an int or a long. It all depends on how accurate you want to be, or how much numeric precision you want.

Numeric precision is an important topic and should never be dealt with lightly. Consider the following example: every country takes a census of its people, and when the census is compiled, we learn some interesting facts. For example, in Canada, 31% of people will divorce. Canada has a population clock that says every minute and 32 seconds, someone is born. At the time of this writing, the population was 32,789,736. Thus, at the time of this writing, 10,164,818 people will divorce. Think a bit about what I just wrote. I said that there is a direct relationship of people who will divorce to the number of births in Canada (31%, in fact). You should be amazed that the births and divorces are timed to the point where 10,164,818—not 10,164,819 nor 10,164,820—people will divorce. Of course, I'm being cynical and just trying to make the point that numbers are just that: numbers that you round off.

I can't say 10,164,818 people will divorce, because I can't be that accurate without performing an actual count. I could probably say 10,164,818 plus or minus 100,000 will divorce. Using the plus or minus, the range is 10,064,818 to 10,264,818, or roughly speaking, 10.2 million people. The number 10.2 million is what a newsperson would report, what literature would say, and what most people would use in conversation. So, if I add 10.2 million and 1,000, can I say that the total is 10,201,000? The 10.2 is a roundoff to the nearest tenth of a million, and adding a thousand means adding a number that is less than the roundoff. The answer is that I cannot add 1,000 to 10.2, because the 1,000 is not significant with respect to the number 10.2. But I can add 1,000 to 10,164,818, to get 10,165,818, because the most significant value is a single whole number.

Relating this back to numeric types, it means integer-based numbers have a most significant single whole number. Adding 1.5 to 1.5 as whole numbers results in 2, as illustrated in Figure 2-15.

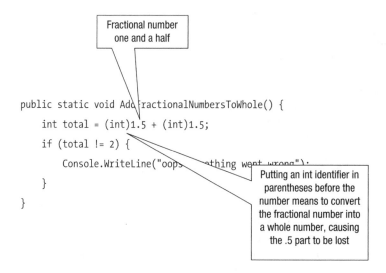

```
public static void AddFractionalNumbersToWhole() {
    int total = (int)1.5 + (int)1.5;
    if (total != 2) {
        Console.WriteLine("oops, something went wrong");
    }
}
```

Fractional number
one and a half

Putting an int identifier in
parentheses before the
number means to convert
the fractional number into
a whole number, causing
the .5 part to be lost

Figure 2-15. *Adding fractions using the int data type*

Let's extend this concept of significant digits to a floating-point number type, float, and consider the example shown in Figure 2-16.

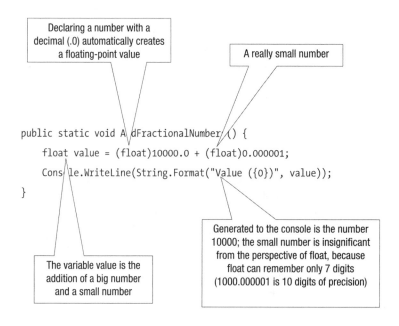

```
public static void AddFractionalNumber() {
    float value = (float)10000.0 + (float)0.000001;
    Console.WriteLine(String.Format("Value ({0})", value));
}
```

Declaring a number with a
decimal (.0) automatically creates
a floating-point value

A really small number

The variable value is the
addition of a big number
and a small number

Generated to the console is the number
10000; the small number is insignificant
from the perspective of float, because
float can remember only 7 digits
(1000.000001 is 10 digits of precision)

Figure 2-16. *Adding fractions using the float data type*

As shown in Figure 2-16, if you want to keep the precision of adding a small number to a large number, you will need to switch number types to double. But even double has limits and can remember only 15 to 16 digits of precision.

If you want even more precision, you could use decimal, but decimal is more suitable for financial calculations. With financial calculations, you will run into the problem of having very large numbers added to small numbers. Imagine being Bill Gates and having a few billion in your bank account. When the bank calculates the interest, you will want to know how many pennies you have accumulated, because pennies, when added over a long period of time, make a big difference. In fact, some programmers have "stolen" money from banks by collecting the fractional pennies and accumulating them.

Now that you've seen some of the complexities involved when working with numbers, let's finish the calculator.

Finishing the Calculator

The original declaration of the Add() method for the calculator worked, but had some serious limitations on what kinds of numbers could be added. To finish the calculator, we need to declare the Add() method using a different type, and then add the remaining operations.

We could use one of three types to declare the Add() method:

- long: Solves the problem of adding two very large numbers like 2 billion, but has the problem that you cannot add fractional numbers like 1.5 plus 1.5.

- double: Solves the problem of adding two very large or small numbers, and can be used to add fractional numbers. Generally speaking, double is a good choice, but can suffer from significance problems if a very large number is manipulated by a very small number.

- decimal: A generally good approach and suitable for all types of precision, but also the slowest when adding, subtracting, or performing other mathematical operations.

The simplest all-around numeric data type to use is double, as it provides good precision and is relatively fast. The complete implementation of the calculator is as follows:

```
public class Operations {
    public static double Add(double number1, double numer2) {
        return number1 + number2;
    }
    public static double Subtract(double number1, double number2) {
        return number1 - number2;
    }
    public static double Divide(double number1, double number2) {
        return number1 / number2;
    }
    public static double Multiply(double number1, double number2) {
        return number1 * number2;
    }
}
```

The four operations are methods with different identifiers, but identical function signatures, making it easy to remember how to use each method. Each of the operations would have an appropriate set of tests verifying the correctness of the implementation. The tests are not reproduced here, but they are implemented in the sample source code. I advise you to take a quick look at the tests to make sure you understand the individual pieces.

The Important Stuff to Remember

In this chapter, you learned about developing a class library that is used to perform some calculations. The following are the key points to remember:

- Organization of your thoughts, projects, and features makes all the difference when writing software.

- When writing software, stay focused. It is very easy to drift around in software development, because software lets you stray easily. A successful developer will always be organized and focused.

- Software is designed using an architecture that could be implemented top-down or bottom-up.

- Within an architecture, individual pieces are called *components*, and they fit together to create a complete application.

- You write tests because you cannot verify the functionality of a component based on its identifier, parameters, or return value.

- When implementing components, you develop tests before, during, and after writing the source code.

- A test is a piece of source code that calls a component using targeted input data, and the results from the component are verified with targeted responses. If the results do not match the targeted responses, the component has failed.

- The CLR offers many different data types, with the major distinction being between value and reference types.

- The CLR has many different number types, but all number types are value types.

- Numbers can overflow or underflow. You should activate a compiler setting to make sure that the CLR will catch those situations.

- When deciding on a specific number type, a large part of the decision is based on how much precision is desired.

Some Things for You to Do

The following are some things to consider related to what you've learned in this chapter:

1. When you write code, how should you organize your code? For example, do you enforce certain naming identifiers? Do you enforce a coding scheme? Do you enforce the use of code comments?

2. In the development community, there is a discussion of whether organization of your software should involve formal structures or should be ad hoc. Think about how software should be organized.

3. In general, how would you test whether or not a component that uses a database worked properly? Outline the process with bulleted points.

4. In general, how would you test the correctness of writing data to a file? To help understand the nature of the problem, how do you know that an operating system manipulates files properly?

5. If the CLR did not provide for a mechanism to catch overflow and underflow conditions, how would you ensure that overflow and underflow didn't happen?

6. For a Pentium CPU (32 bits), which number type would result in the fastest calculations?

7. In this chapter's example, the class Operations is designed to perform arithmetic using the double type. How would you change this so that the calculations are generic?

CHAPTER 3

■■■

Learning About String Manipulations

In the previous chapter, you learned the basics of how data is stored and managed by .NET, including the difference between value and reference types. .NET has three major data types: number-related, custom-defined, and string. The previous chapter focused on the number-related types. This chapter will focus on the string type.

As you'll learn in this chapter, the string type has some special characteristics. If you were to look at the bits and bytes of the string type, you would not realize that they were letters. In an abstract description, a string type is a number type with a special grammar. Since a computer understands only numbers, it uses lookup tables that map a set of letters to a set of numbers.

The example in this chapter is a multilingual translation program. The translation program will not be sophisticated, nor will it be capable of much. However, it will illustrate many of the issues that you will be confronted with when working with strings.

Organizing the Translation Application

As emphasized in the previous chapter, the first step in developing an application is to get organized. We need to understand and define the features of the sample application we are going to develop. The multilingual translation program will implement the following features:

- Translate greetings into three different languages: French, German, and English.

- Convert numbers into the three different languages.

- Convert a date into the three different languages.

From a feature perspective, the first feature is logical, but the second and third features are not as obvious. We generally think of translation as translating one word to another word(s). Yet, languages also can represent numbers and dates in different ways. Translation will mean two things: translate a word from one language to another, and translate a number or date from one language to another.

As in Chapter 2, we'll create the solution as components, with three pieces: a Windows application, a testing console application, and a class library. After you have created each of the projects, your workspace should look like Figure 3-1. Remember to add a reference to the LanguageTranslator class library (right-click References and choose Add Reference ➤ Project ➤ LanguageTranslator). Also remember to set TestLanguageTranslator as the startup project.

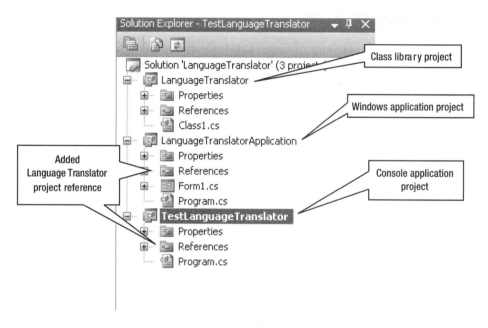

Figure 3-1. *Structure of projects for the translation application in Visual C# Express Solution Explorer*

Building the Translator Application

The translation application, like the calculator application example in the previous chapter, is built in pieces: the class library that performs translations based on data delivered by the user interface, the tests, and the user interface. The individual pieces are components that can be fit together like a jigsaw puzzle to create an application.

■**Note** Components are a core part of your development toolbox. As you will see throughout the book, components allow you to reuse and modularize functionality. Components result in applications that are maintainable and extendable. Of course, there are limits, and the advantages are not automatic. You will need to properly design your application to benefit from using components.

Creating the Translator Class

When working with Visual C# Express, or one of the other Visual Studio products, using the default templates for creating a class library results in the creation of a file named Class1.cs. It is good that a default file is created for a class library, but the identifier Class1.cs does not imply much. Therefore, you should go ahead and delete that file from the project. In its place, create the Translator class, as follows:

1. Right-click the LanguageTranslator project.

2. Click Add ➤ New Item.

3. Select Class.

4. Rename the file Translator.cs.

5. Click Add to create the file and add it to your project.

Notice how quickly you managed to create a C# class using the Visual Studio IDE. The speed of creating a class file lets you focus on adding source code to the file. But do not be misled into believing that by creating a number of class files, your code will automatically work and be a masterpiece. You still need to think about which files, projects, classes, and tests to create.

Translating Hello

The first feature we will implement is the translation of the text "hello." Since "hello" is English, the first translation will be English to German. The following is the code to implement this feature. It is added to the Translator.cs file in the LanguageTranslator project.

```
public class Translator {
    public static string TranslateHello(string input) {
        if (input.CompareTo("hello") == 0) {
            return "hallo";
        }
        else if (input.CompareTo("allo") == 0) {
            return "hallo";
        }
        return "";
    }
}
```

Translator is the main class that is exposed to other components or pieces of source code. Think of it as the identifier of the black box. The black box has a single method: TranslateHello. TranslateHello() is the method used to convert the French "allo" and the English "hello" to the German "hallo." The method's input is a string type, which is a reference object type.

In the implementation of TranslateHello, we use CompareTo() to compare the contents of the input buffer to the parameter "hello". If the comparison is equal, meaning that the strings are equal, 0 is returned. As you'll learn in the "Investigating the String Type" section, string is an object, and objects typically have methods. One of the string type's methods is CompareTo(). The caller of TranslateHello does not know how you managed to translate one word to another language. The caller actually does not care; it cares only that the method behaves as expected.

The abstract intent of the `TranslateHello()` method is to accept some text and, if the text is matched, return a German "hallo."

Creating the Test Application

Without questioning the abstract intent, the written code needs some testing. The test code is added to the test application, which is the project `TestLanguageTranslator`.

The following code is added to the `Program.cs` file

```
static void TestTranslateHello() {
    string verifyValue;

    verifyValue = LanguageTranslator.Translator.TranslateHello("hello");
    if (verifyValue.CompareTo("hallo") != 0) {
        Console.WriteLine("Test failed of hello to hallo");
    }
    verifyValue = LanguageTranslator.Translator.TranslateHello("allo");
    if (verifyValue.CompareTo("hallo") != 0) {
        Console.WriteLine("Test failed of allo to hallo");
    }
    verifyValue = LanguageTranslator.Translator.TranslateHello("allosss");
    if (verifyValue.CompareTo("") != 0) {
        Console.WriteLine("Test to verify nontranslated word failed");
    }
    verifyValue = LanguageTranslator.Translator.TranslateHello("  allo");
    if (verifyValue.CompareTo("hallo") != 0) {
        Console.WriteLine("Test failed of extra whitespaces allo to hallo");
    }
}
```

The source code contains four tests. Each calls the method `TranslateHello()`, with some input, and receives the output. The test happens when the output is verified against an expected result. The verification tests use the `CompareTo()` function to test for correct translation.

Notice the third test:

```
verifyValue = LanguageTranslator.Translator.TranslateHello("allosss");
if (verifyValue.CompareTo("") != 0) {
    Console.WriteLine("Test to verify nontranslated word failed");
}
```

This test expects an explicit failure. You need to write successful tests that fail. Successful tests that are meant to fail ensure that your code does not generate false positives. A *false positive* is when your code is supposed to fail and it does not.

The tests are within a method that needs to be called from the `Main` method, as in the following example:

```
static void Main(string[] args)
{
    TestTranslateHello();
}
```

If you compile and run the tests, you will find that one of the tests fails. The failing test is the fourth one, which attempts to translate a word that has whitespace. Whitespace is space that we humans don't notice, but is necessary to distinguish words, sentences, and so on. Before we can solve the whitespace problem, we need to determine which part of the application is not working properly.

Answering the Question of Responsibility

The whitespace problem is an interesting one. The caller explicitly put in the extra spaces, but is the whitespace a bug, or is it data that is passed in incorrectly?

The problem can be defined in the context of reasonable usage. Imagine that you've just bought a car and you're driving it on the highway. If the car breaks down, the warranty will be in effect and cover the costs of the car repair. Now imagine the situation where you think you are one of the Dukes from the *Dukes of Hazzard*. And being a Duke, you drive your new car as fast as you can and then perform a flying jump. The car will jump into air, which looks quite spectacular, but then the car lands. After that, the shocks collapse, and the car cannot be driven any further. Even though the car is brand new, the Duke did not use the car as envisioned by the car manufacturer, and thus invalidates the warranty.

Getting back to the translation component, it exposes the method `TranslateHello()` and has responsibilities. And the caller of `TranslateHello()` has the responsibility of being reasonable about what can be expected to be translated. So, is whitespace sent by the caller reasonable?

If the whitespace is a normal circumstance, then the failed test is a bug in the component. But if the whitespace is not a normal circumstance, the caller is wrong and must be fixed. The answer is that the caller is being reasonable, and the component is not acting properly. We have a bug in the component that needs to be fixed. How do I know that the caller is not being reasonable? I made it up, because that is how I expected the contract to be implemented. The key is in defining a good contract.

The bug in the component relates to the problem of how a word is being translated. We used the `CompareTo()` method, which means that each character is compared, position for position. The test failed because the caller passed in a string with whitespace, and the component expected no whitespace. This bug is not a surprise, because we humans ignore the whitespace, but computers cannot.

Before I explain how to fix the bug, I need to take a step back and talk about what a string is and how you can figure out what a string can do.

Investigating the String Type

A `string` is an object, and thus a reference type. A `string` is a type that has methods and properties. Value types like `double` and `int` have methods and properties, but `string` is the first type you are encountering that is an actual object that you need to investigate.

To investigate a type, you can read the documentation or you use IntelliSense. Reading the documentation is not a bad idea, but it is the slowest and most cumbersome. IntelliSense is an integrated development environment (IDE) approach, in which a defined type's methods and properties are presented to you in an easy-to-comprehend manner.

The first time you use IntelliSense, it can be nerve-wracking, because it seems like the IDE has a life of its own. There is a convention on how to use IntelliSense, as illustrated in Figure 3-2. I advise that you take a few moments to experiment with it. I also recommend that you keep IntelliSense active in Visual C# Express.

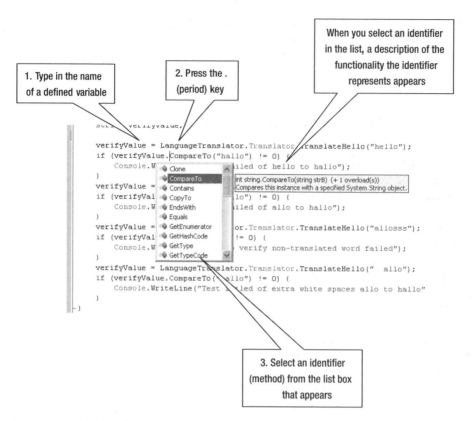

Figure 3-2. *Using IntelliSense on a string typed variable*

IntelliSense works on only identified variables that have types. In Figure 3-2, IntelliSense worked because the IDE parsed the code and had the ability to read the metadata associated with the type. *Metadata* is data that describes your source code. Whenever you define a class, methods and properties are associated with it. The method and property descriptions are pieces of metadata that is displayed by IntelliSense. One of the strengths of .NET is that all types have metadata.

The Basis of All Types: Object

By default, everything in .NET is an object with a few basic properties and methods. Four basic methods are associated with every object:

- Equals(): Verifies the equality of two objects (see Figure 3-3).

- GetHashCode(): Retrieves a unique number describing the object (see Figure 3-4). Two objects with the same contents will return the same hashcode.

- GetType(): Retrieves the metadata associated with an object (see Figure 3-5). Allows the program to play "Are you a . . .?" to dynamically determine which methods and properties a type has. It is used by IntelliSense to display a list box.

- ToString(): Converts the contents of the type into a string (see Figure 3-6). Note that the default CLR ToString() implementations work only for value types.

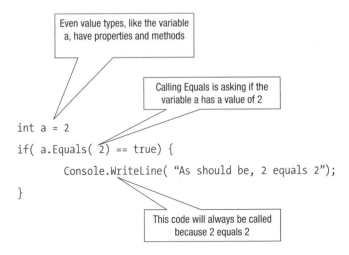

```
int a = 2
if( a.Equals( 2) == true) {
        Console.WriteLine( "As should be, 2 equals 2");
}
```

Figure 3-3. *Equals() is used to verify the equality of two objects.*

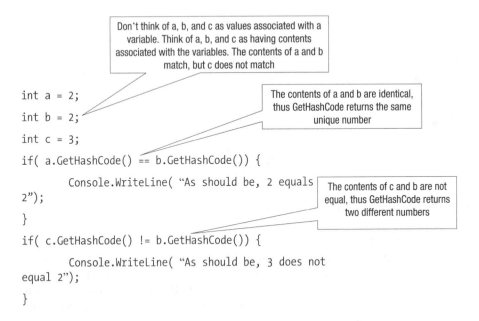

```
int a = 2;
int b = 2;
int c = 3;
if( a.GetHashCode() == b.GetHashCode()) {
        Console.WriteLine( "As should be, 2 equals
2");
}
if( c.GetHashCode() != b.GetHashCode()) {
        Console.WriteLine( "As should be, 3 does not
equal 2");
}
```

Figure 3-4. *GetHashCode() retrieves a unique number describing the object.*

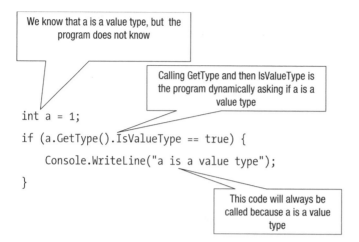

Figure 3-5. *GetType() retrieves the metadata associated with an object.*

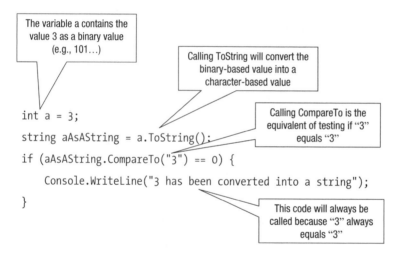

Figure 3-6. *ToString() converts the contents of the type into a string.*

The four basic methods can be called on every variable that you declare. You will use ToString() when debugging or inspecting the state of an object instance during runtime. ToString() returns a human-readable string that contains the state of the object instance.

You might use the GetType() method occasionally, but your IDE and other tools will use it all the time. Using GetType(), you have the ability to figure out the capabilities of a variable during the execution of a program. In technical terms, GetType() returns the formal metadata description of the type.

From reading the description of Equals() and GetHashCode(), you would get the impression that these two functions serve the same purpose. However, this is not the case.

Let's say you're moving and you've packed two boxes containing kitchen items. Both boxes contain five red dishes, three silver forks, two copper knives, and two wineglasses. If you compare the boxes, both Equals() and GetHashCode() will return equality, indicating the boxes contain the same number and color of items. It is important to understand that even though the two boxes are unique instances containing unique articles, their contents are identical. When you compare object instances using Equals() or GetHashCode(), you are comparing the metadata and value attributes, not the unique instances.

Now imagine the situation where one of the boxes has wineglasses from IKEA and the other has wineglasses from Pier 1. If you use the Equals() method to compare the boxes, it will return false, because the box content details are not identical. The difference lies in how the glasses are described. In contrast, calling GetHashCode() will indicate that the contents of the boxes are identical. This is because GetHashCode() is doing a quick contents identification.

The difference between the Equals() and GetHashCode() functions is perspective. In the example, from the perspective of the moving company, the boxes are identical because the moving company does not care whether the wineglasses are from IKEA or Pier 1; it will not distinguish wineglasses from different companies.

The fact that GetHashCode() can return identical numbers for what would seem dissimilar object contents can confuse developers. The way to understand GetHashCode() is that, rather than being useful to verify equality, it helps you verify *inequality*. If two objects return dissimilar hashcode values, then you know the contents are not identical. The intent of a hashcode is to generate a quick fingerprint of the contents of an object. It is not completely reliable, but works for the most part.

WHEN INTELLISENSE IS NOT ENOUGH

IntelliSense is very good and will even display comments that explain what the method does (as illustrated in Figure 3-2). Another place to find answers is the Microsoft documentation itself, which you can access by selecting Help ➤ Index. You can use the Look For box to search for a specific type. For example, if you type "String class" in the Look For box, you will see details of the String class, which you can then filter using the links at the top of the page.

The Microsoft documentation is part of the Microsoft Developer Network (MSDN) (http://msdn. microsoft.com). The MSDN web site contains documentation that helps you figure out the .NET standard software development kit (.NET SDK) application programming interface (API). There are literally thousands of types, with an explosion of methods and properties. You will probably not use all of them in a single application, but you will always use the .NET SDK.

In most cases, MSDN will be enough to help you figure out when you don't know about a specific type. If you want to learn more about concepts, you can surf to a web site such as Code Project (http://www. codeproject.com). Code Project contains plenty of examples for almost every development topic that suits your fancy.

The Problem: Character-by-Character Comparison

Let's get back to the bug of the whitespace. The method that caused problems was CompareTo(). Looking at the MSDN documentation, you see the following definition for this method (found by scrolling down the String class page and clicking the CompareTo link):

Compares this instance with a specified object.

This definition does not tell you much, so you will need to click another method name under the Reference heading. (Other method declarations often cross-reference each other and explain general concepts.) Click the Compare() link, and then click the Compare(string, string) link. In the explanation of the Compare() method, you find the following text:

> *The comparison terminates when an inequality is discovered or both strings have been compared. However, if the two strings compare equal to the end of one string, and the other string has characters remaining, then the string with remaining characters is considered greater. The return value is the result of the last comparison performed.*

■**Note** Looking up the meaning of a method is not a long process, even though it may seem like that from the description in this section. With experience, you don't even notice the extra clicks.

The CompareTo() method failed because of the character-by-character comparison, which is illustrated in Figure 3-7.

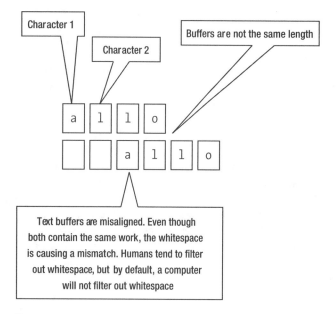

Figure 3-7. *How CompareTo() fails to compare strings that appear identical but have extra characters*

Strings are stored in buffers, with one space in the buffer allocated to one character. As you can see from Figure 3-7, whitespace takes up one space in the buffer. We can take advantage of this sometimes, as you'll see in the next section.

Now that you know what the problem is, the next step is to find a solution.

Solving the Extra Whitespace Problem

You can solve the whitespace problem in multiple ways. Which way you use depends on your needs. Let's look at several solutions and see which works best for our translation program.

Trimming the Whitespace

The first solution we'll look at is to trim the whitespace using a method intended for that purpose. The whitespace problem is not unique and is well known. The string type has a method that can be used to remove, or trim, the whitespace from a buffer. You can remove whitespace at the beginning, end, or both sides of the buffer.

As tempting as it is to change the original implementation of TranslateHello(), don't do that, because you might fix something that is not broken. When you develop code, you have multiple possible ways to solve a problem. If you start messing around with the original source code, by the time you reach the third or fourth solution, the code might be a complete mess. Your fixes might make things worse, and trying to backtrack in your source code becomes very difficult.

■**Note** To manage your source code, you should use version control. However, even with version control, when you delete past attempts, ideas get lost. Thus, while your source code will be clean, you might forget something you did three or four hours ago. Trust me, this happens, because developing source code is an intensive thought process.

The solution is to create a shim that calls the TranslateHello() method. The shim is used to fix the bug. The following shim code is a temporary solution:

```
public static string TrimmingWhitespace (string buffer) {
    string trimmed = buffer.Trim();
    return LanguageTranslator.Translator.TranslateHello(trimmed);
}
```

TrimmingWhitespace() is a temporary method that trims whitespace from the string to be translated. buffer.Trim() is new functionality that preprocesses the buffer. Finally, we call the original method, TranslateHello(), to perform the translation.

Of course, we need to test the new method to see if it trims the string to be translated. The following is the corresponding test code.

```
verifyValue = TrimmingWhitespace("  allo");
if (verifyValue.CompareTo("hallo") != 0) {
    Console.WriteLine("Test failed of extra white spaces allo to hallo");
}
```

The test calls the work-in-progress method, TrimmingWhiteSpace(), to see if everything works. The verification code does not change.

So that you get predictable results, remember to call the shim and not the original method. If you run the test code, you'll see that the shim works, and thus we have a solution.

Finding a Substring

Another solution to the whitespace problem is to find a specific substring in a buffer. Think of it as a search solution, where a method iterates over a string and attempts to match elements of a buffer to some text that is being searched. The work-in-progress code is shown in Figure 3-8.

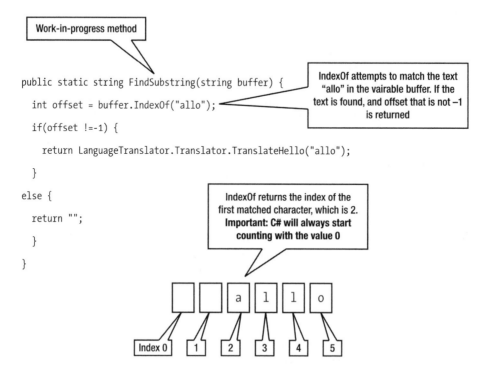

Figure 3-8. *Finding a substring to solve the whitespace problem*

The test code is not shown here, because it is similar to that for the previous solution, with the difference being the method being tested.

Which Is the Best Solution?

Take a moment to think about which is the best solution: trimming the whitespace or finding a substring. The answer is neither is perfect; each solution has its problems. This is a very common occurrence when you are developing software. You think you have all the corners covered, and then another scenario causes your software to fail.

Again, I want to stress that you need to write more tests to figure out which scenarios might cause your software to fail. For the solution of trimming whitespace, writing another test causes it to fail, as shown in the following code. It cannot be tweaked to make the test succeed.

```
verifyValue = TrimmingWhitespace("a  allo");
if (verifyValue.CompareTo("hallo") != 0) {
    Console.WriteLine("Test failed: cannot parse multiple words");
}
```

In the test, the leading "a" is considered the first character and is not trimmed. The verification will fail because CompareTo() cannot verify the misaligned buffer caused by the leading "a."

If the new test were executed against the substring solution, it would succeed and find the word "allo." Because the new test caused the first solution to fail, it would seem that solution is a no-go. Our confidence has been increased in the second solution because the old test and the new test did not fail. But don't be so hasty to consider. The substring solution fails with the following test.

```
verifyValue = FindSubstring("allodium");
if (verifyValue.CompareTo("hallo") != 0) {
    Console.WriteLine("Test failed: cannot parse multiple words");
}
```

The word tested, "allodium", contains the characters allo. The verification will succeed, and this is an example of a false positive.

Note It is important to have many tests that verify a multitude of different scenarios. You should have tests that are supposed succeed and those that are supposed to fail.

The conclusion is that neither of the solutions works properly. With extended testing, each solution created new problems. We need to find another solution.

DEVELOPMENT FRUSTRATIONS

It would seem that creating solutions and then creating tests that nullify the solution is a lesson in frustration. You create code that does not solve the problems. What you must realize and take to heart is that this is part of software development. There are those who write code and don't worry about the tests, but those developers give software development a bad name.

You want to be a trustworthy developer who tests your code. I have been, and my wife is, a software development manager. In her words, "I can deal with slow developers, but I cannot deal with developers who I cannot trust to write stable and robust code. The problem with untrustworthy developers is that I cannot let them release code into production and always have to have somebody looking over their shoulders."

Writing the Tests Before Writing the Code

The reason the previous solutions failed is because each solution was a knee-jerk reaction. Knee-jerk reactions are those where when you encounter a bug, you solve the bug—no more and no less. Instead, you should figure out what the bug is trying to tell you. The original bug with the leading whitespace was not a whitespace bug, but a bug that was saying, "Hey, what if my text is not aligned, or part of a sentence, and so on?"

To solve the bug, you don't write code, but you think of all of the tests that your code needs to pass. You need to assign responsibility and define contexts that succeed and fail. In the translation example, the appropriate implementation approach would be to write the tests before writing the code. Table 3-1 shows the contexts that fail and succeed.

Table 3-1. *Appropriate Tests for the Translation Program*

Test	Verification Result
allo	Success
" allo "	Success
word allo	Fail: You can't translate a single word without translating the other words
word allo word	Fail: Same reason as with word allo
prefixallo	Fail: Different word
alloappend	Fail: Different word
prefixalloappend	Fail: Different word

As you can see in the table, most test cases are failures because the translation component is meant to translate single words only. The test cases seem complete, but in fact, we are missing one more set of cases, which are outlined in Table 3-2.

Table 3-2. *The Missing Test Cases for the Translation Program*

Test	Verification Result
Allo	Success
" allO "	Success

Text can contain mixed cases, and from a human perspective, mixed case is still the same word. However, the computer considers mixed case as a completely different buffer, and so we must be able to cope with this situation.

Figure 3-9 shows the working solution.

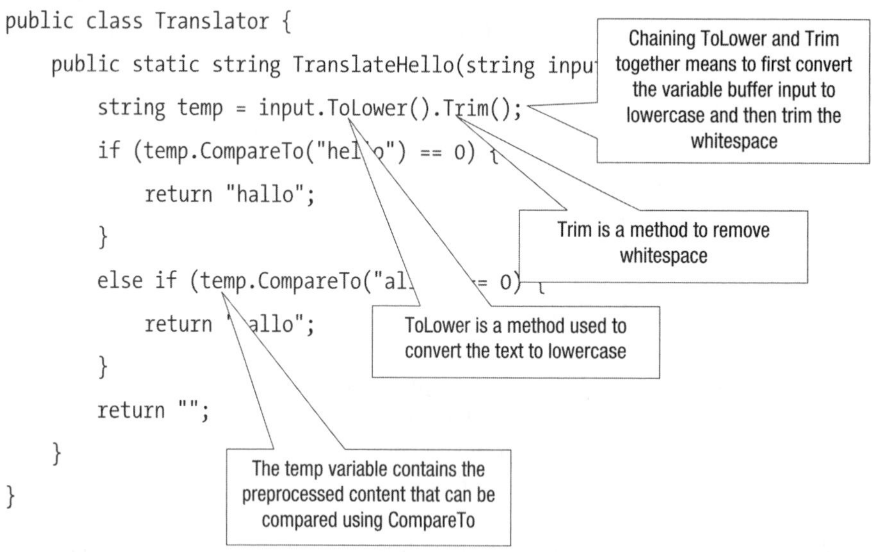

```
public class Translator {
    public static string TranslateHello(string input) {
        string temp = input.ToLower().Trim();
        if (temp.CompareTo("hello") == 0) {
            return "hallo";
        }
        else if (temp.CompareTo("allo") == 0) {
            return "allo";
        }
        return "";
    }
}
```

Chaining ToLower and Trim together means to first convert the variable buffer input to lowercase and then trim the whitespace

Trim is a method to remove whitespace

ToLower is a method used to convert the text to lowercase

The temp variable contains the preprocessed content that can be compared using CompareTo

Figure 3-9. *The final translation solution*

Looking at the solution, you see that there are elements from the first solution, which was discounted because it did not work properly. This is an example of how quickly solving a bug, seeing that code fail, and discounting the solution can be incorrect. You need to think through why something fails, and not just fix the bug to get rid of it.

■Note All of the solutions involved using `string` type methods. The `string` type is very sophisticated and supports many operations that are commonly performed on text.

At this point, we are finished with the translation of the greeting. Next, I'll point out a couple of additional items that you need to keep in mind when dealing with strings.

Quoting Strings

You might have noticed the use of a double quotation marks and single quotation marks (quotes, for short) when the method `CompareTo()` was called. Which type of quote you use makes a very big difference. If you use a double quote, as in the following example, then you are defining a `string` type:

```
"using double quotes"
```

If you use a single quote, as in the following example, you are defining a character:

```
'a'
```

The single quote can be used only with a single character. Think of a single character as a letter, but don't become too attached to that definition, since not all languages have letters. If you attempt to use the single quote to define a buffer of multiple characters, the C# compiler will generate an error, more commonly called a .NET *exception*.

Character Mapping

A single character takes 16 bits of space, and the space that a string consumes depends on the number of characters in a buffer. If a buffer is 10 characters long, then the entire buffer takes up 160 bits of space. A `string` type is a reference type, not a value type.

A single character is 16 bits long so that a buffer can store text in a multitude of different formats. The standardized length is due to a standard called Unicode.

Consider the character *a*. Philosophically, how do you know that an *a* is an *a*? For humans, that's easy because our brains are trained to recognize the curve and look of an *a*. Now look at the Russian letter shown in Figure 3-10.

И

Figure 3-10. *A Russian letter*

What letter does Figure 3-10 show? It looks like an *H*, right? But comparing it to the English language, it is an *N*. The Russian language has its own set of letters, and someone has determined that a Russian *H* is an English *N*. Figure 3-11 is a mapping of the Russian letters to the English letters.

Russian	English transliteration	Russian	English transliteration
а	a	р	r
б	b	с	s
в	v	т	t
г	g	у	u
д	d	ф	f
е / ё	e	х	kh
ж	zh	ц	ts
з	z	ч	ch
и / й	i	ш	sh
к	k	щ	shch
л	l	ъ	ʹʹ
м	m	ы	y
н	n	ь	ʹ
о	o	э	e
п	p	ю	iu
		я	ia

Sennaya.com

Figure 3-11. *Mapping of Russian letters to English letters*

If I were learning Russian, I would want the mapping provided in Figure 3-11. The mapping gives me an idea of what each letter in Russian represents. You could think of Figure 3-11 as a lookup table. The computer has the same sort of need, because a computer does not understand letters. A computer understands only numbers and thus uses lookup tables that map a set of letters to a set of numbers.

There are many lookup tables, such as American Standard Code for Information Interchange (ASCII). For example, using ASCII, the letter *a* maps to the number 97. The problem with ASCII is that it works well for English, but works horribly for other languages. ASCII was extended to deal with Western European languages, but still fails for languages such as Chinese, Russian, or Arabic.

The solution chosen by .NET is Unicode. Unicode is the definition of a set of lookup tables that map to letters for all of the languages of the world.

For the most part, you will not have to concern yourself with the Unicode, because .NET manages everything transparently. This was not the case many years ago, when programmers had to manage the lookup tables themselves. So consider yourself lucky that you did not experience this pain in developing multilingual applications.

Dealing with Languages and Cultures

Managing strings in .NET does not stop with Unicode. .NET is very innovative in that it understands concepts such as culture and language, which are a reflection of how humans speak and live. The ideas of culture and language do not exist in other programming environments.

Consider Switzerland, which is a country in the middle of Europe, and is the size of Vermont and New Hampshire combined. Throughout Switzerland, there are mountains that happen to separate four individual languages: German, Italian, Romansch, and French. Even with the four languages, the Swiss all trade the same currency and write numbers the same way.

In previous programming environments, the language would be tied to a particular country. This works fine for France, Germany, and the United States, but fails miserably for Canada, Switzerland, Belgium, and India. You need to separate language from culture, because multiple languages are used in different cultures. For example, Italian is spoken in Switzerland and Italy. French is spoken in France, Switzerland, Luxembourg, and Canada. German is spoken in Germany, Switzerland, and Austria.

Setting Culture and Language in Windows

The Windows operating system allows you to set the culture and language of your computer, regardless of the language in which Windows is operating. Figure 3-12 shows an example.

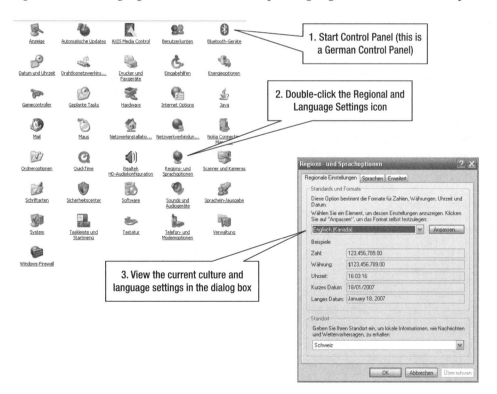

Figure 3-12. *Setting the culture and language in Windows*

The example in Figure 3-12 is running a German version of Windows in Switzerland. The language is English, and the culture is Canada. It would seem that Windows would get confused, but in fact, if you write your .NET application properly, multilanguage support is simple.

Parsing and Processing Numbers

The culture and country become important when interacting with numbers and dates that are stored as strings. Imagine retrieving a string buffer with an embedded number and then attempting to perform an addition, as illustrated by Figure 3-13.

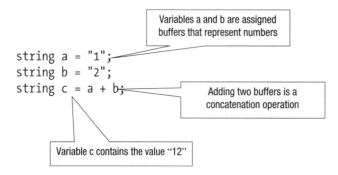

Figure 3-13. *Performing arithmetic on numbers represented as strings can lead to unexpected results.*

Adding numbers is performing a mathematical operation. When the add operation is performed on strings, it always results in a buffer concatenation. The add operation is a very simple way to concatenate string buffers together.

However, concatenation is not the aim of the example. The aim is to treat the strings as numbers and then add the numbers so that c contains the value 3 (1 + 2 = 3). The rewritten version of the example is shown in Figure 3-14. This code parses a string into an integer.

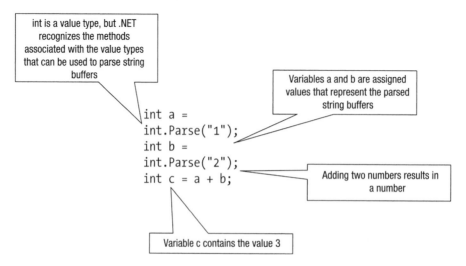

Figure 3-14. *Parsing strings into integers before doing the arithmetic*

The type int has a Parse() method that can be used to turn a string into an integer. The parsing works only if the buffer is a valid number. If the buffer contains letters or an invalid number, an error will be generated.

If the code can cope with a failed string conversion, the solution used by the parsing routines is to generate an exception that a program could process. Alternatively, a fail-safe way that can be used to parse a number without needing an exception block is to use TryParse(), as in the following example.

```
int value;
if(int.TryParse("1", out value)) {
}
```

The method TryParse() does not return an integer value, but instead returns a bool flag, indicating whether the buffer could be parsed. If the return value is true, then the buffer could be parsed, and the result is stored in the parameter value that is marked using the out identifier. The out identifier is used in .NET to indicate that the parameter contains a value after calling TryParse(). You can parse other number types using the same techniques (for example, float.TryParse()).

There are more variations in how a number can be parsed. For example, how would the number 100 be parsed, if the number 100 is hexadecimal? (Computers use hexadecimal numbers.) Here is an example of hexadecimal conversion:

```
using System.Globalization;
...
public void ParseHexadecimal() {
    int value = int.Parse("100", NumberStyles.HexNumber);
}
```

This example uses a variant of Parse(), which has an additional second parameter that represents the format of the number. In this case, the second parameter indicates that the format of the number is hexadecimal (NumberStyles.HexNumber, from the System.Globalization namespace). In the example, the buffer represents the decimal number 256, which is verified by using Assert.AreEquals().

■**Note** If you are wondering how 100 maps to 256 at the hex level, use the calculator that comes with the Windows operating system. Switch the calculator to scientific view and click the Hex radio button, enter the number 100, and then click the Dec radio button.

The enumeration NumberStyles has other values that can be used to parse numbers according to other rules. For example, some rules handle the use of parentheses surrounding a number to indicate a negative value. Other rules deal with whitespace. Here is an example:

```
public void TestParseNegativeValue(){
    int value = int.Parse( " (10) ",
    NumberStyles.AllowParentheses |
    NumberStyles.AllowLeadingWhite |
```

```
    NumberStyles.AllowTrailingWhite);
}
```

The number " (10) " in this example is complicated in that it has whitespace and parentheses. Attempting to parse the number using `Parse()` without using any of the `NumberStyles` enumerated values will not work. The enumeration `AllowParentheses` processes the parentheses, `AllowLeadingWhite` ignores the leading spaces, and `AllowTrailingWhite` ignores the trailing spaces. Then, when the buffer has been processed, a value of –10 will be stored in the variable `value`.

Other `NumberStyles` enumerated values allow you to process decimal points for fractional numbers, positive or negative numbers, and so on. This then raises the topic of processing numbers other than `int`. Each of the base data types, such as `boolean`, `byte`, and `double`, has associated `Parse()` and `TryParse()` methods. Additionally, the method `TryParse()` can use the `NumberStyles` enumeration. (See the MSDN documentation for details on the `NumberStyles` enumerated values.)

Parsing integer values is the same, regardless of the country. Parsing double values or dates is not the same. Consider the following example, which tries to parse a buffer that contains decimal values.

```
public void TestDoubleValue() {
    double value = double.Parse("1234.56");

    value = double.Parse("1,234.56");
}
```

In this example, both uses of the `Parse()` method process the number 1234.56. The first `Parse()` method is a simple parse, because it contains only a decimal point separating the whole number from the partial number. The second `Parse()` method is more complicated in that a comma is used to separate the thousands of the whole number. In both cases, the `Parse()` routines did not fail.

If you test this code, it's possible that an exception will be generated. In this case, the culture of the application is to blame. The numbers presented in the example are encoded using en-CA, which is English-Canadian notation.

Working with Cultures

In .NET, culture information is made up using two identifiers: language and specialization. As I mentioned earlier, in Switzerland, there are four spoken languages, which means that there are four different ways of expressing a date, time, and currency. This does not mean that the date is different for German speakers and French speakers. The date format will be identical, but the words (*Maerz* or *Mars* for the month March) will be different. The words for the date are the same in Austria, Switzerland, and Germany, but the format is not identical. This means multilanguage countries such as Canada (French and English) and Luxembourg (French and German) need to be able to process multiple encodings, hence the need for the two identifiers.

To retrieve the current culture, use the following code:

```
CultureInfo info =
    Thread.CurrentThread.CurrentCulture;
Console.WriteLine(
    "Culture (" + info.EnglishName + ")");
```

The method `Thread.CurrentThread.CurrentCulture()` retrieves the culture information associated with the currently executing thread. As a side note, it is possible to associate different threads with different cultural information. The property `EnglishName` generates an English version of the culture information, which would appear similar to the following:

```
Culture (English (Canada))
```

Consider the following number:

```
1,234
```

The number with an American or Canadian culture is one thousand two hundred thirty-four, but with a German culture, it is one point two three four (for those who do not know about German formatting, a comma is used as a decimal separator, and a period is used as a thousands separator). One way to change the culture is with the dialog box shown earlier in Figure 3-12. The second way to change the culture is at a programmatic level, as in this code:

```
Thread.CurrentThread.CurrentCulture =
    new CultureInfo("en-CA");
```

In the example, a new instance of `CultureInfo` is instantiated with the culture information en-CA.

Next is an example that processes a double number encoded using German formatting rules:

```
public void TestGermanParseNumber() {
    Thread.CurrentThread.CurrentCulture =
        new CultureInfo("de-DE");
    double value = Double.Parse("1,234");
}
```

This example assigns the de-DE culture information to the currently executing thread. Then whenever any of the parsing routines are used, German from Germany is used as the basis for the formatting rules. Changing the culture information does not affect the formatting rules of the programming language.

It is also possible to parse dates and times using the `Parse()` and `TryParse()` routines, as demonstrated by the following examples:

```
public void TestGermanParseDate() {
    DateTime datetime = DateTime.Parse("May 10, 2005");
    Assert.AreEqual(5, datetime.Month);
    Thread.CurrentThread.CurrentCulture =
        new CultureInfo("de-DE");
    datetime = DateTime.Parse("10 Mai, 2005");
    Assert.AreEqual(5, datetime.Month);

}
```

Notice how the first `DateTime.Parse()` processed English-Canadian formatted text and knew that the identifier May equaled the fifth month of the year. For the second `DateTime.Parse()` method call, the culture was changed to German, and it was possible to process 10 Mai, 2005. In both cases, processing the buffer posed no major problems, as long as you knew that the buffer was a German or English-Canadian date. Where things can go awry is when you have a German date and an English culture.

Converting a data type to a buffer is relatively easy in .NET 2.0 because the `ToString()` methods have been implemented to generate the desired output. Consider the following example, which generates a buffer from an integer value:

```
public void TestGenerateString() {
    String buffer = 123.ToString();
    Assert.AreEqual("123", buffer);
}
```

In the example, the value 123 has been implicitly converted into a variable and does not actually represent the variable 123. The value 123 can then have its `ToString()` method called, which generates a buffer that contains `"123"`. The same thing can be done to a double number, as in this example:

```
double number = 123.5678;
String buffer = number.ToString("0.00");
```

Here, the number 123.5678 is converted to a buffer using the method `ToString()`, but the method `ToString()` has a parameter, which is a formatting instruction that indicates how the double number should be generated as a buffer. The desired result is a buffer with a maximum of two digits after the decimal point. Because the third digit after the decimal is a 7, the value is rounded up, resulting in the buffer 123.57.

Let's see an example where the culture information also applies to generating a buffer. Here, a double value is generated in the format of the culture:

```
public void TestGenerateGermanNumber() {
    double number = 123.5678;
    Thread.CurrentThread.CurrentCulture =
        new CultureInfo("de-DE");
    String buffer = number.ToString("0.00");
    Assert.AreEqual("123,57", buffer);
}
```

As in the previous examples, the `CurrentCulture` property is assigned the desired culture. Then when the double variable number has its `ToString()` method called, the buffer `"123,57"` is generated.

The Important Stuff to Remember

In this chapter, you learned about strings and writing code. Here are the keys points to remember:

- Writing tests is an important part of your development practice. A test is not just a mechanism to catch errors, but also a mechanism used to understand the dynamics of your code.

- The `string` type is a special reference type that has many methods and properties. You are advised to look at the MSDN documentation to see what a string can do.

- IntelliSense and the MSDN documentation are your best bets when you want to find out about specific methods, properties, or types. Books and web sites such as Code Project are good resources to help you understand concepts.

- All variables and types are based on the object type.

- When writing code, you need to define responsibilities and contexts. Don't fix bugs or write code using knee-jerk reactions.

- All strings are based on Unicode. Each Unicode character is 16 bits wide.

- When translating buffers, you need to deal with the translation of text and the translation of numbers and dates.

- .NET includes sophisticated technology to help you translate numbers and dates using a combination of language and culture information.

Some Things for You to Do

The following are some exercises that relate to what you've learned in this chapter.

1. Finish the application to translate from one language to another language, allowing the user to choose which direction the translation takes.

2. Extend the `LanguageTranslator` component to be able to translate the words *au revoir* and *auf wiedersehen* to *good bye*.

3. You can combine strings by using the plus sign, but doing many additions will slow down your code. Use the `StringBuilder` class to concatenate two buffers together. Hint: you want to convert the code `string c = a + b`, and make a and b use the `StringBuilder` class. The result of the `StringBuilder` is assigned to the variable c.

4. Create a test that demonstrates what happens when a number value is added to a string value. Write the appropriate tests to verify your conclusion.

5. Extend the `LanguageTranslator` component to include methods to translate American numbers into German numbers.

6. Extend the `LanguageTranslator` component to include methods to translate dates from American or Canadian dates into German dates. Note that the added wrinkle is that you could input an American or Canadian date.

7. Implement the Windows application that calls the `LanguageTranslator` component.

■■■

CHAPTER 4

Learning About Data Structures, Decisions, and Loops

When you are creating applications, the source code will need to make decisions, such as: Should you open the file or save the file? And if you open the file, what kind of iterative code is going to read the contents of the file? These sorts of questions are answered by employing data structures, decisions, and loops.

The easiest way to demonstrate how to make a decision is to write a miniature artificial intelligence (AI) system. The AI system will be extremely primitive, but AI is interesting because it makes extensive use of decision and loop constructs. The AI system iterates and makes decisions based on data defined in a neat and orderly custom data structure.

Using the example of creating an algorithm, the following topics will be covered in this chapter:

- Data structures, including custom types

- The restrictions of value types

- Algorithm design

- Class constructors, which allow you to initialize an object

- The for loop, which allows you to iterate over sets of data

- The if statement, which allows you to execute specific code based on logic

Understanding the Depth-First Search Algorithm

AI involves searching for data, and a core algorithm of AI is searching. The search algorithm that we will develop for this chapter's example is a depth-first search system. AI has other types of searches, such as an A* or a breadth-first search, but they are all based on the same idea as the depth-search algorithm. This idea is searching for information that is arranged in a tree structure.

■Note An *algorithm* is a logical set of finite, repeatable steps for completing a task. The term is usually applied in relation to formal problems such as searching, but most, if not all computer programs, use algorithms of one sort or another.

Before we write any code, you need to understand what the depth-first search algorithm does and why you would use it. The problem to solve is how to get from point A to point B in the most efficient manner. This problem can be stated generally as, "how to solve task A when you have X options."

Imagine you are about to drive to work and you are at the front door of your house. You don't know where your keys are, and thus you begin a search for the keys in the house. Of course, you try to remember, but your memory is not working that early in the morning. You try to retrace your steps, and think of logical places where you could have placed your keys. When you retrace your steps, you follow your memory's logic. Simply put, your search algorithm is based on your memory's suggestion of where the keys might be. The data structure that you are navigating is the rooms of your house. Your brain-based search algorithm could create a search pattern like that shown in Figure 4-1.

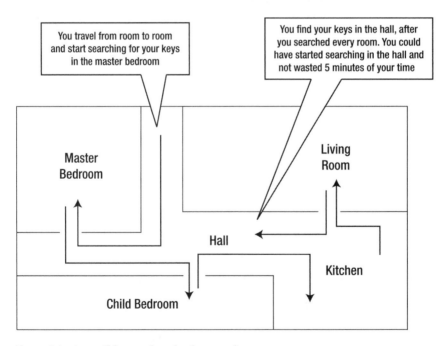

Figure 4-1. *A possible search order for your keys*

In Figure 4-1, you found the keys in the hall, but yet your search algorithm led you astray for a while, since you searched the hall last. The cynic could say that you kept walking around the keys without realizing that they were so close to you. But this is the crux of the problem, because you didn't know you developed a search algorithm that would lead you astray this time. And the same algorithm might not lead you astray next time.

█Note Searching using different strategies is very similar to how you will write computer algorithms. There is no single best algorithm; there are only good algorithms that have certain compromises. When you implement an algorithm, you need to consider the one that best suits your needs with the least number of compromises that could cause problems.

As Figure 4-1 illustrates, you searched in a counterclockwise manner. Another strategy would have been to go clockwise or even in a zigzag, or you could have searched some rooms multiple times.

Let's convert Figure 4-1 into a program that has a search algorithm and a data structure. The search algorithm will be depth-first, and the data structure will be based on a path between the respective rooms. The data structure representing the house in Figure 4-1 is illustrated in Figure 4-2.

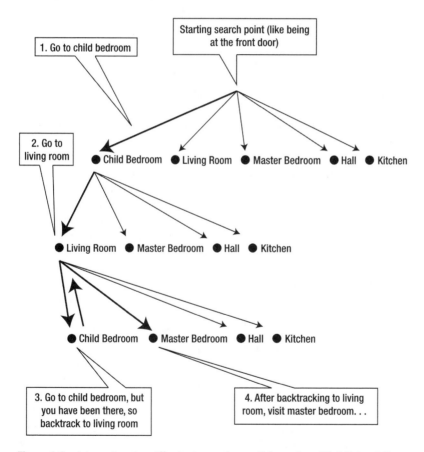

Figure 4-2. *A tree structure illustrates each possible action. Highlighted lines represent a depth-first search, and each circle represents a destination.*

In the tree structure shown in Figure 4-2, each node represents a destination that can be reached from a particular place in the house. From each room, you can reach the other room. But this structure is recursive. From the child bedroom, you can reach the living room, and then you can reach the child bedroom again. Even though you navigated down the tree, you moved from one room to another and back to the original room. This is perfectly acceptable from a data structure perspective, even though you are probably saying, "But that is wrong since rooms will show up multiple times."

■ Note The tree representation in Figure 4-2 is by no means complete, because from each room you can go to the other room. A full tree representation would be a combinatorial explosion.

The structure is the way it is because the data structure is a representation of the house. For example, let's say that you were searching the house. Would you be able to move from one room to another and back again? Sure you would. Would you do it? No, because your search algorithm would say, "Hey dude, you are repeating yourself." And therein lies the trick when writing applications. You have a data structure and an algorithm that operates on the data structure. I call this building an application in layers. You have the lowest level, which is an intelligent data structure, and a higher level that uses the functionality of the intelligent data structure.

By *intelligent data structure*, I mean that the structure is always consistent and does not corrupt itself. In this example, a room will not point to itself, a room will be present in the structure only if it is present in the house, and so on. The higher-level algorithm would be responsible for figuring out how to find information in the tree. It should be smart enough to realize that constantly traveling between two rooms is not going to achieve anything other than wasted time.

The search logic is where you go down the tree traversing one room after another. It is called a *depth-first* search algorithm because you iterate the tree by going down the tree one level after another. You stop traversing down the tree once you reach a room that you have already traversed. Then you go back one level and traverse the room beside the room that you have already traversed. This could mean the search path found by the computer would be similar to Figure 4-1. That's because the computer is as dumb as you are, albeit the computer is not saying to itself, "If only I had started in the hall."

Realize that there is no magic wand to find the keys for you. The technique that you and the computer used is called *brute force*, and it is computationally expensive and typically avoided. In this case though, brute force is the only real solution, because you don't know where the keys are—they could be anywhere in the house. It just happened to be your bad luck that the keys were found in the last place you looked.

Let's try to improve the situation. Imagine for a moment that your keys are tagged with a clapper. The idea is that with your keys going "beep, beep, beep," you will be able to instantly find them and avoid the brute-force searching. But suppose that the keys are in the upper-right corner of the child bedroom. Listening for the beeping, you think that you hear the keys either in the kitchen or the child bedroom. So, where do you go first?

Which path comes first or is the most efficient is a common problem, and you may witness it every day if you have a global positioning system (GPS) for your car. A search algorithm is commonly used in GPS devices. You punch in a set of coordinates, and the GPS device will attempt to find the quickest or shortest way. In the abstract sense, the search algorithm the GPS makers apply is identical to the search algorithm that we are going to develop in this chapter.

Implementing User-Defined Types

The data structure on which the algorithm will operate is a user-defined type. In the examples up to this point, we have been using types like `double` and `string`, which are CLR-provided types. For the example in this chapter, we will define our own type, which we will use to represent a node in the tree.

Declaring Structs and Classes

A user-defined type can be implemented in one of two ways: as a structure or as a class. An example of each is shown in Figure 4-3.

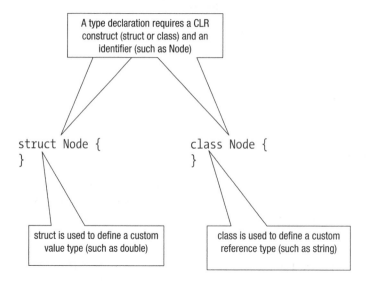

Figure 4-3. *Choices for implementing the Node custom type*

As shown in Figure 4-3, you can choose to create a user-defined type as a value (`struct`) or reference (`class`) type. For the most part, developers use a reference type, because it has fewer constraints and is easiest to use in a general context. A value type has some constraints due to its behavior of storing everything on the stack, as discussed in the following sections.

Value Type Constraints

The constraints of using a value type relate to the fact that data is copied. This impacts what happens when you embed reference types in value types and use value types as parameters to methods.

The Effects of Copying Data

When one custom value type is assigned to another custom value type, the contents of the custom value types are copied. To see this in action, consider the declarations in Figure 4-4.

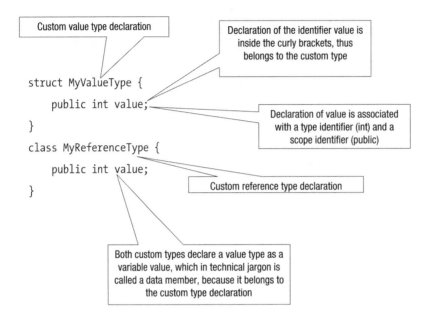

Figure 4-4. *Declaring custom types*

When declaring user-defined types, the data members and methods are declared between the curly brackets ({ }). You can think of the declaration as the writing on the outside of the box, curly brackets as the box, and anything in the curly brackets as the contents of the box. Everything between the curly brackets is the meat of the type. The identifier before the first curly bracket is the name of the type.

As the types are declared in Figure 4-4, they do not have a scope identifier. Think of a scope identifier as defining who has access to your pockets and wallet. In the case of the types in the example, the scope is like saying that your spouse is allowed to peek into your wallet, but strangers cannot.

If the `public` keyword had been in front of the type identifier, then the user-defined type would be exposed like a wallet that is allowed to be peeked into by the general public. In the case of the wallet, it's a bad idea to have public scope, but sometimes public scope is desirable when you are able to control its access. And you do this every time you pay for something by handing a credit card to the cashier. In that case, you are publicly exposing parts of your wallet under your supervision.

Next, consider the code in Figure 4-5. It instantiates `MyValueType` and assigns it to another variable of the same type.

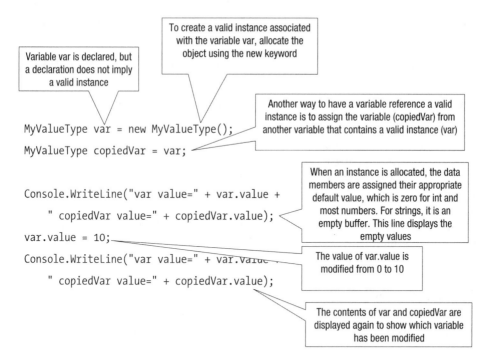

Figure 4-5. *Using a custom value type*

The example in Figure 4-5 illustrates what happens to two variables when one is instantiated and assigned to the other, and then the other is modified. You want to understand how each data type is modified when an interaction with another type occurs.

As a comparison, the same operations can be carried out using a reference type, where the reference code is as follows:

```
MyReferenceType val = new MyReferenceType();
MyReferenceType copiedVal = val;

Console.WriteLine("val value=" + val.value +
    " copiedVal value=" + copiedVal.value);
val.value = 10;
Console.WriteLine("val value=" + val.value +
    " copiedVal value=" + copiedVal.value);
```

So, if two code pieces are functionally identical, with the single difference being their type (value type versus reference type), will they generate the same results?

Running both code pieces results in the following output:

```
var value=0 copiedVar value=0
var value=10 copiedVar value=0
val value=0 copiedVal value=0
val value=10 copiedVal value=10
```

Looking closely at the results, you see that two functionally identical code pieces that differ only in the variable type they use generate completely different results:

- When you assign and modify a value type, only the contents of the modified variable change.

- When you assign and modify a reference type, the contents of the original and assigned variable change.

This example demonstrates that when defining user-defined types, you need to be careful how you treat value and reference types.

As you learned in Chapter 2, a value type is stored on the stack. Thus, declaring a user-defined value type means the full contents of the user-defined type are stored on the stack, and when you assign one value type variable to another value type variable, you are copying the complete contents of the value type. This copying was obvious in our example when we used simple numeric number types (such as double), but when you copy complete structures with contents, the side effects might not be what you expect.

Value Types That Contain Reference Types

Value types copy the contents when you assign variables, but there is a caveat in that this rule does not apply if the value type contains a reference type. Consider the following declaration.

```
struct MyValueTypeWithReferenceType {
    public int value;
    public MyReferenceType reference;
}
```

The first line is the value type declaration that contains a single value type (int) and reference type (MyReferenceType). The third line is the data member declaration that is a reference type. The declaration implies that the value type is stored on the stack, but the reference type is on the heap.

The value type that contains a reference type is manipulated using the following test code.

```
MyValueTypeWithReferenceType var = new MyValueTypeWithReferenceType();
var.reference = new MyReferenceType();
MyValueTypeWithReferenceType copiedVar = var;

Console.WriteLine("var value=" + var.reference.value +
    " copiedVar value=" + copiedVar.reference.value);
var.reference.value = 10;
Console.WriteLine("var value=" + var.reference.value +
    " copiedVar value=" + copiedVar.reference.value
```

It is important to realize that allocating MyValueTypeWithReferenceType does not imply an allocation of the embedded custom type. In the test code, the allocation of the MyValueTypeWithReferenceType is the same as the previous code examples, but a second allocation of MyReferenceType is required because MyReferenceType is a reference type. Had MyReferenceType been a value type, the allocation would not have been necessary. But if you allocate a value type like a reference type, the compiler will ignore the directive.

Running the test code results in the following:

```
value value=0 reference value=10
```

When you assign and modify an embedded reference type, the reference type instance is modified for both variables. In this case, when we assigned the value type, the contents were copied, including the pointer to the reference type.

Table 4-1 summarizes the behavior of types when the allocated variable is assigned to another variable and the data member from the original is modified. For example, if the code is custom2 = custom1; custom1.member = [new value], what's the value of custom2.member?

Table 4-1. *Behavior When the Allocated Variable Is Assigned to Another Variable and the Data Member from the Original Is Modified*

Type	Behavior
Value type	Assigned data member is not modified
Reference type	Assigned data member is modified
Value type embedding value type	Assigned embedded data member is not modified
Value type embedding reference type	Assigned embedded data member is modified
Reference type embedding value type	Assigned embedded data member is modified
Reference type embedding reference type	Assigned embedded data member is modified

Value Types and Parameters

Another value type constraint relates to how variables are stored and manipulated when they are passed via a method. Suppose you create a method that has as parameters a value type and a reference type. If in the method the parameters are modified, what modifications does the caller of the method see? Consider the following code:

```
static void Method(MyValueType value, MyReferenceType reference)
{
  value.value = 10;
  reference.value = 10;
}
```

The caller can pass in instances of a value type and a reference type that are manipulated in the context of the method. Now let's call Method() with the following code:

```
MyValueType value = new MyValueType();
MyReferenceType reference = new MyReferenceType();
Method(value, reference);
Console.WriteLine("value value=" + value.value +
    " reference value=" + reference.value);
```

The calling code instantiates the types MyValueType and MyReferenceType, calls the method Method(), and then inspects the value of the data member value from the value and reference types.

Running the code will generate output similar to the following:

```
value value=0 reference value=10
```

The executed code shows that the value type (MyValueType) data member was not altered, whereas the reference type (MyReferenceType) data member was altered. This is correct, and it demonstrates that when you call a method, you are assigning the parameters of the method to variables in the called method. Looking back at Table 4-1, you can see that when you assign a value to a value type, manipulating the assigned instance does not change the original instance.

This would imply that whenever you use value types, call a method, and alter the value type, you can never see the modifications. This constraint would indicate that for the most part, you should use reference types. However, the CLR offers a solution to this problem through the out keyword, which is associated with the method, as illustrated in Figure 4-6. The out keyword indicates that the variable is assigned when the method returns, rather than when the method is called.

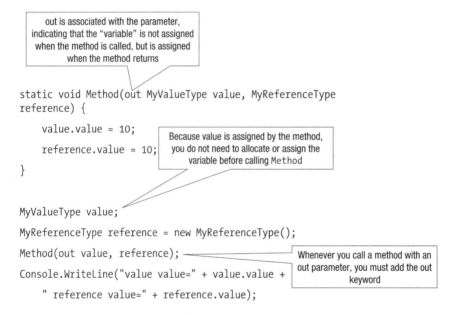

Figure 4-6. *Adding the out keyword*

The upside of using the out keyword is that you can assign a value type in the method and have the caller see the changes. The downside is that the out keyword ignores the assignment of the caller's method parameters. To be able to pass information to the method and then receive information from the method, as with a reference type, you use the ref keyword, as in the following example.

```
static void Method(ref MyValueType value, MyReferenceType reference) {
  value.value = 10;
  reference.value = 10;
}
. . .
MyValueType value = new MyValueType();
MyReferenceType reference = new MyReferenceType();
Method(ref value, reference);
Console.WriteLine("value value=" + value.value +
    " reference value=" + reference.value);
```

When using ref, you are converting the value type into a reference type, and thus to be able to call Method(), you need to allocate the value type.

■**Note** Looking at how the out and ref keywords are used, you can see that C# is an explicit language. You specify the out and ref keywords when declaring the method and when calling the method. Programming in C#, you are always aware of what a parameter, method, variable, or class does and how. This explicitness makes it possible for another person to read your code and understand what you are trying to do.

Now that you have an understanding of the depth-first search algorithm and how the data structure will be defined as a user-defined value type, let's get started building the search algorithm.

Organizing the Search Algorithm

The search algorithm we will write in this chapter deals with the problem of planning a flight from point A to point B. The first step is to figure out the features we need to implement. Here's a summary:

- A data structure implements the node.

- A node can contain references to other nodes.

- Each node has a description and unique identifier to distinguish it from other nodes.

- All of the nodes have flight information.

- An algorithm will traverse the nodes and keep track of its path.

- The path is returned as a list of nodes.

The data structure is based on the problem of planning a flight between two places, as illustrated in Figure 4-7.

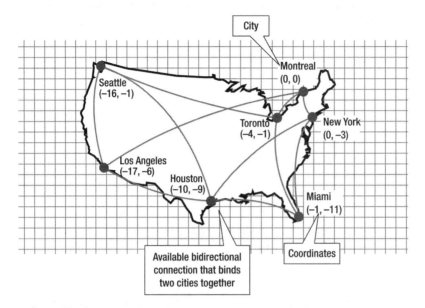

Figure 4-7. *Planning flight routes*

As shown in Figure 4-7, three main attributes describe an individual node in the flight route:

- *City name*: A description that will be used as a key when a user defines a starting and end point.

- *Coordinates:* An illustrative approach used to describe how cities are located in relation to each other.

- *Connections*: A representative connection between two cities. As in real life, not all cities connect to other cities.

For the scope of this chapter, there are only two projects: a class library that contains the depth-first search algorithm and the testing application. The project structure looks like Figure 4-8. As with the examples in the previous chapters, remember to add a reference to the class library (SearchSolution) and to set the test project (TestSearchSolution) as the startup project.

Figure 4-8. *Solution project structure*

Writing the Depth-First Search Code

We will implement the depth-first search algorithm in three main steps. The first step is to define and implement the data structure. The second step is to implement the algorithm and tests. Finally, we'll run the algorithm and see what route has been found.

Defining and Implementing the Data Structure

As I mentioned earlier, for the most part, developers use the class keyword to define a data structure as a reference type, because of the constraints of using a value type. However, for this example, we will start out by using the struct keyword to define Node as a value type. The depth-first search algorithm has two distinct implementation details: data structure and algorithm. Because each detail is separate, it seems appropriate to define Node as a value type. So, at least let's try it and see what happens.

As per the attributes illustrated in Figure 4-7, the data structure that is added to the SearchSolution project is implemented as shown in Figure 4-9.

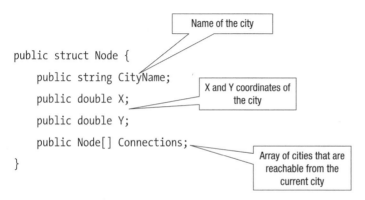

Figure 4-9. *The data structure for the depth-first search*

The data structure is declared as a `struct`, with the connections represented as an array of Node elements. An array of Node elements is formed when one Node contains a list of references to other Node elements. Think of an array as a collection of sticky notes that say, "Here is a reference to A, B, C, and so on." By having one node reference another node, a sort of never-ending tree is created, because it is possible to travel back and forth between two cities. Thus, the depth-first search algorithm will need to avoid repeating itself.

The Connections data member is an array used to define cities that are the next connection. To reference another city, you can create the reference as an array of Node elements, as in the declaration shown in Figure 4-9. An alternative is to use an array of strings that contain the name of the next city, like this:

```
public struct Node {
  public string CityName;
  public double X;
  public double Y;
  public String[] Connections;
}
```

In this declaration, Connections is a string that references other city names and is what humans would see when they look at a table showing all of the connections for a particular city. The problem with using strings is that it is inefficient from a computing perspective. To traverse a tree of cities, you would first traverse the city names, resolve the city name to a Node type, and then traverse the node. The string array approach requires an extra, unnecessary step. So the more efficient and programmatic approach is to have an array of Node instances.

By using the declaration where Connections is an array of Node elements, you have both the city name and available connections in one element. You don't need to develop an algorithm that searches for the city and its connections; rather, you can write an algorithm to navigate a structure without having to do a search and reference operation.

SELF-REFERENCING STRUCTS

An interesting piece of information to keep in mind is that if you had declared the Node structure with a single reference to Node, the C# compiler would have generated an error about a self-referencing node. Here is an example of a self-referencing struct that does not compile:

```
public struct Node {
  public string CityName;
  public double X;
  public double Y;
  public Node Connections;
}
```

The problem in the declaration is that a value type has fixed dimensions, and because you are declaring a Node within a Node, the compiler cannot determine the size of the declared `struct`. The Node declaration with an array reference ([ ]) does compile because the array is explicitly defined as being of unknown length, and the declaration to the array is treated as a reference type.

Instantiating and Initializing a Node

In previous code, you have seen how objects can be instantiated using the new keyword. To instantiate a type, you always use the new keyword. After the new keyword is the type that you want to instantiate, followed by a set of brackets. A node is instantiated using the following code:

```
Node city = new Node();
```

If you look only at the identifier Node with brackets, you would get the impression that you are calling a method that has no parameters. The impression is correct, but it is a special type of method call, and that is made apparent by the use of the new keyword. The method that is being called is known as a *constructor*. Every type has a constructor, and it can be used to initialize the state of the object before being returned to the caller.

■**Note** When I say *class* or *struct*, I am referring to a type declaration. When I say *object*, I am referring to a type declaration that has been instantiated.

In the declaration of Node, there is no defined constructor, and thus a default constructor is provided by the CLR. The default constructor does nothing and has no parameters.

After having instantiated a node, we can assign the data members, as in the following code.

```
city.CityName = "Montreal";
city.X = 0.0;
city.Y = 0.0;
```

Assigning the data members results in setting the city name to Montreal and the coordinates to (0,0).

This is all fine, but shouldn't we need to provide some data members when creating a city node? Does it make sense to instantiate a node without defining the name and coordinates of the city? Technically, a node does not need to be assigned, but logically speaking, an unassigned node is quite useless. And remember that we are working on defining an intelligent data structure, thus a Node instance without city name and coordinates is logically not a valid Node.

You can enforce a verifiable correct initial state by defining a constructor with parameters, rather than using the default constructor, as in the following example. When your code provides a constructor, regardless of the declaration, the default constructor is not generated and is not accessible.

```
public struct Node {
    public static Node[] RootNodes;
    public string CityName;
    public double X;
    public double Y;
    public Node[] Connections;

    public Node(string city, double x, double y) {
        CityName = city;
        X = x;
```

```
        Y = y;
        Connections = null;
    }
}
```

Note The code uses a type called `null`, which is a predefined special type that means the data points to nothing, or programmatically defined as `null`.

To define a constructor, you define a method that has an identifier identical to the type and has no return type. And, in most cases, you will use public scope. The parameters of the constructor represent the three pieces of information that are required to instantiate a valid state. Within the constructor, the data members are assigned the values of the parameters.

The defined constructor has parameters, which means that to instantiate Node, you need to provide the three pieces of data. Thus, to instantiate Node, you need to provide enough data to make the node logical. The original instantiation code would not compile, so to compile the code, you need to modify the instantiation to the following:

```
Node city = new Node("Montreal", 0.0, 0.0);
```

The declaration of the node might reference incorrect data, but that is not the responsibility of the intelligent data structure. An analogy is that a word processor by itself is not responsible for making sure that the text you write makes sense. The role of the word processor is to give you the ability to construct intelligent text.

Examining the Problem of Referencing Using Value Types

As you've learned, a value type is stored on the stack, and its contents are copied, not referenced. When you are trying to build a tree structure with a value type, the problem is that references that were assigned are not updated with the correct information because values are copied. This effect can be demonstrated by going through a longer example of building a data structure of cities that can be reached from another city. To start off, consider the following declaration of all the cities and their coordinates.

```
Node montreal = new Node("Montreal", 0, 0);
Node newyork = new Node("New York", 0, -3);
Node miami = new Node("Miami", -1, -11);
Node toronto = new Node("Toronto", -4, -1);
Node houston = new Node("Houston", -10, -9);
Node losangeles = new Node("Los Angeles", -17, -6);
Node seattle = new Node("Seattle", -16, -1);
```

This code instantiates individual variables that represent all of the cities from Figure 4-7. The individual variables are cities without connections, and the next step is to connect one city to another. We need to allocate and assign the Connections data member.

The following code is used to associate the connections to the cities that are available from Montreal.

```
montreal.Connections = new Node[3];
montreal.Connections[0] = newyork;
montreal.Connections[1] = toronto;
montreal.Connections[2] = losangeles;
```

When you allocate an array, you are allocating space for the type, not the type itself. Think of it as buying an empty wallet and having room to put in your money and credit cards. Thus, you don't call the constructor of the objects, because the objects are not being instantiated.

Once room has been allocated in the array, you can assign the array as you would assign variables. Alternatively, you could instantiate and assign the array.

Notice that square brackets are used to specify an index of an array. Remember that arrays start counting at index 0. So if you have an array of three elements, the first element is at index 0 and the last index is at 2.

Think about what the code is doing. You allocate space for the array and assign the variables representing the cities to the individual elements of the array. Since `Connections` is an array of value types, the connections within the connections are not set, as shown in Figure 4-10.

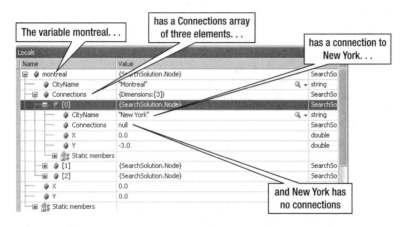

Figure 4-10. *The problem of the missing connections for New York*

The problem is that the `Connections` array for New York is missing. Of course, you could be logical and say it is missing because the `Connections` data member for New York has not yet been defined. But, and it is a big but, think about how data is referenced and think about the behavior summarized in Table 4-1.

Node is a value type, and when a value type is assigned, the values within the type are copied. Because the connections for New York have not been assigned, the Montreal `Connections` array will not contain any connections from New York. And if you modify the original variable for New York and its connections, those changes will not be reflected in the array of connections that Montreal has.

At this point, you might not think this is a problem, but consider the following New York code:

```
newyork.Connections = new Node[3];
newyork.Connections[0] = montreal;
newyork.Connections[1] = houston;
newyork.Connections[2] = miami;
```

In this example, New York has a connection to Montreal, and Montreal has a connection to New York, completing a full circle. Commuters would want this ability to fly back and forth between cities. But because we are using value types, it is not possible to fly back and forth, as illustrated by Figure 4-11.

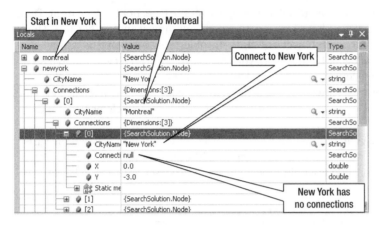

Figure 4-11. *Missing connections for New York*

Figure 4-11 illustrates that recursion with value types does not work. It shows that there are connections from New York to Montreal. But following the connection to Montreal, it would appear that New York has no connections, which is blatantly false, because we can see the connection from New York to Montreal.

When value types are assigned, you are copying contents of the value type and thus getting a snapshot of the state of an object at some period in time. In essence, the code illustrates the chicken-and-egg problem of defining the connections for a particular city and then assigning them. For value types, how can you assign the connection of one city to another when the to-be-assigned connection does not exist? The short answer is you can't. The long answer is you can, but it would mean executing an infinite loop, which is of no use to us, because we want to do something with the data once it has been assigned.

Switching to a Class to Define a Node

To fix the chicken-and-egg problem, we need to use reference types instead of value types. This means we need to change the declaration of Node from a struct to a class, as follows:

```
public class Node {
  public static Node[] RootNodes;
  public string CityName;
  public double X;
  public double Y;
  public Node[] Connections;

  public Node(string city, double x, double y) {
    CityName = city;
    X = x;
    Y = y;
```

```
    Connections = null;
  }
}
```

The change is a one-liner. After the switch, if we executed the same assignment code as in the previous section when Node was a value type, the data structure shown in Figure 4-12 would be created.

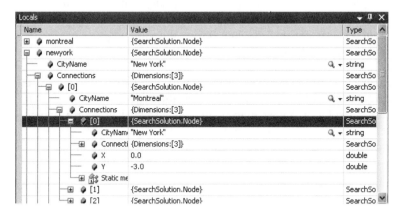

Figure 4-12. *A valid state for the New York Node instance*

Looking at the node structure in Figure 4-12, you can see that New York points to Montreal and back again. The infinite connection does not mean that you are using infinite resources. Instead, it means one reference is being set to another, as illustrated in Figure 4-13.

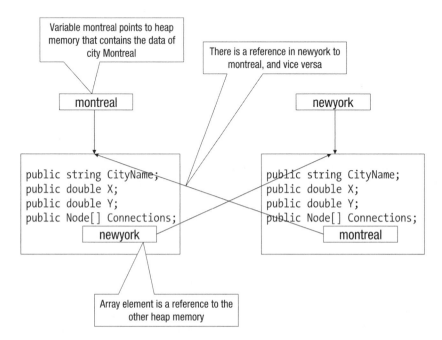

Figure 4-13. *Recursive assignment that seems like infinite resources*

The apparent infinite resources are the cross-reference recursive assignment of two pieces of heap memory. It is fine to do this, and this ability is one of the reasons why people prefer using reference types to value types. Often, when people use value types, they will assume certain variables or data members are being assigned when, in fact, they are not assigned.

Understanding Static Data Members and Methods

You've seen how a constructor can be used to initialize the state of a particular instance of a type. Now we need to define a constructor for the tree structure shown in Figure 4-2. A tree implies a starting point, but the code for the flight connections does not imply a single starting point. Instead, we have the declaration of a number of variables where the identifier of each variable is a city.

The problem with such a declaration is that, if you want to navigate a tree structure, you need to know the individual names of the variables and navigate the tree structure of each variable. This is not a plausible solution. You want to create a single overall point from where all other cities can be referenced.

The solution lies in using an array like that used for the data member Connections. To address the problem of providing a single access point, we declare a static data member, as follows:

```
public class Node {
  public static Node[] RootNodes;
  public string CityName;
  public double X;
  public double Y;
  public Node[] Connections;

  public Node(string city, double x, double y) {
    CityName = city;
    X = x;
    Y = y;
    Connections = null;
  }
}
```

The bold code shows the declaration of a data member with the modifier static to indicate that the data member is static. So, just what does *static* mean in this context?

Let's say that your family consists of your significant other and two kids. One day, you wander into the cell phone store and decide to buy four identical cell phones, as the store is having a family deal. When each phone is activated, the state of each cell phone will be unique. Each person will have an individual number, address book, and so on. In the analogy to objects, the cell phone represents a type; each person has a type, but with a unique state that represents an instantiation of the type.

Some cell phones have a feature called push-to-talk. Essentially, you convert a cell phone into a walkie-talkie. After buying individual cell phones for the family, the push-to-talk feature is activated for everyone in the family. This means if one person is using the push-to-talk feature, all family members will hear the conversation. The push-to-talk feature does not distinguish between the cell phones, so if multiple people talk at the same time, so be it; you'll hear quite a bit of noise. Push-to-talk is a shared resource, not associated with a particular cell phone. In the same way, static refers to a shared resource, not associated with a type instance.

When you associate `static` with a data member, as in the code example, you are saying that, regardless of how many times you instantiate Node, there is always a single instance of the data member RootNodes. You don't even need to instantiate Node to access RootNodes. Static methods are like static data members, in that they are a shared resource and are not associated with a particular object (as illustrated by the Main() method used to start an application).

Figure 4-14 illustrates what you can and cannot do with static and non-static data members.

```
class MyStaticAndNonStaticClass {

    public static int Value;

    public static void MyMethod() {        Assignment allowed because static can
                                                       reference static
        Value = 10;

        InstanceValue = 20;                   Assignment not allowed because static cannot
                                                   reference information that requires a type that has
    }                                             been instantiated using the keyword new

    public int InstanceValue;

    public void MyInstanceMethod() {        Assignment allowed because instance can
                                                       reference static
        Value = 10;

        InstanceValue = 20;                   Assignment allowed because instance can
                                                       reference instance
    }

}

class TestStaticVsNonStatic {               Method call allowed because static means you do not
                                                need to instantiate the type using new keyword
    public void TestSimple() {

        MyStaticAndNonStaticClass.MyMethod();

        MyStaticAndNonStaticClass.MyInstanceMethod();

        MyStaticAndNonStaticClass cls = new       Method call not allowed because
MyStaticAndNonStaticClass();                      method can be called only when
                                                   the type is instantiated using new
        cls.MyInstanceMethod();                    keyword

    }

}
```

Figure 4-14. *Examples of static and non-static data members*

The general rule of thumb is that static data members or methods can be accessed without having to instantiate the type. Also, don't attempt to reference non-static data members or methods in a static method.

Getting back to the Node declaration, the static data member RootNodes is used to define a single root for the search tree. As when instantiating a type, there is a constructor for the static type that is called whenever a static method or data member is referenced. The static constructor is like the previously defined constructor, except the `public` keyword is replaced with `static`. For the search tree case, it is used to initialize the tree and state.

We now have a complete definition of the Node class, with the following source code. Take a moment to look it over and fit the pieces together.

```
public class Node {
  public static Node[] RootNodes;
  public string CityName;
  public double X;
  public double Y;
  public Node[] Connections;

  public Node(string city, double x, double y) {
    CityName = city;
    X = x;
    Y = y;
    Connections = null;
  }

  static Node() {
    Node montreal = new Node("Montreal", 0, 0);
    Node newyork = new Node("New York", 0, -3);
    Node miami = new Node("Miami", -1, -11);
    Node toronto = new Node("Toronto", -4, -1);
    Node houston = new Node("Houston", -10, -9);
    Node losangeles = new Node("Los Angeles", -17, -6);
    Node seattle = new Node("Seattle", -16, -1);

    montreal.Connections = new Node[3];
    montreal.Connections[0] = newyork;
    montreal.Connections[1] = toronto;
    montreal.Connections[2] = losangeles;

    newyork.Connections = new Node[3];
    newyork.Connections[0] = montreal;
    newyork.Connections[1] = houston;
    newyork.Connections[2] = miami;

    miami.Connections = new Node[3];
    miami.Connections[0] = toronto;
    miami.Connections[1] = houston;
    miami.Connections[2] = newyork;

    toronto.Connections = new Node[3];
    toronto.Connections[0] = miami;
    toronto.Connections[1] = seattle;
    toronto.Connections[2] = montreal;
```

```
    houston.Connections = new Node[3];
    houston.Connections[0] = miami;
    houston.Connections[1] = seattle;
    houston.Connections[2] = newyork;

    seattle.Connections = new Node[3];
    seattle.Connections[0] = toronto;
    seattle.Connections[1] = houston;
    seattle.Connections[2] = losangeles;

    losangeles.Connections = new Node[3];
    losangeles.Connections[0] = montreal;
    losangeles.Connections[1] = seattle;
    losangeles.Connections[2] = houston;

    Node.RootNodes = new Node[7];
    Node.RootNodes[0] = montreal;
    Node.RootNodes[1] = newyork;
    Node.RootNodes[2] = miami;
    Node.RootNodes[3] = toronto;
    Node.RootNodes[4] = houston;
    Node.RootNodes[5] = losangeles;
    Node.RootNodes[6] = seattle;
  }
}
```

Defining the Algorithm Test

The Node type is a self-contained type, meaning that the algorithm does not need to instantiate the tree structure. This is an example of good design, because if you had to add more cities, the only changes required would be to Node itself. Any search algorithm that uses the Node type does not need to be changed.

■**Note** When you have the ability to create code that localizes changes without affecting other pieces of code, it is called *decoupling* code. You want to write code that is decoupled from other code, so that when changes are made in one piece of code, other pieces of code continue functioning. As you will experience when developing code, decoupling of code is a daily struggle.

For illustrative purposes, let's try a first stab at the search algorithm and see where things take us. We could start by defining the search class or start by defining the test that will test the search class. Let's define the test first, because it allows us to figure out what shape the search class should take:

```
public static void TestSearch() {
  SearchSolution.SearchAlgorithm.DepthFirstFindRoute("Montreal", "Seattle");
}
```

In the test, the search algorithm is called directly using `SearchAlgorithm.DepthFirstFindRoute()`. Here, `SearchAlgorithm` is the name of the class, and `DepthFirstFindRoute()` is the name of the method. The naming implies that this class will contain all search algorithm implementations. This is wrong, because the entire search algorithm will not be contained within a single method. Most likely, it will require multiple methods. And if each search algorithm requires multiple methods, then maintaining the `SearchAlgorithm` class will become a nightmare.

A better solution would be to identify a single class as being a single implementation of a search algorithm. Then for each class, we can define a common method identifier that is used to find the route between two points. Doing this results in the following modified test:

```
public static void TestSearch() {
  SearchSolution.DepthFirstSearch.FindRoute("Montreal", "Seattle");
}
```

Now the test implies that the class `DepthFirstSearch` has a static method `FindRoute()`. This is acceptable, and if you were to implement `BreadthFirstSearch`, the naming would be `SearchSolution.BreadthFirstSearch.FindRoute`. However, there is another problem, which relates to multiple users being able to use the algorithm during the execution of a program. Going back to the push-to-talk feature of a cell phone, the method `FindRoute()` is static and thus a shared resource. If multiple users do use this algorithm, they will share the resource. This could be problematic if you are storing temporary data in the data members of the `DepthFirstSearch` class. Using a static method could corrupt your found search path.

The more appropriate solution is to define the method `FindRoute()` as a non-static method, implying that `DepthFirstSearch` must be instantiated before we can call `FindRoute()`. We should modify the test again as follows:

```
public static void TestSearch() {
  SearchSolution.DepthFirstSearch cls = new SearchSolution.DepthFirstSearch();
  cls.FindRoute("Montreal", "Seattle");
}
```

To execute the method `FindRoute()`, we need to instantiate `DepthFirstSearch`, allowing multiple users to perform searches without getting state mixed up. At this point, we could pat ourselves on the back and think that we have written a good test that requires a class implementation.

The Problem of Magic Data

Our test is not yet complete, because we don't have access to the route found by the algorithm, but that will be explained in a moment. For the time being, let's say that the found route is pixie dust that just happens to fall on our lap.

In the implementation of `DepthFirstSearch`, a reference to the data structure is necessary. The search algorithm needs to know which tree to navigate. One way to implement a reference to the tree is to directly reference the static data `Node.RootNodes`. An implementation of `DepthFirstSearch()` would be as follows:

```
public class DepthFirstSearch {
    public DepthFirstSearch( ) {
    }
```

```
    public void FindRoute(string start, string end) {
        Node[] startNodes = Node.RootNodes;
    }
}
```

This example declares a variable called startNodes, which represents the starting point and root of the tree as shown in Figure 4-2. The root of the tree is based on the data member Node.RootNodes, and this assignment is called a *magic type assignment*. A magic type is formed when you call a method, and magically, it happens to know how to reference data, even though you never instructed the type. In the case of DepthFirstSearch(), the magic is the ability of DepthFirstSearch() to know to reference the correct data member RootNodes.

The assumption is bad because it couples the data member RootNodes to the method FindRoute(). Imagine if the developer of the Node class later decides to add functionality to load the tree from a file on the hard disk. So that FindRoute() is not broken, the developer would need to explicitly copy the hard-disk-loaded tree to the data member RootNodes.

Or what if two different users wanted to create two different flight trees? Nodes.RootNodes is a shared resource, and thus can process only a single flight tree. The developer of Node might alter RootNodes, and thus FindRoute() would behave erratically.

When you have a case of magic data, whatever data is magic needs to be passed to the type. So the test for the flight route would change to the following:

```
public static void TestSearch() {
  SearchSolution.DepthFirstSearch cls =
    new SearchSolution.DepthFirstSearch(SearchSolution.Node.RootNodes);
  cls.FindRoute("Montreal", "Seattle");
}
```

As the root tree node is required, we change the constructor to require that a caller pass in the root tree node. The test code still uses the static data member RootNodes, but DepthFirstSearch() does not need to know where to find the tree. If the Node developer were to alter the behavior of the data member RootNodes, then only the constructor code to DepthFirstSearch() would need altering, not the DepthFirstSearch() method. Thus, Node and DepthFirstSearch are properly decoupled from each other.

Getting the Found Route

Once you have called the FindRoute() method, you expect an answer. Because the route could involve multiple cities, the found route is stored in an array of Node elements. In programmatic terms, there are two ways of retrieving the array of Nodes. The first is a return parameter value, like this:

```
public static void TestSearch() {
  SearchSolution.DepthFirstSearch cls =
    new SearchSolution.DepthFirstSearch(SearchSolution.Node.RootNodes);
  Node[] foundRoute = cls.FindRoute("Montreal", "Seattle");
}
```

The bold code shows the assignment of the return value to the variable foundRoute.

The second approach is to use a data member, as follows:

```
public static void TestSearch() {
  SearchSolution.DepthFirstSearch cls =
    new SearchSolution.DepthFirstSearch(SearchSolution.Node.RootNodes);
  cls.FindRoute("Montreal", "Seattle");
  Node[] foundRoute = cls.FoundRoute;
}
```

In the second approach, the route is stored in the data member FoundRoute.

Each approach seems fine, and you are not sure which to use. When you have a choice like this, you need to make a decision. The safest way to make a decision is to write tests and see if there are any problems with either approach.

In the example of calculating a single route, either approach is fine. But let's look at the code when multiple routes are being searched. First, consider the code where the found path is a return parameter value:

```
public static void TestSearch() {
  SearchSolution.DepthFirstSearch cls =
    new SearchSolution.DepthFirstSearch(SearchSolution.Node.RootNodes);
  Node[] foundRoute1 = cls.FindRoute("Montreal", "Seattle");
  Node[] foundRoute2 = cls.FindRoute("New York", "Seattle");
}
```

Now take a look at the code that uses the data member:

```
public static void TestSearch() {
  SearchSolution.DepthFirstSearch cls =
    new SearchSolution.DepthFirstSearch(SearchSolution.Node.RootNodes);
  cls.FindRoute("Montreal", "Seattle");
  Node[] foundRoute1 = cls.FoundRoute;
  cls.FindRoute("New York", "Seattle");
  Node[] foundRoute2 = cls.FoundRoute;
}
```

Again, it would seem that both choices are adequate. However, there is a difference; the difference is subtle, but distinct enough to matter. In the test implementation where the found route is a return value, the variables foundRoute1 and foundRoute2 represent routes that relate directly to the route being searched. There is no chance that the variables foundRoute1 can represent the route New York–Seattle. With the data member code, it could happen that foundRoute1 points to the route New York–Seattle, as shown in the following code.

```
public static void TestSearch() {
  SearchSolution.DepthFirstSearch cls =
    new SearchSolution.DepthFirstSearch(SearchSolution.Node.RootNodes);
  cls.FindRoute("Montreal", "Seattle");
  cls.FindRoute("New York", "Seattle");
  Node[] foundRoute1 = cls.FoundRoute;
  Node[] foundRoute2 = cls.FoundRoute;
}
```

By switching the order of the FindRoute() method calls and references to the data member FoundRoute, the variables foundRoute1 and foundRoute2 will reference the same found route, specifically the route New York–Seattle. This is not a good idea. The example shows how data members have no direct relation to methods and can vary independently.

So the choice of returning the found route from a method is the better and more robust approach.

■**Note** Data members are useful when you want to store or retrieve data that spans multiple method calls or is not dependent on the order of how methods are called. When you have data that is dependent on the order of called methods, you should use the return keyword or out parameters.

The following is the complete test case that includes the verification code that searches for a flight from Montreal to Seattle.

```
public static void TestSearch() {
  SearchSolution.DepthFirstSearch cls =
    new SearchSolution.DepthFirstSearch(SearchSolution.Node.RootNodes);
  SearchSolution.Node[] foundRoute = cls.FindRoute("Montreal", "Seattle");
  if (foundRoute.Length != 2) {
    Console.WriteLine("Incorrect route as route has two legs");
  }
  if (foundRoute[0].CityName.CompareTo("Los Angeles") != 0) {
    Console.WriteLine("Incorrect as first leg is Los Angeles");
  }
}
```

■**Note** We've already used the if construct in earlier chapters. It tests a condition and executes the code contained in its curly brackets if that condition is true. The != means does not equal. We'll examine if in more detail later in this chapter, in the "Using the if Statement" section.

Implementing the Depth-First Search Algorithm

The implementation of the depth-first search algorithm involves creating an algorithm that iterates the tree. Here, we'll implement the algorithm in C#. In so doing, we'll use decision statements and for loops to iterate the array data. These are incredibly common in C# programs, and life would be very difficult without them.

We implemented the test code in the previous section, so the next step is to implement a version of DepthFirstSearch() that represents a shell, so that all of the code compiles and runs. The shell is structural and is used to hold up the entire application. It is defined as shown in Figure 4-15.

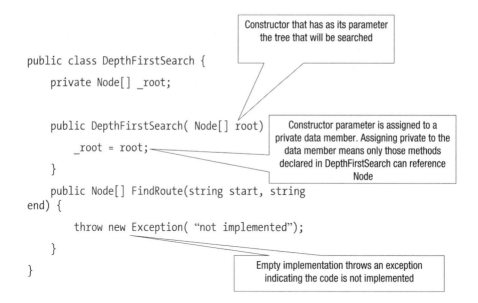

Figure 4-15. *The initial shell of the depth-first algorithm*

With a shell implemented, you could run the application and see if everything works. If you do run the test code, you will get an error, because calling FindRoute() generates an exception that indicates FindRoute() has not been implemented. (Exceptions are discussed in detail in the next chapter.) However, the shell is complete, and we are ready to implement the guts of the algorithm.

Implementing the guts of an algorithm is arguably one of the most difficult steps, as you must go through the logic of what you want to do. Whenever I am confronted with an algorithm that needs implementation and I am not quite sure how to proceed, I just write code, based on an entry point and an exit point.

The Keyhole Problem

In the example, the entry and exit point into the algorithm is FindRoute(). In turn, the entry of FindRoute() is two parameters: start, indicating the beginning city, and end, indicating the destination city. The exit of FindRoute() is an array of Node elements.

The array of Node elements needs to be preallocated with space so that all of the found cities can be added. We can make an assumption at this point that we preallocate the number of nodes to the length of the data member DepthFirstSearch()._root plus one. The assumption is that the longest trip cannot exceed the number of cities available. We know that the root node is an array of all starting point cities, thus the allocation can never be exceeded.

Focusing on the FindRoute() method, the updated code looks like this:

```
public Node[] FindRoute(string start, string end) {
  Node[] returnArray = new Node[_root.Length + 1];
  return returnArray;
}
```

The code with the array allocation is a classic keyhole problem (an idea first introduced by Scott Meyers; see http://www.aristeia.com/TKP/). The problem of a keyhole is that you implement an algorithm based on assumptions that cause you to write code that works for that specific context, but would fail when executed in another context.

The code allocates an array to the length of the root tree structure, and that is making a grand assumption. Imagine if the Node developers decided to introduce connections that could be reached only via another city that is not included in the root nodes. At that point, you could potentially exceed the available space in the array. Another solution would be to allocate an array of arbitrary length X. But then, if there are $X+1$ unique cities, another array could be violated.

The simplest solution would be to not allocate an array, but instead figure out how many elements you need after having found a path. However, this would not work, because then you would have no idea which city you had already visited. Another solution (which will be discussed in Chapter 9) is to use a collection class.

In this case, we are going to wash our hands of the problem and force the Node developers to modify their class. The Node developers are going to add a static method that tells the search algorithm how big the array needs to be. The following is the modified FindRoute() code:

```
public Node[] FindRoute(string start, string end) {
  Node[] returnArray = new Node[Node.GetMaxPossibleDestinationsArraySize()];
  return returnArray;
}
```

Now the code doesn't have a keyhole problem from the perspective of DepthFirstSearch(), because Node will always indicate the appropriate size for the array. If there is still not enough room, the problem will lie with Node. This is not an ideal solution, but sometimes is the only option.

Using the for Loop

The root node (_root) references a list of cities that are available as a starting point. To start off the search, the first step is to match the starting city with the start parameter by iterating over the list of cities. For that, we need the for loop. Here is the modified source code of FindRoute():

```
public Node[] FindRoute(string start, string end) {
    Node[] returnArray = new Node[Node.GetMaxPossibleDestinationsArraySize()];
    for (int c1 = 0; c1 < _root.Length; c1++) {
        if (_root[c1].CityName.CompareTo(start) == 0) {
            returnArray[0] = _root[c1];
            FindNextLeg(returnArray, 1, end, _root[c1]);
        }
    }
    return returnArray;
}
```

The for loop starts counting at 0 and goes to the end of the _root array using the _root.Length property. For each loop iteration, the _root[c1].CityName is tested to see if it is the starting city. Then the starting city is assigned as the first city in the array that represents the found travel route (returnArray[0] = _root[c1];). Finally, the method FindNextLeg() is used to find a possible route to the destination.

A for loop is used to go through a series based on some logic. For the most part, that series involves incrementing or decrementing numbers, but it can use other kinds of logic.

The for loop has the following form:

```
for ([starting condition]; [ending condition]; [modification]) {
        [Operations of doing something]
}
```

where:

[starting condition]: Defines the first initialization of the loop. Think of it as a loop constructor that sets up the state for iteration. For the most part, it is the initialization of a counter to a predefined value.

[ending condition]: Defines the conditions that will terminate the looping. An example loop termination is when a counter reaches the maximum length of an array, and thus no more elements can be referenced.

[modification]: Implements a time series modification. Think of it as what you would do to move the state from the current state to the next state. If your time series state is a counter, then it would mean either incrementing or decrementing the counter by a specific value.

A semicolon separates the conditions and modification from each other.

Other types of loops exist in C#, but the for loop is the only type that is explicitly meant to generate indices to other pieces of information. In the case of iterating over the array, it generated a series of numbers (0, 1, 2, 3, and so on), and each number was then used to reference an array element in _root.

■**Note** The rule of thumb for a for loop is that it is employed to generate an index series that is used to reference another piece of information. The index series could be a direct array element reference, or it could be used to perform a calculation, which is then used to generate a reference to a piece of data. The index series does not need to generate incremental or decremental values. The index series does need to generate a logical index series.

Using the if Statement

When the starting point city has been found, the algorithm will begin to search down the tree. A depth-first search means that the search will travel down the tree as far as it can before backtracking and trying other routes. The recursion of traveling down the tree is managed by the FindNextLeg() method, which is defined as shown in Figure 4-16.

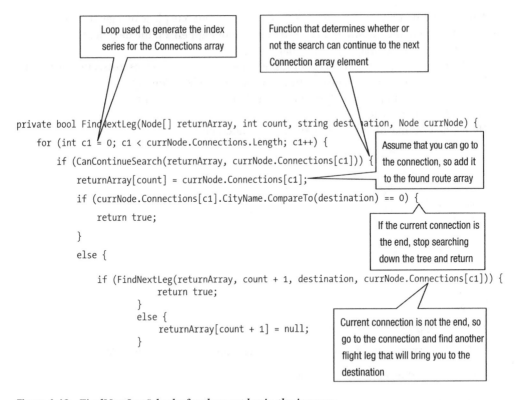

Figure 4-16. *FindNextLeg() looks for the next leg in the journey.*

The big idea here is to create a flight route by traveling the tree of connections in the hope that one of the connections will cause you to end up at your end point. Notice that for each leg, the parameter count is incremented, so as you progress a level deeper in the tree, you assign the city at the level to the found route array.

What makes this function tick is the decision code represented by an `if` code block. The `if` code block says, "If this decision test is true, then execute the code within the curly brackets associated with the `if` block; otherwise, move to the code right after `if` block."

An `if` statement has the following form:

```
if( [condition] ) {
   [Do action]
}
else if( [condition]) {
   [Do action]
}
else {
   [Do action]
}
```

The statements if, else if, and else together represent one piece of logic (for example, if this cannot happen, then test the else if; if that cannot happen; do the default in the else). The statements after the first if are optional.

The [condition] must return a true or false value. A true value means to execute the actions within the block, and a false value means to try the next code statement.

The else statement is a sort of default catchall that is executed if none of the other if statements prove to be true.

Here is an example of logic executed in an if statement:

```
if(test1) {
  // Code1
}
else if(test2) {
  // Code2
}
else {
  // Code3
}
// Code4
```

The following code steps are executed:

- If test1 is true, then execute Code1. After executing Code1, execute Code4.

- If test1 is false, jump to else if with test2.

- If test2 is true, then execute Code2. After executing Code2, execute Code4.

- If test2 is false, jump to else.

- Execute Code3. After executing Code3, execute Code4.

Here is another example:

```
if(test1) {
  // Code1
}
else {
  // Code2
}
// Code3
```

The executed code steps are:

- If test1 is true, then execute Code1. After executing Code1, execute Code3.

- If test1 is false, jump to else.

- Execute Code2. After executing Code2, execute Code3.

And here is one more example:

```
if(test1) {
  // Code1
}
if(test2) {
  // Code2
}
else {
  // Code3
}
// Code4
```

The executed code steps are as follows:

- If test1 is true, then execute Code1. After executing Code1, jump to if with test2.

- If test1 is false, jump to if with test2.

- If test2 is true, then execute Code2. After executing Code2, execute Code4.

- If test2 is false, jump to else.

- Execute Code3. After executing Code3, execute Code4.

The following code is illegal:

```
else {
  // Code2
}
// Code3
```

And this is also illegal:

```
else if(test2) {
  // Code2
}
else {
  // Code3
}
```

It is possible to have one if statement embedded within an else, if, or else if to create a more complex multilevel decision tree.

The condition or test[*N*] variables are Boolean values that can contain true or false. You have already seen examples of these, like this:

```
if (CanContinueSearch(returnArray, currNode.Connections[c1]))
```

The if statement says that if the method CanContinueSearch() returns true, then execute the code within the curly brackets.

Here is another example of a condition:

```
if (returnArray[c1] != null)
```

This if statement says that if the array element returnArray[c1] does not have a value of null, then execute the code within the curly brackets.

In both examples, either the method or comparison must return a Boolean value. If a Boolean value is not returned, the C# compiler will generate an error indicating that the code does not generate a true or false value.

It is easy to see how a method can generate a true or false value, but the array element not equal to null statement is a bit more complicated. The statement is an example of using operators to perform a comparison. Comparisons test if things are equal to each other or not equal to each other. Table 4-2 shows the comparison operators and what they mean.

Table 4-2. *Comparison Operators*

Expression	Description
a == b	Does a equal b?
a != b	Does a not equal b?
a > b	Is a greater than b?
a < b	Is a less than b?
a >= b	Is a greater than or equal to b?
a <= b	Is a less than or equal to b?
!a	A change operator that says if a is true then false, and if a is false then true

Additionally, you can use the following operators in the context of a decision:

- AND (&&): If both sides of the comparison are true, then return true; otherwise, return false.

- OR (||): If both sides of the comparison are false, then return false; otherwise, return true.

Expressions do not have to remain simple. They can be combined, like this:

```
if((a == b) && (b == c))
```

This example includes two expressions that test for equality. The tests are enclosed in parentheses, so equality is tested and the results are stored temporarily. Then the results are compared using the AND (&&) operator. If both results are true, then the AND operator will return true. In a nutshell, the decision tests if a equals b equals c.

Preventing Repetition in the Route

The FindNextLeg() method contains a reference to the CanContinue() method, which is designed to halt the search. In the case of our depth-first search algorithm, the purpose is to not fly to the same city twice. Contained within the function is code similar to FindNextLeg():

```
private bool CanContinueSearch(Node[] returnArray, Node city) {
  for (int c1 = 0; c1 < returnArray.Length; c1++) {
    if (returnArray[c1] != null) {
      if (returnArray[c1].CityName.CompareTo(city.CityName) == 0) {
        return false;
```

```
        }
      }
    }
    return true;
}
```

The logic is that `CanContinueSearch()` will iterate through the `returnArray` and see if the city being considered (variable `city`) is already in the found path. If the city is in the path, then we stop searching that part of the tree; otherwise, we continue searching.

Running the Depth-First Search Algorithm

Everything has been implemented, including tests, so we are ready to run the test of finding the flight between Montreal and Seattle. Looking at Figure 4-2 there are two paths: Montreal to Los Angeles to Seattle, or Montreal to Toronto to Seattle. However, running the algorithm generates the following peculiar result (you have not seen how to display the results, but that is done easily enough with a `for` loop that iterates over `foundRoute`):

- Montreal

- New York

- Houston

- Miami

- Toronto

- Seattle

Looking at the result, you are probably thinking that the algorithm does not work, because the proposed flight includes every city except Los Angeles. If a travel agent were to propose such a flight route to you, you would probably have a panic attack.

The algorithm did not fail; rather, the `CanContinueSearch()` function did not include functionality to optimize the flight. Right now, the algorithm says to perform a depth-first search, meaning to go down the tree before backtracking. So let's go through the structure in the `Node` static constructor again.

We started our route in Montreal, which had the following `Connections` definitions:

```
montreal.Connections = new Node[3];
montreal.Connections[0] = newyork;
montreal.Connections[1] = toronto;
montreal.Connections[2] = losangeles;
```

Applying our depth-first algorithm, it means the first array element of the tree is considered a connection, and thus our route takes us to New York. New York has the following flight connections:

```
newyork.Connections = new Node[3];
newyork.Connections[0] = montreal;
newyork.Connections[1] = houston;
newyork.Connections[2] = miami;
```

The first connection from New York is Montreal, which is already in the flight route. Thus, the second array element is searched, which is Houston. Houston has the following flight connections:

```
houston.Connections = new Node[3];
houston.Connections[0] = miami;
houston.Connections[1] = seattle;
houston.Connections[2] = newyork;
```

Following the flight route from Houston, we travel to Miami, which has the following connections:

```
miami.Connections = new Node[3];
miami.Connections[0] = toronto;
miami.Connections[1] = houston;
miami.Connections[2] = newyork;
```

Following the flight route from Miami, we travel to Toronto, which has the following connections:

```
toronto.Connections = new Node[3];
toronto.Connections[0] = miami;
toronto.Connections[1] = seattle;
toronto.Connections[2] = montreal;
```

At Toronto, the first connection is Miami, where we have already been. The second connection is Seattle, and that is our end destination.

So from the perspective of the algorithm, everything worked. From the perspective of the traveler, it's not ideal. This demonstrates yet again how important it is to write test routines, as algorithms might be correct, but they will generate responses that you might not have anticipated. Improving the example is one of the exercises at the end of the chapter.

The Important Stuff to Remember

In this chapter, you learned about data structures and algorithms. Here are the key points to keep in mind:

- When developing a program, you need to think of the data structures and algorithms that are involved.

- A single best data structure and a single best algorithm do not exist. Every data structure and algorithm has compromises. You need to choose the data structure and algorithm that best suits your needs with the least number of critical compromises.

- Data structures and algorithms do not need to be the same class. They can be different types and often are.

- Data structures can be implemented using value (struct) or reference (class) types.

- Value types when used as data structures have three constraints that you need to be aware of that relate to the fact that data is copied, what happens when you embed reference types in value types, and what happens when you use value types as parameters to methods.

- For the most part, you will use reference types, but you can also use value types. When using value types, you need to be aware of how a value behaves; otherwise, you might get undesirable interactions.

- A constructor is a special type of method that is called when a type is being instantiated. You would assign parameters to a constructor when you want to enforce a verifiably correct state for the object.

- A rule of thumb when using value and reference types is to consider the context. Are you creating a simple assign-once structure, or are you creating a complex navigable structure? If your structure is complex, then use a reference type; otherwise, a value type is fine.

- When you instantiate a type, each object has its own instance of methods and data members. When a type has methods or data members declared with the static keyword, that type has a single instance of the method or data member and is not associated with a type instance.

- Writing the test before the type implementation allows a developer to get a feeling of how the type should look and behave, and gives some guidance.

- When you write methods, you don't want to rely too heavily on magic data making everything work. When writing classes, you need to think in terms of IKEA furniture (assembly required), as that will make your code more flexible and a candidate for reuse.

- When you write a for loop, think of the statements in the brackets as being code that generates an index that is used to retrieve the actual information being iterated over.

- Decisions are implemented using a combination of if, else if, and else statements.

Some Things for You to Do

The following are some exercises to practice what you learned in this chapter:

1. Node was declared to be a reference type. Can you think of where in the declaration of Node it would be more appropriate to use a value type? And if you can think of it, rewrite Node.

2. The static data member Node.RootNodes is exposed for every class to consume. Is there a way to decouple RootNodes so that the user of Node is not aware of the location of the tree?

3. We discussed a keyhole problem regarding the allocation of an array. Yet there is also a coupling problem between Node and DepthFirstSearch. Explain why there is a coupling problem and outline an alternative algorithm that does not have the coupling problem.

4. Fix the CanContinueSearch() function so that an optimal flight path is found for any two cities. Note that you should extend your test cases to test various scenarios.

5. Implement the breadth-first search algorithm. The breadth-first algorithm will search each connection before going down further in the tree. Hint: modify the behavior of FindNextLeg().

CHAPTER 5

■■■

Learning About C# Exception Handling

Source code can have thousands, hundreds of thousands, or millions of lines of source code, and no single human could keep track of it all. To keep track of all the source code, you need a team of developers, and that means code written by one developer is going to be used and modified by another developer. Since the two developers can't perform a Vulcan mind meld, they must have a well-understood and useful form of communication. But that's just part of the solution. The code itself must be easy to understand.

The challenge of writing software is not creating a perfect piece of code, but writing code that can be understood by other developers and used by other pieces of software. The goal isn't to be clever and write software that can do everything, but to write simple, robust, and easy-to-understand software. The "keep it simple" approach is the best way forward.

Having understandable code is particularly important when things go wrong. Your code should generate the appropriate errors. For example, suppose your code relies on a file being present. When the file is not present, your code should generate a clear and distinct error, such as "File XYZ is not present and thus I cannot continue." Upon seeing such an error message, another developer would know that he should check whether the file is actually there.

This chapter explains exceptions, as errors in an application are technically known, and how to handle them. We'll begin with an overview of how exceptions fit into the structure of a program.

Understanding Errors, Exceptions, and Exception Handling

An error is when something is not right and could be the result of incorrect data or an incorrect calculation. However, the .NET CLR does not understand errors; it understands only exceptions.

For example, if an error is caused by multiplying two numbers rather than adding them, your program will continue to function, but will produce the wrong results. A similar error occurs when a user enters the wrong data—the answer will be wrong, but the program will still run.

In the case of a serious problem that is beyond the control of the user or that threatens to crash your program, the CLR steps in and treats this as an exception. This halts the program and allows your code to deal with the problem, rather than letting the program crash. (Some would argue that an exception will not halt your entire program, but a thread of your program;

while this is technically true, it's not an important distinction for this introduction to exceptions.) This is called exception handling.

To understand how code organization affects exception handling, think of an application as a large corporation. A corporation has a chief executive officer (CEO), then first-level managers, then mid-level managers. Corporations and management within corporations understand that to get anything done, they must develop a game plan and then carry out the game plan. The CEO or highest level manager will know about the overall game plan. The company is organized so that lower-level managers and workers can carry out discrete tasks as defined in the game plan. In other words, these organizational units carry out the implementation of the plan.

Translating this to software, your code contains two types of methods: methods that organize the functionality and methods that implement the functionality. You create organizational code so that you have the ability to separate each task from the others. The work of one does not affect the other, and thus the code has been modularized.

■**Note** As with corporation reorganization, management code is constantly being reorganized to fix bugs and implement new pieces of functionality. For example, you might reorganize code so that it becomes more streamlined and efficient.

Now we need to put exceptions into the picture. Errors occur when something does not go according to plan. In the management hierarchy, if an error occurs, the CEO is not automatically told. For example, if the company ran out of staples, most likely the CEO would not want to hear about it. If, however, one of the manufacturing plants fell off the side of a cliff, then the CEO would definitely want to know. The information about the error is passed up the chain of command just as far as it needs to go.

Relating this to the different types of methods, in your hierarchical code, the implementation code is responsible for making sure all errors are reported, and the organizational code is responsible for either fixing the error or propagating it to a piece of code that is higher in the hierarchy. The higher piece of code should either fix the problem or delegate it again to a higher piece of code, depending on the seriousness of the error.

For the remainder of this chapter, we'll look at the various ways of dealing with exceptions. The idea is to give you practical solutions that you can use without getting too bogged down in theoretical what-ifs.

When working with exceptions, it is often useful to run the application in Visual C# Express's debugger, so let's start there.

Running the Debugger

The Visual C# Express debugger runs the application, but adds the ability to monitor what the application is doing. To start the debugger, either select Debug ➤ Start Debugging from the menu bar or press F5.

Your application will run as normal, but the Solution Explorer will disappear, and the Locals and Call Stack panes will appear, allowing you to see what is going on in the application. From the perspective of the application, you will not see a difference in its behavior. The application executes in the same way, regardless of whether it is being run or being debugged. To stop debugging, just close your application normally.

You can also start the debugger at a certain point in your code by setting a breakpoint, as shown in Figure 5-1. When Visual C# Express reaches this breakpoint, it goes into *debug mode*; this mode is different from *application mode*—the state it is in before it reaches the breakpoint and after it leaves the breakpoint. To leave debug mode, you can either press the F5 key to switch to application mode and continue executing the application, or press Shift+F5 to stop debugging and stop executing the application.

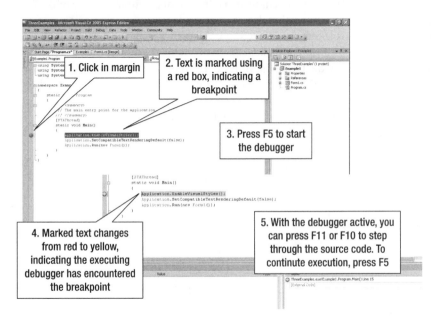

Figure 5-1. *Debugging an application with a breakpoint*

Running an application in the debugger is useful when tracking down exceptions, as you'll see in the next section.

Handling Exceptions

Those who recall the "good old days" of Windows 3.0 and its 16 bits will also remember the dreaded three-finger salute. The three-finger salute refers to pressing Ctrl+Alt+Delete to reboot Windows when a program crashed. You did not have the chance to save your work; you just had to watch everything go down the drain.

If you missed those computing days, count yourself lucky. Nowadays, we have mechanisms to catch unexpected errors and make sure that the program or operating system keeps on processing. The big deal with modern operating systems and programming environments like the CLR is that they can stop a single task from disrupting the operation of the CPU.

Catching Exceptions

If you go back to Chapter 2 and look at Figure 2-13, you'll see how Visual C# Express interrupted the flow of the program by catching the exception generated by a mathematical overflow situation. This is like your driving teacher realizing you are making a mistake and pressing hard on the brake, so you don't hit a tree, person, or another car. So, in a sense, you can think of the CLR exception-handling mechanism as the teacher stepping on the brake when something devastating is about to happen.

Stepping on the brake stops the devastation, but you, as the driver, will get a shock because of the error that you were about to make. Likewise, when an exception is triggered, the program gets a shock. How you deal with the shock determines the fate of the program. In the example of the overflow error in Figure 2-13, the shock was captured by the IDE, and thus a friendly, easy-to-understand user interface was presented.

Consider the source code shown in Figure 5-2, which generates an exception. This is referred to as *throwing* an exception.

```
class MyType {
    public int DataMember;
}
class Tests {
    public void GeneratesException() {
        MyType cls = null;
        cls.DataMember = 10;
    }
    public void RunAll() {
        GeneratesException();
    }
}
```

Class declaration with a single data member

Class is declared but not instantiated using new

Data member of the class is being assigned, even though the class has not been instantiated. This will cause a null reference exception

Figure 5-2. *Throwing an exception*

If the RunAll() method were executed, the exception shown in Figure 5-3 would be generated in Visual C# Express (use F5 to run the debugger).

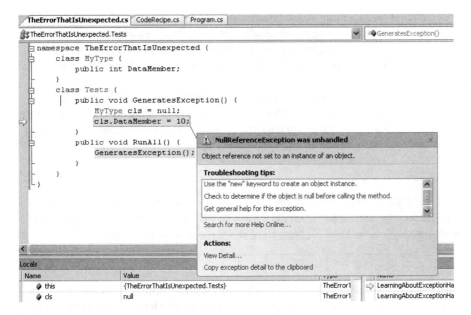

Figure 5-3. *An exception generated by a null reference*

The exception did not cause the operating system or Visual C# Express to crash, because Visual Studio's built-in exception handler caught it. Visual Studio hit the brake and made sure that only your program stopped working.

Imagine if Visual Studio were not running. The generated exception would cause the program to stop in its tracks, and a messy error message would appear, referencing objects, line numbers, and the stack. Most users would have no idea what happened, and be left with a program that was not working anymore.

What you want to do is catch the exception as Visual Studio did. For example, if you knew that an exception could occur in RunAll(), you could modify the code as follows:

```
class MyType {
    public int DataMember;
}
class Tests {
    public void GeneratesException() {
        MyType cls = null;
        cls.DataMember = 10;
    }
    public void RunAll() {
        try {
            GeneratesException();
        }
        catch (Exception) {
            ;
        }
    }
}
```

The bolded code is an *exception block*, which catches an exception and allows you to respond to it. In this example, nothing happens after catching the exception. If you run this program, Visual C# Express will not generate an exception warning, and the program will run without any problems. From the perspective of Visual C# Express, everything worked and is running OK.

But if you stop and think about it, is everything really OK? Even though the program continued to execute, was the program logically correct? The answer is no, because what the program did was swallow an exception without doing anything to remedy the problem. You should never do such a thing, because it implies sloppy programming.

■**Note** In practice, there are some cases when you need to swallow errors because you cannot process the data in any other way. This can happen when you are dealing with network connections, database operations, and the like. However, in the majority of cases, you should not swallow the exception.

A real-world example of when you might want to throw an exception is because a parameter is not valid. As you will learn in the "Filtering Exceptions" section later in this chapter, there is an exception type for just this purpose, ArgumentException(). Developers who received that exception would then be able to easily figure out that they must fix a parameter. This saves debugging time and reduces overall development time.

The real work in exception handling is adding all of the possible exceptions that could occur. But what is better: hunting down the cause of the error or adding the code to help you find the error easily? In the long run, adding the code to help track down the error saves time and avoids frustration.

Implementing Exception Handlers

An exception handler is implemented using the try, catch, and finally keywords. When you implement an exception handler, you are saying that for a specific code block, if an exception is generated, you will catch it and process the exception.

An exception handler has the following form:

```
[action 1]
try {
    [action 2]
}
catch (Exception exception) {
    [action 3]
}
[action 4]
```

The notation of an exception handler is simple. The try keyword and the curly brackets ({}) define a region of code, or *block*, that is protected. *Protected* means that any generated exception will need to pass through the exception handler. If an exception is thrown by protected code, the code in the catch block will execute and allow you to process the exception. catch is the keyword defined immediately after the try block, and the catch block specifies which exception is caught and defines the steps to take when an exception occurs.

If code within the try block (action 2 in the example) calls another method, then the code within the called method is protected. This is the case even if the code is not protected from the perspective of the method. Figure 5-4 illustrates how exceptions are caught when multiple methods are involved.

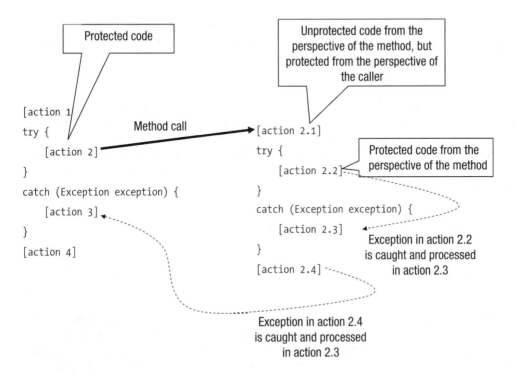

Figure 5-4. *Exceptions and calling methods that generate exceptions*

In Figure 5-4, the protected code of action 2 calls a method that has action 2.1, action 2.2, and action 2.4. action 2.2 executes in the context of an exception block, and thus if action 2.2 throws an exception, it will be caught and processed by action 2.3. The catch block containing action 3 is not aware an exception occurred. From the perspective of the called method, action 2.1 and action 2.4 are not protected, but because the called method is called from action 2, which is protected by the catch block containing action 3, action 2.1 and action 2.4 are considered protected. If action 2.1 or action 2.4 had thrown an exception, then the catch block with action 3 would have caught the exception. This example illustrates two things:

- Exceptions can span method calls.

- When an exception is thrown, the handler will catch it closest to the place where the exception occurred.

An example of how exceptions function is our legal court system. Let's say that you want to slap someone with a lawsuit. If the lawsuit is a civil case, it will be heard by the local court. You cannot bring a civil lawsuit directly to the supreme court level until it has been heard by the lower court levels. If the lawsuit is a criminal case, most likely it will be heard at the state/provincial level first. The local municipality will not hear the case because it is not in the jurisdiction of that court.

The same behavior occurs with exceptions and exception handlers. An exception might be caught and processed by one exception handler, without the exception being processed by a higher-level exception handler. This situation is illustrated in Figure 5-3 where an exception was thrown and caught by the IDE. An exception that was thrown several method calls deep was caught at the highest level.

In previous examples, an exception was thrown because the code did something that it was not supposed to do. However, you can throw an exception on purpose by using the following syntax:

```
throw new Exception();
```

When you throw an exception like this, you instantiate a type that is related to the base type `Exception`. Associating the `throw` keyword with an object creates an exception that can be caught by a higher-level catch block.

In most cases of throwing an exception, you will instantiate the exception type as you throw it. The previous example uses the parameterless `Exception()` constructor, but other variations are available, as shown in the following code.

```
try {
    throw new Exception("Exception in action 2.4.");
}
catch (Exception thrown) {
    throw new Exception("Exception in action 2 has been caught.", thrown);
}
```

The first variation, `Exception("Exception in action 2.4.")`, uses the string description constructor parameter that passes text describing what went wrong. The text is meant for human understanding, so don't use text like "Error 168: something went wrong." The second variation, `Exception("Exception in action 2 has been caught.", thrown)`, includes the original exception as an additional constructor parameter in a newly thrown exception. This allows you to pass on even more information.

The generated output of this code looks like this:

```
Unhandled Exception: System.Exception: Exception in action 2 has been caught.
---> System.Exception: Exception in action 2.4.
```

The generated exception tells you clearly where the exception occurred and where it was processed. You have a complete flow of the actions.

■**Note** An experienced developer may say that the flow is also presented by the stack that is dumped by the program if the exception is not caught. Yes, you could see the program flow based on this stack dump, but it is not much fun to decipher the stack of 10 or 15 method calls.

Consider the following amendment to the code, which reduces the amount of information.

```
try
{
    throw new Exception("Exception in action 2.4.");
}
catch (Exception thrown)
{
    throw new Exception("Exception in action 2 has been caught");
}
```

The results are not as enlightening:

```
Unhandled Exception: System.Exception: Exception in action 2 has been caught.
```

If you want to gain access to the error string, you can use the Message property of an exception.

```
try
{
    throw new Exception("Exception in action 2.4.");
}
catch (Exception thrown)
{
    Console.WriteLine(thrown.Message);
    throw new Exception("Exception in action 2 has been caught.");
}
```

You still have the more specific message, but not as part of the flow of exceptions:

```
Exception in action 2.4.
```

```
Unhandled Exception: System.Exception: Exception in action 2 has been caught.
```

DON'T REPEAT ERROR MESSAGES

When you throw exceptions, make sure that you don't use the same error message twice. Imagine the situation where you deliver a program into production and the error message "File not found" is generated. If this text is used in multiple places, when the user calls tech support, the support staff will have no idea which file was not found. Instead, in the error message, tell the user which file was not found and why. The more details you deliver, the easier it is for the support desk to help users get around the problem.

If you do need to use the same text in multiple places, add a context identifier. For example, you could generate a load error fault in the context of loading a file using a dialog box. Or you could generate a load error in the context of loading a file based on a command-line argument. Specify each context as an additional piece of information appended or prefixed to the exception text, much like the previous code illustrated when catching an exception in action 2.

Safeguarding Against Stack Unwinding

Exception handling makes it simple for you to stop your program from crashing, but it does not help you ensure that the state of your application is still intact. Consider the example shown in Figure 5-5, which illustrates how program state can be corrupted due to an exception that is caught and swallowed..

```
class MyType {
    public int DataMember;                  ┌─ DataMember represents state 1 ─┐

}
class Tests {                               ┌─ LocalDataMember
                                               represents state 2 ─┐
    public int LocalDataMember;
    public void GeneratesException() {      ┌─ State 2 is assigned ─┐
        LocalDataMember = 10;
        MyType cls = null;                  ┌─ State 1 should also be assigned, but
                                               the exception that is raised causes the
        cls.DataMember = 10;                   assignment to never happen ─┐
    }
    public void RunAll() {                                    ┌─ At this point, state 1 and 2
        Console.WriteLine("LocalDataMember=" + LocalDataMember);   are not assigned ─┐
        try {
            GeneratesException();
        }
        catch (Exception) {                                  ┌─ At this point, state 1 is not
            ;                                                    assigned but state 2 is assigned,
        }                                                        thus indicating a corrupted state ─┐
        Console.WriteLine("LocalDataMember=" + LocalDataMember);
    }
}
```

Figure 5-5. *Exceptions can corrupt the state of a program.*

When an exception is caught, the stack is unwound. Consider the example shown in Figure 5-6, where the unwinding of the stack can have the side effect of jumping over a method call.

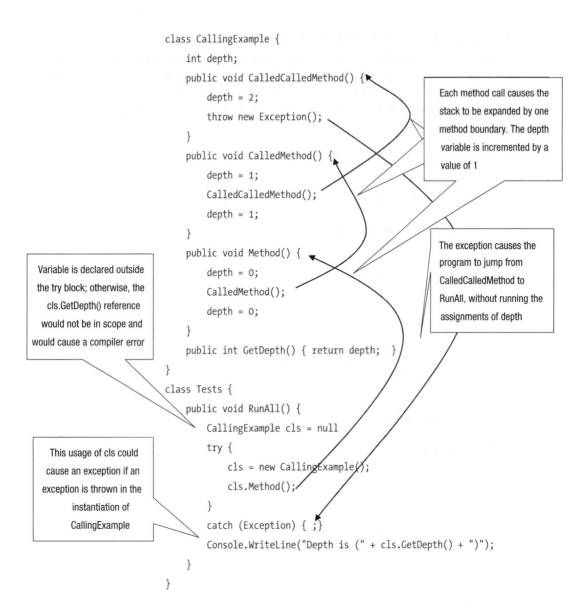

```
class CallingExample {
    int depth;
    public void CalledCalledMethod() {
        depth = 2;
        throw new Exception();
    }
    public void CalledMethod() {
        depth = 1;
        CalledCalledMethod();
        depth = 1;
    }
    public void Method() {
        depth = 0;
        CalledMethod();
        depth = 0;
    }
    public int GetDepth() { return depth; }
}
class Tests {
    public void RunAll() {
        CallingExample cls = null
        try {
            cls = new CallingExample();
            cls.Method();
        }
        catch (Exception) { ;}
        Console.WriteLine("Depth is (" + cls.GetDepth() + ")");
    }
}
```

Each method call causes the stack to be expanded by one method boundary. The depth variable is incremented by a value of 1

The exception causes the program to jump from CalledCalledMethod to RunAll, without running the assignments of depth

Variable is declared outside the try block; otherwise, the cls.GetDepth() reference would not be in scope and would cause a compiler error

This usage of cls could cause an exception if an exception is thrown in the instantiation of CallingExample

Figure 5-6. *Unwinding the stack can cause a method call to be skipped.*

In the example in Figure 5-6, the methods are called sequentially, starting with RunAll(), and then when a single exception is thrown, the code in the RunAll() method's catch block is executed immediately. So, depth has a value of 2 instead of a value of 0 (the value you would expect if no exception were thrown) when execution finishes. You can see that the stack has unwound too fast, leaving the program with unpredictable results.

The stack unwinding problem causes corruption and can wreak havoc on your program. A seemingly working program might corrupt itself and slowly fail or generate incorrect data. Fortunately, there are a couple ways to protect against stack unwinding.

Using finally to Process Unfinished Tasks

The simplest solution to the stack unwinding problem is to use the `finally` keyword, which indicates that you want to guarantee a piece of code executes, whether or not an exception is thrown. The following shows how you could rewrite the example in Figure 5-6 using `finally`. When executed, this code will set the `depth` data member to the correct value.

```csharp
class CallingExample {
    int depth;
    public void CalledCalledMethod() {
        depth = 2;
        throw new Exception();
    }
    public void CalledMethod() {
        depth = 1;
        try {
            CalledCalledMethod();
        }
        finally {
            depth = 1;
        }
    }
    public void Method() {
        depth = 0;
        try {
            CalledMethod();
        }
        finally {
            depth = 0;
        }
    }
    public int GetDepth() {
        return depth;
    }
}

class Tests {
    void TestCallingExample() {
        CallingExample cls = null;
        try {
            cls = new CallingExample();
            cls.Method();
        }
        catch (Exception) { ;}
        Console.WriteLine("Depth is (" + cls.GetDepth() + ")");
    }
    public void RunAll() {
        TestCallingExample();
```

```
        }
    }
```

In this example, each `finally` keyword is associated with a `try` block. You don't need to associate a `catch` block with a `try` block if you are using `finally`. If the `try` block is entered, when the code leaves the `try` block, regardless of whether it ran successfully or threw an exception, the code within `finally` is executed. Thus, if stack unwinding occurs, it is possible to reset or assign state to a consistent value before the exception is processed elsewhere.

■**Note** When the `finally` block is called, you don't know if it is called due to an exception or successful code execution. Thus, you shouldn't assume that `finally` is called because an exception was thrown.

Sandboxing Your Code

The sandboxing technique is similar to playing with an Etch A Sketch, in that you attempt to build a state, and if you make a mistake, you can throw the state away. This requires that you separate your code into three distinct steps: declaration, manipulation, and integration. Figure 5-7 illustrates the three steps in sandboxing your code.

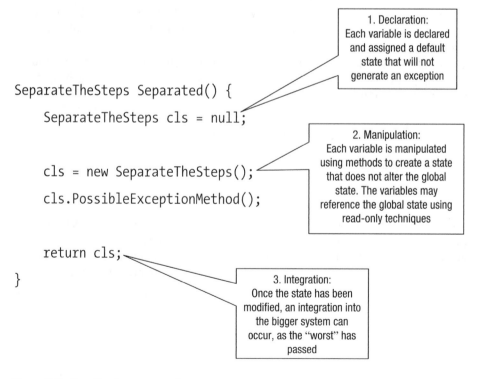

Figure 5-7. *Sandboxing your code*

Figure 5-7 illustrates one way of performing a sandboxing operation, but there are many other possible implementations. In each of the different implementations, the objective is the same: you want to perform the operations that could cause an exception apart from the main code. Then if you do have an exception, it will be localized to the separate code. When the stack unwinds, the other code won't be corrupted.

■**Note** The rule of thumb with sandboxing your code is to keep all of the code manipulations that could generate an exception separate from any existing state that could be corrupted. Once the manipulations have been carried out, you integrate the objects into the global state using method calls that are extremely unlikely to generate exceptions. For those situations when you must manipulate existing state, use a `finally` handler, so that the previous existing state can be re-created if necessary.

Filtering Exceptions

In all of the examples in this chapter, the `catch` statement used the `Exception` type:

```
catch (Exception) { ;}
```

`Exception` will catch every exception.

In Figure 5-3, the IDE caught an exception, referencing `NullReferenceException`, which is a specific type of exception. When you use it in a `catch` block, you will catch only null reference exceptions.

By specializing the exception, you have the ability to filter which exception you want to catch. For example, `NotSupportedException` will catch only instances of `NotSupportedException` exceptions. Here is an example:

```
try {
    throw new NotSupportedException("There is no code");
}
catch(NotSupportedException ex) {
    ;
}
```

If the code within the `try` block threw an instance of `Exception`, the `catch` block would not trigger, because the `catch` block was looking for a specific exception type.

Exception types can be combined to provide specific filtering capabilities. The specific exception type should be the first exception after the `try` block, as in this example:

```
try {
    // ...
}
catch( NotSupportedException ex) {
    ;
}
catch( Exception ex) {
    ;
}
```

By combining multiple exception filters, you don't need to figure out which kind of exception is being thrown. For example, without the filtering capabilities of a catch block to catch NotSupportedException exception types, you would need to write this code:

```
try {
    throw new NotSupportedException( "There is no code");
}
catch (Exception ex) {
    if (ex is NotSupportedException) {
        // ...
    }
    else {
        throw ex;
    }
}
```

Table 5-1 lists common exception types in the System namespace that you can throw or can be thrown. There are many more exceptions, and you can even generate your own exceptions, by subclassing Exception. An exception type is defined as an exception type because the identifier Exception is appended to the description identifier of the exception.

Table 5-1. *Common Exception Types*

Exception	Description
Exception	Plain vanilla exception; a general container for all exceptions. When you get one of these exceptions, look at the Message property for the exact details. If you throw this type of exception, it is important to supply an easy-to-understand string to the exception constructor.
ArgumentException	Thrown if you call a method and one of the arguments is not valid. Typically, in the Message property you can find the problem with the arguments. If this exception is thrown, it is because the contents of the argument are wrong.
ArgumentNullException	Thrown if you call a method where one of the arguments is a null value. This could be because you are passing the null value to the method or one of the arguments has a null value.
ArgumentOutOfRangeException	Thrown if you call a method where one of the arguments is not in the expected range. While this exception sounds similar to ArgumentException, it is more specialized and targets whether an argument is in an acceptable range. Check the documentation of the method or the method implementation on what the acceptable range is. If you throw this exception, note the valid range in the error message.
ArithmeticException	Thrown if a mathematical error is generated.
DivideByZeroException	Thrown if you attempt to divide by zero.
FormatException	Thrown if the format of the parameter is not correct. For example, if a method expects a number to be formatted with a period and you use a comma, an exception is generated.

Continued

Table 5-1. *Continued*

Exception	Description
IndexOutOfRangeException	Thrown if you attempt to reference an index of an array that would be beyond the limits of the array. This exception is thrown if you have not allocated an array and then attempt to reference an element, or if you attempt to reference a negative index of the array.
InsufficientMemoryException	Thrown if not enough memory is available. Although this exception is not generated often, it can be generated if you attempt to allocate an array when you specify something along the lines of 5 trillion elements (due to an improperly assigned array size variable).
InvalidCastException	Thrown if you attempt to cast one type to another type that is not supported. This exception is very common when you use inheritance and attempt a cast.
NotImplementedException	Thrown when using methods or properties without an implementation. Often, you don't have time to implement all of the code at once. For those properties or methods that have not been implemented, don't leave an empty property or method implementation. Instead, throw an exception. Then you will know if you have forgotten to implement something.
NotSupportedException	Thrown when you attempt to use an interface instance and a method that cannot work. For example, if you open a read-write buffer to a read-only CD-ROM, you will get this exception when writing to the CD-ROM. If you attempt to read from the interface instance, an exception will not be thrown.
NullReferenceException	Thrown when you attempt to call a method or property of a variable that has not been assigned with a valid type instance.
OutOfMemoryException	Similar to InsufficientMemoryException.
OverflowException	Thrown when you attempt to perform numeric operations that are not supported, such as adding 2 billion to 2 billion using a 32-bit integer.
SystemException	Thrown by the operating system. Do not attempt to derive from this class.

Writing Exception-Safe Code

Now that you've seen how to implement exception handlers, we'll look at an even better approach to exceptions: not generating them. We'll focus on how you can make your code safer and less likely to generate exceptions.

Writing Defensive Code

All too often, developers get exceptions such as NullReferenceException because they didn't make sure that the state in a piece of code was valid. And if the state is not valid, an exception will occur. In fact, in this chapter, one of the previous examples has just such a situation, which you may have noticed. Here is the code that has a dumb little exception possibility:

```
void TestCallingExample() {
    CallingExample cls = null;
    try {
        cls = new CallingExample();
        cls.Method();
    }
    catch (Exception) { ;}
    Console.WriteLine("Depth is (" + cls.GetDepth() + ")");
}
```

The problem is in the bolded line, which assumes that cls will always reference a valid instance of CallingExample. This is an assumption that you cannot afford to make. If an exception occurred while instantiating CallingExample, cls will still be null, and the catch block will catch the instantiation exception, saving a program crash. However, the use of cls.GetDepth() right after that throws your protection out the window, as cls is null and will generate a NullReferenceException. Here's a better way to write this code:

```
void TestCallingExample() {
    CallingExample cls = null;
    try {
        cls = new CallingExample();
        cls.Method();
    }
    catch (Exception) { ;}
    if (cls != null) {
        Console.WriteLine("Depth is (" + cls.GetDepth() + ")");
    }
}
```

The bolded code illustrates defensive coding that tests if cls is not null, and if so, then allows the referencing of cls.GetDepth(). Now the code is exception-safe. It does not mean exceptions cannot occur, because calling GetDepth() could still generate an exception internally, but with respect to the TestCallingExample() method, you have made everything as safe as possible, and have assumed GetDepth() is a low exception-risk method.

Missing from the TestCallingExample() method is an indication of whether the processing worked. It is assumed from the perspective of the caller of TestCallingExample() that calling TestCallingExample() will always result in something being done. The caller of TestCallingExample() has no way of knowing that something failed, other than if an exception was thrown.

Code that tells you if something went wrong using an exception is both a blessing and a curse. It is a blessing because the code is telling you that something went wrong. But it is a curse because sometimes you know something could go wrong, and that it is OK, but you don't want the exception to travel up the program hierarchy. In these cases, you need to catch the exception, which makes your code more complicated.

For example, say you wanted to parse a number. The .NET parsing routines tend to give a result if everything worked OK, but generate an exception if things are not OK. There is no return value, nor out parameter, just an exception. But when parsing a number, you do know that things could go wrong, so you will need to write an exception handler. Following is some source code that parses a number.

```
int TestGetValue(string buffer) {
    int retval = 0;
    try {
        retval = int.Parse(buffer);
    }
    catch (FormatException ex) {
        Console.WriteLine("Exception (" + ex.Message + ")");
    }
    return retval;
}
```

In the example, the code realizes that if Parse() is called and the string cannot be converted into a number due to incorrect letters or numbers, an exception will be thrown. The exception will be caught, processed (using the exception's Message property to obtain the problem), and then the value of retval will be returned to the caller. But what if an exception does happen? The variable retval is initialized to a default value of 0, which is a valid formatted number and can be interpreted as the result of a successful format processing.

The problem in the code is that a developer is caught in a bind. By capturing the exception, the method TestGetValue() is saying, "I will always return to the caller a valid value." Yet there are instances when a valid value is not available. In the case of parsing a number, an exception is thrown. So by capturing an exception, you are doing the completely wrong thing, because you should be letting the exception be caught by a higher-level caller. But things can become sticky here. Do you really want to inform the caller that a parse cannot occur? Perhaps the caller is more interested in whether a valid value is returned. It's like saying to the CEO, "Oops, we just ran out of staples." Sure, staples might be important, and maybe the company will not run as smoothly, but do you really want to inform the CEO about every little problem?

Microsoft developers know about this problem with parsing, and use an approach that you can use as well. As you learned in Chapter 3, there are two variations of parsing a number:

- Parse() returns a valid number if the buffer could be parsed, and an exception if a number could not be parsed.

- TryParse() returns a true or false value indicating the result of the parse.

Here's how you could rewrite the TestGetValue() method to use TryParse():

```
bool TestGetValue(string buffer, out int val) {
    bool retval = false;
    if (int.TryParse(buffer, out val)) {
        retval = true;
    }
    return retval;
}
```

In the modified example, TestGetValue() returns a true or false to indicate a success or failure when parsing a number. If a true is returned, the parameter val will point to a valid number; otherwise, val should be not be used.

Some of you might have caught that my use of Parse() and TryParse() is not very creative. The method TestGetValue() could have been reduced to a single line:

```
bool TestGetValue(string buffer, out int val) {
    return int.TryParse(buffer, out val);
}
```

Using Default State

Default state is a useful technique to guard against exceptions that developers often ignore. When developers are writing their code, they will often return null when things don't work out. Using null is not a bad idea, but it adds unnecessary baggage. For example, consider the following code:

```
class DefaultStateWrong {
    string[] Tokenize(string buffer) {
        return null;
    }

    public void IterateBuffers(string buffer) {
        string[] found = Tokenize(buffer);
        if (found != null) {
            for (int c1 = 0; c1 < found.Length; c1++) {
                Console.WriteLine("Found (" + found[c1] + ")");
            }
        }
    }
}
```

The problem in this example is Tokenize(), which is a method used to convert the parameter buffer into a series of string tokens. Using safe exception coding, if the data could not be parsed, you could throw an exception, or you could return a null value indicating that the buffer could not be parsed.

The caller code knows that there is the possibility of a null value when calling Tokenize(), and thus has an if block to check for the null value. The if block is defensive coding, but it also adds complexity because you need to verify for a null value.

What if Tokenize() were a bit smarter and decided to return an empty array to indicate an empty result set? The logic of this is not incorrect, because the caller expects either a result set with items or a result set with nothing in it. If a dramatically bad parsing error has occurred, the only recourse is to throw an exception. Here is the rewritten code:

```
class DefaultStateRight {
    string[] Tokenize(string buffer) {
        return new string[0];
    }

    public void IterateBuffers(string buffer) {
        string[] found = Tokenize(buffer);
        for (int c1 = 0; c1 < found.Length; c1++) {
            Console.WriteLine("Found (" + found[c1] + ")");
        }
    }
}
```

In the rewritten code, Tokenize() returns an empty array that, when iterated using a for loop, will cause zero iterations. This is exception-safe code with improved readability.

But what happens if Tokenize() does throw an exception? With Tokenize() throwing an exception and the lack of a try/catch block in IterateBuffers(), it looks like IterateBuffers() is written incorrectly. However, IterateBuffers() is not written incorrectly, because Tokenize() will throw an exception only if something really problematic has occurred. A big problem is beyond the scope of the IterateBuffers() method, and thus needs to be handled at a higher level. Think of it as the situation where you have a criminal case and the local municipal court automatically delegates the case to the provincial or state level, because those courts are equipped to deal with such a case.

Processing Errors That Are Warnings

One of the silliest things that programs do is exit when they could have continued working. It reminds me of when my family lived on the French Rivera, where it does not rain too often. Our two bulldogs were used to the nice weather, and at the slightest hint of moisture in the air, they would refuse to go outside. Our male dog Big Boss (Man) would stand in the doorway, stick his nose out slightly, and take a few deep breaths. If he sensed the slightest bit of moisture, instantly you were dragging an 80-pound concrete block.

The point is that, like our bulldogs, programs sometimes overreact to situations. For fear of having problems or not doing something correctly, they instantly shut down.

Let's say that you have a program that requires a configuration file to run. What happens when the configuration file does not exist? One approach is to panic and exit. The panic approach will work, but what if multiple problems follow from the first one? Then you are painstakingly hitting one error after another. Another approach is to use a default action. In this example, the default action could be to display a dialog box asking the user to select a configuration file, or the program could create a default file, as in this example:

```
try {
    LoadConfiguration();
}
catch(ConfigurationException ex) {
    CreateDefaultConfiguration();
}
```

Here, the LoadConfiguration() method is in a try/catch block, but the catch block catches only ConfigurationException failures (a built-in C# exception). If there is a ConfigurationException failure, then a default configuration is created. With a default configuration, the program can continue processing. Using the filtering capabilities of exceptions, if another exception is thrown in LoadConfiguration(), then some higher-level exception handler will process it.

When processing an error that is a warning, the important steps are to filter for the specific exception and implement an appropriate exception handler that has been properly tested. Don't try to implement a fix-all exception handler, because you will never be able to implement a proper handler and thus will cause more problems. In the handler to fix the problem, make sure that you don't generate an exception. If you do, that exception will be sent to a higher method caller.

The Important Stuff to Remember

In this chapter, you learned about errors and exceptions. Here are the key points to keep in mind:

- Errors and exceptions will always occur in your programs.

- Your code is split into a tree very much like a management hierarchy. The hierarchy contains two types of code: code that organizes and code that implements.

- Exceptions are caught using try/catch blocks.

- The finally block is used to execute code, regardless of whether an exception is thrown, and to reset state.

- Code that implements has the responsibility of throwing exceptions. Code that implements does not try to fix or swallow the exception. This means code that implements will implement a finally block to reset state, but usually not a catch block.

- Code that organizes has the responsibility of being aware that exceptions might occur. This means code that organizes will implement catch blocks to catch exceptions and process them. Usually, this code will not have a finally implementation, but it may filter exceptions.

- Exceptions can be filtered to determine which exceptions will be captured and which cannot be captured.

- You can help make your code exception-safe by implementing sandboxing functionality.

- Implement default state so that your code is easier to read and maintain.

- Code that implements an error that is a warning is typically organizational code and is used to fix an exception.

Some Things for You to Do

To apply what you've learned in this chapter, here's what you can do, summed up in a single step:

1. Rewrite all of the code examples in Chapter 4 to be exception-safe.

CHAPTER 6

Learning the Basics of Object-Oriented Programming

At this point, you should be comfortable with writing basic C# code, but your coding style would solve problems directly without considering reusability or other more advanced concepts. You could code yourself out of a wet paper bag, but once you were out of the bag, you would have no idea what to do next. (In case you're interested, the phrase, "You couldn't do [fill in topic] out of a wet paper bag" implies that your skills in a certain area are so weak that a wet paper bag is more overpowering. The reference to wet paper bag comes from the fact that wet paper bags have no holding power and will tear at the slightest nudging.)

This chapter focuses on reusing base functionality, where two classes share methods and properties in common to solve a particular problem. To demonstrate the concepts, we will create a simple currency exchange application. This application will use object-oriented programming, a powerful set of techniques common in modern programming languages such as C#.

In this chapter, you'll learn about the following topics:

Object-oriented programming: Object-oriented, often abbreviated as OO, refers to a way of building applications using instantiated types. First, you define the type and its behavior. Then, when instantiated, the type has a state. When you are developing, you don't know the state of the object, so you can only guess at it.

Data member scopes: Types have methods, and methods can be called by other types. But do you want to let all types call all of a type's methods? Think of it as follows. When you are at a party, do you want to allow everyone to grab into your pockets? No, you want to control access to your pockets, just as you want to control access to your type's methods.

Properties: There are methods, and there are properties. Methods are supposed to do things to a type. Properties are external state representations of a type.

Base classes: The term *base class* denotes common functionality. We use the word *base*, because in object-oriented programming, hierarchy is defined from the base upwards. We use the word *class*, because class is the basic type that contains functionality.

Let's begin with some background on how currency exchange works, which applies to the currency converter application we'll develop in this chapter to demonstrate object-oriented programming concepts.

Understanding Currency Spreads

This chapter's sample application deals with exchanging different currencies. Did you know that when you exchange one currency for another, you never have to pay a processing fee? Whether you are exchanging currencies at some airport or on an exchange, you should not be charged any processing fees. It makes you wonder how people earn money by accepting one currency and then giving out another currency. The answer lies in how currency exchange works.

When dealing with currencies, you are always dealing with currency pairs. This is different from something like buying a stock, when you are dealing with only that stock. A currency by itself is actually quite useless. Suppose you have a $100 in your hand. What will it be worth one year from now? The answer is simple: $100. Yes, you can argue that the $100 dollars will not buy as much next year, but that would be complicating the issue with concerns not related to this discussion. The fact is that if you have 100 dollars, 100 yen, 100 euros, and so on into infinite time, you will always have 100 currency units.

Currency exchange involves comparing one currency to another currency. The value of a currency is what one person would give in comparison to another currency.

Foreign exchange (forex) market traders make their money by dealing in *spreads*. Spreads are tricky because as the exchange rate moves up or down, so does the spread. For example, hotels always give you horrible rates, and you may wonder why they are ripping you off. But hotels are not ripping you off; they are hedging themselves on the safe side.

Consider the following example of a spread:

EUR.USD   1.3141   1.3142

The EUR.USD term means you are converting one euro into a number of US dollars (USD). The first number is the bid, which means that a trader is willing to give 1.3141 US dollars for every euro. The second number is saying a trader wants 1.3142 US dollars for every euro. Essentially, the buyer and seller are 0.0001 US dollars apart. The exchange spread is normal, and it moves around because some might be willing to sell at a lower conversion rate, and others might be willing to buy at a higher conversion rate.

Let's say one day you enter a hotel in Austria on a skiing holiday. In your hand, you have 1,000 US dollars (USD), but Austria belongs to the European Union (EU). To buy anything in the EU zone, you need euros (EUR). Being clever, you decide to go on the Internet and check out the going spread. It turns out to be the one you've just seen.

Standing in the hotel foyer, you have US dollars in your pocket and you need to buy euros. Thus, you will need to go in the direction USD.EUR. The way to do that is to divide one by the posted spread values. This calculation gives the following conversion rates:

USD.EUR   0.7610   0.7609

The numbers are a bit wrong, because the buyer is willing to give a higher value than the seller. Granted, this happens at times on the forex markets, but here, it's because we used a raw conversion of EUR.USD. The market might be a bit higher and lower, but generally speaking, you have a feeling of what to expect.

You advance to the hotel desk, and you kindly ask what the going rate is for US dollars to euros. The concierge gives the following exchange rate:

USD.EUR   0.75120

EUR.USD   1.29340

Doing your calculations, this rate doesn't seem right. The hotel is giving you 751.20 euros for your 1,000 US dollars, but the forex market clearly says the traders would be willing to give you 761.00 euros. The hotel is ripping you off by 10 euros.

The hotel is not ripping you off; rather, it is hedging its risks. The spot conversion rates will go up and down during the day, and the hotel is not in the business of exchanging money. The hotel is in the business of giving you room and board. The hotel managers need to make sure that when they go to the bank to exchange your dollars for euros, they don't lose money in the process. They ensure this by giving you less money.

Whenever you exchange monies, you should always look at the spreads. Sometimes the spreads are good; sometimes they are horrible. I have found the best spreads are at the banks. It is a bit more work to get money from your home bank, but usually worth the effort. Another option is to pull the money from your credit card; however, sometimes credit cards charge interest on the money you withdrew.

Now that you have an idea of what's involved in currency exchange, let's see what our sample application will do.

Organizing the Currency Exchange Application

The currency application takes a number of currency units and converts it to a number of other currency units. The application will implement the following features:

- Accept and store a currency exchange rate.

- Store the currency unit identifiers.

- Convert to a currency and back to the original currency.

- Distinguish between active currency traders and hotel currency traders.

- Implement a spread for hotel currency traders.

As in the examples in the previous chapters, the project structure of the currency application will consist of two projects: a console testing application, named `TestCurrencyTrader`, and a library component, named `CurrencyTrader`, which contains the functionality of the hotel trader and the active trader.

Writing Tests for the Currency Exchange Application

Since we don't exactly know how the implementation will appear, let's start by writing some tests that will use our implementation. We want to build the application incrementally, so we'll write some tests, write some code, test the code, and continue. The overall big picture is to be able to convert from one currency to another.

Getting Started with Structural Code

At the heart of the application is an exchange rate, currency units, and a calculation that combines the exchange rate with the currency units. Thus, a logical first step would be to write test code that combines these elements, something like this:

```
CurrencyTrader cls = new CurrencyTrader();
cls.ExchangeRate = 1.31;
double haveUSD = 100.0;
double getEUR = cls.Convert(haveUSD);
Console.WriteLine("Converted " + haveUSD + " USD to " + getEUR);
```

This code is unique in that the test code has all of the responsibility of making sure the correct data is assigned to the structure. To clarify this, here is the same code with random variable names used instead of the identifiers for the currency variables:

```
CurrencyTrader cls = new CurrencyTrader();
cls.ExchangeRate = dddddedfasffsdf;
double ukfkisd = 100.0;
double didkfdbnfd = cls.Convert(ukfkisd);
Console.WriteLine("Converted " + ukfkisd + " USD to " + didkfdbnfd);
```

This code is structural, rather than architectural. *Structural* code is code that requires an intelligent programmer—a programmer who knows what the individual items mean. *Architectural* code, on the other hand, is more idiot-proof and requires less knowledge, because many parts are encapsulated. The user needs to understand only how to use the classes. Put another way, structural code is knowing how to add two numbers. Architectural code is knowing how to punch in the two numbers and hit the plus sign on a calculator. You can argue that by not knowing how to add and relying on the calculator, you have no idea if the calculator is doing its job properly. That is a valid point, and that is why tests are important to ensure that the calculator is doing its job properly.

Understanding Base Classes

The first test code, which is structural, is not wrong. Structural code forms the basis of what is called a *base class*. A base class is a class that provides certain functionality that will be reused by other classes. In this case, converting the currency units is functionality that we will need in both the active trader and hotel trader. You define base classes so that you get consistent behavior when performing identical operations. In lieu of base classes, you would need to copy and paste the functionality to reuse it.

Base classes have some very important characteristics:

- Only developers who understand what the base class code is trying to do should use the base class code. To control access, we will use scope.

- Base classes describe properties and methods. To make use of the base class, the descriptions are assembled to perform a calculation. For example, to perform a currency conversion, you need to manually define the exchange rates and currency units, and execute the conversion method. The manual step-by-step approach gives the developer flexibility.

- Base classes need extensive testing because their functionality will be used throughout your code. If the base classes have bugs, most likely a large chunk of your code will have bugs.

■**Note** Base classes are a general concept that only developers understand fully. A general concept is called a *design pattern*. Design patterns create a developer lingo where words like *factory*, *state*, and *visitor* refer to specific coding concepts that developers understand without needing to explain the coding concept. I suggest that you learn more about design patterns. The Data & Object Factory web site (`http://www.dofactory.com/Patterns/Patterns.aspx`) has some excellent coding examples of essential patterns used by developers.

In the current example, the `CurrencyTrader` class needs to be converted into a base class that can be used only by knowledgeable developers. You want to prevent your source code from being used in the wrong context.

One way to stop usage in the wrong context is to declare the `CurrencyTrader` class as abstract. The `abstract` keyword says that the class in question cannot be instantiated. You can reference the class, but you cannot instantiate the class. Consider the following code, which declares `CurrencyTrader` as `abstract`.

```
abstract class CurrencyTrader { }
```

Using `abstract` implies that someone needs to create a class that can be instantiated, using a mechanism called *inheritance*. From a developer perspective, the idea behind `abstract` is to embed reusable logic used by some other class. Using `abstract` implies inheritance.

Understanding Inheritance

Inheritance is similar to a genealogy tree, in that you have a tree structure where there is a parent, and the descendants of the parent are children. And like the genealogy tree, the structure can have multiple levels. However, inheritance is not quite like genealogy, because genealogy requires a pair of humans to create a tree.

A class uses inheritance to gain functionality from the base class and becomes a subclass of that base class. Inheritance, and in particular .NET, has a tree structure where there is only a single root parent. When you use inheritance, you can gain functionality, but you can also *override* functionality, as illustrated in Figure 6-1.

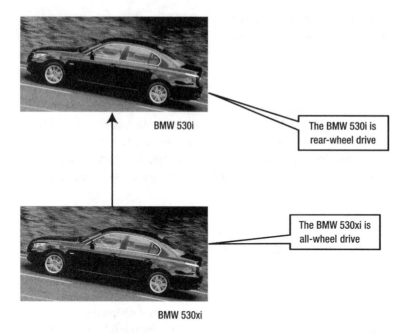

Figure 6-1. *Simple two-level inheritance example using the awesome BMW 530i and 530xi*

The pictures in Figure 6-1 seem to illustrate the same car, but in fact, they are two different models with a major difference in power train. From an inheritance perspective, the BMW 530i could be considered the parent of the BMW 530xi.

■**Note** The order of which is the parent and which is the child is my logic; some might disagree. This disagreement is healthy and part of the object-oriented design process.

The first model that you would design would probably be the rear-wheel-drive model, since it is simpler to design, cheaper, and more popular. You would consider all-wheel-drive as a feature. The all-wheel-drive model is not a completely new car. Both the 530i and 530xi would share the same tires, motor, steering wheel, body trim, and so on. What would be different is that the 530xi replaces the power train, thus changing the behavior of the car.

Let's say that you are a driver sitting in the seat driving your BMW, and it's a snowy night in Canada. Whether you are driving the 530i or the 530xi, you would use the same steering wheel, blinkers, gas pedal, brake, and so on. But the behavior of the 530i and 530xi would be different—the rear-wheel-drive car might slide around a bit more than the all-wheel-drive car. The power train overrides behavior, which means the consumer of the hierarchy sees the same interface (for example, methods and properties), but gets different behavior.

Another way to use inheritance is not to replace functionality, but to enhance functionality, as illustrated in Figure 6-2. This is called *overloading* behavior.

Figure 6-2. *A more extensive inheritance tree illustrating how functionality can be enhanced*

In Figure 6-2, all of the cars are related in that they are the 530 line. The new model is the BMW 530xi Sports Wagon, which, from an inheritance perspective, is based on the functionality of the BMW 530xi. But here is the twist: the functionality of the 530xi Sports Wagon requires you to get accustomed to the Sports Wagon. For example, even though you press a single button to open the trunk, the Sports Wagon's trunk is slightly different from the trunk in the 530xi and 530i, and thus exposes the driver to a slightly different user interface and behavior.

When you use inheritance to overload functionality, you are adding functionality that is called in the same way, but is used and behaves differently. With this form of inheritance, you don't just change behavior, you also change the user interaction.

In our example, we will use inheritance to extend functionality, and not override or overload.

Using C# Properties

So far, the test code would call a data member reference, as in this line:

```
cls.ExchangeRate = 123.45;
```

The data member would be implemented as follows:

```
public abstract class CurrencyTrader {
    public double ExchangeRate;
}
```

Exposing the data member using a public scope worked in previous chapters, but we don't really want to do this because we are exposing the internal state of the object. In object-oriented programming, exposing the internal state is a bad idea (as explained in more detail shortly).

Rather than expose the data member publicly, we will change the test code to use properties. Properties also expose the internal state of an object, but they provide a layer of abstraction. As you will learn, some properties expose both internal state and external state. This is the case with the ExchangeRate property that we will use to access and modify the exchange rate. If we did not use the ExchangeRate property, we would need to create a method that assigns the exchange rate and a method that retrieves the exchange rate. The methods would behave like the property, but they are not as convenient to use.

Rewriting the Test Code to Use Properties

The interesting thing about C# properties is that they look and behave like data members. This means with C# properties, the test code does not need to be rewritten, as the test code still assumes a direct access to the variable. Consider the rewritten CurrencyTrader that exposes ExchangeRate as a C# property, shown in Figure 6-3.

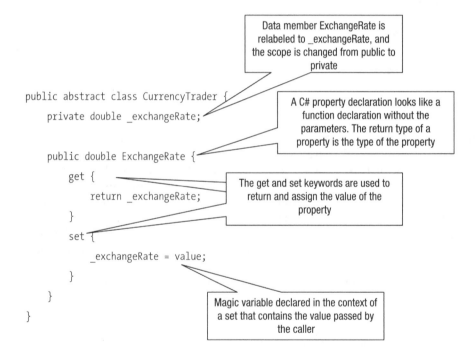

Figure 6-3. *Exposing ExchangeRate as a C# property*

To completely fool the test, the name of the property must be identical to the name of the previously declared data member. So that there is no identifier collision, the data member ExchangeRate is renamed to _exchangeRate and the scope changes from public to private.

Properties look like methods without parameters, but have a return value. Also, each property must have at least a get code block or a set block (it can have both), which are called *getters* and *setters*. If a property has only a get code block, you have created a read-only property. If a property has only a set code block, you have created a set-it-and-forget-it property. Within the context of a property, you can have only the get or set keyword. You cannot add any other code.

The following code will execute the code defined in the get code block and retrieve the state from the class to the variable.

```
value = cls.ExchangeRate;
```

And the following code will execute the code in the set code block and assign the state from the variable to the class.

```
cls.Exchange = value;
```

Each code block has special features. The get code block must always return data to the caller and thus requires use of the return keyword. The set code block has no requirements to do anything. However, if you want to know what data is being passed to the property, you can use the value variable, which is not declared in your code, but is instead implied. Consider this as a situation where the magic variable value is made available to you by the C# programming language.

Understanding the Problems with Properties

Many programmers feel that properties promote bad programming practices. Properties expose the internal state of an object. Looking at the previous source code, you will see that the data member _exchangeRate has a one-to-one relationship to the property ExchangeRate. If the caller assigns the property ExchangeRate, then the private data member _exchangeRate is immediately assigned. This exposes the internal state, even though the exposure is indirect.

As an example, say that you want to preheat an oven to a certain temperature to bake something. The simplest way to preheat the oven is to monitor the temperature and create a property Temperature, like this:

```
class Oven {
    private int _temperature;

    public int Temperature {
        get {
            return _temperature;
        }
        set {
            _temperature = value;
        }
    }
}
```

The class Oven exposes its temperature as a property, which is a direct reference to the variable _temperature. The caller of Oven would periodically ask the oven for its temperature and decide when the oven has been preheated.

So, is Oven in its current implementation actually a structural class? The user of Oven has quite a bit of responsibility in that it must periodically query the temperature and decide if the oven is preheated. A better implementation is to define a class that takes care of itself. The caller would then just need to ask, "Are you ready?" Here's how that code would look:

```
class Oven {
    private int _temperature;
```

```
    public void SetTemperature(int temperature) {
        _temperature = temperature;
    }
    public bool AreYouPreHeated() {
        // Check if oven temperature matches prescribed temperature
        return false;
    }
}
```

In the modified implementation of Oven, the data member _temperature is not externally exposed. And in this situation, the role of the data member _temperature is not to represent the temperature of the oven, but to act as an upper limit to which the oven should be heated. The upper limit is assigned using the SetTemperature() method. To check the temperature of the oven, you don't retrieve the temperature of the oven, but call the AreYouPreHeated() method. The caller receives either a true or false value to indicate whether or not the oven is ready.

The caller of Oven has the responsibility only of setting the upper temperature and asking if the oven is preheated. From this example, it would seem that you don't need properties. However, you still need properties because Oven in its current form represents an easy-to-use class that can be integrated at the architectural business-logic level.

The challenge of the developer is to bridge the gap between a raw structural class and the exposure of an architectural business-logic-level class. That challenge will be met when the hotel currency trader and active currency trader are implemented.

Even with these arguments and the distinction between base class and architectural business-logic-level classes, some still naysay properties. The reason has to do with controlling access.

Suppose you are in a grocery store, waiting at the cash register. The cashier tallies up the items, arrives at a total, and asks you to pay. Do you open your purse or wallet and let the cashier get the credit card or cash? Along the same lines, why can't you just place the cash into the cash register? The answer to these questions is one of trust. As trustworthy as the cashier and shopper might be, we feel better when we know we have the control.

Let's go back to an example I mentioned at the beginning of the chapter: allowing people to grab into your pockets. The previously defined Temperature property is allowing someone to grab into your pockets. You wouldn't generally allow it, but what if that person were your spouse or your mom? Would you still disallow it? The answer is very different, because you probably trust your mom or spouse. In the same way, often state and its exposure are a matter of trust and using the right scope.

■**Note** In this discussion of properties and object-oriented design, my goal is to explain that there is a place and time for both, and you should not feel biased toward one approach or the other. When you design a type that does not reveal its state, you are designing a type that fulfills an abstract intention. When you design a type that reveals its state (to some extent) through properties, you are designing a type that is used at the lower technical level. Also keep in mind that sometimes internal state is external state, such as the exchange rate example. You cannot abstract away the exchange rate state because it is a number used in a calculation.

Understanding Inheritance and Scope Modifiers

At this point, the ExchangeRate property is a mechanical property that will be used by any class that subclasses CurrencyTrader. So now we need to decide whether access to the property should be restricted. The answer is that it should be restricted to only those developers who truly understand how to convert currencies. Access should be restricted to those classes that will subclass CurrencyTrader. Following is the rewritten version of CurrencyTrader.

```
public abstract class CurrencyTrader {
    private double _exchangeRate;

    protected double ExchangeRate {
        get {
            return _exchangeRate;
        }
        set {
            _exchangeRate = value;
        }
    }
}
```

The bolded code highlights three examples of scope access:

public: The type, method, or property can be accessed and referenced by any other type. In the context of a crowd of people, it means anyone can reach into your pocket and inspect your wallet.

private: The method or property can be accessed and referenced only by the type declaring the method or property. In the context of a crowd of people, it means only you can reach into your pocket and inspect your wallet.

protected: The method or property can be accessed and referenced by the type declaring the method or property or by types that subclass the declaring type. In the context of a crowd of people, it means only you and people who you have allowed can reach into your pocket and inspect your wallet.

If you happen to declare a type, method, or property without a scope modifier, the default is assumed, which means private is implied.

The private and protected modifiers cannot be assigned to a type. You'll learn more about other modifiers and details about type scope declarations in the next chapter.

Using C# Inheritance to Subclass Another Type

The rewritten version of CurrencyTrader will cause the test code to break, because it uses the abstract keyword, and abstract types cannot be instantiated directly. Here is the broken code:

```
CurrencyTrader cls = new CurrencyTrader();
cls.ExchangeRate = 123.44;
```

The code will not work for two reasons:

- CurrencyTrader is abstract and thus cannot be instantiated.

- ExchangeRate is protected and cannot be referenced externally.

This broken code puts us in a bind. Up to this point, whenever we tested code, we assumed all of the pieces that were to be tested could be referenced. One solution would be to change the scope declarations and remove the abstract and protected keywords. Yes, that solves the problem, but it is a cop-out. The better approach is to test CurrencyTrader as it was intended to be used: as a class that is derived from. So, the solution is to use inheritance and create a test class that derives from CurrencyTrader, as follows:

```
class TestCurrencyTrader : CurrencyTrader {
    public void InitializeExchangeRate() {
        ExchangeRate = 100.0;
    }
}
```

TestCurrencyTrader is a test class that is added to the test source code. A colon (:) separates the class identifier from the subclassed class identifier, CurrencyTrader.

To expose a method outside the class declaration, you use the public modifier, even though the class does not have a public modifier.

Inheritance means identifiers that are scoped protected or public can be referenced in the subclassed type. For example notice how ExchangeRate seems to be all on its own, without any object reference. The lonely reference to ExchangeRate is fine, because the base class CurrencyTrader has an identifier with that name. The property ExchangeRate can be referenced locally because of its protected scope The identifier ExchangeRate has an implied this reference (this.ExchangeRate), so it is not necessary to add that, unless you have multiple identifiers with the same name, or you want to explicitly reference a certain identifier.

And now the tests will not test CurrencyTrader, but will test TestCurrencyTrader, which should contain some verification code to make sure everything works correctly.

Understanding Private, Protected, and Public Scope

Let's dig a bit deeper into how the three types of scope work. To start, consider the CurrencyTrader implementation:

```
public abstract class CurrencyTrader {
    private double _exchangeRate;

    protected double ExchangeRate {
        get {
            return _exchangeRate;
        }
        set {
            _exchangeRate = value;
        }
    }
    protected double ConvertValue(double input) {
```

```
        return _exchangeRate * input;
    }
    protected double ConvertValueInverse(double input) {
        return input / _exchangeRate;
    }
}
```

The new class ActiveCurrencyTrader subclasses CurrencyTrader and is written as follows:

```
public class ActiveCurrencyTrader : CurrencyTrader {
}
```

The data member CurrencyTrader._exchangeRate is declared as private, and thus can be referenced only in CurrencyTrader. If _exchangeRate had no declaration, private scope would be implied. For example, the following code would not compile.

```
public class ActiveCurrencyTrader : CurrencyTrader {
    public void Method() {
        _exchangeRate = 100.0;
    }
}
```

The ActiveCurrencyTrader class is not part of CurrencyTrader, and thus _exchangeRate cannot be referenced.

Considering the ActiveCurrencyTrader class, ExchangeRate, which has been declared as protected, could be referenced as follows:

```
public class ActiveCurrencyTrader : CurrencyTrader {
    public void Method() {
        ExchangeRate = 100.0;
    }
}
```

Protected scope means only those classes that derive from a class can view the methods, properties, or data members. How many times and levels a class subclasses another class is not important.

Public scope is the loosest and simplest of all scopes. You use public whenever you want to expose functionality that other classes or derived classes want to reference.

Here are some guidelines for using each scope:

Private scope: You will use private for most data member declarations because data member declarations imply the state of an object. Sometimes, when developing algorithms, you will break apart the logic into several methods. The broken-apart methods are used to solve a problem, and thus should be used only in the context of the class, implying the methods need to be declared using private.

Protected scope: You will use protected whenever you want to enforce an inheritance architecture. Very often, protected and abstract go hand in hand, as both are intended for inheritance. The main objective behind protected is to offer a derived class access to the private state of a parent class, or to offer reusable functionality that should be used only by knowledgeable developers.

Public scope: As a rule, think carefully before using public. You will use public scope for the most part, but it is also the scope that can cause the most problems. For example, once you declare something as public, trying to later change the scope could wreak havoc in the code that uses the class. It might be harder to develop using the other scopes, but you will have code that will have fewer maintenance issues. It all comes down to what methods and properties you want to expose to the outside world.

Handling Verification

To run the test class TestCurrencyTrader, the following code is used.

```
TestCurrencyTrader cls = new TestCurrencyTrader();
cls.IntializeExchangeRate();
```

The modified test code entails instantiating TestCurrencyTrader and then calling the method InitializeExchangeRate(). But is this a test? After all, the InitializeExchangeRate() method doesn't have a parameter or return value. Think of it as sending a letter via mail. You don't know if the letter will arrive, but it probably will. Tests that are probably passed are a really bad idea.

We need to move the verification code from the test routine to the TestCurrencyTrader class, like this:

```
class TestCurrencyTrader : CurrencyTrader {
    public void InitializeExchangeRate() {
        ExchangeRate = 100.0;
        if (ExchangeRate != 100.0) {
            throw new Exception("100.0 verification failed");
        }
    }
}
```

The bolded code illustrates the verification code used to ensure that the value assigned to ExchangeRate is the same one that is retrieved.

■**Note** The tests we're using are becoming more complicated, and you may wonder, "Why do it that way?" For this book, we are writing tests and creating our own testing framework. Normally you would not do that. You would use a testing framework such as NUnit (http://www.nunit.org) or the Microsoft Visual Studio Professional tools to help create the tests. But here I want to demonstrate how to use C#, not a testing tool. By learning how to write the tests from the ground up, you will understand what to expect from testing frameworks.

Using Conditional Statements

Having verification code within a class is acceptable in the context of the test class TestCurrencyTrader. However, the problem of testability is still present in those classes that do not expose their state.

To understand the problem, let's return to the code for preheating the oven that you saw earlier in the section about the problems with properties. Imagine rewriting Oven to include a verification test, like this:

```
class Oven {
    private int _temperature;

    public void SetTemperature( int temperature) {
        _temperature = temperature;
        if( _temperature != 100.0) {
            throw new Exception( "100.0 verification failed");
        }
    }
    public bool AreYouPreHeated() {
        // Check if oven temperature matches prescribed temperature
        return false;
    }
}
```

The bolded code illustrates a verification much like that used in CurrencyTrader, which verifies the parameter temperature for a specific value. While the verification is useful for a particular test, it is not useful in the big picture. As the code is written, the only valid value of temperature is 100.0; anything else will generate an exception. It is definitely not a solution.

To get around this problem, you could use the C# conditional statements. Conditional statements are special keywords that allow a developer to define whether a piece of source code is compiled. Following is an example of source code that includes conditional statements.

```
class TestCurrencyTrader : CurrencyTrader {
    public void InitializeExchangeRate() {
        ExchangeRate = 100.0;
#if INTEGRATE_TESTS
        if (ExchangeRate != 100.0) {
            throw new Exception("100.0 verification failed");
        }
#endif
    }
```

The conditional statement always starts with a hash character (#), immediately followed by a keyword—if in this example. Between the #if and #endif is code that is conditionally compiled. This is known as a *preprocessor directive*. In this example, the condition means to compile the code contained within the #if and #endif block if the value INTEGRATE_TESTS is true.

You can define a compilation identifier like INTEGRATE_TESTS in the source code or in your IDE. In Visual C# Express, you can assign INTEGRATE_TESTS as follows:

1. Right-click your project and select Properties.

2. Click the Build tab.

3. Add the INTEGRATE_TESTS value to the Conditional Compilation Symbols box.

Using Partial Classes for Verification

Conditional compilation is useful when you want to include or remove code depending on a configuration. However, some programmers will frown upon having conditional compilation code within a function, as that would be a maintenance nightmare. Another solution is to use the partial class keyword in conjunction with conditional compilation statements.

Thus far in all of the examples, whenever we defined a class, all of the methods and code were declared between the curly brackets of the class. By using *partial* classes, it is possible to declare a class in multiple places. When the C# compiler compiles the source code, the individual class pieces will be assembled into a single class definition. For our test code, we can create an implementation partial class and a conditionally compiled test partial class implementation. The following is the modified TestCurrencyTrader class that could be used to test the state without exposing the state.

```
partial class TestCurrencyTrader : CurrencyTrader {
    public void InitializeExchangeRate() {
        ExchangeRate = 100.0;
    }
}

#if !INTEGRATE_TESTS
partial class TestCurrencyTrader : CurrencyTrader {
    public void VerifyExchangeRate(double value) {
        if (ExchangeRate != value) {
            throw new Exception("ExchangeRate verification failed");
        }
    }
}
#endif
```

The keyword partial prefixes the class keyword. The first implementation of TestCurrencyTrader is an example of not exposing state. The second implementation of TestCurrencyTrader, which is declared in the context of a conditional compilation statement, contains the method VerifyExchangeRate(). This is a verification method that tests the ExchangeRate property for a particular value.

■**Note** You can use partial classes only in the context of a single assembly, as the partial keyword cannot be used across assembly boundaries. When I say "single assembly," I am referring to the compiled pieces of .NET source code illustrated in Chapter 1. In other words, if you define a partial class in a library, then all pieces of the partial class need to be defined in the library.

Partial classes make it simple to separate functionality into various source code files, where the modification of one source code file does not affect another source code file. This example demonstrates using partial classes to manipulate internal state of a class without violating the do-not-expose-internal-state rule. Another use of partial classes is in the context of code generators, where one source code file contains the custom code, and the other source code file contains the generator code.

Finishing the Base Class

The `ExchangeRate` property is one of the pieces of shared functionality. Another piece of shared functionality we want to implement is the calculation of the exchange rate. We'll do this with `ConvertValue()` and `ConvertValueInverse()` methods, which convert a currency from one value to another using multiplication. The following shows the methods in the completed base class implementation of `CurrencyTrader`.

```
public abstract class CurrencyTrader {
    private double _exchangeRate;

    protected double ExchangeRate {
        get {
            return _exchangeRate;
        }
        set {
            _exchangeRate = value;
        }
    }
    protected double ConvertValue(double input) {
        return _exchangeRate * input;
    }
    protected double ConvertValueInverse(double input) {
        return input / _exchangeRate;
    }
}
```

The bolded code highlights the methods that convert the currency from one unit to another. Notice that there is no declaration of currency units, because the base class is a utility class used to help us realize an active trader or hotel trader implementation.

■Note Base class functionality, even when appearing trivial, is defined to ensure consistency in implementation. Without consistency, you encounter the problem where one implementation does one thing and another implementation does something completely different.

This completes our test code. Now we will implement the active trader and hotel trader components of the currency exchange application.

Writing the Active Trader and Hotel Trader Currency Converters

With the `TestCurrencyTrader` test solution completed, it's time to turn our attention to the `CurrencyTrader` solution. As mentioned earlier, this consists of the active trader and hotel trader currency converter components. Here, you'll see more clearly what it means to use inheritance.

Implementing ActiveCurrencyTrader

The `ActiveCurrencyTrader` class implements the logic of the active currency trader. To begin, we'll add its constructor.

Adding a Constructor to ActiveCurrencyTrader

To give `ActiveCurrencyTrader` some default state, we use a constructor. However, the constructor will serve another purpose, in that any class that instantiates `ActiveCurrencyTrader` will consider the instance as immutable. *Immutable* means that once data has been assigned to the instance, it cannot be altered. In other words, it is unchangeable.

■**Note** The `string` type is immutable because once a string variable has been assigned, it cannot be changed. Take a look at the methods associated with `string`, and you will see nothing that allows you to modify the contents. An immutable type is good because it allows you to implement a set-it-and-forget-it object, and it prevents other classes from accidentally changing the contents. Overall, an immutable type is robust and predictable.

The following is the constructor code.

```
public class ActiveCurrencyTrader : CurrencyTrader {
    string _fromCurrency;
    string _toCurrency;

    public ActiveCurrencyTrader(double currExchange, string fromCurrency,
        string toCurrency) {
        ExchangeRate = currExchange;
        _fromCurrency = fromCurrency;
        _toCurrency = toCurrency;
    }
}
```

The constructor has three parameters: `currExchange` represents the current exchange rate, `fromCurrency` indicates the source currency (for example, USD), and `toCurrency` indicates the destination currency (for example, EUR). These three parameters are assigned to data members, whereby only the current exchange rate is assigned to the base class `CurrencyTrader`. `ExchangeRate`.

Defining Informational Read-Only Properties

The strings that represent the from currency and to currency are stored as strings, and are purely for informational purposes. For example, let's say that you have instantiated a bunch of currency pairs so that the trader can comprehend the currency pair in which the values of _fromCurrency and _toCurrency will be presented. This means that the currency strings are read-only properties and are coded as follows:

```
public class ActiveCurrencyTrader : CurrencyTrader {
    string _fromCurrency;
    string _toCurrency;

    public ActiveCurrencyTrader(double currExchange,
        string fromCurrency, string toCurrency) {
        ExchangeRate = currExchange;
        _fromCurrency = fromCurrency;
        _toCurrency = toCurrency;
    }
    public string FromCurrency {
        get {
            return _fromCurrency;
        }
    }
    public string ToCurrency {
        get {
            return _toCurrency;
        }
    }
}
```

The naming of the properties corresponds closely to the naming of the data members (FromCurrency, ToCurrency). I do this throughout my code so that I know what each piece of code means. My notation is to use a leading underscore to name private data members, but you can use a different notation if you prefer.

Adding the Conversion Methods

The last step to make the ActiveCurrencyTrader class complete is to add the functionality to convert a value from or to a currency pair. The ActiveCurrencyTrader class will use the exact currency exchange rate. The ConvertValue(), and ConvertValueInverse() methods have protected scope, and thus are not exposed. ActiveCurrencyTrader needs to define a pair of publicly scoped methods that will call the protected scope methods. The complete ActiveCurrencyTrader implementation is as follows.

```
public class ActiveCurrencyTrader : CurrencyTrader {
    string _fromCurrency;
    string _toCurrency;
```

```
    public ActiveCurrencyTrader(double currExchange,
          string fromCurrency, string toCurrency) {
        ExchangeRate = currExchange;
        _fromCurrency = fromCurrency;
        _toCurrency = toCurrency;
    }
    public string FromCurrency {
        get {
            return _fromCurrency;
        }
    }
    public string ToCurrency {
        get {
            return _toCurrency;
        }
    }
    public double ConvertTo(double value) {
        return ConvertValue(value);
    }
    public double ConvertFrom(double value) {
        return ConvertValueInverse(value);
    }
}
```

The ConvertTo() and ConvertFrom() methods are wrappers to the ConvertValue() and ConvertValueInverse() methods, and provide no added value. But remember the problem of the cashier and credit card. Just because it seems like there is no added value, the reality is that you are writing code that is acting as a gatekeeper and giving yourself flexibility.

For example, suppose that CurrencyTrader.ConvertValue(), and CurrencyTrader.ConvertValueInverse() were declared using public rather than protected. Then any user of ActiveCurrencyTrader could use the functionality exposed by CurrencyTrader. Suppose someone decided to change the functionality of ConvertValue() and ConvertValueInverse(). At that point, you would have problems, because the changes to CurrencyTrader automatically imply changes in ActiveCurrencyTrader. By defining your own methods, you are controlling and making sure that if things change in the future, you can accommodate them without needing to change the callers of ActiveCurrencyTrader.

We have now completed the functionality of ActiveCurrencyTrader, so let's implement HotelCurrencyTrader.

Implementing HotelCurrencyTrader

The difference in features between HotelCurrencyTrader and ActiveCurrencyTrader is the existence of a sizable spread.

Adding a Constructor to HotelCurrencyTrader

Again, we'll begin by adding a constructor. The HotelCurrencyTrader constructor needs an additional parameter value referencing a spread. Following is the code for the HotelCurrencyTrader constructor, including the informational properties.

```
public class HotelCurrencyTrader : CurrencyTrader {
    string _fromCurrency;
    string _toCurrency;
    double _spread;

    public HotelCurrencyTrader(double currExchange, double spread,
        string fromCurrency, string toCurrency) {
        ExchangeRate = currExchange;
        _fromCurrency = fromCurrency;
        _toCurrency = toCurrency;
    }
    public string FromCurrency {
        get {
            return _fromCurrency;
        }
    }
    public string ToCurrency {
        get {
            return _toCurrency;
        }
    }
}
```

In the constructor of HotelCurrencyTrader, you can see the additional parameter spread. The spread parameter is assigned to the data member _spread and represents a calculation that modifies the exchange rate.

Adding the Conversion Methods to HotelCurrencyTrader

Remember in the previous section how the methods ConvertTo() and ConvertFrom() seemed to add no extra value. For HotelCurrencyTrader, they will add value and illustrate why it is useful to create indirect exposure. Calculating what people will receive for their currency depends on the exchange rate, and in the case of the hotel, the exchange rate has a spread. As explained earlier in this chapter, this means you will never get as much as you hoped and will always pay more than you expected.

The following is the source code for the HotelCurrencyTrader implementations of ConvertTo() and ConvertFrom().

```
public class HotelCurrencyTrader : CurrencyTrader {
    string _fromCurrency;
    string _toCurrency;
    double _spread;

    public HotelCurrencyTrader(double currExchange, double spread,
        string fromCurrency, string toCurrency) {
        ExchangeRate = currExchange;
        _fromCurrency = fromCurrency;
        _toCurrency = toCurrency;
    }
```

```csharp
    public string FromCurrency {
        get {
            return _fromCurrency;
        }
    }
    public string ToCurrency {
        get {
            return _toCurrency;
        }
    }
    public double ConvertTo(double value) {
        double realExchange = ExchangeRate;
        ExchangeRate = realExchange - _spread;
        double retval = ConvertValue(value);
        ExchangeRate = realExchange;
        return retval;
    }
    public double ConvertFrom(double value) {
        double realExchange = ExchangeRate;
        ExchangeRate = realExchange + _spread;
        double retval = ConvertValueInverse(value);
        ExchangeRate = realExchange;
        return retval;
    }
}
```

The ConvertTo() and ConvertFrom() methods have the added logic in that the spread will be added or subtracted from the exchange rate. The methods read the current exchange rate, assign it to a temporary variable, define a new exchange rate taking into account the spread, calculate the currency, and then reassign the exchange rate.

The ConvertTo() and ConvertFrom() methods swap values to achieve the desired calculations. There is absolutely nothing wrong with doing this, and you will often swap values in your own code. What is important is to restrict access on what classes can do this. Because ExchangeRate is a property with protected access, it means only those classes that subclass can assign and change the value of ExchangeRate. And this implies that the class doing the subclassing knows what it is doing to the data. It is a valid assumption and one that you can use to your benefit. The caller is not aware of this swapping, because HotelCurrencyTrader is taking advantage of the object-oriented technique to not expose the state of the type.

That's it—we're finished with the currency exchange application. For the remainder of this chapter, I will fill in some extra details that are important.

Learning More About Preprocessor Directives, Properties, and Abstract Methods

Some details about preprocessor directives, properties, and the abstract keyword that did not come up in this chapter's example are worth mentioning. These are things you should know about when writing your own code.

More Preprocessor Directive Details

Earlier in the chapter, you saw how you can use the hash character (#) and conditional statements to conditionally include code during compilation. The technical term for this jargon is called *preprocessing* the code, and the statements are called *preprocessor directives*. Table 6-1 shows the preprocessor directives you can use.

Table 6-1. *Available Preprocessor Directives*

Hashcode	Description
#define	Used to define the compilation identifier, such as the INTEGRATE_ TESTS identifier used in this chapter's example. You would define this at the top of a source code file to activate conditional preprocessor statements used throughout the source code file. Using a #define directive does not span multiple source code files.
#undef	Used to undefine an identifier. You would use #undef if you wanted to change a global setting. Let's say that an identifier is set globally, but for a particular source code file, you want the behavior as if the identifier were not set. In that case, you use #undef. Another way to achieve this behavior is to use the ! character in front of the identifier.
#if and #endif	Used to conditionally include or not include a piece of source code. You would use a conditional directive whenever you wanted to define source code configurations, such as for debug or production builds.
#elif	Instead of a single #if block, you could have multiple tests for code inclusion. You would use #elif when you have more than a single preprocessor directive, such as for debug, production, and performance builds.
#else	A default code block that is included if the other #if statements did not trigger.
#region and #endregion	These have absolutely nothing to do with the compilation of the source code. They are used by Visual Studio to create regions of source code that can be "folded." Folding means to collapse a block of code out of sight temporarily. Source code files can become long, and constantly paging up and down becomes tedious. By folding the code, you are reducing the amount of times that you need to page up and down, even though the code still exists.

The following example demonstrates how to use the preprocessor directives.

```
#define ACTIVATE_1
#undef ACTIVATE_2

namespace TestDefine {
    class Example {
#if ACTIVATE_1
        int _dataMember;
#elif !NO_ACTIVATE_10
        int _dataMember3;
#else
        int _defaultValue;
```

```
#endif
    }
}
```

In general, you will use preprocessor directives when you are building debug mode or release mode code. *Debug mode* means that the code is compiled such that it can be debugged and analyzed using pretty symbols. *Release mode* means when the code is compiled, the code can still be debugged, but the pretty symbols are missing.

■**Note** Visual C# Express does not give you the flexibility to choose debug mode or release mode for development. To get this feature, you need the full version of Visual Studio.

Think of the pretty symbols as milestones on the road. Every time your code executes in debug mode, the code is saying, "You are now calling this method in this source code file," or "Oops, that property code in the source code file is not working properly." In release mode, the pretty symbols are more like road signs saying, "Place X y Miles/Kilometers." The signs help guide you, but the information you get from them is very limited; that is, you don't know which towns you're passing.

More Property Scope Details

In this chapter's examples, the get and set parts of the properties always had the same scope. However, properties can have mixed scope; that is, the get and set parts can have different scopes. Scope splitting works only if you specify both the get and set parts of the property. The idea behind splitting the scope is to enable the implementation of the logic where classes in the inheritance chain are allowed to assign a property, and classes external to the inheritance chain are allowed only to read the property. The following is an example where a property is declared as public and the assignment of the property is protected.

```
class PropertyScopeExample {
    int _value;

    public int Value {
        protected set {
            _value = value;
        }
        get {
            return _value;
        }
    }
}
```

More abstract Keyword Details

In this chapter's example, the keyword abstract was used to declare a class that could be referenced, but not instantiated. It is also possible to use the abstract keyword to define methods that need to be implemented. The idea behind declaring abstract methods is that it allows a developer to define an intention in a base class that can then be implemented in the subclass.

In the implementation of HotelCurrencyTrader and ActiveCurrencyTrader, two methods were defined: ConvertTo() and ConvertFrom(). A developer could come to the conclusion that the methods are common to both classes, and thus they could be defined in the base class CurrencyTrader. That is not a bad idea. Let's revisit the CurrencyTrader class and see how these two methods could be added to CurrencyTrader as abstract methods.

```
public abstract class CurrencyTrader {
    private double _exchangeRate;

    protected double ExchangeRate {
        get {
            return _exchangeRate;
        }
        set {
            _exchangeRate = value;
        }
    }
    protected double ConvertValue(double input) {
        return _exchangeRate * input;
    }
    protected double ConvertValueInverse(double input) {
        return input / _exchangeRate;
    }
    public abstract double ConvertTo(double value);
    public abstract double ConvertFrom(double value);
}
```

An abstract method is declared without an implementation, and requires that the class declaring the method(s) be declared as abstract.

Any class that subclasses CurrencyTrader is required to implement ConvertTo() and ConvertFrom(). In the case of HotelCurrencyTrader and ActiveCurrencyTrader, this is not a problem, because the methods are already implemented. However, the methods need to be changed slightly, as follows:

```
public override double ConvertTo(double value) {
    // ...
}
public override double ConvertFrom(double value) {
    // ...
}
```

The slight change is the addition of the keyword override to indicate that the ConvertTo() and ConvertFrom() methods in HotelCurrencyTrader and ActiveCurrencyTrader override the functionality in CurrencyTrader.

While you have seen all of the technical aspects, the bigger question is why you would do this in the first place. Let's go back to the implementation of ActiveCurrencyTrader, which has no abstract method implementations. To use the class and the method ConvertTo(), you would write the following code.

```
ActiveCurrencyTrader cls = new ActiveCurrencyTrader();
double converted = cls.ConvertTo( 100.0);
```

Imagine the situation where the values to convert to and from are text. To keep things general, you would write the following code.

```
public double ConvertToTextField(ActiveCurrencyTrader cls) {
    return cls.ConvertTo(int.Parse(text1.Text));
}
```

The implementation of ConvertToTextField() makes one major mistake in that it assumes that you will always be converting a currency using the ActiveCurrencyTrader implementation. If you wanted to use the class HotelCurrencyTrader, you would need to implement another method with a parameter of type HotelCurrencyTrader.

This problem is the classical *polymorphism* problem and is solved by using abstract methods. Consider the following rewritten ConvertToTextField() method.

```
public double ConvertToTextField(CurrencyTrader cls) {
    return cls.ConvertTo(int.Parse(text1.Text));
}
```

This implementation of ConvertToTextField() uses the CurrencyTrader base class, and since ConvertTo() and ConvertFrom() are declared, they can be referenced.

How you call ConvertToTextField() and how you instantiate HotelCurrencyTrader or ActiveCurrencyTrader will not be covered in this chapter, because polymorphism is the subject of the next chapter. Just keep what you've learned about the abstract keyword in mind as you read that chapter, which covers concepts such as interfaces, because you can do the same types of things with it.

The Important Stuff to Remember

In this chapter, you learned some of the basics of object-oriented programming. The following are the key points to remember:

- Your code will be composed of structural or base class functionality, and architectural business-related functionality.

- Base class functionality is focused on a particular problem. The problem might be solved in a general manner, but only the particular problem is solved. Base class functionality requires specific knowledge of the field. Think of it as implementing a calculator where your main concern is ensuring that the calculations are correct.

- Architectural business-related functionality is higher-level functionality where general business knowledge is needed. The idea is to take the base classes, or base class–related classes, and use them to solve a business problem. Think of it as using a calculator and your main concern is getting the results of the calculations.

- Properties should be used instead of exposing data members publicly.

- Many dislike properties because they promote bad programming practices. You need to get beyond those comments and think in terms of the credit card and the cashier. Properties have their time and place.

- Classes should, in general, not expose their state. To get around exposing state, create methods that implement the general intent of the purpose of the class.

- Inheritance is a fundamental part of C# and you will need to know how to use it. One way to implement inheritance is through the use of the abstract keyword.

- Overriding is when you keep the interface the same and change behavior.

- Overloading is when you derive a class and define an identifier that happens to be the same as some base class identifier. Your overloaded identifier may change behavior and usage.

- Conditional compilation statements can be effective when you want to include code in certain configurations.

- Partial classes are very useful when you want to separate functionality that serves a specific purpose. In this chapter's example, it meant having the ability to add test code without violating the rule of exposing state.

Some Things for You to Do

To apply what you've learned in this chapter, you can do the following:

1. The code for HotelCurrencyTrader.ConvertTo() and HotelCurrencyTrader.ConvertFrom() contains a potentially big bug. Identify the bug and fix it.

2. In the examples, the exchange rate is assigned by the caller of the HotelCurrencyTrader and ActiveCurrencyTrader. Implement functionality such that the exchange rate can be retrieved dynamically. Hint: think of converting ExchangeRate into a property that references an abstract base class that can be used as a directory to look up an exchange rate pair.

3. The currency ExchangeRate property is a double. Implement ExchangeRate using the decimal type.

4. Write test code for ActiveCurrencyTrader and HotelCurrencyTrader.

■■■

CHAPTER 7

Learning About Components and Object Hierarchies

The previous chapter covered the basics of object-oriented programming. You learned how one class can subclass another class, thus building a hierarchy. Using an object hierarchy, classes can share functionality.

This chapter will focus on the details of object hierarchies, including how to extend them so that derived classes can specialize shared functionality. To demonstrate these concepts, we will build a tax application. This type of application is a good example of using object hierarchies, because the general idea of paying taxes is identical, regardless of the country, but the details are different.

From a technical perspective, we'll cover the following topics:

- Interfaces, which are the basis of software components

- Details of overloading and overriding methods

- How and when to use factories

We'll begin with some basic tax concepts that relate to our sample application.

Understanding Some Basic Tax Concepts

Taxes and death are two sure things in life. Regardless of where you live, the government has managed to create a system where you pay taxes (for the good of the people, of course). As a result, people hate paying taxes, and many figure out creative ways to not pay taxes. Honest people who would normally not break the law find clever ways of bending the law in their favor. In some countries, they even expect that you will cheat, and will calculate your "true" tax figure.

Taxes seem like a complex topic, but they are rather simple. What makes taxes complicated are the volumes of rules associated with them. Taxes boil down to the fact that if you buy or do X, then you can deduct or charge Y. Sometimes, the taxes make sense; sometimes they don't. Overall though, the tax rules are similar in logic, and that means a hierarchy of objects can be designed.

Taxable income is the sum of monies that you earned for which a tax rate is applied. The taxable income may or may not be equal to the sum of money that you earned during a year. Taxable income can be less due to deductions and income deferment. And in some cases, taxable income can be more due to deferment.

Deductions are items that can be charged against taxable income. People mistakenly believe that deductions can be charged directly against the tax payable amount. Or they mistakenly believe a tax deduction is always an advantage. For example, let's say you have $1,000 of tax deductions. If your income is $2,000,000, then the deduction is not worth much, since your taxable income is still $1,999,000.

Partial taxation is when a partial amount of earned monies is added to the total taxable income. Often, partial taxation is applied to capital gains. Capital gains refers to when you have bought something like a property and then sold it at a higher price than you paid for it. The difference between the two prices is subject to capital gains tax.

A variation of partial taxation is income splitting so that a lower tax rate is achieved. Let's say that you have a household of two people. One of the two earns the income, and the other stays at home. In such a case, the household would be taxed at the same level as a single-person household. Yet the two-person household has more expenses. Thus, some countries allow a household to declare a single tax, where in effect, a single earner in a two-person household is taxed at half the rate.

When calculating the total tax, some countries linearly increase the taxation rate. Typically, the linear tax rate is less for lower incomes and more for higher incomes. Another approach is to divide income in chunks with different tax rates for each. This means that those monies earned up to a certain amount are taxed at a certain rate. Monies above that amount and below another higher amount are taxed at a higher rate. This chunking of the amounts and rates keeps on being calculated until a highest tax rate is reached, where any amounts over that upper limit are taxed at the highest rate.

Organizing the Tax Application

As a general rule, in each country, you must pay an income tax, which is calculated against your total income. From your income, you can deduct certain expenses, thus lowering your taxable income. What differs from country to country are what you can deduct and the individual tax rate. These will be addressed by the tax application we will build in this chapter.

For the tax application, the following features will be implemented:

- Define a taxable income.

- Define a series of deductions.

- Implement a tax-calculation engine that has the ability to account for families or single earners.

As in previous examples, the project structure of the taxation application will consist of two projects: a console testing application and a library component that contains the functionality. The library component will be in a solution called LibTax, and the testing application will be in a solution called TestTax.

Before we start coding, however, you need to understand the concepts of interfaces and components.

Programming Using Ideas

At this moment, we don't have a clue where to start building the tax application, because the problem is in the details of the implementation. Unlike previous examples, where it was possible to gauge what tests were needed, in this example, we simply do not know. We could start by implementing the general tax rules, and then applying them to a specific system. But what if our general tax rule implementations didn't actually work out? We would have wasted time writing code that we would end up throwing out.

Consider the following situation: you write a series of base classes that represent a generic taxation kernel based on the information in the "Understanding Some Basic Tax Concepts" section. The base classes need a task, and thus wait for a client. A little while later, an individual from the United Kingdom desires a tax program based on the base classes. The developers, eager to show off the usefulness of their base classes, implement the tax program. The idea is that you save time by using the base classes to implement something specific. Without the base classes, you would, in theory, have a longer development time.

Experience has shown that unless the base classes are developed from highly experienced business analyses, the odds of the base classes helping you are rather slim. What most likely will happen is your base class code will need to be warped, twisted, and fitted to make the program work. The result is that if another client from another country asks for a tax program, the base classes will yet again need to be warped, twisted, and fitted to make the program work. The managers, seeing this brute-force technique, start to realize that the monies invested in the base classes were not such a good idea.

Who is at fault? Is it the fault of the developers who created the base classes? Is it the fault of the complexity of implementing a tax program? The answer is that it is the fault of the idea of the base classes. The original developers wanted to create base classes based on a problem that does not exist. It is like trying to build the foundation of the bridge across the water before you have an idea of how many people will use the bridge and what kind of people would use the bridge. Logically, engineers don't start building bridges before they figure out the details of the bridge. Yet, in the software industry, time and time again, we see projects focusing on developing a general framework without having a concrete problem to solve.

I am not saying that base classes themselves are a bad idea, nor is the idea of developing a general framework. What I am saying is that to be able to develop useful base classes, you need to understand the domain of the base classes. If you don't, then you should not be writing base classes.

But how do you gain experience in the domain to write well-designed base classes? You can start by writing down some ideas as C# constructs and then implementing the ideas. Coming up with ideas and then implementing them is part of the development process called *test-driven architecture*.

To start test-driven architecting, you think of the requirements and then come up with a general solution. In the case of our example, the requirement is to create a tax engine to calculate income tax. Generally speaking, it means figuring out what the total taxable income is, subtracting the total deductions, and applying a tax rate to the remaining sum to calculate the total tax.

In programming terms, the general ideas are converted into source using C# *interfaces*.

Representing Ideas Using C# Interfaces

Think of C# interfaces as programmatic constructs you can use to jot down ideas. When you jot down ideas to solve a problem, you usually implement a bread-crumb trail approach—you start with one idea, and then follow it to another idea, which leads to another idea, until you have jotted down all of your ideas.

Your first idea is the central idea. In our tax application, the central idea is the tax engine itself. The tax engine is used to perform a tax calculation and to pull together all of the other pieces. The other pieces are some nebulous things that you need to complete the tax engine. I like to call these other pieces *dependencies*. The dependencies are ideas that you need to finish the previous idea, hence the metaphor of following bread crumbs to your solution.

Ideas by themselves are designs that solve a particular problem or give an inkling of how to solve the particular problem. When an idea is converted into source code, it becomes a blueprint that forces the implementation to take a certain shape. Ideas when coded are C# interfaces, which cannot be executed by themselves. From a programmatic point of view, an interface is like an abstract base class in that you can reference an interface, but you cannot instantiate an interface. To get a working idea, you write an implementation, or implement an interface.

The following is an example of a C# interface.

```
interface IExample { }
```

The keyword `interface` is associated with an identifier `IExample`, and from a syntax perspective is used like the `class` keyword. You can associate the public scope with an interface. The interface contains methods and properties that determine the behavior of the classes that implement the interface. Consider the following source code that defines an interface with a single method and single property.

```
interface IExample {
    void Method();
    int Property { get; set; }
}
```

Between the curly brackets after the identifier, an interface can define methods and properties. The methods and properties don't have curly brackets after the identifiers, because you are defining only a signature of a method or property that will be implemented by the class. It is like defining an abstract method of an abstract base class.

The following code is a rudimentary implementation of the defined interface.

```
class ExampleImplementation : IExample {
    public void Method() {
    }

    public int Property {
        get {
        }
        set {
        }
    }
}
```

`ExampleImplementation` implements the `IExample` interface using inheritance, like the sample abstract base class presented in the previous chapter.

■**Note** C# and the CLR are single-inheritance models in that a class can subclass only a single class. But a C# class can implement as many interfaces as necessary. If a class subclasses another class and interface, the class is the first identifier after the colon. Using another form will generate a compiler error.

When implementing an interface, all of the methods and properties of the interface must be implemented in the class. If they are not, then when the source code is compiled, the compiler will complain about missing methods or properties and consider the implementation as incomplete.

As inheritance is used, you can think of `IExample` as a base class that has no implementation. The following code illustrates how to instantiate the implementation and assign the instance to an interface.

```
IExample cls = new ExampleImplementation();
cls.Method();
```

In the example, the class `ExampleImplementation` is instantiated and assigned to a variable `cls` of type `IExample`. This instantiation and assignment is a downcast from a derived class to a base class, or more accurately, a *base type*. A *downcast* is when you cast a type from subclassed type in the inheritance chain (for example, `ExampleImplementation`) to a base class in the inheritance chain (for example, `IExample`). The automatic downcast works because `ExampleImplementation` can be expressed as being of the type `IExample`. Think of it as saying, "I am instantiating `ExampleImplementation` and assigning the instance to the type `IExample` that is in my inheritance hierarchy." When the method `cls.Method()` is called, the caller is really calling the `ExampleImplementation.Method()`, although the caller would not know that, as it is using the base type `IExample`.

The mechanics of defining an interface and its associated implementation are straightforward, but why would you do it? To explain, I'll use a real-life analogy.

Let's say that you are going to a restaurant for an evening of fine dining. When you are sitting at the table, you expect a waiter to take your order, serve your food, remove the used dishes, and give you the bill. All of these actions are ideas used to run a restaurant that serves a clientele. You make use of the idea, as do millions of other clients. The idea is applied across all restaurants.

Think about this a bit. The idea is a waiter, but the implementation is a human. When you sit down, your waiter may introduce himself by his name, but do you ever use the name? Most people don't, because they think of the waiter as a human that takes their order, serves their food, and so on. The point is that the human is the implementation, but you really only care about a waiter fulfilling the scope of the task. For example, while you might be sympathetic that your waiter is having a bad day, you want him to be chipper and happy, and to do his job of taking your order, serving your food, and so on. Bluntly put, you probably would not care if the waiter's puppy had been run over by a truck.

This is exactly what interfaces and implementations are about. The interface defines a role of tasks that an implementation is supposed to implement. You don't care if the implementation is capable of doing more, or if the implementation is "having a bad day." All you care about is that the implementation does what the interface says it should do.

What you have is a decoupling of the idea from the interface, just like at the restaurant, where you don't care if Tom, Dick, Mary, or Jane is your server. In fact, would you care if the human waiter was replaced by a robot? Probably not, because what you really care about is eating the food. This is an important aspect of interfaces and implementations, in that implementations are replaceable, and you want to be able to swap one implementation for another.

When you use interfaces and types that implement interfaces, you are writing component-oriented software. Components and inheritance are two different object-oriented techniques. You use inheritance to implement interfaces, but components serve the purpose of making ideas happen.

Understanding How Inheritance and Components Work

Inheritance is the act of defining base classes with functionality that may or may not be over-ridden or overloaded, as explained in the previous chapter. Components define subsystems that are put together like pieces of a puzzle. The idea behind components is to be able to associate two interface instances and make them work with each other without knowing what the other does.

To get a feeling of the difference between inheritance using classes and components that use interfaces and classes, we will look at a classic example of inheritance and how that example translates to components.

Illustrating Inheritance Using a Shape, Rectangle, and Square

One of the most popular examples of using inheritance involves shapes and how to calculate the area of a shape. The starting point of this inheritance is an abstract base class that has a single property and method to indicate a single dimension and its associated area. For example, the following would be an appropriate abstract base class definition.

```
abstract class Shape {
    public abstract double CalculateArea();
}
```

The method CalculateArea() is used to calculate the area of the shape. It is declared as abstract and must be implemented by a derived class.

For starters, let's define Square, which represents the square shape.

```
class Square : Shape {
    double _width;
    public double Width {
        get {
            return _width;
        }
        set {
            _width = value;
        }
    }
    public override double CalculateArea() {
```

```
        return Width * Width;
    }
}
```

A square has only one dimension, Width, which represents the width of a particular shape. In the case of a square, width means one of the four sides. We've implemented the CalculateArea() method, which calculates the surface area of the square by multiplying the Width property by itself.

A rectangle is a form of square, and therefore Rectangle derives from Square:

```
class Rectangle : Square {
    double _length;
    public double Length {
        get {
            return _length;
        }
        set {
            _length = value;
        }
    }

    public new double CalculateArea() {
        return Width * _length;
    }
}
```

Rectangle cannot be described using a single dimension, thus we need to add the property Length. In the implementation of the Rectangle.CalculateArea() method to calculate the area, the length is multiplied by the width.

Take a good look at how CalculateArea() is declared. In the case of Rectangle.CalculateArea(), the new keyword is used, not override. This is because you want to enforce calculation consistency. Calculation consistency is when you perform a specific calculation on a type and get the answer expected of that type, and not some other type.

So, say you instantiate Rectangle, and then downcast to Square. When you call CalculateArea, you want it to calculate as if the rectangle were a square, not a rectangle. Thus, by adding the new keyword in the Rectangle CalculateArea method, a square is calculated as a square, and a rectangle is calculated as a rectangle.

But there is a consequence. Let's say Rectangle is downcast to Shape. As the inheritance is declared when calling CalculateArea, the area of a square is calculated, which is not correct. Thus it would seem that using new is incorrect, and override should be used instead. So using override solves the Shape.CalculateArea problem, but when a rectangle is converted into a square, the area represents a rectangle and not square. You have a situation where you can't win.

To illustrate the differences, assuming the use of new, look at the following source code, which calculates the area of a Rectangle.

```
Rectangle cls = new Rectangle();
cls.Width = 20;
cls.Length = 30;
double area = cls.CalculateArea();
```

In the example, Rectangle is instantiated, and the properties Width and Length are assigned values of 20 and 30, respectively. When the CalculateArea() method is called, the found area is assigned to the variable area.

The source code does what we expect. It instantiates a rectangle, assigns the rectangle dimensions, and calculates the area of the rectangle. But a Rectangle type can also be a Square type. Consider the following modified source code, which makes a Square out of a Rectangle.

```
Rectangle rectangle = new Rectangle();
rectangle.Width = 20;
rectangle.Length = 30;
Square square = rectangle;
double area = square.CalculateArea();
Console.WriteLine("Square Area is " + square.CalculateArea() +
    " Rectangle Area is " + rectangle.CalculateArea());
```

In the example, the variable rectangle is of type Rectangle. The dimensions of the rectangle are assigned, and then the rectangle is converted into a square and assigned to the variable square. Using the keyword new, the area is 400, which is correct because when we ask for the dimensions of the square, we get a width of 20.

Now suppose that we used the keyword override and type cast to Square. The width would still be 20, but the area would be 600. And if we were to write tests to test the area calculation of the square, we would get a failure.

The shape example demonstrates that even though you think a square is like a rectangle, you can't have one derive from the other without some type of trouble. Rather than being a base class, Shape should be an interface. And Square is a base class for Rectangle, but each class implements the Shape interface. Then we would get consistent behavior. Here is the solution:

```
interface IShape {
    double CalculateArea();
}

class Square : IShape {
    double _width;
    public double Width {
        set {
            _width = value;
        }
        get {
            return _width;
        }
    }
    public double CalculateArea() {
        return _width * _width;
    }
}

class Rectangle : Square, IShape {
    double _height;
    public double Height {
```

```
    set {
        height = value;
    }
    get {
        return _height;
    }
}
public new double CalculateArea() {
    return Width * _height;
}
}
}
```

This modification of the inheritance using both interfaces and classes will result in a consistent CalculateArea, regardless of how an instance of Rectangle is cast. Following is the code that we could execute to verify that there are no consistency problems.

```
Rectangle rectangle = new Rectangle();
rectangle.Height = 30;
rectangle.Width = 20;
Square square = rectangle;
IShape shapeCastFromRectangle = rectangle;
IShape shapeCastFromSquare = square;

Console.WriteLine("Area Rectangle (" + rectangle.CalculateArea() +
    ") Area Square (" + square.CalculateArea() +
    ") Area Cast From Rectangle (" +
        shapeCastFromRectangle.CalculateArea() +
    ") Area Cast From Square (" +
        shapeCastFromSquare.CalculateArea() + ")");
```

The various techniques used in this example are explained in the remainder of this chapter.

■**Note** The example illustrates that by using inheritance, you can downcast a type and get the appropriate behavior. But this works only if you design your inheritance hierarchy properly. You need to understand that behavior depends on the type that you have from the inheritance tree. And if you are not careful, you can get some very odd side effects. C# allows you to explicitly define what each method does, and you should think very hard about what each method should do.

Illustrating Components Using a Shape, Rectangle, and Square

Another way to implement a shape is to use components. Using components means to define an idea, and then define an implementation of the idea. Designing and implementing components is not similar to designing and implementing inheritance trees. With inheritance, you need to consider type casting, base class functionality, and how to override or overload methods or properties. (*Type casting* is when you cast to a specific type with or without an explicit cast operator.) With components, you need to think in terms of ideas and how they would be implemented as interfaces.

Having looked at the Shape, Rectangle, and Square implementation, you might define an interface (named IShape) as follows:

```
interface IShape {
    double CalculateArea();
    double Width { get; set; }
}
```

For the IShape declaration, you might even add a Length property, but the overall idea of the IShape interface is wrong. When you think of a shape, do you think in terms of length and width? Probably not. Rather, you think in terms of area, perimeter, and other features that are common to all shapes. Length and width are not common to all shapes. A circle has a radius or diameter; a triangle has base width, height, and triangle peak offset. The point is that the idea of a shape is not the idea of a rectangle or a square.

The correct way to define the ideas as interfaces would be as follows:

```
interface IShape {
    double CalculateArea();
}

interface ISquare : IShape {
    double Width { get; set; }
}

interface IRectangle : IShape {
    double Width { get; set; }
    double Length { get; set; }
}
```

This code contains three interfaces: IShape, which defines a shape; IRectangle, which describes a rectangle; and ISquare, which defines a square. The IRectangle and ISquare interfaces subclass the IShape interface, indicating that an IRectangle is also an IShape. The ISquare interface is separate from the IRectangle interface, because a square is not a rectangle, even though the shapes might appear similar (a square is a rectangle, but a rectangle is not necessarily a square).

This separation of the square and rectangle interface illustrates that when designing interfaces, you need to focus on the specific behavior of the interface. You don't want to focus on the general behavior. The general behavior is managed when you design the classes. The modeling of your real-life experiences are defined in the implementations, as illustrated by the following example.

```
class SquareImpl: ISquare, IRectangle { }
class RectangleImpl: IRectangle { }
```

The SquareImpl class implements the behavior of ISquare and IRectangle, and models real life, where a square is also a rectangle. And RectangleImpl implements only the behavior IRectangle, illustrating that a rectangle can only be a rectangle and not a square.

Now you cannot write code where the implementation produces inconsistent results. For example, the following code would not be possible.

```
IRectangle rectangle = new RectangleImpl();
ISquare square = (ISquare)rectangle;
```

But the following code is possible.

```
IRectangle rectangle = new SquareImpl();
ISquare square = (ISquare)rectangle;
```

■**Note** When defining ideas, the resulting interfaces could be considered as behavior characteristics that an implementation can have. It is entirely possible for an implementation to have multiple behavior characteristics. For example, this could mean that an implementation could be both a square and rectangle at the same time. In terms of the restaurant, waiters are humans with hobbies, feelings and desires, although you don't know these other aspects, as you see only the waiters.

An optimization could have been to have the following interface inheritance.

```
interface ISquare : IShape {
    double Width { get; set; }
}

interface IRectangle : ISquare {
    double Length { get; set; }
}
```

or:

```
interface ISquare : IRectangle {
}

interface IRectangle : IShape {
    double Width { get; set; }
    double Length { get; set; }
}
```

However, this isn't a good idea, because at the interface level, you are implying that a square and rectangle are related. They might be at the implementation level, but they also might not be. For example, imagine you are creating a super shape that has the characteristics of a rectangle and a triangle. When creating a relationship between interfaces, you are implying that the super shape depending on the interface inheritance used must have the characteristics of a square, even though it might not. Thus, when using inheritance with interfaces, IShape as a base interface of IRectangle and ISquare is acceptable, but a relation between IRectangle and ISquare is not. Remember that an implementation can create that relation, and a type cast can extract that relation.

Now that you have an idea of the differences between inheritance and components, we can get started with our tax application. As we work through the example, you'll learn the details of implementing interfaces.

Implementing a Tax Engine

So far, we've discussed some basic tax concepts; the features of the tax application; and the theory of inheritance, interfaces, and components. We're ready to implement the tax engine. The preferred approach is to design the core idea and then create the other pieces, or dependencies.

Defining the Interfaces

Putting everything together and starting with the tax engine, we can create the following interface structure.

```
public interface ITaxEngine {
    double CalculateTaxToPay(ITaxAccount account);
    ITaxDeduction CreateDeduction( double amount);
    ITaxIncome CreateIncome( double amount);
    ITaxAccount CreateTaxAccount();
}
public interface ITaxAccount {
    void AddDeduction(ITaxDeduction deduction);
    void AddIncome(ITaxIncome income);
    double GetTaxRate( double income);
    ITaxDeduction[] Deductions { get; }
    ITaxIncome[] Income { get; }
}
public interface ITaxIncome {
    double RealAmount { get; }
    double TaxableAmount { get; }
}
public interface ITaxDeduction {
    double Amount { get; }
}
```

The structure has four interfaces: ITaxIncome, ITaxDeduction, ITaxEngine, and ITaxAccount. ITaxIncome and ITaxDeduction are pure behavioral interfaces. *Pure behavioral* means the interface does one thing, but it might be implemented in conjunction with other interfaces. ITaxEngine and ITaxAccount are behavioral functional interfaces. *Behavioral functional* means that the interfaces are typically implemented by themselves, and usually not with another interface.

■**Note** Generally speaking, the naming convention used to define a type is verbose and self-explanatory. I use names like TaxEngine, BaseTaxEngine when defining classes. But when I define interfaces, I use identifiers prefixed with a capital I, like ICanadaEngine and ITaxEngine. The capital I is a common convention used to identify interfaces. You should use this notation to be consistent with other .NET code.

For example, you might implement a Swiss tax system where there are two classes, defined as follows:

```
class SwissTaxEngine : ITaxEngine { }
class SwissTaxAccount : ITaxAccount { }
```

And if you wish to implement an American tax system, the two classes would be defined as follows:

```
class AmericanTaxEngine : ITaxEngine { }
class AmericanTaxAccount : ITaxAccount { }
```

The user of either the American or Swiss tax system will not know the specific details of those tax systems. Initially, users would need to determine which tax system they wished to use. This decision is made using something called a factory, as explained in the upcoming "Abstracting Instantiations with Factories" section.

Implementing a Base Class Tax Engine

Whenever you define interfaces, you will need to implement them. In most cases, you will create an abstract base class that provides a certain amount of default functionality. The abstract base class serves the same purpose as outlined in the previous chapter: to provide a certain amount of basic functionality.

In the case of the tax engine, we need to implement the ITaxEngine interface and provide default implementations for some methods, and for some abstract methods that the derived class needs to implement in other methods. The following is the complete base class implementation.

```
public abstract class BaseTaxEngine : ITaxEngine{
    protected double _calculatedTaxable;

    public BaseTaxEngine() { }
    public virtual double CalculateTaxToPay(ITaxAccount account) {
        _calculatedTaxable = 0.0;
        foreach (ITaxIncome income in account.Income) {
            if (income != null) {
                _calculatedTaxable += income.TaxableAmount;
            }
        }
        foreach( ITaxDeduction deduction in account.Deductions) {
            if (deduction != null) {
                _calculatedTaxable -= deduction.Amount;
            }
        }
        return account.GetTaxRate( _calculatedTaxable) * _calculatedTaxable;
    }

    public virtual ITaxDeduction CreateDeduction(double amount) {
        return new TaxDeduction(amount);
    }
```

```
    public virtual ITaxIncome CreateIncome(double amount) {
        return new TaxIncome(amount, 1.0);
    }
    public abstract ITaxAccount CreateTaxAccount();
}
```

The base class must implement all interface methods, regardless of whether or not the method has an implementation. The `CalculateTaxToPay()`, `CreateDeduction()`, and `CreateIncome()` methods have implementations. The `CreateTaxAccount()` method does not have an implementation and is declared as `abstract`. The methods with implementations have a `virtual` keyword associated with them, indicating any class derived from `BaseTaxEngine` can override the functionality if they don't like the default functionality.

In the implementation of `CalculateTaxToPay()`, the income (`account.Income`) is added together and deductions (`account.Deductions`) are subtracted from the income. The resulting total is used as a query amount (`account.GetTaxRate()`) to retrieve the actual tax rate used to calculate against the payable tax.

▌Note The implementation of `CalculateTaxToPay()` is a shared functionality, which implies that there cannot be any code specific to a derived type. All of the calculations and data manipulations are executed against an interface, making it possible to generalize operations. Whenever you implement base class methods or shared pieces of code, you should try to keep the source code derived class agnostic.

Overriding for Specialized Functionality

In the base class implementation, the data member `_calculatedTaxable` is declared as `protected`. As you learned in the previous chapter, this means that `_calculatedTaxable` can be manipulated in a derived class. However, if you look at how the data member is used, you will see that only `CalculateTaxToPay()` assigns the data member. The purpose of the data member is to provide information about the operation `CalculateTaxToPay()` without giving the exact details of the operation.

The idea behind `_calculatedTaxable` and the declaration of `CalculateTaxToPay()` is to provide a mechanism where the derived class does not need to calculate things again. Consider the example of a country where, if your taxable income is above 400 currency units, a surtax of 10 currency units is calculated. You don't know what your taxable income is until the function `CalculateTaxToPay()` is executed, and that function returns only the total payable taxes. So how do you know if you should apply the surtax in this situation? One solution is to reverse-calculate the payable taxes, but that would involve quite a few additional steps. An easier solution is to write some code in the base class method of `CalculateTaxToPay()` that stores the taxable income so the subclass has access to it.

The original implementation of `CalculateTaxToPay()` does not consider a surtax, so the derived class must contain that functionality. Since `CalculateTaxToPay()` can be overridden without the data member `_calculatedTaxable`, the derived class would need to implement the functionality in the base class to calculate whether or not the surtax applies. Following is an example derived class implementation of the tax engine for such a situation, stored in a namespace called `LibTax.Surtax`, to distinguish it from the base functionality.

```
namespace LibTax.Surtax
{
    internal class TaxEngine : BaseTaxEngine {
        public override double CalculateTaxToPay(ITaxAccount account) {
            double taxToPay = base.CalculateTaxToPay(account);
            if (_calculatedTaxable > 400) {
                taxToPay += 10;
            }
            return taxToPay;
        }
        public override ITaxAccount CreateTaxAccount() {
            throw new Exception("The method or operation is not implemented.");
        }
    }
}
```

In the implementation of CalculateTaxToPay(), we replace the virtual keyword with override, implying that the functionality of TaxEngine replaces the functionality of BaseTaxEngine. However, if TaxEngine is called, and the TaxEngine.CalculateTaxToPay() implementation is empty, then tax is not calculated. Since our fictional country calculates the basic tax similarly to most countries, the functionality of BaseTaxEngine.CalculateTaxToPay() can be used. Thus, the first line of TaxEngine.CalculateTaxToPay() is base.CalculateTaxToPay(), meaning the base class (BaseTaxEngine) method CalculateTaxToPay() is called.

Calling the base class results in calculating a basic tax to pay amount. We need to figure out if a surtax applies, and that is where the protected data member _calculatedTaxable comes into play. Having called BaseTaxEngine.CalculateTaxToPay(), the data member _calculatedTaxable is assigned and contains the amount that is being taxed. Thus, TaxEngine. CalculateTaxToPay() can make a decision if more than 400 currency units have been earned. And if so, then the variable taxToPay is incremented with another 10 currency units. Had _calculatedTaxable not existed, TaxEngine.CalculateTaxToPay() would have needed to call the base class functionality to get the basic tax rate, and then recalculate the taxable monies to figure out if the surtax applied.

■Note When you override methods, you are saying that you need something special. This does not imply that the base class functionality will be called. It implies that you might call the base class functionality and perform some additional operations. Thus, when designing base class functionality, it is important to track calculations or operations using protected data members. The data members avoid having derived classes perform the same operations multiple times, slowing down the application and avoiding potential errors.

USING NAMESPACES

Namespaces are used to define blocks of functionality that belong together. You will need to use namespaces in the case of tax engines, because there would be an American tax engine, Swiss tax engine, and so on, and each should have its own namespace. Sometimes you might even create a custom assembly for each set of interface implementations, but you would still need to create a namespace. Creating a namespace is independent of the fact of whether or not you create a separate assembly.

In the examples, I use namespaces like `LibTax.Surtax` and `LibTax.Canada`. These namespaces are typically created by adding folders using the Add ➤ New Folder context menu item in the Solution Explorer of Visual Studio.

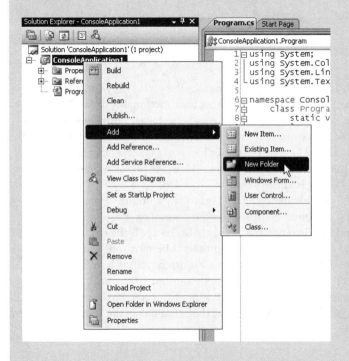

The source code examples don't illustrate the `using` keyword and assume that you have created them at the beginning of the source code. You can take a look at the source code and inspect the namespaces to see how they are used.

Abstracting Instantiations with Factories

Take a good look at the scope declaration of the tax engine shown earlier and compare it with the scope declaration for the `ITaxEngine` interface. What you will notice is that `ITaxEngine` is declared as public scope, as is `BaseTaxEngine`, and `TaxEngine` is declared as `internal`. Going back to our project structure, this scope declaration implies that any reference to `LibTax` will see the interface `ITaxEngine` and `BaseTaxEngine`, but not `TaxEngine`. For example, the following test code will not work.

```
ITaxEngine taxengine = new LibTax.Surtax.TaxEngine();
```

The reason the test code will not work is that any type that is not declared with public scope is private to the solution containing the declaration. You may be thinking, "That's great—you declare a type that you cannot instantiate, So, how can I use that type?"

The scope declarations are not a mistake and illustrate a design pattern called a *factory*. A factory is a way of abstracting the instantiation away from the caller so that the interface can vary from its implementation. In our restaurant analogy, it means when you want a waiter, you don't want to need to know his name. You would rather have a generic mechanism where the restaurant presents to you the waiter. Otherwise, to eat at a restaurant, you would need to know the name of your waiter before being able to order something. That would be inefficient.

The correct way of defining a factory is as follows:

```
namespace LibTax {
    public static class EngineCreator {
        public static ITaxEngine CreateSurtaxTaxEngine() {
            return new LibTax.Surtax.TaxEngine();
        }
    }
}
```

The factory is typically declared as a static method (CreateSurtaxTaxEngine()) on a class. So that the factory is never instantiated, you add the static declaration to the front of the class declaration. In the implementation of CreateSurtaxTaxEngine(), the type LibTax.Surtax. TaxEngine is instantiated, and the instance is downcast to the interface type ITaxEngine.

■Note Adding a static declaration that is prefixed to the class is a good way to ensure a type does not get inadvertently instantiated. From a design perspective, static is like abstract in that they both enforce a particular usage.

The EngineCreator class is declared with public scope, implying any code that references the assembly can see the class. Thus, the test code can be rewritten as follows:

```
ITaxEngine taxengine = EngineCreator.CreateSurtaxTaxEngine();
```

After calling EngineCreator.CreateSurtaxTaxEngine(), the test code has a valid instance of ITaxEngine. It's very important to note that the test code has no idea what type implemented the interface. This allows the assembly to change which type is referenced in the implementation of CreateSurtaxTaxEngine() without having to inform the caller of the method.

Putting this into the context of the restaurant, it means waiters can be replaced. So if you repeatedly visit a restaurant and get a waiter called John, but one day John gets sick and is not working, you can still order and receive your food from the waitress called Mary. It would be a bad idea for a restaurant to depend on a particular server for a particular guest.

Using Default Implementations

In some cases, base classes are not necessary. Sometimes you can create a default implementation that could span multiple subsystems. In the case of the tax engine, an income is an income in Canada, an income in the United States, and an income in Germany. What varies is how the income is treated in each country when calculating taxes. Another consistency across countries is that if income is a capital gain, not all of the income is taxable.

In the case of income, you can create an implementation that would be identical across different tax engines, as follows:

```
sealed class TaxIncome : ITaxIncome {
    double _amount;
    double _taxableRate;

    public TaxIncome(double amount, double taxableRate) {
        _amount = amount;
        _taxableRate = taxableRate;
    }
    public double RealAmount {
        get {
            return _amount;
        }
    }

    public double TaxableAmount {
        get {
            return _amount * _taxableRate;
        }
    }
}
```

The ITaxIncome interface has two properties that are implemented in TaxIncome: RealAmount and TaxableAmoun. The values for the two properties are considered read-only and are defined by the constructor of TaxIncome. The purpose of the constructor is to assign two values, and then consider the object as immutable. If you wanted to change the values of the ITaxIncome interface, you would need to instantiate a new instance of TaxIncome. While it sounds like a pain to need to instantiate a new instance whenever you want to change the value of the RealAmount and TaxableAmount properties, this approach has some advantages in terms of performance and resource management.

In the sample code, the TaxableAmount property is the result of multiplying the data members _amount and _taxableRate. For example, when calculating the taxable income of a capital gain in Canada, you multiply the total amount by 50%. Thus, the data member would have a value of 0.50.

Another item to note is that the declaration of TaxIncome is lacking a public scope, but has a sealed keyword prefixed to the identifier. When a class is prefixed with sealed, it means that the class cannot be subclassed. From a design perspective, the code is saying TaxIncome is a shared class that should not be subclassed lest it affect the shared behavior.

The sealed keyword can also be applied to a method, which means that the method cannot be overloaded or overridden. You would use sealed on a method when you do not want a derived class to change the behavior of the method.

The implementation of ITaxDeduction is similar to ITaxIncome:

```
sealed class TaxDeduction : ITaxDeduction {
    double _amount;

    public TaxDeduction(double amount) {
        _amount = amount;
    }
    public double Amount {
        get {
            return _amount;
        }
    }
}
```

TaxIncome and TaxDeduction are sealed classes because the functionality will be shared among implementations. But is it wise to expose the interfaces and not the classes themselves? Interfaces are used to separate implementation from ideas. Interfaces change very little, whereas implementations can and will change more often. But if an implementation behaves like an interface in terms of changing interface signature, why not just expose the class itself? The answer is that sometimes you will expose the class, and sometimes you will expose the interface. For the tax engine, exposing the sealed classes TaxIncome and TaxDeduction would probably have been fine. The rule of thumb is that you expose classes only when you are sure that the interface signatures of methods and properties will not change very often.

Implementing a Base Tax Account

The ITaxAccount interface is also a candidate for base class functionality. The implementation of this interface looks like this:

```
abstract class BaseTaxAccount : ITaxAccount {
    ITaxDeduction[] _deductions;
    ITaxIncome[] _incomes;

    public BaseTaxAccount() {
        _deductions = new ITaxDeduction[ 100];
        _incomes = new ITaxIncome[ 100];
    }

    public void AddDeduction(ITaxDeduction deduction) {
        for( int c1 = 0; c1 < 100; c1 ++) {
            if( _deductions[ c1] == null) {
                _deductions[ c1] = deduction;
                break;
            }
        }
    }
```

```
public void AddIncome(ITaxIncome income) {
    for( int c1 = 0; c1 < 100; c1 ++) {
        if( _incomes[ c1] == null) {
            _incomes[ c1] = income;
            break;
        }
    }
}

public ITaxDeduction[] Deductions {
    get {
        return _deductions;
    }
}

public ITaxIncome[] Income {
    get {
        return _incomes;
    }
}

public abstract double GetTaxRate(double income);
}
```

Let's take stock of what has been accomplished and decide if the tax engine is complete from a base functionality perspective.

- Ideas have been defined for a complete tax engine.

- Some interfaces have been implemented in the form of base classes.

- Some interfaces have been implemented as sealed default implementations.

The tax engine can be considered complete because all of the interfaces have been defined and accounted for from a base functionality perspective as either base classes or default implementations. It is does not mean that interfaces will always be implemented. Sometimes some interfaces will not have a base functionality or base classes.

The important aspect to remember when defining the base functionality is to account for all interfaces to serve a purpose. Do not define an interface as a placeholder for potential future functionality. A user when seeing an interface expects it to serve some type of purpose.

■**Note** The rule of thumb for interfaces is that once defined and put into production, they are not changed. This rule of thumb is almost written in concrete. You never change interfaces once they are in production because doing so would wreak havoc—all the code that uses the interface would need to be updated. In general, if you feel the need to change an interface, create a new one.

With base functionality complete, we are ready to implement a tax system for a particular country.

Using the Base Functionality of the Tax Engine to Calculate Taxes

We will use the base functionality of the tax engine to calculate Canadian taxes. I chose the Canadian tax system because that is the system that I happen to know and understand, and there is plenty of online documentation on how to calculate the tax rate.

SOME BACKGROUND INFORMATION ON CANADIAN TAXES

The first thing I would like to say about Canadian taxes is that Canadians pay too much—way too much. The second comment is that Canadian taxes are simple, in that they don't let you write off many deductions (for example, interest payments on your house), which brings us back to the first point that Canadians pay way too much. Of course, people in other countries would probably say the exact same thing.

Canadian taxes are based on calculating the tax rate at the federal level and at the provincial level. Thus, to calculate your taxes, you need to know in which province and in which year you are paying your taxes. Canadian taxes change quite a bit depending on the year. From an implementation perspective, it means the tax engine must know about provincial taxes, federal taxes, and which year.

Capital gains in Canada are calculated on a 50% basis. This means if I made a capital gain of 200 Canadian dollars, then only 100 Canadian dollars are declared as taxable monies.

Implementing a Tax Engine and Tax Account

Implementing a Canadian tax engine means deriving a class from BaseTaxEngine, and that means implementing the CreateTaxAccount() method. The implementation of the Canadian tax engine implies creating a new namespace, and a good name would be LibTax.Canada. The code will not show the namespace details, as they are implied.

The implementation is as follows:

```
internal class TaxEngine : BaseTaxEngine {
    public override ITaxAccount CreateTaxAccount() {
        return new TaxAccount();
    }
}
```

In the implementation of the CreateTaxAccount() method, the TaxAccount class is instantiated. TaxAccount is a class that derives from BaseTaxAccount and thus implements the ITaxAccount interface. The implementation of TaxAccount is as follows:

```
internal class TaxAccount : BaseTaxAccount {
    Province _province;
    int _year;

    public TaxAccount() {
    }
    public override double GetTaxRate(double income) {
        if (_year == 2007) {
```

```
            if (_province == Province.Ontario) {
                return OntarioTax2007.TaxRate(income);
            }
        }
        throw new NotSupportedException("Year " + _year + " Province " +
            _province + " not supported");
    }
}
```

The purpose of the GetTaxRate() method is to return the applicable tax rate for the given amount. In Canada, the tax rate is determined by which province you live in and the year. The calculation in GetTaxRate() has the ability to calculate the taxes for the year 2007 in the Ontario province.

Yet there is a problem, and it involves the data members _province and _year. The data members are used in the calculation GetTaxRate(), but they are not assigned. This is a problem.

Assigning State When the Interface Cannot

The problem of the Canadian tax account is a common one that you will encounter in many situations. The essence of the problem is the need to assign state that is specific to an implementation without violating the intention of the general interface.

To illustrate the problem, let's say that the method GetTaxRate() will include a reference to the province and year. The rewritten ITaxAccount interface would be as follows:

```
public interface ITaxAccount {
    void AddDeduction(ITaxDeduction deduction);
    void AddIncome(ITaxIncome income);
    double GetTaxRate(double income, Province province, int year);
    ITaxDeduction[] Deductions { get; }
    ITaxIncome[] Income { get; }
}
```

The bolded code illustrates the added parameters that are used to calculate Canadian taxes. But is this a good solution? No, it's a particularly bad solution. The parameters are specific to an implementation, and particularly to a Canadian implementation.

The parameter year could be justified because most countries do have specific tax rates and implementations that are dependent on a year. Yet the parameter province has no justification. Imagine trying to implement a British tax system and needing to specify a province, when Britain does not collect income tax at a local level.

A solution might be to redefine the interface as follows:

```
public class Specifics {
    public Province CanadianProvince;
    public State AmericanState;
}
public interface ITaxAccount {
    void AddDeduction(ITaxDeduction deduction);
    void AddIncome(ITaxIncome income);
    double GetTaxRate(double income, int year, Specifics specifics);
```

```
    ITaxDeduction[] Deductions { get; }
    ITaxIncome[] Income { get; }
}
```

This new implementation has a specifics parameter, which is of type Specifics. The purpose of Specifics is to define a class that is a hodgepodge of information that is needed to determine the correct tax rate. However, the Specifics approach is wrong, for the following reasons:

- It requires knowing the implementation, which in the case of the interface is a bad idea. It is like going to a restaurant and saying you would like a waitress with blond hair.

- Even if the type Specifics were acceptable, you would be adding and removing data members depending on how many tax systems you have implemented. That is a bad idea and introduces maintenance issues.

The proposed solutions are not acceptable. Additionally, there is still the problem of having to figure out which tax rate to use.

Implementing Ideas with Specifics

To implement a solution, let's first start by fixing the TaxAccount class. The modified version will have some type of functionality that has data members that reference the year and province. Here is the modified and correct implementation of TaxAccount:

```
internal class TaxAccount : BaseTaxAccount {
    Province _province;
    int _year;

    public TaxAccount(Province province, int year) {
        _province = province;
        _year = year;
    }
    public override double GetTaxRate(double income) {
        if (_year == 2007) {
            if (_province == Province.Ontario) {
                return OntarioTax2007.TaxRate(income);
            }
        }
        throw new NotSupportedException("Year " + _year + " Province " +
            _province + " not supported");
    }
}
```

The fix is to add a constructor that has province and year as parameters. This sort of fix is quite common, in that you don't change the interfaces, rather you change how the implementations are instantiated. Remember that when you instantiate a specific implementation, you know what functionality you want, and thus can give the additional parameters. Once you are at the interface level, you should need to use only general ideas.

Now the TaxEngine class needs to be fixed. TaxEngine is responsible for instantiating TaxAccount, and thus to instantiate a Canadian TaxAccount, TaxEngine needs additional parameters, as follows:

```
internal class TaxEngine : BaseTaxEngine {
    public override ITaxAccount CreateTaxAccount() {
        return new TaxAccount(Province.Ontario, 2007);
    }
}
```

In the implementation of CreateTaxAccount(), the province Ontario and year 2007 are assumed. Thus, whenever TaxEngine is instantiated, you need to make sure that the person is in Ontario and paying taxes for the year 2007. The implementation solves nothing and skirts the issue of having to figure out how to deal with someone paying their taxes in British Columbia and the year 2008.

If you look at the implementation of TaxEngine, you will notice it is short. One obvious solution would be to create a TaxEngine type for each province and each year. Here are two examples:

```
internal class Ontario2007TaxEngine : BaseTaxEngine {
    public override ITaxAccount CreateTaxAccount() {
        return new TaxAccount(Province.Ontario, 2007);
    }
}
internal class BritishColumbia2008TaxEngine : BaseTaxEngine {
    public override ITaxAccount CreateTaxAccount() {
        return new TaxAccount(Province.BritishColumbia, 2008);
    }
}
```

This solution is not that bad, because to be able to instantiate the correct tax engine, you just need to define a factory that knows which class to instantiate. But for the problem at hand, this solution is extremely tedious, as you could end up with hundreds, if not thousands, of TaxEngine definitions. You would use the specific implementation approach when you have fewer than a dozen variations.

The better approach is to add an interface specific to the Canadian tax system. Think of it as follows. When you are instantiating the tax engine, you will need to know which tax system to use. The factory protects you from needing to know which type to instantiate, but there is nothing wrong with giving some extra information that could be used by a factory.

Thus, the solution is to define a new interface called ICanadaTaxEngine. The purpose of ICanadaTaxEngine is to add factory methods that are used to instantiate types with parameters specific to the implementation. Following is the definition of the ICanadaTaxEngine.

```
public enum Province {
    Alberta,
    BritishColumbia,
    Manitoba,
    NewBrunswick,
    NewfoundlandLabrador,
```

```
        NovaScotia,
        Nunavut,
        Ontario,
        PrinceEdwardIsland,
        Quebec,
        Saskatchewan,
        Yukon
    }

    public interface ICanadaTaxEngine {
        ITaxAccount CreateTaxAccount(Province province, int year);
        ITaxIncome CreateCapitalGain(double amount);
    }
```

The definition of ICanadaTaxEngine contains two additional methods:

- CreateTaxAccount() is used to instantiate a tax account specific to a province and year.

- CreateCapitalGain() is used to instantiate an income using the Canadian capital gain calculation.

Thus, the implementation of TaxEngine becomes the following.

```
internal class TaxEngine : BaseTaxEngine, ICanadaTaxEngine {
    public override ITaxAccount CreateTaxAccount() {
        return new TaxAccount(Province.Ontario, 2007);
    }
    public ITaxAccount CreateTaxAccount(Province province, int year) {
        return new TaxAccount(province, year);
    }
    public ITaxIncome CreateCapitalGain(double amount) {
        return new TaxIncome(amount, 0.50);
    }
}
```

In the modified implementation of TaxEngine, the class still derives from BaseTaxEngine, fulfilling the requirement of being a general tax engine. However, for the additional requirements of the Canadian tax system, we implement the ICanadaTaxEngine interface.

Defining a specific interface that implies a certain implementation is fine, because the specific interface is not bound to a certain implementation. The better way to understand this implementation technique is to consider the specific interface as a characteristic that an implementation is capable of supporting. This goes back to the shape example, where a square can support both the ISquare and IRectangle interfaces.

Using the Tax Engine

The last step is to use the tax engine to calculate some taxes. The following is an example of calculating the taxes for Ontario in 2007.

```
ITaxEngine engine = EngineCreator.CreateCanadianTaxEngine();
ICanadaTaxEngine canadaEngine = engine as ICanadaTaxEngine;
ITaxAccount account = canadaEngine.CreateTaxAccount(Province.Ontario, 2007);

ITaxIncome income = engine.CreateIncome(100);
ITaxIncome capitalGain = canadaEngine.CreateCapitalGain(100);
account.AddIncome(income);
account.AddIncome(capitalGain);

ITaxDeduction deduction = engine.CreateDeduction(20);
account.AddDeduction(deduction);
double taxToPay = engine.CalculateTaxToPay(account);
Console.WriteLine("Tax to pay (" + taxToPay + ")");
```

Notice the definition of the variables engine and canadaEngine. This is fine, because what we are doing with the interfaces is choosing a characteristic that can be dynamically queried.

Learning More About Inheritance and Type Casting

This chapter introduced interfaces and components, and delved deeper into inheritance. Here, I'll provide more details about inheritance and type casting.

More Inheritance Details

In this section, I am going to clearly lay out how inheritance works in C#. I will present examples of usage for seven scenarios. Each example is followed by a list explaining the key points to understand. My goal is to illustrate all of the possible scenarios so that you have a reference to how inheritance works.

■**Note** All of the examples demonstrate using methods, but it is possible to apply the same inheritance techniques using properties.

Scenario 1: *Overloading Base Class Functionality*

```
class Base {
    public void Method() {
        Console.WriteLine("Base.Method");
    }
}
class Derived : Base {
    public new void Method() {
        Console.WriteLine("Derived.Method");
    }
}
```

```
class Test {
    public static void Run() {
        Derived derivedCls = new Derived();
        Base baseCls = derivedCls;

        // Calls Derived.Method
        derivedCls.Method();
        // Calls Base.Method
        baseCls.Method();
    }
}
```

- Keywords used: new in the derived class to indicate the method is being overloaded.

- Overloading a method means to change the functionality of the method in the derived class.

- Which method is called in the inheritance depends on the type of the object on which the method is called. Thus, if the variable is of type Base, Base.Method() is called; if the variable is of type Derived, Derived.Method() is called.

Scenario 2: *Overriding Base Class Functionality*

```
class Base {
    public virtual void Method() {
        Console.WriteLine("Base.Method");
    }
}
class Derived : Base {
    public override void Method() {
        Console.WriteLine("Derived.Method");
    }
}

class Test {
    public static void Run() {
        Derived derivedCls = new Derived();
        Base baseCls = derivedCls;

        // Calls Derived.Method
        derivedCls.Method();
        // Calls Derived.Method
        baseCls.Method();
    }
}
```

- Keywords used: `virtual` in the base class to indicate the method behavior can be changed in the derived class. `override` is used in the derived classes to indicate a method with the new behavior. Multiple levels of inheritance require multiple usages of `override`.

- Overriding a method means to change the behavior of the method in the base class to that of the derived class. If there are multiple levels of inheritance, then the functionality used is the instantiated type.

- You can also define a `virtual` base class method using the `abstract` keyword. The difference between `virtual` and `abstract` is that `virtual` has a method or property implementation, whereas `abstract` has no implementation.

Scenario 3: *Implementing an Interface*

```
interface IInterface {
    void Method();
}
class Implementation : IInterface {
    public void Method() {
        Console.WriteLine("Implementation.Method");
    }
}

class Test {
    public static void Run() {
        Implementation implementation = new Implementation();
        IInterface inst = implementation;

        // Calls Implementation.Method
        implementation.Method();
        // Calls Implementation.Method
        inst.Method();
    }
}
```

- Keywords used: none.

- The class that implements the interface has a behavior, like when a class subclasses and implements an abstract method.

- Whether you have a reference to the interface instance or the class itself, the method `Implementation.Method()` is called.

Scenario 4: *Implementing Two Interfaces with the Same Method/Property Name*

```
interface IInterface1 {
    void Method();
}
interface IInterface2 {
```

```
        void Method();
}
class Implementation : IInterface1, IInterface2 {
    void IInterface1.Method() {
        Console.WriteLine("Implementation.IInterface1.Method");
    }
    void IInterface2.Method() {
        Console.WriteLine("Implementation.IInterface1.Method");
    }
}

class Test {
    public static void Run() {
        Implementation implementation = new Implementation();
        IInterface1 inst1 = implementation;
        IInterface1 inst2 = implementation;

        // Cannot be called
        //implementation.IInterface1.Method();
        // Calls Implementation.IInterface1.Method
        inst1.Method();
        // Calls Implementation.IInterface2.Method
        inst2.Method();
    }
}
```

- Keywords used: special notation for the implementation of a particular interface method (for example, IInterface1.Method() and IInterface2.Method()).

- Special notation involves specifying the identifier of the interface before the method name. The method must not be prefixed with a scope identifier, as the method must be private to the class.

- The methods are not callable using standard class method calls. The individual methods can be called only by performing a type cast to the appropriate interface. The next section discusses type casting in more detail.

- It is not necessary to use this notation when implementing two interfaces with the same method or property name. You can use a Method() declaration as in previous examples, except then the same method or property is called for each interface.

Scenario 5: *Implementing an Interface in a Derived Class*

```
interface IInterface {
    void Method();
}
class BaseImplementation {
    public void Method() {
        Console.WriteLine("Implementation.Method");
```

```
        }
    }
    class ImplementationDerived : BaseImplementation, IInterface {
    }

    class Test {
        public static void Run() {
            ImplementationDerived implementation = new ImplementationDerived();
            IInterface inst = implementation;

            // Calls Implementation.Method
            implementation.Method();
            // Calls Implementation.Method
            inst.Method();
        }
    }
```

- Keywords used: none.

- When implementing an interface, it is not necessary to have the base class subclass the interface. You can define a base class with the appropriate method and property signatures. In the derived class, when the C# compiler searches for appropriate interface methods and properties, the complete inheritance tree will be searched.

- Using this technique can have odd side effects if you are not careful with how methods are overridden and overloaded.

Scenario 6: *Implementing an Interface That Allows Overriding*

```
    interface IInterface {
        void Method();
    }
    class Implementation : IInterface {
        public virtual void Method() {
            Console.WriteLine("Implementation.Method");
        }
    }
    class ImplementationDerived : Implementation {
        public override void Method() {
            Console.WriteLine("ImplementationDerived.Method");
        }
    }

    class Test {
        public static void Run() {
            ImplementationDerived implementation = new ImplementationDerived();
            IInterface inst = implementation;
```

```
            // Calls ImplementationDerived.Method
            implementation.Method();
            // Calls ImplementationDerived.Method
            inst.Method();
        }
}
```

- Keywords used: virtual and override.

- By default, when you implement an interface without using the virtual keyword, you are saying that the derived class can overload only the method. In many cases, this is appropriate, as you will want to override the method and thus will need to use the virtual and override keywords.

- This is a common problem, and most beginning C# programmers are puzzled by the overloading behavior.

Scenario 7: *An Inheritance Tree That Overrides and Overloads*

```
class Base {
    public virtual void Method() {
        Console.WriteLine("Base.Method");
    }
}
class Derived1 : Base {
    public override void Method() {
        Console.WriteLine("Derived1.Method");
    }
}
class Derived2 : Derived1 {
    public new virtual void Method() {
        Console.WriteLine("Derived2.Method");
    }
}
class Derived3 : Derived2 {
    public new virtual void Method() {
        Console.WriteLine("Derived3.Method");
    }
}

class Test {
    public static void Run() {
        Derived3 derivedCls = new Derived3();
        Base baseCls = derivedCls;
        Derived2 derived2cls = derivedCls;

        // Calls Derived3.Method
        derivedCls.Method();
        // Calls Derived.Method
```

```
            baseCls.Method();
            // Calls Derived3.Method
            derived2cls.Method();
        }
    }
```

- Keywords used: virtual, override, and new.

- This inheritance hierarchy confounds most C# programmers and requires careful attention.

- The inheritance hierarchy is saying that Derived1.Method() overrides the behavior of Base.Method(). Derived2.Method() overloads the behavior of Derived1.Method(), while establishing a new overriding base method. Derived3.Method() overrides the behavior Derived2.Method(), and not Base.Method() (very important).

- When confronted with a complex inheritance hierarchy as illustrated by scenario 7, it is important that you start at the base class and work up the inheritance hierarchy.

More Type-Casting Details

This chapter illustrated some type-casting examples. In C#, you have two ways to type cast:

- A forced type cast, which can also be used on value types

- A type cast that queries if a type cast is possible

Consider this hierarchy:

```
class Base {
    public void Method() {
        Console.WriteLine("Base.Method");
    }
}
class Derived : Base {
    public new void Method() {
        Console.WriteLine("Derived.Method");
    }
}
```

The next step is to instantiate the type Derived and cast the instance to the base type:

```
        Derived derivedCls = new Derived();
        Base baseCls = derivedCls;
```

When casting from a derived type to a base class type, a type cast is not necessary and you can assume it is implied.

A type cast is necessary when you want to cast a base class instance to a derived class instance. Following is the source code for a forced type cast, assuming the inheritance hierarchy from the previous cast.

```
DerivedClass backToDerived = (DerivedClass)baseCls;
```

The forced cast is the right side of the equal sign. The cast is the desired type enclosed in parentheses. The cast is forced because a conversion to the desired type will occur, regardless if it is possible or not. If the cast is not possible, a cast exception is thrown.

Another way to perform a type cast is to use a query cast, as illustrated by the following code, again assuming the inheritance hierarchy of this section.

```
DerivedClass backToDerived = baseCls as DerivedClass;
```

In the code, the cast involves using the keyword as and the type to which to cast. This cast is a query because a cast will be attempted. If the cast is successful, then an instance of the type is assigned to the variable backToDerived. If the cast is not possible, then backToDerived is assigned a null value. No exception is thrown. This casting technique is possible only for reference types.

The Important Stuff to Remember

In this chapter, you learned about interfaces and implementations. You should keep the following points in mind:

- Using interfaces is not like using inheritance. They are two separate designs, even though interfaces will use inheritance.

- Interfaces at an abstract level imply ideas of how you would like your application to work.

- Ideas when implemented as interfaces should be general and applicable to multiple application implementations for the domain.

- Ideas are implemented using C# interfaces. And interfaces are implemented using classes or structures. But note that interfaces are reference types. Interfaces and implementations are components.

- Factories are used to instantiate implementations and return an interface instance. Using a factory means that the user of an interface does not need to know which implementation to instantiate.

- Interfaces can be considered as attributes that might be targeting a specific characteristic of an implementation. However, as illustrated in the previous chapter, interfaces do not expose internal state or the internal workings of the implementations.

- Components are a fundamental way of developing code and should be your primary way of writing code. For the remainder of this book, interfaces will be used whenever possible. Take notice and try to understand what the idea behind the interface is.

Some Things for You to Do

Here are some things for you to do to apply what you've learned in this chapter:

1. Implement your own tax system using the predefined base classes.

■Note Because of the number of possible tax systems, I do not provide an answer for exercise 1. If you want me to review your answer, please send it to me at christianhgross@gmail.com.

---

2. *Boxing* refers to what happens implicitly when casting value types to reference types. Illustrate an example where boxing happens. (Boxing isn't explained in this chapter, but it is discussed in Chapter 9, and you can also easily research the topic on the Internet.)

3. Add functionality to the tax engine's base classes that implements the behavior of a minimum tax-free amount. This means if your income is not above the minimum tax-free amount, you do not pay taxes.

4. Implement the shape system using interfaces for four shapes: square, rectangle, circle, and triangle.

CHAPTER 8

■■■

Learning About Component-Oriented Architecture

So far, you have learned the essentials of C#. With the essentials, you can write a functional application that uses classes, objects, interfaces, and inheritance. In this chapter, you'll learn about a C# programming technique that some developers define as *structural*. A structural programming technique is when the code does not directly serve to solve a business problem, but solves a problem relating to building the application.

Another purpose of this chapter is to give you more experience with developing component-oriented code. In particular, you'll learn how to develop a kernel. Developing a kernel demonstrates the power and flexibility of the component-oriented development approach. You can build a working system even though you might not know what all of the implementations are ahead of time. This type of development makes it possible to modularize development, in that individual teams are responsible for certain interfaces. Then once the pieces have been implemented, they are fitted together like a jigsaw puzzle. Of course, interfaces and components do not guarantee success, but they do ensure one team does not need to wait for another team to finish its code.

Two other C# programmatic concepts that will be discussed are indexers and the `yield` statement. An indexer gives a type the ability to appear like an array. The `yield` keyword is used in conjunction with `foreach` and makes it possible to perform iterations on types that may not necessarily support collections.

To demonstrate all of these concepts, we'll build an application that controls lighting in buildings, using the kernel programming approach.

Understanding Kernels

Imagine you are the owner of a house or commercial building, and you want to reduce your electricity bill. One way of doing that is to automate the lighting system of your building so that lights are on when they need to be. What is unique about this system is that you have a controller and the devices that are controlled.

The controller controls devices that it does not know about ahead of time, but fulfills a contract. The lighting system is a controller, programmatically called a *kernel*, because the rooms that it controls are not known initially. The rooms are known when the controller is used to manage the lighting system. The kernel programming approach is one where a core of functionality is developed. The core functionality by itself does not work, because it relies on other pieces to perform certain tasks. In programming terms, this is called developing components that use interfaces and implementations.

Components are implemented at the technical level using interfaces and classes that subclass the interfaces. The interface represents an idea, and the classes represent the implementation of an idea. A class could implement multiple interfaces, where each interface represents a unique characteristic of the class implementation. Ideas and interfaces also represent contracts or standards. The kernel defines a standard, and the component has the responsibility of implementing that standard.

Implementing a kernel is like being a coach. A coach thinks of where to place players in the field and develops strategies that the players need to implement. But on game day, the players will do what they think is best, and the coach is powerless. A coach can teach the players, but whether they apply that knowledge is up to the individual players.

In programming terms, the kernel is the coach, and the external implementations to manipulate are the players. When designing interfaces that other pieces of functionality will implement, you cannot watch over the shoulders of the programmers and make sure they do things correctly. You need to trust, but you also need to implement a mode of programming where you assume the programmers are going to do things incorrectly. This has nothing to do with the personal abilities of the other programmers. It has to do with the ability to make sure your kernel continues functioning, even when someone makes a mistake.

Remember that when implementing a kernel, you are implementing a controller, and you are devising the strategy of the application. You are just not doing all of the implementations.

When you write production code, and you have been put in charge of writing a kernel, count yourself lucky. But remember with the job of building a kernel comes great responsibility. If your kernel is buggy or badly designed, then the external implementations will also be buggy and potentially badly designed. The kernel is the rock and foundation of the application.

Organizing the Lighting Application

For the moment, imagine we are not developing software, but actually building a house. And in this house, we are going to add a central lighting system. The make of light bulbs, lamps, and lighting controller are not identical. This is interesting in that multiple companies make products that work with each other's device. This works because all companies adhere to a particular standard.

The process of standardization is all around us, and is as simple as the electricity that comes out of our electrical outlets. However, what is a standard in one country is not necessarily the standard in another country. Different countries will have different standard voltages. In terms of software, the kernel represents a standard that allows the integration of components.

The lighting application will include these features:

- A room where the light can be controlled using either a simple on/off switch or a gradual light-intensity mechanism.

- The controller represents a building, and the rooms within the building can be grouped, making it simpler to perform group operations.

- Rooms are associated with identifiers that allow each room to be isolated individually.

- Rooms can be associated with a set of attributes that indicate the behavior they do and do not support.

The source code will implement the controller as a library project named LibLightingSystem. This library project will also define the interfaces that the components will implement. To demonstrate building a complete working application, two other projects implement the interfaces and represent components: Museum and Home. The key characteristics of a museum are that some rooms are made dark at night and are completely managed by the controller, while other rooms are controlled individually in the room itself and also can be managed by the controller. The key characteristics of a home are that all of the rooms are individually controlled, but they have sensors that allow automatic control. Some of the lighting associated with the house depends on certain prerequisites being fulfilled. For example, night-lights might turn on depending on the time of year, or room lights might be turned on and off automatically when no one is home. As usual, we will use a testing console application, named TestLightingSystem, to test the three assemblies. Figure 8-1 shows the project structure.

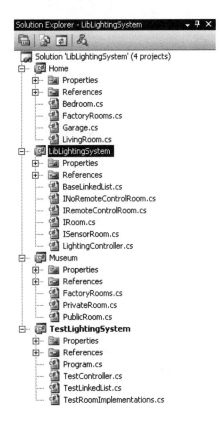

Figure 8-1. *Lighting system application project structure*

Building the Kernel

The lighting system is a two-part implementation. The first part is that we must write code that works properly. The second part is to integrate code that someone else has written and make sure that if that code does not work properly for some reason, those problems will not affect the code that we wrote.

This application is complicated by the fact that we are dealing with the unknown. In the previous examples, we had control of every class, interface, and definition. This time, we are not in control, and thus we need to use a defensive style of programming. This means we need to write many tests and keep certain information private.

Defining the Interfaces

The core of the lighting controller is to control the lighting in a room that is part of the building. We can define and organize the rooms by using interfaces. We need four interfaces:

- IRoom: A placeholder interface for the idea of a room

- INoRemoteControlRoom: An interface for rooms that should not be controlled by the lighting controller

- IRemoteControlRoom: An interface for rooms that should be completely controlled by the lighting controller

- ISensorRoom: An interface for rooms whose control is based on state (whether or not a person is in the room)

The interfaces for the rooms where lighting may be controlled, IRemoteControlRoom and ISensorRoom, will depend on certain pieces of logic. The interfaces will need to provide input data and accept output data. The logic might also seek input from other sources, such as time of day or amount of sunlight outdoors. It boils down to defining some type of logic that the kernel implements. This is key, and it relates to the children-and-parent issue. While you accept your children as being intelligent beings that can make decisions, at the end of the day, it is usually the parent who makes the final decisions. Likewise, while your kernel might accept input and potential decisions, the kernel makes the final decisions.

Defining IRoom, a Placeholder Interface

For design purposes, the simplest and base idea is the room itself, which can be defined as follows (in the controller library LibLightingSystem):

```
public interface IRoom { }
```

The interface does not have any methods or properties. It is called a *placeholder* interface. A placeholder type serves no other purpose than identifying that the implementation is of a certain type. Placeholder interfaces make it simpler to group objects that have certain capabilities.

Imagine defining objects without a placeholder interface, something like this:

```
class Type1 { }
class Type2 { }
```

Looking at Type1 and Type2, you cannot see any correlation between the two types; there is no way to say that Type1 and Type2 have some similar attribute. (Well, technically there is a correlation in that both types are derived from Object, but that type of correlation is like saying that all people are humans.) Using a placeholder interface, Type1 and Type2 can be correlated, as follows:

```
class Type1 : IRoom { }
class Type2 : IRoom { }
...
IRoom[] rooms = new IRoom[ 10];
rooms[0] = new Type1();
rooms[1] = new Type2();
```

Having Type1 and Type2 implement the IRoom interface, which means do nothing other than subclass IRoom, establishes a correlation between Type1 and Type2. The correlation is that both Type1 and Type2 are rooms. We have no idea what kind of rooms, and we have no idea if the rooms are in the same building. We only know that they are rooms.

The use of placeholder interfaces is very important in kernel design. Placeholders establish that a type wants to be part of a grouping. The kernel can use that grouping to define a list of elements that are all similar. It is like knowing the age of people to determine whether they are eligible to drive. The age does not indicate the sex or intelligence, nor if they are good or bad drivers. The age is a placeholder that says, "Yes you are part of a grouping that is allowed to take a driving test to give you the right to drive."

In the case of our lighting control, defining the IRoom placeholder interface is saying that whatever instance is associated with IRoom is indicating its interest in being part of the lighting controller kernel. When you have identified a type using a placeholder interface, you are saying your type can be used in a certain context. The context is determined by the placeholder interface.

Defining the INoRemoteControlRoom Interface

Although the purpose of the lighting system is to control the lighting, some rooms should not be controlled by the system. Perhaps the room is private, or controlling its lighting would cause problems.

For example, should a bedroom in a house be controlled by the lighting controller? If the lighting controller controls the lighting in the bedroom, it might turn off the lights while a person is reading. Or maybe it will turn on the lights when the person has decided to sleep in. Of course, the person could just switch the light on or off manually, but that is disruptive. The inconvenience of the controller getting it wrong outweighs the benefit of the controller getting it right, so the controller should not deal with this room.

The definition of an interface that indicates that the controller should do nothing is as follows (in the controller library LibLightingSystem):

```
public interface INoRemoteControlRoom: IRoom { }
```

As you can see, INoRemoteControlRoom lacks methods and properties, like our placeholder interface IRoom. However, in this case, there are no methods or properties because the kernel system does not require them. The idea behind the INoRemoteControlRoom interface is to indicate that the type implementing the interface is a room, but a room that should not be managed by the controller. Using the bedroom as an example, the implementation is as follows (defined in the Home project):

```
class Bedroom : INoRemoteControlRoom {
}
```

The definition of the bedroom allows the kernel to use an instance of a room, as follows:

```
IRoom[] rooms = new IRoom[ 10];
rooms[0] = new Bedroom();
...


if( rooms[0] is INoRemoteControlRoom) {
    // Do nothing and potentially change course in code
}
```

This code creates an array of rooms and assigns the index 0 to an instance of Bedroom. The if statement asks if the IRoom instance in index 0 is of type INoRemoteControlRoom.

■**Note** Using placeholder interfaces and inheritance sets up a very powerful architecture that allows you to create groupings. You can then filter individual instances based on refinements of the grouping. All of this is possible in the C# language using the keywords as and is, which allow queries of subclassed types of an instance. The queries are noninvasive and do not cause exceptions to be thrown. The queries give you the ability to make decisions based on whether an instance would like to be associated with a particular grouping based on an interface.

Defining the IRemoteControlRoom Interface

Another type of room is one where the lighting is completely managed by the controller. The controller does not seek the input of the room and manages the lighting based on the logic that seems appropriate to it.

For example, a public-viewing area in a museum does not require light at certain times of day. When the museum is closed, and the cleaners are finished, the lights can be turned off. When the museum is open, the lights are turned on. This is a simple logic and can be completely managed by the controller.

The interface for the controlled room is defined as follows (in LibLightController):

```
public interface IRemoteControlRoom : IRoom {
    double LightLevel { get; }
    void LightSwitch(bool lightState);
    void DimLight(double level);
}
```

The only input that IRemoteControlRoom provides is information about whether the light is on, off, or at a certain level. This is through the LightLevel property. The LightLevel property is read-only (it just has a get), because the controller and the light level might become out of sync.

For example, suppose it's time for the museum to close, and the lights are switched off in the public-viewing area. But today, the cleaners took a little while longer than usual. They turn the lights back on so that they can see what they are doing. The local device can do one of two things: allow the light to be turned on without the approval of the controller, or not allow the light to be turned on, requiring a controller intervention. The best approach is to allow a local override and let the cleaners turn on the light. The `LightLevel` property is necessary so that the controller can verify if the state of the light is what the controller expects it to be.

■**Note** When you are defining a kernel, sometimes it is necessary to add functionality into an interface that verifies the state of the implementation. Because the kernel is not in control of the implementation, the kernel should not assume the state, as the state could change for some reason. In the case of the lighting system, the change could be due to a cleaner turning on the light after it was turned off.

The `IRemoteControlRoom` methods `LightSwitch()` and `DimLight()` turn the light on or off and set the light to a certain level, respectively. These methods are used to control the state of the implementation.

Defining the ISensorRoom Interface

Another type of room is one that can be controlled under certain circumstances. Let's go back to the cleaner example where the cleaner turned on the light. If the controller notices that the light is on, even though it was turned off, should the controller turn off the light? You might say sure, the controller should turn off the light. However, that is not completely correct. Imagine the situation where the cleaner turns on the light and the controller turns it off. The cleaner would immediately turn the light back on, and the controller would turn it off. The cleaner would tape the light switch down so that a constant battle of the light going on and off ensues (because this battle is in milliseconds, the light remains on). A smarter approach would be to allow a timing of the light. But how much time—a quarter of an hour, a half hour, an hour?

Another approach is not to use a time interval, but to enhance the interface and allow the controller to figure out the state. This enhanced interface, called `ISensorRoom`, is defined as follows (in `LibLightController`):

```
public interface ISensorRoom : IRemoteControlRoom {
    bool IsPersonInRoom { get; }
}
```

The `ISensorRoom` interface has a single property `IsPersonInRoom`, which is a `bool` property. If the property has a value of `true`, then a person is in the room; otherwise, no person is in the room. How the implementation determines whether or not a person is in the room is not the problem of the kernel. The kernel assumes the implementation knows how to figure this out.

■**Note** As a general rule of thumb, the kernel can communicate with the implementation only via the interface. The kernel should never assume a certain implementation of an interface. The kernel should take the approach that what it sees is what it gets. Thus, if the kernel needs additional information, the interface should be extended during design, or another interface should be implemented. Of course, this does not mean for every piece of state the interface should be extended. Sometimes, you will need to define a specific interface, such as in the tax application example in the previous chapter (`ICanadianTaxEngine`).

Now that we've created the interfaces, we're ready to implement the kernel.

Implementing the Kernel

In this example, the kernel will be a single class that contains all of the functionality of the controller. This definition means that the individual implementations, testing, and applications will interact with a single class.

Here is an example of implementing the light-dimming method using the LightingController class:

```
public class LightingController {
    public void DimLights(object grouping, double level) {
    }
}
```

The user of LightingController would dim a light using this code:

```
LightingController controller = new LightingController();
object grouping = null;
controller.DimLights(grouping, 0.50);
```

The user code instantiates the type LightingController directly and uses the method DimLights() directly. Using classes directly has the cost that the controller code cannot change without affecting the users, as there is a tight coupling between the user code and the kernel. And this is why I have been writing at length about using interfaces, ideas, and implementations. Yet, the controller appears to throw all of that out of the window.

The reason for using a class goes back to the previous chapter's example and the interfaces ITaxDeduction and ITaxIncome. That example had only a single implementation of each interface, and those implementations were not going to change. As I explained in the previous chapter, the interfaces could have been represented as classes. The same logic applies with respect to the controller. The controller is not going to change much from a method and property signature perspective, and there is going to be only a single implementation of the controller. Therefore, an interface is not necessary. Using a class is completely acceptable, and the approach we're using in this chapter. However, I'll talk about when you might want to implement the kernel as an interface a little later in the chapter, in the "Defining the Kernel As an Interface Instead of a Class" section.

The controller represents a building that has the ability to organize rooms into groupings. Based on the groupings, the controller can perform operations such as turning the lights on or off, or setting lights to a specific dimness. When each of these operations is executed, the controller must respect the intentions of the individual rooms, by querying for a particular interface as defined by the previous section.

The controller has two main responsibilities: calling the appropriate interface methods and organizing the interface instances. The organization of the instances involves using collections, arrays, or a linked list. We'll use a linked list in this example.

Storing a Collection Using a Linked List

In the examples in previous chapters, we created a collection of objects using an array, like this:

```
MyType[] array = new MyType[10];
array[0] = new MyType();
array[2] = new MyType();
```

This creates an array that can contain 10 elements at most (MyType[10]). If you needed to store 20 elements, you would need re-create the array, and copy the references from the old array to the new array. Another feature of an array is that you don't need to assign the elements in a sequential manner. The example assigns the first and third positions, with the second position being null. Thus, some code that iterates the array will need to verify that the array element is not null. The sample code generates the structure illustrated in Figure 8-2.

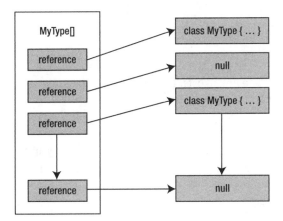

Figure 8-2. *Array structure of referenced elements*

Figure 8-2 reveals a very important aspect of reference types: an array holds a reference to the object and not the value of the object. If the array were value types, then the entire value would be stored in the array.

The array could just as easily have been some object with a number of variables, like this:

```
class MyTypeArray {
    public MyType Element1;
    public MyType Element2;
...
}
```

Since array elements are a bunch of references stored in a type, you could make use of this knowledge to create a type that serves no other purpose than referencing a list of elements, more commonly called a *linked list*.

In a linked list, the individual objects are linked together and reference another element nearby. A doubly linked list will only ever hold references to two other objects: the next one and the previous one. (Another type is a singly linked list, which holds a reference to only one other object: the next one.)

In a doubly linked list, the type will always have two data members: Next and Prev. Each of these data members is used to reference another element in the list, as illustrated in Figure 8-3. To iterate a list, you start from either the left or right side and then go to the Next or Prev data members, respectively. Here is an example:

```
MyType curr = GetHeadOfList();
while(curr != null) {
    // Do something with curr
    curr = curr.Next;
}
```

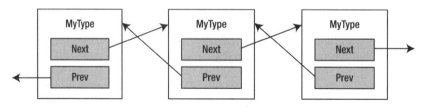

Figure 8-3. *Structure of doubly linked list*

As you can see, you can easily add elements to linked lists. The drawback is that it is expensive to find a particular object, as that requires iterating through the list.

■**Note** For the most part you will be using the List class, but there is also a LinkedList class. If you're interested, you can find information about the .NET version of System.Collection.Generic.LinkedList in the MSDN 3.0 documentation.

For our application's kernel, we'll use a doubly linked list to link together a number of rooms into a set of groupings.

Creating a Linked List

The Next and Prev data members for the doubly linked list could be coded individually, but it's more efficient to define a base class. The initial structure of the BaseLinkedList class is as follows (defined in LibLightingSystem):

```
public abstract class BaseLinkedList {
    private BaseLinkedList _next;
    private BaseLinkedList _prev;

    public BaseLinkedList Next {
        get {
            return _next;
        }
    }
    public BaseLinkedList Prev {
        get {
            return _prev;
        }
    }
}
```

BaseLinkedList is declared as abstract to indicate that using this class implies that you derive a class. Prev and Next are C# properties that can only read the values of the private data members of _prev and _next.

Inserting and Removing Linked List Items

Inserting an object into a linked list or removing an object from a linked list requires some careful coding. You need to make sure that the actions will not corrupt the list. This is not a task that you want to delegate to the users of the linked list, as they could unintentionally corrupt the list. The following is the code to insert and remove an object from a linked list, and is part of the BaseLinkedList class.

```
public void Insert(BaseLinkedList item) {
    item._next = _next;
    item._prev = this;

    if (_next != null) {
        _next._prev = item;
    }
    _next = item;
}
public void Remove() {
    if (_next != null) {
        _next._prev = _prev;
    }
    if (_prev != null) {
        _prev._next = _next;
    }
    _next = null;
    _prev = null;
}
```

The Insert() method assumes that you want to insert an object into a list where there is at least one element. The Insert() method assumes the following code at a minimum.

```
BaseLinkedList singleElement = GetHeadOfList();
BaseLinkedList anotherElement = CreateListElement();
singleElement.Insert(anotherElement);
```

The first step is to assign the data members (_next, _prev) of the object (item) that is going to be added to the list.

■**Note** Notice how in the Insert() method, it is possible to assign the private data members of another object instance. You learned that private scope means that only the declared type can read private properties and methods. This rule has not been violated, because the rule implies types can read the private data members and private methods of other instances of that type.

Once the data members of the item have been assigned, the item is integrated into the list, by redirecting the _prev property of the next object (if it is not null), and then assigning the local _next property to the object to be inserted.

The Remove() method does the same as Insert(), but in reverse. The first step is to redirect the _next and _prev properties of the previous and next objects, assuming that they are not null. And then the object to be removed has its _next and _prev properties assigned to null.

■**Note** The declaration of Prev and Next is a common architecture where data members can be read, but to assign them, you need to use methods. Using read-only properties is one way to make sure that the internal state cannot be corrupted, if you must expose the internal state.

Testing the Linked List

BaseLinkedList is a core class and serves a utility purpose. This makes the class eligible to be declared in the kernel or a definitions assembly. As the class is a core class, it means you need a more exhaustive testing framework to ensure that there will be no problems. In this section, we will go through one test that demonstrates what you should be testing for and how you should be testing a core class.

BaseLinkedList is declared as abstract and needs an implementation. The purpose of the implementation is to give us enough information on the state and context of the object. In this case, we want to define an object that tests every part of the class BaseLinkedList. If you have ever seen pictures of a test car tire hooked up to dozens of wires, then you will understand what the test class needs to do. Following is a sample implementation, placed in the TestLightingSystem project. Remember to include a reference to LibLightingSystem (right-click References in TestLightingSystem and select Add Reference ➤ Projects ➤ LibLightingSystem).

```
...
using LibLightingSystem;

namespace TestLightingSystem
{
    class LinkedItem : BaseLinkedList {
        private string _identifier;
        public LinkedItem(string identifier) {
            _identifier = identifier;
        }
        public string Identifier {
            get {
                return _identifier;
            }
        }
        public override string ToString() {
            string buffer;
            buffer = "this(" + _identifier + ")";
```

```
            if (Next != null) {
                buffer += " next(" + ((LinkedItem)Next).Identifier + ")";
            }
            else {
                buffer += " next(null)";
            }
            if (Prev != null) {
                buffer += " prev(" + ((LinkedItem)Prev).Identifier + ")";
            }
            else {
                buffer += " prev(null)";
            }
            return buffer;
        }
    }
}
```

The LinkedItem class has a single data member declaration, _identifier, which is used to identify the instance. The test code will call the Insert() and Remove() methods, and then generate a visual representation of the linked list. The visual representation is used to understand what the problem might be if anything goes wrong. You will not write tests against the visual representation because that would overcomplicate the testing.

To generate a visual representation of the object, the ToString() method is overridden. By default, all objects have a ToString() implementation, which does absolutely nothing other than spit out the identifier of the object reference. To make ToString() do something useful, you need to override it. In the example, ToString() will generate a buffer that contains the BaseLinkedList identifier and the next and previous object identifiers. These three pieces of information tell you the structure of the linked list.

The next step is to write a test in TestLightingSystem's Program.cs that verifies that the Insert() method works properly, and it is implemented as follows:

```
namespace TestLightingSystem
{
    class Program
    {
        static void Main(string[] args)
        {
            TestInsert();
        }

        public static void TestInsert() {
            Console.WriteLine("**************");
            Console.WriteLine("TestInsert: Start");
            LinkedItem item1 = new LinkedItem("item1");
            LinkedItem item2 = new LinkedItem("item2");
            LinkedItem item3 = new LinkedItem("item3");
```

```
            string toString = item1.ToString();
            Console.WriteLine(toString);
            if(item1.Next != null || item1.Prev != null) {
                throw new Exception(
                    "TestInsert: Empty structure is incorrect");
            }

            item1.Insert(item2);
            toString = item1.ToString();
            Console.WriteLine(toString);
            if(!(item1.Next == item2 && item1.Prev == null)) {
                throw new Exception(
                    "TestInsert: Item 1->Item2 structure is incorrect");
            }
            toString = item2.ToString();
            Console.WriteLine(toString);
            if(!(item2.Next == null && item2.Prev == item1)) {
                throw new Exception(
                    "TestInsert: Item 2->Item1 structure is incorrect");
            }
            item2.Insert(item3);
            toString = item2.ToString();
            Console.WriteLine(toString);
            if(!(item2.Prev == item1 && item2.Next == item3)) {
                throw new Exception(
                    "TestInsert: Item2->Item1, Item3 structure is incorrect");
            }
            toString = item3.ToString();
            Console.WriteLine(toString);
            if(!(item3.Prev == item2 && item3.Next == null)) {
                throw new Exception(
                    "TestInsert: Item3->Item2, structure is incorrect");
            }

            toString = item1.ToString();
            Console.WriteLine(toString);
            toString = item2.ToString();
            Console.WriteLine(toString);
            toString = item3.ToString();
            Console.WriteLine(toString);
            Console.WriteLine("TestInsert: End");
        }
    }
}
```

This test generates pretty output like this:

```
**************
TestInsert: Start
this(item1) next(null) prev(null)
this(item1) next(item2) prev(null)
this(item2) next(null) prev(item1)
this(item2) next(item3) prev(item1)
this(item3) next(null) prev(item2)
this(item1) next(item2) prev(null)
this(item2) next(item3) prev(item1)
this(item3) next(null) prev(item2)
TestInsert: End
```

The pretty output is not a verification of what went right. Rather, the extensive output makes it simpler to perform postmortem debugging to understand why something failed.

In the TestInsert() method, a situation is created where three LinkedItem instances are instantiated: item1, item2, and item3. Initially, the three items are not linked, but we use the Insert() method to link them into a structure, as shown in Figure 8-4.

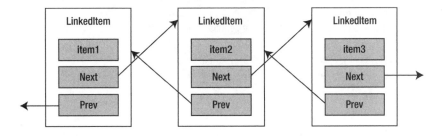

Figure 8-4. *Testable doubly linked list structure*

But to get to the structure in Figure 8-4, some intermediate steps are required, and in the implementation of the method TestInsert(), those intermediate steps are tested. The Next and Prev properties for each and every item are tested for the proper values at each step. If some of the values don't match, an exception is thrown to indicate an improper structure. If an exception is thrown, the generation of the visual structure becomes important. As an aside, while developing the Insert() and Remove() algorithms, the visual structures and test code helped me figure out a bug.

The TestInsert() method is an example of an exhaustive test of a context. The downloadable source code contains several other examples of exhaustive tests.

DEBUGGING AND TESTING TOOLS

Some of you might be thinking that to figure out why a test failed, you should use a debugger. However, with proper tests that are part of an extensive testing framework and that generate an extensive output, the need for a debugger is reduced. Among the people who believe in a test-driven development (TDD) environment (including me), there is a question on the merits of a debugger. According to Wikipedia's Test-Driven Development entry (http://en.wikipedia.org/wiki/Test-driven_development), "Programmers using pure TDD on new ('greenfield') projects report they only rarely feel the need to invoke a debugger. Used in conjunction with a Version control system, when tests fail unexpectedly, reverting the code to the last version that passed all tests is almost always more productive than debugging."

A debugger is good for finding problems, but bad for understanding the nature of the problem. Good tests verify scenarios. The more scenarios, the more tests, and the more tested your code is. If a particular scenario fails, you know that you have a problem. And if everything was OK until you made a slight change that caused the tests to fail, you know you have a problem. Test scripts are signposts that tell you what is working and what might not be working. By using a debugger, you are often testing large chunks of code where you need to labor to find the bug. A debugger has its uses, but when writing good tests in many scenarios, you will rarely need to use it.

And speaking of writing tests, as I noted in Chapter 6 in this book, I could introduce a testing framework like NUnit (http://www.nunit.org) or Microsoft Visual Studio Team System (http://msdn2.microsoft.com/en-us/vstudio/default.aspx). When you are writing production code, you will probably use such a testing framework. They do not help you to write your tests, but rather help you by providing support code to generate errors, log problems, and indicate progress of the tests. Do not get misled by tools that say they can write the tests for you. No tool can write your tests, because that would imply the tool understands the context of your code. And since such a tool does not yet exist, you will need to write your own tests.

Implementing Room Groupings

Room groupings are collections of rooms that fall into a specific organization. The idea behind a grouping is to perform group operations without having to explicitly sort a room before performing an operation. For example, in the case of the museum, we don't need to figure out whether a room is public or private each time a global operation is being performed.

The organization of the collection is that there can be multiple room groupings that are linked together, and within a grouping, there are multiple rooms that can be grouped together. The linked list structure has two levels and is coded as follows (in LibLightingSystem):

```
class RoomGrouping : BaseLinkedList {
    public Room Rooms;
    public string Description;
}


class Room : BaseLinkedList {
    public IRoom ObjRoom;
}
```

The class declaration Room represents an individual room. But notice how it derives from BaseLinkedList, which seems to imply that Room is actually many rooms. This is part of the linked list implementation; it is like a chain, where the chain is created by individual links.

The RoomGrouping class has two data members: Rooms, which represents the list of rooms in the grouping, and Description, which represents an easy-to-understand description of the grouping. The single data member for Room is a reference to an IRoom interface instance. This data member does not know about the collection and is managed by another object that references the individual IRoom instances, like an array of IRoom instances.

The room groupings are managed by the LightingController class. An initial implementation of LightingController is as follows:

```
public class LightingController {
    private BaseLinkedList _roomGroupings = new RoomGrouping();
}
```

When dealing with linked lists, you have a problem: which is the first element of a list? When you use arrays, an empty list of arrays is an array with no references. But there is an explicit array object. Using the linked list, an empty linked list is a list that does not exist. Thus, when you want to create a list, you need a room. In LightingController, the first element is an instance of RoomGrouping, which is not a room grouping, but serves as a placeholder. To insert a room grouping, you could simply use this code:

```
_roomGroupings.Insert(newRoomGroup);
```

Without the placeholder, you would need to write the following code whenever you wanted to add an element into the list.

```
if(_roomGroupings == null) {
    _roomGroupings = newRoomGroup;
}
else {
    _roomGroupings.Insert(newRoomGroup);
}
```

The code that uses the placeholder is shorter and simpler; however, it also requires a dangling instance of RoomGrouping that has no real value. I chose the dangling approach because I am making the decision that a room grouping with no identifier is the default room grouping.

Adding a Room Grouping

The following code adds a room grouping (added to the class LightingController).

```
public object AddRoomGrouping(string description) {
    RoomGrouping grouping = new RoomGrouping {
            Description = description,
            Rooms = null
        };
    _roomGroupings.Insert(grouping);
    return grouping;
}
```

To add a new room grouping, you instantiate `RoomGrouping`, assign the data members, and then call the method `_roomGroupings.Insert()` to insert the new room grouping into the linked list.

Let's look at the technique for assigning data members, called *object initialization*. In previous examples, when an object was instantiated and we wanted to assign default values, we would create a constructor with the appropriate parameters. However, another way is to instantiate the object and define a block that assigns the appropriate data members or properties. In the case of `RoomGrouping`, there are two publicly defined data members: `Description` and `Rooms`:

```
Description = description,
Rooms = null
```

The `Description` and `Rooms` data members have assign access, which is important as this technique only works with properties that are not read-only. To assign a data member or property, the parentheses are dropped when you use the new keyword. In its place are curly brackets with a series of key/value pairs that are separated by commas. The key represents the data member property to assign, and the value is the data that is assigned to the data member or property.

Another technique of interest in the code to add a room grouping is the definition of a data handle when passing information:

```
return grouping;
```

In the implementation of `AddRoomGrouping()`, the variable grouping is assigned an instance of `RoomGrouping`. The declaration of the `RoomGrouping` class limits its scope to the `LibLightingSystem` assembly only, while the declaration of `LightingController` is public. If the method `AddRoomGrouping()` had attempted to return an instance of `RoomGrouping`, the compiler would have marked this as an error, because the scope is inconsistent. Assuming for the moment that you did want to return an instance of `RoomGrouping`, your only solution would be to declare `RoomGrouping` as `public`. The declaration change is the wrong solution, because `RoomGrouping` is a class without declared methods (other than the base class methods) and has public data members. It is a class for a specific purpose and should not be shared.

Declaring `RoomGrouping` as `public` is the wrong approach, so another solution is needed. You could add a counter data member to the `RoomGrouping` declaration and return an `int` value indicating the `RoomGrouping` instance you are referring to in the list. However, that would mean having access to the list somewhere, and then needing to iterate to find the appropriate `RoomGrouping` instance.

The solution is to declare the method as returning a type `object`. When you use `object`, you are defining that your method is giving you an object instance. You may or may not know what the instance type is, and in the case of `AddRoomGrouping()`, you don't. But that is fine, because you, as the user, will consider the instance as a key that is managed by the class `LightingController`. In technical jargon, the object instance is a *handle* that you hold and pass to some other component that knows what to do with it. In the example, it means giving the handle to `LightingController` because it knows that the handle is an instance of `RoomGrouping`.

■**Note** Handles were very popular in the C programming days and were consider pointers to memory. The caller did not know what the pointer pointed to, but kept using it when interacting with an API. These days, handles have lost significance as we have objects, .NET generics, and other programming constructs. However, at times, handles are very useful. They can help you to avoid the problem of having to expose the internal state of your API, while not having to maintain an object hierarchy to watch which objects are being referenced.

Finding a Room Grouping

When a number of room groupings have been added, you will want to find a room grouping with a particular description. As room groupings are a doubly linked list, it means needing to iterate the list, as follows (added to LightingController):

```
public object FindRoomGrouping(string description) {
    RoomGrouping curr = _roomGroupings.Next as RoomGrouping;
    while (curr != null) {
        if (curr.Description.CompareTo(description) == 0) {
            return curr;
        }
        curr = curr.Next as RoomGrouping;
    }
    return null;
}
```

In the iteration code, the iteration is similar to the code illustrated earlier in the "Storing a Collection Using a Linked List" section. The one difference is that the curr variable is of type RoomGrouping, and because Next is of type BaseLinkedList, a type cast is necessary. Then an iteration using a while loop is carried out; during each iteration, a test comparing curr.Description to the parameter description is made. If an object is found, the handle to the RoomGrouping is returned, and if nothing is found, a null is returned, indicating that the RoomGrouping could not be found.

This method would be used as follows:

```
object foundHandle = controller.FindRoomGrouping("description");
```

However, the linked list of room groupings is a collection that could be accessed as an array. C# has constructs that make it possible to convert the class LightingController into a class that has array functionality. The following method in LightingController declares array-like functionality, which is called an *indexer*.

```
public object this[string description] {
    get {
        return FindRoomGrouping(description);
    }
}
```

A C# indexer is defined like a property, except that the property identifier is this and is followed by a set of square brackets that contain the array parameters. The return type of the indexer is the identifier before the this keyword. In the example, the indexer has only the get part defined, thus the indexer is read-only. You could use this indexer as follows:

```
object foundHandle = controller["description"];
```

Therefore, an indexer gives you the ability to define array access that does not need to be numerically based.

Note Indexers are utility-based and best added to classes that manage collections. In the case of the LightingController, which manages a collection of room groupings, use of an indexer is appropriate.

To find a particular room grouping, you would use the methods or indexer of LightingController. However, sometimes a user would like to know all of the room groupings that are available. You could define an indexer with a numeric value, as in the following code, and iterate the individual elements.

```
public string this[int index] {
    get { }
}
```

The previous indexer example and the FindRoomGrouping() method returned an object handle. However, this indexer example returns a string. When you iterate the room groupings, you don't want a handle, because you don't know what the handle represents. If you call the FindRoomGrouping() method and you search based on a description, the handle that is returned is cross-referenced with the description. If you iterate using a numeric indexer, the returned object handle means nothing to you other than being associated with a specific index. What you really want to know is what descriptions are available, and thus the numeric indexer will return a string, which cross-references with the room grouping description.

Note A type can have multiple indexer definitions, but each indexer definition must have different array parameters.

Suppose we implemented a numeric indexer. To iterate the individual room groupings, we would need to use the following code.

```
for(int c1 = 0; c1 < controller.Length; c1 ++) {
    string description = controller[c1];
}
```

This iteration code is acceptable and something that we could use, but it involves adding the property Length to the LightingController class. Another approach is to use foreach, as follows:

```
foreach(string description in controller.RoomGroupingIterator()) {
    // Do something with the description
}
```

The foreach syntax is simpler. It doesn't matter that we've lost the information about which offset is which description, because that information is useless. Remember we are dealing with a linked list that can change its order however it pleases. Thus, having a numeric identifier is completely meaningless. The only reliable way to find a room grouping is to know its description or hold a specific index for the collection.

Note Unless you are absolutely sure that the collection you are manipulating does not move elements around, holding an index as a unique description of the object can be dangerous, and potentially could corrupt the state of an application. In this chapter, I have already illustrated two other techniques that can be used to reference a particular object: a handle and an indexer.

The LightingController class has no foreach functionality built in. Here is where the yield keyword comes in. The yield keyword is a powerful construct that allows you to add foreach support to a type. The following is the code to implement an iterator using the yield keyword (you'll also need to add using System.Collections; to the top of the LightingController file, to gain access to the IEnumerable interface).

```
public IEnumerable RoomGroupingIterator() {
    RoomGrouping curr = _roomGroupings.Next as RoomGrouping;
    while (curr != null) {
        yield return curr.Description;
        curr = curr.Next as RoomGrouping;
    }
}
```

In the iterator, another while loop using the curr variable is created, but the magic is the bolded code. The yield keyword is used in conjunction with the return keyword. Don't think the return exits the function, but consider the yield/return combination as a way of doing some message passing.

The yield keyword always boggles the mind of developers. The easiest way to understand it is by exploring how it works in conjunction with the foreach keyword:

1. The code encounters a foreach statement and sets up a context where a collection of elements is being iterated. The context involves retrieving a collection and making space for an individual element.

2. The code calls the collection iterator, which in the example means calling the method RoomGroupingIterator().

3. RoomGroupingIterator() assigns the curr variable to the head of the room groupings doubly linked list.

4. A loop is performed as long as curr is not equal to null.

5. The code encounters a `yield return` statement, which means to take the result after the `return` keyword and store it in the space for the individual element (step 1).

6. The code creates a bookmark of the last executed code in the iterator and jumps back into the `foreach` statement.

7. The `foreach` statement continues and executes code, which in the example is the comment `// Do something with description`.

8. When the `foreach` attempts another iteration, the previous bookmark is retrieved and the code immediately after the bookmark is executed. This results in the code `curr = curr.Next as RoomGrouping` in the method `RoomGroupingIterator()` being executed.

9. The loop continues, and steps 4 through 9 are executed until `curr` is `null`.

10. When `curr` is `null`, the iterator exits, causing an exit of the `foreach` loop.

The hard part to comprehend is the mechanism used when `yield return` causes an exit and then resumption of execution. Programmers are not used to the idea that you can jump in and out of method and resume execution. Keep in mind that this works only in the context of a `foreach` and `yield return` combination. There is no other situation in C# where this applies, and it works because C# uses a bookmarking mechanism.

The example illustrates `yield` in the context of a loop, but a loop is not necessary. The following code is a collection of three numbers: 1, 2, and 3.

```
public IEnumerable NumberIterator() {
    yield return 1;
    yield return 2;
    yield return 3;
}
```

WHY LEARN ABOUT INDEXERS AND YIELD?

This chapter's example demonstrates how you can use indexers and the `yield` keyword to make the type look and feel like a standard collection. The example serves a purpose. However, was it a fair example? I am trying to teach you how to write software in a very professional manner, which means software engineering. A linked list is part of that software engineering, but do people use linked lists today? Not really. Should people know about linked lists? Sure, just like you should know about how to add, even though you are going to use a calculator.

So, if the example serves a purpose of illustrating some features of C#, and the example is not like what you are going to do, are the features useful? Yes, the features are useful. The difference with the illustrated features and the examples is that I showed you how to write infrastructure code. Imagine building a house, and you need to create a number of trusses. To speed production of the trusses, you create jigs. Jigs serve no purpose in the building of the house other than making the mundane quicker. Similarly, indexers and `yield` make it simpler for you to develop classes that fit into the standard C# programming paradigm.

You may need to create structural classes that do nothing other than keep all of the other pieces that do something working. And when you create structural classes, you will use indexers, and you will use the `yield` keyword. So in the end, when you think of indexers and the `yield` keyword, think of providing a mechanism to a class that makes your multiple elements appear like a C# collection.

Adding Rooms to Groupings

The data handle that we defined when adding the grouping is used when we add a room to a grouping. The idea of the handle is to provide a reference that the kernel can use. Since the handle is an instance of a RoomGrouping type, whenever a room is added to a grouping based on a handle, it is not necessary to find the room grouping. The handle is the room grouping, and all that is necessary is a type cast. The following demonstrates how to add a room to a room grouping.

```
public void AddRoomToGrouping(object grouping, IRoom room) {
    RoomGrouping roomGrouping = grouping as RoomGrouping;
    if (roomGrouping == null) {
        throw new Exception(
          "Handle grouping is not a valid room grouping instance");
    }
    Room oldRooms = roomGrouping.Rooms as Room;
    if (oldRooms == null) {
        roomGrouping.Rooms = new Room {ObjRoom = room };
    }
    else {
        roomGrouping.Rooms.Insert(new Room {ObjRoom = room });
    }
}
```

In the implementation of AddRoomToGrouping(), the first step is to cast the handle grouping to an instance of RoomGrouping. The cast used is the as operator, so that if the cast fails, it is only necessary to test if roomGrouping is not null. Executing the null test is absolutely vital; otherwise, you might perform operations that will cause an exception to be thrown.

Once the handle has been cast to a RoomGrouping instance, to add a room to the linked list is trivial. Adding a room involves only assigning the head of the list if there are no rooms in the list, or calling the method Insert() if there are rooms.

Performing Operations on a Group

With a grouping defined, you can perform global operations that affect all rooms of a grouping. One example is turning off the lights in all the rooms in a grouping, which is based on the IRoom interface instance. Here is the code to turn off all of the lights in a grouping:

```
public void TurnOffLights(object grouping) {
    foreach (IRoom room in RoomIterator(grouping)) {
        IRemoteControlRoom remote = room as IRemoteControlRoom;
        ISensorRoom sensorRoom = room as ISensorRoom;
        if (sensorRoom != null) {
            if (!sensorRoom.IsPersonInRoom) {
                continue;
            }
        }
        else if (remote != null) {
            remote.LightSwitch(false);
```

```
        }
    }
}
```

Notice that the handle is not converted into a `RoomGrouping` instance. The handle is passed to the method `RoomIterator()`, which, like the `RoomGroupingIterator` method, uses the `yield` keyword to allow `TurnOffLights()` to use a `foreach` statement to iterate the individual rooms.

■Note The combination of `yield return` and `foreach` is a powerful and easy way to iterate a collection of data. The advantage of `yield return` is that the data being iterated does not need to be in a loop or a collection. The data could be algorithmically generated or based on a fixed number of elements.

For each iteration of the `foreach` loop, the `IRoom` instance room is cast into the types `IRemoteControlRoom` and `ISensorRoom`. A cast to both of these types is necessary because, depending on the room type, certain algorithms need to be executed. For example, if the room is of type `ISensorRoom` and the property `IsPersonInRoom` is `true`, then the lights should be left as is. If the lights are to be left as is, that means performing the next iteration using the `continue` keyword.

If the processing continues, we check if the room can be remotely controlled, which implies implementing the interface `IRemoteControlRoom`. If `remote` is not `null`, then we can call the `LightSwitch()` method with a parameter of `false` to turn off the lights. The iteration continues for all rooms in the grouping.

This completes the kernel, but before you see how it fits with a lighting application, I would like to discuss an alternative approach to implementing the kernel.

Defining the Kernel As an Interface Instead of a Class

As I noted earlier, rather than defining the kernel as a class, another approach would be to define the kernel as an interface that is implemented. If a company were to distribute multiple implementations of a controller, an interface would be appropriate, but only if the multiple implementations of the interface used the same set of methods.

Do not confuse multiple implementations with multiple implementations that offer a completely different feature set. For example, controller version 1 and controller version super-duper 1000 might control the same room types, but the inputs, outputs, logic, and algorithms contained in each might be completely different. In that case, using an interface gains no advantage. You might use a version 1 interface on a version super-duper 1000 for legacy integration, since the old interface has older ideas.

You would use an interface for the controller when multiple controllers implement the same interface. You would use an interface if you want the flexibility to later implement multiple implementations using the same interface. On the other hand, if there will only ever be a single implementation for a single interface declaration, it's much easier to use a class declared as `public`.

If you do decide to declare the controller using an interface and implementation, you need to structure the project differently than the organization used for this chapter's example. The reason is that you cannot declare the interfaces and implementations in the same project.

Imagine trying to offer multiple kernel implementations, but for the users to be able to use the interfaces, they must reference a project that contains a particular kernel implementation.

You will need to modularize the structure and have an organization similar to that shown in Figure 8-5.

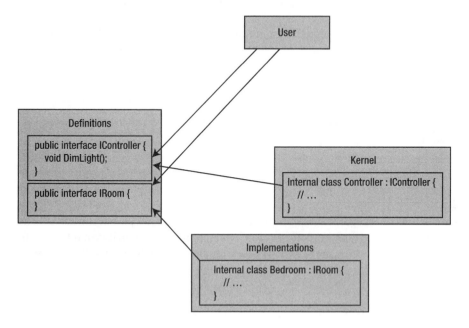

Figure 8-5. *Organization of a modular interface and implementation architecture*

In Figure 8-5, the individual boxes represent a single .NET assembly. Each assembly serves a unique purpose:

- Definitions: An assembly that contains all interfaces used by all of the other assemblies. This represents a single assembly that changes very rarely and is a cornerstone of the application. Along with interfaces, you would add general utility classes that all assemblies would reference.

- User: The main application that interacts with the interfaces of objects that are implemented in either the Kernel or Implementations assemblies. The User assembly is responsible for wiring all of the types together (for example, responsible for assigning interface instances from the Implementations assembly to the Kernel assembly).

- Kernel: An assembly that defines the main functionality of the application and manipulates instances that implement interfaces from the Definitions assembly. The kernel does not know where the interfaces are implemented, and it expects some other piece of code to know where the implementations are.

- Implementations: An assembly that contains the implementations of the interfaces that the kernel manipulates. The programmer may create a single implementation assembly or multiple assemblies. The implementations are only aware of the Definitions assembly, and are unaware of the Kernel assembly.

Building a Complete Application

All of the code illustrated thus far is related to the kernel, and it would seem that our application is complete. In reality, the kernel has done nothing other than organize and manipulate the rooms. The kernel has not defined any implementations for a particular room. Now let's see how to define some rooms and use the rooms in the context of the kernel.

The idea is to enable a developer to add functionality to the kernel without affecting the code of the kernel. The example that we will go through defines a couple of rooms in a museum (the Museum project).

■Note The implementation of the Home project is not discussed here, but it is available in this book's downloadable source code.

Defining Some Rooms

The rooms are defined in a separate assembly called Museum and are not part of the kernel. The following is an example of a room implementation. Again, remember to include a reference to LibLightingSystem (right-click References in Museum and select Add Reference ➤ Projects ➤ LibLightingSystem).

```
...
using LibLightingSystem;

namespace Museum
{
    class PrivateRoom : INoRemoteControlRoom {
    }
    class PublicRoom : ISensorRoom {
        public bool IsPersonInRoom {
            get { return false; }
        }

        double _lightLevel;

        public double LightLevel {
            get { return _lightLevel; }
        }

        public void LightSwitch(bool lightState) {
            if (lightState) {
                _lightLevel = 1.0;
            }
            else {
                _lightLevel = 0.0;
            }
        }
    }
```

```
    public void DimLight(double level) {
        _lightLevel = level;
    }
  }
}
```

The two room declarations, `PrivateRoom` and `PublicRoom`, are both internal to the assembly. Each room implements the interface that it deems appropriate. `PrivateRoom` implements the interface `INoRemoteControlRoom`, indicating that `LightingController` should leave the room alone.

`PublicRoom` implements `ISensorRoom`, indicating that it will tell the controller when a person is in the room and allow itself to be controlled. The implementation of `PublicRoom` is trivial and frankly not that useful, but it illustrates the bare minimum of what needs to be implemented. In a production environment, `PublicRoom` would have access to external devices such as a heat sensor and lights. The objective of `PublicRoom` would be to give and take signals from the `LightingController` and take action. It is not up to `PublicRoom` to ask whether or not a decision is correct. For example, if `LightingController` indicated to turn the light off even though a person is in the room, then `PublicRoom` would not ask why the light is being turned off.

■**Note** When you are designing a kernel-like architecture, the implementations are realizations of ideas and should never question the controller. The implementations might not be aware of a bigger picture and thus might prevent an algorithm from functioning properly. Of course, the exception to this rule is if the decision would cause physical damage or cause the program to crash. In that case, the implementation should throw an exception, indicating that the decision is faulty.

Instantiating PublicRoom and PrivateRoom

As described in the previous chapter, when you are developing components, you want to separate the interfaces from the implementations. This gives you the flexibility to change the implementation in an assembly without requiring the users of the assembly to recompile their code.

To instantiate the implementations, you need a factory, and the museum with its `PrivateRoom` and `PublicRoom` implementations is no different. However, a builder method that assembles a building of potential `PrivateRoom` and `PublicRoom` combinations will be offered with the museum. The builder method is useful because it predefines a canned building that has all the room groupings and rooms properly added.

■**Note** Think of a builder method as a way of creating a predefined structure, thus saving users from having to do that themselves. A builder method is only a starting point, and you should be able to manipulate the structure afterwards for fine-tuning purposes.

The following is the implementation of the museum factory, which is added to the project Museum.

```
public static class FactoryRooms {

    public static IRoom CreatePrivateRoom() {
        return new PrivateRoom();
    }

    public static IRoom CreatePublicRoom() {
        return new PublicRoom();
    }

    public static LightingController CreateBuilding() {
        LightingController controller = new LightingController();
        object publicAreas =
            controller.AddRoomGrouping("public viewing areas");
        object privateAreas =
            controller.AddRoomGrouping("private viewing areas");
        controller.AddRoomToGrouping(publicAreas, new PublicRoom());
        controller.AddRoomToGrouping(privateAreas, new PrivateRoom());
        return controller;
    }
}
```

The implementation has three methods: `CreatePrivateRoom()`, `CreatePublicRoom()`, and `CreatingBuilding()`. The fact that `CreatePrivateRoom()` and `PrivateRoom` have similar naming is purely coincidental. The method could just as well have been called `CreateNonControlledRoom()`. The `CreatePrivateRoom()` and `CreatePublicRoom()` methods are intended to define method identifiers that users can understand. What is instantiated in the method must return an `IRoom` instance.

The `CreateBuilding()` method is a builder method, and it returns a `LightingController` instance. It is fine to return a `LightingController` instance, because it is a globally defined type and can serve as a basis for the builder method. In the implementation of the builder method, the room groupings and rooms are instantiated and added to the `LightingController` instance. This is the work that the builder should save the end user. Additionally, by providing a builder method, you avoid creating museum structures that have glaring errors in their structures.

Note Factory types serve to instantiate types and define builder methods, but can also be used to perform generic structural operations. Let's say that in your museum there is a wing, which contains three public rooms and a private room. You could define a builder method that creates a wing, and the wing is added to an already created building. The general idea behind the factory type is to avoid errors and centralize repeated instantiations.

Learning More About Private Classes and Object Initialization

In this chapter, you learned how to apply interfaces, implementations, and components in a kernel-type situation. This is very much the type of programming that you will encounter as you continue using C#. Here, I will provide a few more details about using private classes and initializing objects with nested data types.

Private Classes

The RoomGrouping and Room classes are defined in the LibLightingController project and are private to the library. This is because RoomGrouping and Room are classes only LightingController needs to support its functionality. The declaration of each class is internal to the assembly, which is good, but it still means that some developers could use the classes within the kernel assembly for their own purposes. Sometimes that is a desirable feature; sometimes it is not.

In the case of LightingController, another approach is to declare the classes in the context of LightingController, as follows:

```
public class LightingController {
    private class RoomGrouping { }
    private class Room { }
}
```

The Room and RoomGrouping classes are declared within the class, and their declarations are private. This means that only LightingController can instantiate and use the classes, and there can never be the situation where another class will instantiate the types. In the case of LightingController, this would have been a better solution.

Private classes are also used in the factory context. For example, imagine the situation where you don't ever want anyone but the factory to instantiate a room. A possible IRoom declaration and factory could be as follows:

```
public static class Factory {
    private class MyRoom : IRoom { }
    public static IRoom CreateMyRoom() {
        return new MyRoom();
    }
}
```

In this implementation of MyRoom, you can be sure that only Factory can ever instantiate MyRoom, and you can always be sure that the only way to manipulate MyRoom is through the IRoom interface. All too often, developers become lazy and instantiate types within the assembly, and switch to the implementation type whenever the interface does not have the methods or properties that they want.

Object Initialization with Nested Data Types

In this chapter, you saw how to use object initialization to assign data members in lieu of a constructor. Object initialization also works using nested data types. Consider the situation where a type references another type. Using object initialization, you can instantiate and assign multiple levels of objects.

Suppose you had this source code:

```
class MyType {
      int _dataMember;

      public MyType() { }
      public int DataMember {
         get {
             return _dataMember;
         }
         set {
             _dataMember = value;
         }
      }
}

class EmbeddedMyType {
    MyType _embedded;

    public EmbeddedMyType() {
    }

    public MyType MyType {
       get {
           return _embedded;
       }
       set {
           _embedded = value;
       }
    }
}
```

The type EmbeddedMyType has a property that references MyType. If you were to instantiate EmbeddedMyType, you would probably also want to instantiate and assign the property MyType. You can do that with object initialization, like this:

```
EmbeddedMyType cls = new EmbeddedMyType
{
    MyType = new MyType
    {
        DataMember = 10
    }
};
```

The Important Stuff to Remember

In this chapter, you learned about writing a kernel, using C# indexers, and the `yield` keyword. The main items to remember are as follows:

- A kernel is a component-oriented architecture where you are not in control of certain implementations. Components make it possible to modularize a development process so that separate teams have their own tasks.

- Interfaces are contracts between modules, and you test against the interface, not the implementation.

- Placeholder interfaces are used to make it simpler to group object instances.

- Indexers and the `yield` keyword are structural, and thus are like a tool to help you accomplish a task quicker.

- Indexers make it possible for your type to behave like an array.

- The `yield` keyword is used in conjunction with `foreach` and makes it possible to perform iterations on types that may not necessarily support collections. For example, a mathematical series could be iterated.

Some Things for You to Do

Here are some exercises that will help you apply the concepts you learned in this chapter:

1. The `LightingController.AddRoomGrouping()` method has a mistake. Write some tests to find the error, and then fix the code and rerun your tests to verify that the error has been fixed.

2. The `TestInsert()` test method is one example of an insertion test, but not all variations have been tested. Write another test method that implements the remaining variation(s) that need to be tested.

3. The declarations of `RoomGrouping` and `Room` are not optimal. Fix the declarations.

4. Implement a general collection class based on the experience of using the class in the class `LightingController`. Hint: look at how the linked list for `Room` is declared and figure out a way to abstract that into some general collection class.

5. When the method `LightingController.AddRoom()` is called, the method is tested internally to see if the handle is of type `RoomGrouping`. Can you think of a more defensive programming technique to make sure that the code someone else passes to the kernel will not cause the kernel to fail? Hint: think about the methods to turn on or off the lights and think of what could go wrong.

■ ■ ■

CHAPTER 9

Learning About Lists, Delegates, and Lambda Expressions

One of the most common pieces of code that you will write is code that manages many object instances. In the previous examples, many object instances were managed using an array. In Chapter 8, you learned that a linked list used in conjunction with an indexer and the `yield` keyword could make a plain-vanilla object look like a collection. This chapter introduces the .NET collection classes, which provide an easy way to manage a set of object instances. Think of a collection class as an infinite sack where things can be added, iterated through, and retrieved.

The chapter begins with a discussion of how to manage collections. Then we'll look at an example of "code that feels wrong" and improve it by using delegates, then anonymous methods, and finally lambda expressions.

The project structure used in this chapter is a single console application. As we will not be building an overall application, but rather a set of sample code snippets, no tests or libraries are involved.

Managing Collections

When you have a collection, what you actually have is an object that happens to point to many other objects. Compare that to a relational database, where a result set can contain a single record, no records, or multiple records. To interact with a database, you use the Structured Query Language (SQL), which considers everything as a collection. There is no such thing as a single record. (On various database implementations, SQL has been extended to allow interaction with a single record, but the performance hit for doing that is generally high.) The performance in a C# collection is good, but the ease of use is not.

C# provides collection classes for managing collections. C# 2.0 introduced a different approach to collections, which solved many of the problems that came up in earlier C# versions. Here, we'll look at managing collections both before and after C# 2.0, which will help you to understand how collections are used.

Managing a Collection Before C# 2.0

Before C# 2.0, the main collection classes were stored in the namespace `System.Collections`. The following are some of the classes and interfaces in that namespace:

- `ArrayList`: A general collection that manages all of the referenced objects using an internal array. This class manages the problem of increasing the size of an array.

- `HashTable`: A collection class where the individual objects are stored using key/value pairs. In the previous chapter, the indexer was used to retrieve a room grouping based on its identifier. You could use a `HashTable` to accomplish the same thing.

- `ICollection`: An interface implement by `ArrayList` that provides basic functionality that copies the references to another array.

- `IDictionary`: An interface implemented by `HashTable` that allows a programmer to associate a key with a value.

- `IList`: An interface implemented by `ArrayList` that provides a general-access mechanism for manipulating a collection of items.

- `Queue`: A collection that implements the first in, first out (FIFO) mechanism. You could use a queue when you are processing a set of instructions. The first instruction to process would be the first instruction added to the collection.

- `Stack`: A collection that implements the last in, first out (LIFO) mechanism. Think of it as a stack of papers. When one piece of paper is laid on top of another, the first piece of paper that is processed is the last piece of paper added to the stack of papers.

All of the collection types—`ArrayList`, `HashTable`, `Queue`, and `Stack`—implement a way to store a set of types. The difference in the collection types lies in how the individual objects are stored and retrieved from the collection. For examples of using these collection types, see the "Learning More About Collection Types" section later in this chapter.

A Simple Collection Example

Let's walk through an example of using collections in pre-C# 2.0 style. Begin by creating a console application and call it `OneToManySamples`. Then add a new class (right-click your console application project and select Add ➤ Class ➤ Class). Call it `Example.cs` and add all of the following code to it:

```
using System.Collections;
...
class Example {
    int _value;

    public int Value {
        get {
            return _value;
        }
        set {
            _value = value;
```

```
            }
        }
    }

static class Tests {
    static void PlainVanillaObjects() {
        IList objects = new ArrayList();

        objects.Add(new Example { Value = 10 });
        objects.Add(new Example { Value = 20 });

        foreach (Example obj in objects) {
            Console.WriteLine("Object value (" + obj.Value + ")");
        }
    }
    public static void RunAll() {
        PlainVanillaObjects();
    }
}
```

This is the type of code written before C# 2.0, and it follows a standard set of steps:

1. You define a custom type (Example in this example).

2. You instantiate the custom type and add the instances to a collection. In the example, two instances of Example are added to the collection type ArrayList.

3. The collection is manipulated to allow you to access and manipulate the instances of the custom types. In the example, the collection ArrayList is an interface instance of IList.

The bolded code in the example is where the action takes place. Instantiating the type ArrayList is the instantiation of a collection manager. The ArrayList instance is then assigned to the variable objects, which is of type IList. IList is an interface making it possible to use the collection in the context of a component-oriented development environment. To add two objects to the collection, we call the Add() method twice. To iterate the elements in the collection, we use the foreach statement.

■**Note** The fact that the collection classes can be used in the context of a component-oriented application is no coincidence. When Microsoft created its .NET library, components were an essential part of the library.

To run the tests, open Program.cs in your console application and edit it as follows:

```
class Program
{
    static void Main(string[] args)
    {
```

```
        Tests.RunAll();
    }
}
```

Press Ctrl+F5 to run the application and see the results.

The Problem of Mixed Types

What is unique about the sample code is that the foreach statement works and happens to know that the objects in the collection are of type Example. However, the following code adds a different object to the collection, which will cause the iteration to fail.

```
class Another { }

IList objects = new ArrayList();

objects.Add(new Example { Value = 10 });
objects.Add(new Example { Value = 20 });
objects.Add(new Another());
foreach (Example obj in objects) {
    Console.WriteLine("Object value (" + obj.Value + ")");
}
```

The bolded code illustrates how the collection object contains two instances of Example and one instance of Another. The code will compile, which misleads you into believing everything is fine. If you try to run the application (either normally or in debug mode), you will see the following:

```
Unable to cast object of type 'Another' to type 'Example'.
```

So, should a collection contain multiple types? There are arguments for and against the idea, but the problem is not the ability to mix types. The problem is that you can mix types, even if you don't really intend to do that.

Using the foreach keyword with mixed types will result in an exception, because for each iteration, the object in the collection is cast to a type Example. As the last item in the collection is of type Another, the cast will fail, and an exception will be generated. Collections before .NET 2.0 could not enforce type consistency, and that was a problem.

Had you desired to mix types, the proper foreach loop would have been as follows:

```
foreach (object obj in objects) {
    if( obj is Example) {
        // ...
    }
    else if( obj is Another) {
        // ...
    }
}
```

The Problem of Value Types

Another issue with pre-C# 2.0 collections is that they have performance problems. Consider the following code that manipulates value types.

```
IList objects = new ArrayList();
objects.Add(1);
objects.Add(2);
foreach (int val in objects) {
    Console.WriteLine("Value (" + val + ")");
}
```

In the example, an ArrayList is again instantiated, but this time, the numbers 1 and 2 are added to the collection. Then, in the foreach statement, the integers are iterated. The code works, but there is a hidden performance hit. The items added to the collection are value types, which means you are manipulating stack-based memory.

However, the definition of IList uses objects:

```
public interface IList : ICollection, IEnumerable
{
    // Methods
    int Add(object value);
    void Clear();
    bool Contains(object value);
    int IndexOf(object value);
    void Insert(int index, object value);
    void Remove(object value);
    void RemoveAt(int index);

    // Properties
    bool IsFixedSize { get; }
    bool IsReadOnly { get; }
    object this[int index] { get; set; }
}
```

How IList is defined and how a value type is defined should raise alarms. An object is a reference type, and thus you have a conflict: IList stores reference types, but int is a value type.

What's happening is that the .NET environment knows that there is a conflict and adds a fix. Don't think of the fix as a hack, but as a way of solving a problem that all virtual machine environments like .NET need to address. The .NET environment uses the terms *boxing* and *unboxing* to denote converting a value type into a reference type and then back again, respectively.

To understand boxing and unboxing, let's consider the context. You are creating a list that references value types. The array is a reference type that is stored on the heap, but value types are stored on the stack. If you get the array to reference data on the stack, you will have a consistency issue, since the stack changes. Thus, you will need to move the memory from the stack to the heap, but that would violate the principle behind value types. The solution is the compromise of boxing and unboxing.

To illustrate what boxing does, I have written some code that is similar to the boxing of a value type. The difference is that my code is explicit and boxing is done automatically.

```
class ReferenceHeap {
    public int Value;
}
...
public static void Method() {
    int onStack = 1;
    ReferenceHeap onHeap = new ReferenceHeap { Value = onStack };
}
```

In the example, Method() declares a value type onStack, which is allocated in the context of a method and is thus on the stack. The type ReferenceHeap is a class, and thus a reference type, and automatically all of its data is stored on the heap. When the variable onHeap is allocated and initialized, the value from onStack is moved to the heap and assigned to the instance onHeap. This is what boxing does, except C# does it automatically and transparently. When you use a pre-C# 2.0 list, all the value types are automatically boxed and unboxed.

■**Note** It is important to remember that when you box and unbox, you are transferring values. Thus, if the variable onStack is changed, the value of onHeap does not change.

Unboxing refers to moving the value from the heap to the stack, which in the case of the example, means transferring the value from the variable onHeap to onStack.

Boxing/unboxing happens automatically, but it has a performance penalty, since memory is allocated and assigned.

Managing a Collection After C# 2.0

The two problems of storing mixed object types and the performance penalty of boxing/unboxing required Microsoft to carefully consider a solution. After much debate and thinking, Microsoft introduced .NET generics. In a nutshell, .NET generics solve both collection problems by enforcing a type. (.NET generics solve broader problems as well.)

Collections are an ideal application of .NET generics because collections are utilitarian. You don't use collections to solve the problem of calculating taxes. You use collections to solve the problem of how to create a collection of incomes and a collection of deductions.

Here is an example of how to use .NET generics-based collections:

```
IList<Example> lst = new List<Example>();
lst.Add(new Example { Value = 10 });
lst.Add(new Example { Value = 20 });
foreach(Example item in lst) {
    Console.WriteLine( "item (" + item.Value + ")");
}
```

The bolded line represents the .NET generics-based code. The code used to add an object and the foreach loop are identical to that used in the pre-C# 2.0 example.

Between the angle brackets (<>) is an identifier that is the specialization of the general approach. Whatever is inside the brackets when you declare an IList or List is saying, "I want my collection to contain instances of the type defined inside the brackets." You cannot add a type that is not related to the type defined in IList or List, so the following code would not compile.

```
lst.Add(new Another());
```

This is because the .NET generics collection is type-safe and does not allow mixed types. It allows only objects of type Example.

When you declare a list like this:

```
IList<Example> lst;
```

you are saying that the list has a method declared like this:

```
void Add(Example item);
```

If you are programming C# 3.0, you should use C# 2.0 and later collection classes. The non-.NET generics collection classes are, to a large degree, legacy code. Whenever possible, use .NET generics-based collection classes.

Now that you know how to manage a collection of objects, the next section will present a common collection-related problem and then demonstrate how to solve the problem.

The Case of the Code That Feels Wrong

Let's start out with a common problem: addition of all elements in a collection. Consider the following code.

```
IList<int> elements = new List<int>();

elements.Add(1);
elements.Add(2);
elements.Add(3);

int runningTotal = 0;
foreach (int value in elements) {
    runningTotal += value;
}
```

This code has three parts: initialization of elements, adding of numbers to elements, and iteration of all values in elements that are added to the variable runningTotal. The code seems acceptable. But let's say that you need to write another piece of code where, instead of calculating the running total, you need to find the maximum value, like this:

```
IList<int> elements = new List<int>();

elements.Add(1);
elements.Add(2);
elements.Add(3);

int maxValue = int.MinValue;
foreach (int value in elements) {
```

```
    if (value > maxValue) {
        maxValue = value;
    }
}
```

The difference between the two code pieces is the bolded code. The initialization is different, and that is OK, but the inner loop is different, and that is not as OK. In the code bases, the repetition is not apparent, but what if you wanted to combine the code bases? The following code adds all elements and finds the maximum value.

```
IList<int> elements = new List<int>();
elements.Add(1);
elements.Add(2);
elements.Add(3);
int runningTotal = 0;
foreach (int value in elements) {
    runningTotal += value;
}
Console.WriteLine("RunningTotal (" + runningTotal + ")");
int maxValue = int.MinValue;
foreach (int value in elements) {
    if (value > maxValue) {
        maxValue = value;
    }
}
Console.WriteLine("Maximum value is (" + maxValue + ")");
```

Another variation is as follows:

```
IList<int> elements = new List<int>();
elements.Add(1);
elements.Add(2);
elements.Add(3);
int runningTotal = 0;
int maxValue = int.MinValue;
foreach (int value in elements)  {
    if (value > maxValue)  {
        maxValue = value;
      }
      runningTotal += value;
    }
}
```

Regardless of the variation used, you are using copy and paste as a way of solving the problem. For one or two instances, writing the foreach loop is not that problematic, but it would be if you needed to use the iterator code in a dozen places. This type of code is harder to maintain and extend. One way of being more efficient is to delegate the code to an abstract base class that is implemented to calculate the running total or maximum value. Following is the complete code (you can place the three classes in separate files called IteratorBaseClass.cs, RunningTotal.cs, and MaximumValue.cs if you want to test this).

```csharp
abstract class IteratorBaseClass {
    IList<int> _collection;

    protected IteratorBaseClass(IList<int> collection) {
        _collection = collection;
    }
    protected abstract void ProcessElement(int value);
    public IteratorBaseClass Iterate() {
        foreach (int element in _collection) {
            ProcessElement(element);
        }
        return this;
    }
}

class RunningTotal : IteratorBaseClass {
    public int Total;
    public RunningTotal(IList<int> collection)
        :
        base(collection) {
        Total = 0;
    }
    protected override void ProcessElement(int value) {
        Total += value;
    }
}

class MaximumValue : IteratorBaseClass {
    public int MaxValue;
    public MaximumValue(IList<int> collection)
        :
        base(collection) {
        MaxValue = int.MinValue;
    }
    protected override void ProcessElement(int value) {
        if (value > MaxValue) {
            MaxValue = value;
        }
    }
}

static void Main(string[] args)
{
    IList<int> elements = new List<int>();
    elements.Add(1);
    elements.Add(2);
    elements.Add(3);
```

```
        Console.WriteLine("RunningTotal (" +
            ((new RunningTotal(elements).Iterate()) as RunningTotal).Total +
            ") Maximum Value (" +
            ((new MaximumValue(elements).Iterate()) as MaximumValue).MaxValue +
            ")");
}
```

The rewritten code is much longer, even though the bolded code, which represents the user code, is much shorter. However, this code still isn't right. The code is ill fitting because the problem that it addresses can be solved using another, simpler technique. So, in a nutshell, you can say the problem is that you want to solve a single particular technical problem using an elegant piece of code that does not include repeated sections that have been copied and pasted. In the next sections, you'll see how to use delegates, anonymous delegates, and lambda expressions to solve the problem. The idea is to show a practical example where the use of each feature is a natural fit.

WEIGHING THE ADVANTAGES OF REUSING CODE

Very often, when you write code, the code that performs the task directly is shorter and to the point. When you abstract the code and develop general classes, the code will begin to bloat and expand, but the advantage is that the code can be reused. So, when is abstracting code worth the effort?

Consider the analogy of building a house. You are constructing the trusses for the house. You have a blueprint that indicates that you need to build 50 trusses. You could build each of the 50 trusses individually, or you could build a jig to speed up building the trusses. And herein lies the problem. If the trusses can be built without a jig in 10 hours, and with the jig in 2 hours, you would think building the jig was a good idea. But not so fast. What if building the jig takes 20 hours? Then the time that you saved by using the jig you lost by building the jig.

Software is no different. Sometimes, even though the code is more complicated and bloated, if the code is reused often enough, abstracting it saves time, as the end-user code is simplified. Experience will tell you when to code specifically or when to write general code that can be reused. A rule of thumb is to start out by solving the problem, and if it looks like the code can be reused, then abstract the specific code.

Using Delegates

Since the beginning of C#, there has been a concept called a *delegate*. A delegate is a method without a type. For example, consider the following type definition.

```
interface IExample {
    void Method();
}
```

If the interface were converted into a delegate, it would look like this:

```
delegate void Method();
```

A delegate and interface share the same role, in that they are types without implementations and are used to build components. An interface can have multiple methods and properties. A delegate is a method declaration and can define only the parameters and return types. The purpose of delegates is to be able to define a generic method-calling mechanism without needing to add the baggage of implementing an interface.

The approach used in the delegate solution to the problem presented in the previous section is to define a chunk of functionality that performs the iteration, called an *iterator*. And then to do something with the iteration, another chunk of functionality is integrated via a delegate. The result is that you have two separate pieces of functionality that are integrated using a component methodology.

Following is the complete rewritten foreach code that uses delegates.

```
public delegate void ProcessValue(int value);

public static class Extensions {
    public static void Iterate(this ICollection<int> collection,
                               ProcessValue cb) {
        foreach (int element in collection) {
            cb(element);
        }
    }
}

static class Tests {
    static int _runningTotal;

    static void ProcessRunningTotal(int value) {
        _runningTotal += value;
    }

    static int _maxValue;
    static void ProcessMaximumValue(int value) {
        if (value > _maxValue) {
            _maxValue = value;
        }
    }

    static void DoRunningTotalAndMaximum() {
        List<int> lst = new List<int> { 1, 2, 3, 4 };
        _runningTotal = 0;
        lst.Iterate(new ProcessValue(ProcessRunningTotal));
        Console.WriteLine("Running total is (" + _runningTotal + ")");

        _maxValue = int.MinValue;
        lst.Iterate(new ProcessValue(ProcessMaximumValue));
        Console.WriteLine("Maximum value is (" + _maxValue + ")");
    }
```

```
    public static void RunAll() {
        DoRunningTotalAndMaximum();
    }
}
```

Declaring the Delegate and Using Extension Methods

The beginning of the code is the single line that contains the delegate keyword:

```
public delegate void ProcessValue(int value);
```

The declaration of the delegate is outside the scope of a class or interface, but the usage of a delegate must be in the context of a class. Therefore, while a declaration requires no surrounding type, the implementation does.

The type of the delegate is the identifier of the method, which in our case is ProcessValue. The delegate will be used in the code example to provide a general callback mechanism in the iterator. The iterator is declared as follows:

```
public static class Extensions {
    public static void Iterate(this IList<int> collection,
                               ProcessValue cb) {
        foreach (int element in collection) {
            cb(element);
        }
    }
}
```

The class Extensions is a static class that has a static method. As explained in Chapter 4, this means Extensions can never be instantiated as a type, and to call the method Iterate(), you need to use the following syntax.

```
Extensions.Iterate(...);
```

The first parameter of the Iterate() method is the list to iterate, and the second parameter is a delegate instance. Notice that the first parameter is declared with the this keyword. Imagine declaring the method without using this, and using the method as a static method. The calling structure would be as follows:

```
IList<int> collection;
ProcessValue cb;
Extensions.Iterate(collection, cb);
```

The syntax is a bit clunky because it explicitly implies knowing that there is a method that operates on a list. It would be better if you could declare a list, and then, using IntelliSense, see the availability of the method. In C# 3.0, this is possible via *extension methods* that allow a developer to make it appear as if a type were extended, without extending it. Thus the extension methods allow you, in the context of the example, to write the following code.

```
IList<int> collection;
ProcessValue cb;
collection.Iterate(cb);
```

The Iterate() method appears to be an extension of IList, without having to change IList. Extension methods are declared by having a static class with a static method, and the first parameter prefixed with this. This first parameter is no longer needed in the method call, but represents the type to be extended.

■**Note** Extension methods are utilitarian and thus should be used only when you want to extend types without changing the types. This could be because you are using standard .NET types like int, double, and IList, or because changing types would be too costly. Extension methods are used only for functionality that is reused throughout the code. You could use them in context of one or two usages, but doing that in the long term might prove problematic, as there could be overlap or conflicts.

In the implementation of Iterate(), each element of the collection is iterated using foreach, and then in the loop, the variable cb is called as if it were a method. The calling of cb is what separates the iterator from the processing of the iteration. Imagine having implemented a method that calculates the running total or maximum. To iterate all of the elements, you would instantiate the delegate with the method and call Iterate(), as follows:

```
lst.Iterate(new ProcessValue(ProcessRunningTotal));
...
lst.Iterate(new ProcessValue(ProcessMaximumValue));
```

With the delegate and the extension method, we've created a compact and simple general solution. The code that wants to automatically iterate code must provide only a delegate implementation.

Implementing the Delegate

Implementing a delegate is straightforward in that you need to declare only a method in a class that has the same method signature. A delegate can be implemented using a static method or an instance method; it does not matter. The following code demonstrates implementing the ProcessValue delegate using both types of methods.

```
class DelegateImplementations {
    void InstanceProcess(int value) { }
    static void StaticProcess(int value) { }

    public static ProcessValue StaticInstantiate() {
        return new ProcessValue(StaticProcess);
    }
    public ProcessValue InstanceInstantiate() {
        return new ProcessValue(InstanceProcess);
    }
}
```

In the example, the InstanceProcess() and StaticProcess() methods are implementations of the delegate ProcessValue. A delegate lacks association. When you implement a method of an interface in a class, you know which methods belong to which interfaces. With a delegate, you have no such luck. If you have two delegates with identical parameter and return type signatures, then a method with the same signature can be used for either delegate definition.

To have the methods be recognized as a delegate, you need to look at the methods StaticInstantiate() and InstanceInstantiate(). Each method instantiates the delegate using the new keyword, and each instantiation has a single constructor parameter, which is the method to associate with the delegate instance. Notice how StaticInstantiate() instantiates the delegate with the method StaticProcess(). This is possible because both methods involved are static. Because static methods are converted into delegates, it does not matter how many times the delegate is instantiated; the same method instance is called.

The implementation of InstanceInstantiate() instantiates a delegate that wraps the InstanceProcess() method. You might think that InstanceInstantiate() and StaticInstantiate() behave similarly, as their code is similar, but there is a big difference between the two instantiation methods: to execute InstanceInstantiate(), you need to instantiate DelegateImplementations. This is a very important consideration. Consider the following source code, which uses an instantiated DelegateImplementations.

```
public ProcessValue GetMeADelegate() {
    DelegateImplementations cls = new DelegateImplementations();
    return cls.InstanceInstantiate();
}
```

In the implementation of GetMeADelegate(), the class DelegateImplementations is instantiated and the method InstanceInstantiate() is called. Because the scope of cls is in the context of the GetMeADelegate() method, you would think that cls would be garbage-collected after the method call has finished. That is not what happens. When the method InstanceInstantiate() is called, a delegate is instantiated and references the method InstanceProcess(). Even though the delegate references a method, the class instance cls is referenced and cannot be garbage-collected.

■**Note** The rule of thumb with delegates is that if the delegate references an instance method, the delegate maintains a reference to the object, and thus the object is not eligible for garbage collection.

Now let's look at the running total and maximum value example and see how the delegates are implemented.

```
static class Tests {
    static int _runningTotal;
    static void ProcessRunningTotal(int value) {
        _runningTotal += value;
    }

    static int _maxValue;
    static void ProcessMaximumValue(int value) {
```

```
            if (value > _maxValue) {
                _maxValue = value;
            }
        }
    }
```

The `ProcessRunningTotal()` and `ProcessMaximumValue()` methods both have the same signatures as `ProcessValue()`, and therefore are delegate candidates. In each delegate implementation, the running total is calculated or the maximum value is found. The following code uses the delegates.

```
static void DoRunningTotalAndMaximum() {
    List<int> lst = new List<int> { 1, 2, 3, 4 };
    _runningTotal = 0;
    lst.Iterate(new ProcessValue(ProcessRunningTotal));
    Console.WriteLine("Running total is (" + _runningTotal + ")");

    _maxValue = int.MinValue;
    lst.Iterate(new ProcessValue(ProcessMaximumValue));
    Console.WriteLine("Maximum value is (" + _maxValue + ")");
}
```

In the example, the `DoRunningTotalAndMaximum()` method instantiates and assigns `lst` using the object initializer notation. Then to iterate the individual elements, the `lst.Iterate()` method is called with the delegate for the `ProcessRunningTotal()` method. After having calculated and presented the running total, the maximum value is calculated and displayed.

The delegate solution is more compact than the previous abstract base class solution. The big advantage is the ability to solve a problem using a smaller, piecemeal approach. It is not hard to implement a delegate, and it is not hard to use a delegate.

Using Anonymous Delegates

Starting with C# 2.0, the usage of delegates could be streamlined by using anonymous methods. In the previous delegate examples, the code to calculate the running total or find the maximum value was defined in explicit methods contained within a type. When you use anonymous methods, the code of the method is defined within a method call.

The anonymous method approach still uses the same class iterator and delegate `ProcessValue`. What changes is how the iterator and `ProcessValue()` are used. The delegate implementation methods `ProcessRunningTotal()` and `ProcessMaximumValue()` are not necessary. The calling code changes as follows:

```
            List<int> lst = new List<int> { 1, 2, 3, 4 };
            int runningTotal = 0;
            lst.Iterate(
                delegate( int value) {
                    runningTotal += value;
                });
            Console.WriteLine("Running total is (" + runningTotal + ")");
```

```
int maxValue = int.MinValue;
lst.Iterate(
        delegate(int value) {
            if (value > maxValue) {
                maxValue = value;
            }
        });
Console.WriteLine("Maximum value is (" + maxValue + ")");
```

The anonymous methods are the bolded code. An anonymous method is a complete method declaration in the context of another method. The signature of the method is the identifier delegate, followed by the parameters of the defined delegate. You don't need to define the return value because it is implied from the declaration of the delegate ProcessValue().

The theory behind an anonymous method is a bit obtuse because anonymous method code is code that is not executed when the anonymous method is declared. The best way to understand an anonymous method is to think of it as way of declaring code that will be executed at some later point in time.

Look at the first section of bolded code, and you will see the implementation that is identical to that of the ProcessRunningTotal() method. By declaring an anonymous method for the running total, your code is saying, "Hey whenever you are ready to do something, here is the code you should be executing." Look at the implementation of both anonymous methods, and you will see the references to state that is declared in the context of the parent method. The great advantage of anonymous methods is that you have the ability to share state.

The reason you would use anonymous methods, rather than formally defined methods, is that you have the ability to write compact code that solves your problem without having to sacrifice portability.

Multicasting with Delegates

In the examples, there is a one-to-one relationship with a delegate. However, delegates are inherently capable of multicasting. Consider the example of the iterator that maintains a running total and finds a maximum value. It is not necessary to iterate the list twice. The following code is a rewritten example of a single iteration that calls two delegate implementations.

```
List<int> lst = new List<int> { 1, 2, 3, 4 };
int runningTotal = 0;
int maxValue = int.MinValue;

ProcessValue anonymous = new ProcessValue(
    delegate(int value) {
        runningTotal += value;
    });
anonymous += new ProcessValue(
        delegate(int value) {
            if (value > maxValue) {
                maxValue = value;
            }
        });
```

```
lst.Iterate(anonymous);
Console.WriteLine("Running total is (" + runningTotal + ")");
Console.WriteLine("Maximum value is (" + maxValue + ")");
```

In the example, the bolded parts are the assignment and addition of a delegate implementation to a variable. The variable anonymous is a single variable and, when called using the delegate notation, represents a single method call. The .NET runtime understands that a single variable can reference multiple delegate implementations and adds all of the plumbing to handle the multicasting. The result of this multicasting is that you need to call Iterate() only once to execute two operations.

To remove a delegate implementation from a variable, use the -= operator:

```
void RemoveDelegate( ProcessValue toRemove) {
    anonymous -= toRemove;
}
```

Using Lambda Expressions

We are now ready to solve the problem using lambda expressions, which use the same ideas as anonymous methods. Here is the complete code for our example modified to use lambda expressions:

```
public static class Extensions {
    public static void Iterate(this ICollection<int> collection,
                        Func<int, bool> lambda) {
        foreach (int element in collection) {
            lambda(element);
        }
    }
}

static class Tests {
    static void DoRunningTotalAndMaximum() {
        List<int> lst = new List<int> { 1, 2, 3, 4 };
        int runningTotal = 0;
        lst.Iterate(
            (value) => {
                runningTotal += value;
                return true;
            });
        Console.WriteLine("Running total is (" + runningTotal + ")");

        int maxValue = int.MinValue;
        lst.Iterate(
            (value) => {
                if (value > maxValue) {
                    maxValue = value;
                }
                return true;
```

```
        });
        Console.WriteLine("Maximum value is (" + maxValue + ")");
    }
    public static void RunAll() {
        DoRunningTotalAndMaximum();
    }
}
```

The bolded code is the altered code from the anonymous method example. The first major change when writing code that uses lambda expressions is that you don't need to define delegates, as they are predefined. Consider the following declaration.

```
Func<int, bool> MyMethod;
```

The declaration is for a method with a parameter of int and a return type of bool, which would be the following method.

```
bool MyMethod(int value) { return false; }
```

The .NET API allows you to define methods with up to five parameters in the same way. If you had a method with five parameters, there would be six .NET generics parameters—the last one would be the method return type:

```
Func<int, int, bool, int, int, bool> FiveArgs;
```

If you had a method with no parameters, then there would be a single .NET generics parameter representing the return type:

```
Func<bool> NoArgs;
```

It is not necessary for you to declare a delegate identifier, because with .NET generics and the delegate declarations, you can define any combination of method declaration you need. The only method declaration that is not possible is a delegate method with no parameters and no return type.

■Note If you want to define a Func<> with no return types, then you need to define an explicit delegate like void Func(). You can still use lambda expressions, because the C# compiler will adapt and fit the proper code.

Let's look at the lambda expression in the code that has taken the place of the anonymous method implementing the int parameter and bool return type delegate signature:

```
        (value) => {
            runningTotal += value;
            return true;
        });
```

The lambda expression does not have a keyword like `delegate` or a delegate identifier. The identifier and keyword are not necessary; they are implied because a lambda expression is an anonymous method. The parentheses (`()`) are used to define a series of lambda parameters, but the parameters are not typed. The parameter type information is not necessary because it is implied based on the declaration of the `Iterate()` method. We know that the parameter value is an `int` because otherwise `Iterate()` would not compile.

The characters `=>` are used to separate the declaration of the parameter from the implementation of the method. Even though the example has parentheses and curly brackets, it is possible to declare a lambda expression without brackets, and thus the `=>` characters imply an expression follows. The curly brackets, like other pieces of C# source code, imply executable code.

Let's take another look at the identical anonymous method:

```
new ProcessValue(
  delegate(int value) {
    runningTotal += value;
  }
);
```

The anonymous method with its `new`, `ProcessValue`, and `delegate` adds quite a bit of syntax without adding any real value. When I implement an anonymous method, I am constantly counting to make sure I have the right number of brackets. Compare this to the lambda expression, which is compact and easy to read.

Understanding Lambda Expressions

Lambda expressions are not going to make your programming life easier, and they surely are not easy to understand at first. However, once you do understand them, lambda expressions make a certain class of problems trivial to solve.

Lambda expressions are about deferring execution to a later point in time. They say, "When you do operation x, then also do operation y."

This previous section described one scenario where you would use lambda expressions. To demonstrate another use of lambda expressions, let's look at a different problem. Consider a simple spreadsheet where we need to calculate the cells without violating the state of the cells. The spreadsheet arrangement is shown in Figure 9-1.

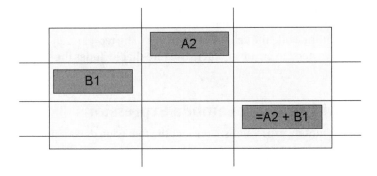

Figure 9-1. *Sample spreadsheet arrangement*

The sample spreadsheet has nine cells, three with values. Cells A2 and B1 have values, and they are added in cell C3. Then the results of C3 are multiplied by 2 and inserted into cell C2. This is a standard spreadsheet operation. Now imagine implementing the source code to calculate the spreadsheet. Take a moment to think about it before you continue reading.

Creating the Algorithm

The problem of Figure 9-1 is that you can't process from one corner to the next corner. Imagine if the cell were represented by the following interface with a single method called Execute().

```
interface ICell {
    void Execute();
}
```

The single method Execute() is magical and knows what to do in the cell itself. A spreadsheet could be represented as the following collection.

```
IList<IList<ICell>> spreadsheet;
```

The collection within a collection declaration creates a two-dimensional list of cells. The declaration illustrates a spreadsheet that has flexible dimensions. Consider the following declaration using a fixed length and width array.

```
ICell[,] spreadsheet;
```

As you can see, there are multiple ways to declare a spreadsheet. For this example, I am going to use the collection within a collection declaration.

To process the spreadsheet, a foreach loop is created and the ICell.Execute() method will be executed:

```
foreach(IList<ICell> rows in spreadsheet) {
    foreach(ICell cell in rows) {
        cell.Execute();
    }
}
```

The algorithm cycles through the collections and executes the cell. But that is not the correct approach, because it would imply cell C2 would be executed before C3. The semantics of the spreadsheet are the reverse, in that C3 must be executed before C2. The reason this algorithm does not work is that it is a top-down execution model.

To make the spreadsheet algorithm work, the cell structure needs to be reorganized so that cell C3 is executed before C2. We need to create another structure that includes the hierarchy of execution.

Implementing the Algorithm Using Lambda Expressions

Another approach would be to use lambda expressions. Consider the following declaration of a spreadsheet.

```
class Spreadsheet {
    public Func<object>[,] Cells;
    public object[,] State;

    public Spreadsheet() {
        Cells = new Func<object>[10, 10];
        State = new object[10, 10];
    }
    public void Execute() {
        for (int col = 0; col < Cells.GetLength(1); col++) {
            for (int row = 0; row < Cells.GetLength(0); row++) {
                if (Cells[col, row] != null) {
                    State[col, row] = Cells[col, row]();
                }
            }
        }
    }
}
```

The spreadsheet has two data members: Cells and State. The data member Cells is a two-dimensional array of lambda expressions that return an object. Each lambda expression will contain some code to execute. The data member State contains the results of the execution and is presented to the user.

The following code is used to assign the cells.

```
static class CellFactories {
    public static Func<object> DoAdd(Func<object> cell1, Func<object> cell2) {
        return () => (double)cell1() + (double)cell2();
    }
    public static Func<object> DoMultiply(Func<object> cell1,
                                          Func<object> cell2) {
        return () => (double)cell1() * (double)cell2();
    }
    public static Func<object> Static(object value) {
        return () => value;
    }
}
```

The CellFactories class has three methods: DoAdd(), DoMultiply(), and Static(), which are used to add, multiply, and calculate a static value in a particular cell, respectively. Look at how DoAdd() is implemented. The lambda expression uses two other lambda expressions to retrieve the values used to generate an additive result.

The way that the lambda expressions are structured results in a chain of execution. This means that if the results for C2 are requested first, C3 is referenced and executed, resulting in a retrieval from the cells A2 and B1. There will never be a violation of cells being calculated improperly. The code to execute the spreadsheet shown in Figure 9-1 is as follows.

```
Spreadsheet spreadsheet = new Spreadsheet();

spreadsheet.Cells[1, 0] = CellFactories.Static(10.0);
spreadsheet.Cells[0, 1] = CellFactories.Static(10.0);
spreadsheet.Cells[1, 2] =
  CellFactories.DoAdd(spreadsheet.Cells[1, 0], spreadsheet.Cells[0, 1]);
spreadsheet.Cells[2, 2] =
  CellFactories.DoMultiply(spreadsheet.Cells[1, 2], CellFactories.Static(2.0));
spreadsheet.Execute();
```

In this code, the factories are used to initialize the base values of 10.0 and 10.0. Notice how 10.0 is used and not 10—omitting the decimal point and zero would cause a cast error. Then in the assignment of Cell[1,2], the method DoAdd() is called with Cells[1,0] and Cells[0,1].

Learning More About Collection Types

In the beginning of this chapter, I talked about the different collection types, but not how to use them. This section presents examples of using the types.

Using a Plain-Vanilla List

A plain-vanilla list is a list of specific types such as int, double, or some other object type. Instantiate the list as follows:

```
IList<MyType> lst = new List<MyType>();
```

The default type List is used for most of your coding situations, but if you are adding and removing elements frequently, the following code is better.

```
IList<MyType> lst = new LinkedList<MyType>();
```

The type LinkedList implements the logic that was presented in the previous chapter, whereas List manipulates a fixed-length array. LinkedList has a downside in that it does not support the IList interface, and the sample code will not compile. Thus, to make the code work, you would need to use ICollection:

```
ICollection<MyType> lst = new LinkedList<MyType>();
```

Add an element to IList as follows:

```
lst.Add(new MyType());
```

To add elements to your list according to an order, use the following form.

```
list.Insert(0, new MyType());
```

This adds an element to the front list. If you are adding elements at the beginning of the list or somewhere in the list, it is better to use the LinkedList type, as it is more efficient. Using the class List incurs an array copy resource penalty.

You can also add one list to another:

```
IList<MyType> lstToBeAdded;
lst.AddRange(lstToBeAdded);
list.InsertRange(0, lstToBeAdded);
```

The AddRange() method is used to append the list lstToBeAdded to lst. The InsertRange() method inserts all of the elements in lstToBeAdded to the front of the list lst.

Delete an element from the list like this:

```
lst.Remove(existingMyType);
```

The Remove() method expects an instance of a type to remove from the list.

To delete a particular element at a particular index, use the following form.

```
lst.RemoveAt(0);
```

This code would remove the element at the front of the list.

Using a Key/Value Pair List

A key/value pair list is a list that has a cross-reference. It is like a dictionary where you have a word and associated meaning. In computing terms, the word is a type and its definition is another type. The word is a key and the definition is a value. Using the spreadsheet described earlier as an example, you could use textual cell definitions like A1 or B1, and the key/value pair definition would be as follows, using the IDictionary interface and Dictionary class.

```
IDictionary<string, object> worksheet =
  new Dictionary<string, object>();
```

You could also use SortedDictionary, but that implies the elements within the list are sorted.

To add static values to the dictionary, use this form:

```
worksheet.Add("A2", CellFactories.Static(10.0));
worksheet.Add("B1", CellFactories.Static(10.0));
```

The following code shows how to reference the cells and add another cell that will add the cell values.

```
worksheet.Add("C3", CellFactories.DoAdd(
    worksheet["A2"], worksheet["B1"]));
```

When using IDictionary, the indexer has been defined as retrieving the key of the list.

When working with IDictionary objects, you might want to know whether or not a key is available. The following code is used to verify if a key exists.

```
if(worksheet.ContainsKey( "A2")) {
    ...
}
```

If you want to iterate the keys, use this form:

```
foreach( string keys in worksheet.Keys) {
}
```

Iterate the values a follows;

```
foreach( object values in worksheet.Values) {
}
```

Using a Stack

A Stack is a special list that behaves like a stack of paper on a table. When you add three items on the Stack, the last one added to the Stack is the first one off the Stack. Here is an example of using a Stack:

```
Stack<string> stack = new Stack<string>();

stack.Push("first");
stack.Push("second");
stack.Push("third");

if(stack.Pop().CompareTo("third) == 0) {
    // This is what we expect
}
```

The code demonstrates using the Push() method to push items on the stack and the Pop() method to remove items from the stack. Remember that Push() is an explicit addition, and Pop() an explicit removal (though a call to Pop() returns the object removed from the stack so you can do something with it, as shown in the code).

If you want to know what is on the top of the stack, use Peek(), which acts like Push(), except it does not remove the item from the list.

Using a Queue

A Queue is another special type of list that behaves like a queue that you would encounter at a ticket counter. As people start queuing, the first person to be served is the one at the front of the line. Here is an example of using a Queue:

```
Queue<string> queue = new Queue <string>();

queue.Enqueue("first");
queue.Enqueue("second");
queue.Enqueue("third");

if(queue.Dequeue().CompareTo("first) == 0) {
    // This is what we expect
}
```

The Important Stuff to Remember

In this chapter, you learned about using delegates, anonymous methods, lambda expressions, extension methods, and lists. The main items to remember are as follows:

- You are using C# 3.0, and thus you should use the .NET generics-based collection classes.

- There are many different types of lists. The main types are the simple object collection, key/value collection, stack, and queue.

- .NET generics-based classes are type-safe and have better performance than old-style collections.

- Delegates are like interfaces without the fancy extras.

- Delegates can be defined and used for multicasting calls without having the caller need to manage the multicasting infrastructure.

- Delegates can be implemented as static methods, instance methods, or anonymous methods. The only important aspect to the method is to make sure the method signature matches the delegate declaration.

- Lambda expressions are a specialized form of anonymous method that enable you to write deferred execution code. The advantage of deferred execution is that the code can contain a state whenever it is executed.

- Lambda expressions are the next step in simplifying complicated programs and are akin to event-driven programming.

Some Things for You to Do

The following are some things for you to do to start applying your budding knowledge of software engineering to improving the code base.

1. Collection classes before C# 2.0 allowed you to mix types. With C# 2.0 and later, the .NET generics classes do not allow you to mix types. Provide a solution where you could mix types with C# 2.0 and later collections.

2. Create a list that contains the numbers 1 to 20. Remove the numbers 15, 10, and 3 to 7.

3. Create a list with an object that is defined as follows:

```
class MyType {
    public string Value;
}
```

Add ten elements to the list, and then sort the list alphabetically from *A* to *Z*. Hint: look at the method Sort() and implement a custom IComparer<>. As part of this excercise, you need to investigate and figure out how to use IComparer<>. My suggestion is to search the MSDN and Code Project web sites.

4. Delegates are capable of multicasting. In terms of the spreadsheet, what does this mean? Hint: look at the Calculate() method and think about the ramifications.

CHAPTER 10

■■■

Learning About Persistence

Your programs will probably need to read and/or write data to some type of storage device. That storage device might be a hard disk, USB drive, or even the network. The key concept is that you are taking information from memory and transferring it to some other location. Later, you will retrieve that information and use it to execute some task.

Taking data from memory and transferring it to another place is referred to as *persistence*. Most examples of persistence involve creating an object, and then saving that object via a file to the hard disk. However, reading and writing an object is not just saving data to the hard disk, even though that is often the result. Reading and writing data to the hard disk is about reading and writing to *data streams*. This chapter focuses on the process of reading and writing data to streams.

This chapter's example is a set of applications for a lottery-prediction system. You'll see how streams are generic concepts that can apply to files, the console, or even the network.

Organizing the Lottery-Prediction System

Let's say we want to predict the next set of lottery numbers. We have a program that saves the numbers drawn, and each week, we run a program that retrieves the drawn numbers and predicts the next set of numbers. Many will argue that lottery numbers are random and thus cannot be predicted. But that doesn't mean that we can't write a program to generate the probabilities, and that usually entails knowing which numbers have been drawn previously.

The lottery-prediction example involves three applications: TextProcessor, which is used to read a messed-up lottery number file that will be cleaned up; Binary2Text, which converts a binary stream into text; and Text2Binary, which converts a text stream into binary. Five projects are defined for these applications:

- Binary2Text: A console program that is used to convert a binary lottery ticket stream into a text stream.

- LottoLibrary: A class library that contains the definition of the Ticket type that represents a lottery ticket in memory.

- ReaderWriter: A class library that contains the infrastructure code for processing streams and command-line arguments.

- Text2Binary: A console program that is used to convert a text lottery ticket stream into a binary stream.

- TextProcessor: A console application that will read and write a text file. This application will become a prototype example of how to write a console-based application. It contains a reference to the ReaderWriter class library.

Piping Data Using a Console

Console applications are not very interactive; for the most part, they are keyboard-based applications. The main advantage of console applications is their ability to dynamically string data-stream manipulations together, a process called *piping*.

For the lottery-prediction example, TextProcessor is a console application that will be fed data by a pipe and generate data using a pipe, as illustrated Figure 10-1. A file feeds a pipe, which feeds the console application that manipulates the data, which then feeds an outgoing pipe that could be used to feed another console application.

Figure 10-1. *Pipeline approach to processing*

TextProcessor will read a file of lottery numbers, clean them up, and remove any duplicates. The console program will not worry about how the data is used. The main focus of TextProcessor is to read data, clean it up, and write out semantically correct data.

Reading Data from the Console

Reading data from the console can happen in two ways:

- Supply the path of the file to be read to the application as a console argument.

- Pipe the data from another application to the console application.

Our example will be able to accept data streams in both ways.

Reading from a File

Reading from a file is programmatically the simplest way of obtaining the data. It requires specifying a command-line argument. For example, to simply load a file named lotto.txt into the TextProcessor program, the command line is as follows:

```
TextProcessor.exe lotto.txt
```

A single command-line parameter, lotto.txt, is passed as a string to TextProcessor.exe. Command-line arguments are separated from each other using spaces. In the context of Windows, this is a problem, because paths can contain spaces. For example, the following command line would be passed as two command-line arguments.

```
TextProcessor.exe c:\My Documents\user\lotto.txt
```

The space between My and Documents tells the console that there are two arguments. To fix that problem, you need to enclose the path in quotation marks:

```
TextProcessor.exe "c:\My Documents\user\lotto.txt"
```

The command line may also include additional parameters, as in this example:

```
TextProcessor.exe -count 10 lotto.txt
```

The parameter -count expects a value, which is 10 in this example. Traditionally, options are specified using key/value pairs, because console applications allow the options to be placed in any order. The exception is the last argument, which is usually the data on which to operate.

Note For more information about the permutations and combinations of command lines, and what a console can do, see http://en.wikipedia.org/wiki/Command_line_interface.

Piping Data

Another solution is to use a command that reads the file and pipes the contents of the file to a stream. The console application reads the stream and processes the data. The following is an example of a command line that pipes data. The pipe operation is indicated by the pipe character (|).

```
type lotto.txt | TextProcessor.exe
```

In the example, the command type, which ordinarily reads a file and displays it on the console, reads in the lotto.txt file and pipes it to the console. Then TextProcessor.exe reads from the console, processes the data, and pipes it back to the console.

For the scope of the TextProcessor application, the command lines listed in Table 10-1 are valid.

Table 10-1. *TextProcessor Command Lines*

Command	Description
`TextProcessor.exe`	Without any arguments, the data will be read from the console pipe and written back to the console pipe.
`TextProcessor.exe [filename]`	Using one argument, the data will be read from the specified file and written to the console pipe.
`TextProcessor.exe -out [filename] [filename]`	Using the `-out` parameter with two arguments, the first file specified is where the data will be written, and the last file specified is the file to read.
`TextProcessor.exe -out [filename]`	Using the `-out` parameter with one argument, the data is read from the console pipe and written to a file. Notice that the output filename is explicitly defined; otherwise, if a single identifier is given, the console application would not know whether you are reading or writing to a file.
`TextProcessor.exe -help`	Outputs to the console how to use `TextProcessor`. The help is also generated when the parameters are specified incorrectly.

Building a Shell

Implementing `TextProcessor` from an architectural perspective involves writing two pieces of code: a module to read/write to a stream and a module to process the stream. By separating the two modules, the processor is not dependent on where the data originated. This also allows the developer to define an interface that is implemented to process the data.

Assembling the Pieces Using an Echo Program

The lottery-prediction program is a case where I know something about the topic, but not all the details. Developing code is a constant challenge of figuring out which APIs to use. In this type of situation, so that I don't get bogged down in API hunting, I first assemble all of the pieces I need for the application. I develop what I call an *echo program*. An echo program has all of its pieces in place, and when called will seem like it functions. The echo part comes in when the end piece of functionality is called and it returns the data that was sent to it. In essence, the end piece is acting like an echo. The cleverness behind the echo is that it requires no implementation, yet it demonstrates the complete flow of data and whether that data flow is workable.

The echo program is not a final program. The echo program is a temporary solution for an intermediate goal. When building an application with intermediate goals, you are using an iterative development technique. The iterations are not visible to your other team members and are completely private. However, the iterations will keep you focused on solving a problem, rather than trying to implement a large piece of code that will not be able to fully test for a while.

Test-driven development, for the most part, is a bottom-up development approach. You develop a core piece of functionality, test it, and then write code that uses the tested piece of functionality. But sometimes you need to develop in a top-down fashion. I typically develop code top-down when I am trying to nail down an overall architecture. The problem with developing top-down is that you don't yet have the bottom code. In other words, you are writing code with no working code. So that your code does have some meaning, you develop an echo. The echo solves the problem of working code and allows you to focus on getting the individual pieces to fit together. Once the pieces are working, and the echo was successful, you can start filling in the implementations. Some developers call the echo a *mock* implementation.

Here, I'll explain developing the sample application by assembling individual pieces in a top-down manner, focusing on getting a single echo implemented. Then once the overall flow is complete, the individual pieces will be implemented completely. Figure 10-2 illustrates a complete architecture for the lottery-prediction program, including the pipeline for the TextProcessor console application.

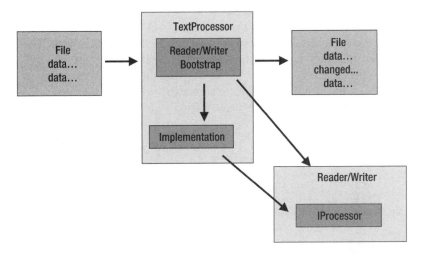

Figure 10-2. *Architecture of a reader/writer application using a general assembly*

Reading and Writing to a Stream

For developing the lottery-prediction application, we'll use a piece of bootstrap code to initiate the reading and writing library, which then calls the specific implementation. *Bootstrap code* is code that does not actually perform the processing, but is responsible for setting up and initiating another piece of source code that will do the processing.

This is the same sort of architecture as we set up in Chapter 8's example, for the application to control the lights of a building. In that case, the controller was a generic piece of software that called an interface, but did not know about the individual implementations. The focus there was on developing the room implementations, and the lighting controller was left as a nebulous to-do task. Here, we'll go through the creation of a complete working application, including the controller and implementation. Note that this chapter is light on testing routines, both for brevity and because one of the exercises at the end of the chapter is for you to come up with a testing plan.

We want to be able to process the following command line.

```
type lotto.txt | TextProcessor.exe
```

If TextProcessor.exe does not read the data from the pipe, an exception will be thrown at the console level, indicating that the piped data was not read.

■Note For the application to work, the lotto.txt and TextProcessor.exe files must be in the same directory. By default, TextProcessor.exe is in the [*Visual Studio project*]\bin\debug directory. Copy TextProcessor.exe into the lotto.txt directory, or vice versa, or you could even copy them both into another directory.

In the architecture of TextProcessor, the bootstrap code is in the ReaderWriter assembly. The TextProcessor console application must call the bootstrap code and instantiate a local type that has implemented the IProcessor interface. The Main() method of TextProcessor is implemented as follows (this is the best time to add a reference to the ReaderWriter project through References ➤ Add Reference ➤ Projects ➤ ReaderWriter):

```
using ReaderWriter;

namespace TextProcessor {
    public static class Program {
        static void Main(string[] args) {
            Bootstrap.Process(args, new LottoTicketProcessor());
        }
    }
}
```

TextProcessor.Main() passes all of the given arguments (contained in the args array) to the actual processing routine (Bootstrap.Process()). The LottoTicketProcessor class implements the IProcessor interface and will serve for the temporary purpose of echoing data. The IProcessor interface is defined as follows:

```
namespace ReaderWriter {
    public interface IProcessor {
        string Process(string input);
    }
}
```

The IProcessor interface has a single method Process(), which accepts a string to be processed, and the return value is the processed string.

The implementation of LottoTicketProcessor is as follows:

```
using ReaderWriter;

namespace TextProcessor {
    // TODO: Finish implementing the class
    class LottoTicketProcessor : IProcessor {
        public string Process(string input) {
            return input;
        }
    }
}
```

The implementation of the Process() method takes the input parameter and returns it as the answer. There is no processing, just a redirection of the data.

For the Bootstrap.Process() method, we could have defined a class EchoProcessor and then passed that class. But remember that right now, we are just trying to assemble pieces, and EchoProcessor is not an actual class that we will be using in the future. The real class is LottoTicketProcessor, except temporarily it will act as an echo.

Now let's look at implementing the ReaderWriter assembly. For this first phase, the reader/writer will also be minimal, so that we can see that all of the pieces are in place and working. The first phase will assume that the data is received on the console and will be sent on the console. Here is the implementation of Bootstrap:

```
using System.IO;

namespace ReaderWriter {
    public static class Bootstrap {
        public static void Process(string[] args, IProcessor processor) {
            TextReader reader = Console.In;
            TextWriter writer = Console.Out;

            writer.Write(processor.Process(reader.ReadToEnd()));
        }
    }
}
```

The implementation performs two main steps: assign the streams and manipulate the streams. In the computing world, streams are wonderful things, because they are a generic concept like string buffers. A stream could be a text file, console input, or even a network connection. A stream can be text-based or binary-based, with or without a formatted protocol. Thus, when processing a stream, you don't work specifically with the console or a file, but use interfaces like System.IO.TextReader and System.IO.TextWriter.

Assigning the console streams involves assigning the data members In and Out to TextReader and TextWriter, respectively. The code that calls the processor.Process() method sends a stream to the processor and awaits a response that is sent as another stream.

Knowing that TextReader and TextWriter are general interfaces, or technically abstract base classes, you could be tempted to redesign the IProcessor interface as follows:

```
namespace ReaderWriter {
    public interface IProcessor {
        void Process(TextReader input, TextWriter output);
    }
}
```

There is nothing wrong with this declaration of IProcessor, but I would not be tempted to use it because it relies on the interfaces TextReader and TextWriter. In the case of our example, that is acceptable, and you might find that it is good enough for your application. But I like to keep things general and then be more specific when necessary. Later in this chapter, when we work with binary data streams, we will need to be specific and will use an interface declaration similar to the one shown here.

■**Note** As a general rule of thumb, it is always easy to write specific code because you have easy access to the methods and properties you need. It is harder from a design perspective to keep things general. The advantage of keeping things general is your code is more flexible and can be used in multiple contexts. However, you shouldn't make it a hard rule that all code will be general. The rule of thumb is to try to stay as general as possible using interfaces and have the implementation define the specifics.

Having implemented all of the pieces, you could compile the source code and run the command to read piped data. The only thing missing is the file that contains the data, lotto.txt. For the example, create a file called lotto.txt and add text such as the following, where each line represents the date of the lottery draw, then the six lottery numbers, and then the bonus number (you could also use the lotto.txt file included with this book's downloadable code).

```
1970.01.10 7 8 12 17 32 40 24
1970.01.17 7 12 22 24 29 40 36
1970.01.24 16 22 25 27 30 35 24
1970.01.31 3 11 21 22 24 39 8
1970.02.07 2 5 11 16 18 38 37
```

Now run the piping command:

```
type lotto.txt | TextProcessor.exe
```

You should see the contents of lotto.txt. If that is what you get, you have a successful round-trip and have created all of the puzzle pieces.

REMEMBERING TO IMPLEMENT ALL THE PIECES

Some readers may argue that having an echo implemented in LottoTicketProcessor is the wrong approach because there might be a communication failure among team members, leading to buggy code. Also, you might miss implementing some code, creating bugs when there should not have been any. Although those risks are involved, this approach has important benefits, and there are ways to mitigate the risks.

One of the challenges of C# developers is knowing not only the language, but also the .NET API. This book will not talk about the API because you could die of old age before you read everything there is to know about the .NET API.

The .NET API is vast, but you will not need to use all of the API all the time. What you need to be aware of are the general classes of the API. What part of the API is used to read and write streams? What part of the API is used to create GUI elements? This means you are not going to ever be an expert on all parts of the API, although you might be an expert C# programmer and understand the general concepts.

When I understand a domain quite well, I develop using a bottom-up approach. This works because I know which interface and implementation need to talk to which other interface and implementation. When I don't understand a domain fully, I develop using a top-down approach. Using a top-down approach, I can figure out what the pieces are in a simplified manner. I create my echo program, which gives a complete round-trip without getting bogged down in the details of the API.

Think of a bunch of guys putting together a barbecue grill. They might look at the instructions, but more likely, they will look at the parts and try to mentally fit the pieces together. They might even put a couple of pieces together to get an idea of what each piece does and how the overall grill should appear. Once they become confident of their prototype, they build the real thing, which hopefully resembles a barbecue grill.

When you use this approach, what you are doing is building a *mockup*, *proof of concept*, or *prototype*. Maybe two or three team members might help develop this prototype, but the fact that your code needs to be declared as a prototype is extremely important.

Visual C# Express and the Visual Studio products help you in that they allow you to embed task markers. Go back to the source code example where `LottoTicketProcessor` was illustrated and look at the comment:

```
// TODO: Finish implementing the class
```

Notice TODO is in all capital letters. That type of comment is special. It is called a *task* and is tracked by Visual C# Express in the Task List window. To open comments in the Task List window, select View ➤ Task List, and then select Comments from the drop-down list at the top of the window.

This allows a team of developers to add markers throughout the entire code base, indicating what is done and not done. That way, you will not forget to do certain tasks.

Some other identifiers that you can use are HACK to identify some code that is not correct, but hacked in so that it works, and UNDONE. If you happen to be using a Visual Studio edition other than Express, you can define your own comment identifiers. For more information, see the MSDN article "Visual Studio How to: Create Custom Comment Tokens" (http://msdn2.microsoft.com/en-US/library/ekwz6akh(VS.80).aspx).

Implementing Stream Reading and Writing

Finishing the stream reading and writing means looking at the possible arguments that can be given, and then implementing the code to process the arguments. Here is the complete source code:

```
#define DEBUG_OUTPUT
using System;
using System.Text;
using System.IO;

namespace ReaderWriter {
    public static class Bootstrap {
        public static void DisplayHelp() {
            Console.WriteLine("You need help? Right now?");
        }
```

```csharp
        public static void Process(string[] args, IProcessor processor) {
            TextReader reader = null;
            TextWriter writer = null;
            if (args.Length == 0) {
                reader = Console.In;
                writer = Console.Out;
            }
            else if (args.Length == 1) {
                if(args[0] == "-help") {
                    DisplayHelp();
                    return;
                }
                else {
                    reader = File.OpenText(args[0]);
                    writer = Console.Out;
                }
            }
            else if (args.Length == 2) {
                if (args[0] == "-out") {
                    reader = Console.In;
                    writer = File.CreateText(args[1]);
                }
                else {
                    DisplayHelp();
                    return;
                }
            }
            else if (args.Length == 3) {
                if (args[0] == "-out") {
                    reader = File.OpenText(args[2]);
                    writer = File.CreateText(args[1]);
                }
                else {
                    DisplayHelp();
                    return;
                }
            }
            else {
                DisplayHelp();
                return;
            }
            writer.Write(processor.Process(reader.ReadToEnd()));
#if DEBUG_OUTPUT
            Console.WriteLine("Argument count(" + args.Length + ")");
            foreach(string argument in args) {
                Console.WriteLine("Argument (" + argument + ")");
            }
```

```
#endif
        }
    }
}
```

In the code, before the first if block, the variables reader and writer are assigned to null, indicating that there is a reader and there is writer, but we don't know whether they will reference streams or files. Then the if blocks go through the different combinations and variations of the command-line arguments (see Table 10-1).

The code follows a truth table approach, which could be considered following a set of conditions and then acting on the conditions. For example, a state could be defined as If A = X, and B != Y then do C. To process the command-line arguments, we define all of the possible states and then all of the possible resulting actions.

■**Note** By going through each and every variation of the command-line arguments in a sequential manner, I am ensuring that I am testing for each situation. When running various tests and then acting on the tests, you need to be explicit and redundant, because the code is easier to follow. All too often, programmers take shortcuts and try to optimize on truth tables, and thus miss a particular test, causing a bug that is extremely hard to track down.

The first if block tests if the argument count is zero, then the second tests if there is a single argument, and so on. Let's look at the first test:

```
if (args.Length == 0) {
    reader = Console.In;
    writer = Console.Out;
}
```

Here, the source and destination of the lottery number data stream are the console input and output streams. The code assigns the reader and writer variables.

If the command line had no arguments or if one of the command-line argument tests has been verified, the IProcessor implementation is called:

```
writer.Write(processor.Process(reader.ReadToEnd()));
```

The code directly executes writer.Write(), processor.Process(), and reader.ReadToEnd(). There is no verification of whether writer, processor, or reader point to actual object instances. There could be a case for adding code that verifies if processor references an actual object instance, but there is absolutely no point to adding code to verify if writer and reader reference actual object instances. Doing so would imply that your truth test block is incomplete and you have not thought through all the permutations that assign writer and reader.

Let's look at the next truth test, which indicates that there is one command-line argument. When there is one command-line argument, you need to verify which of the two command-line variations it is:

```
TestProcessor.exe -help
```

or:

```
TestProcessor.exe lotto.txt
```

The first variation has an explicit command-line parameter -help. The second variation is the identifier of a file that contains the input data. Thus, the second if block contains another if block to test another aspect of the truth test:

```
else if (args.Length == 1) {
    if(args[0] == "-help") {
        DisplayHelp();
        return;
    }
    else {
        reader = File.OpenText(args[0]);
        writer = Console.Out;
    }
}
```

When testing for the -help argument, immediately after calling DisplayHelp(), you must use the return keyword. This is extremely important because, when the console application calls DisplayHelp(), it is saying, "I don't care where the input or output data is coming from since I am doing something else and thus must stop processing." If you were to continue processing, the writer and reader could reference invalid states and cause an exception to be generated.

If all tests have been tried and failed, then the final else calls the method DisplayHelp() to indicate that the command line is incorrect, and the help shows the correct command line.

Doing a complete test and debug of the console application is difficult because of the streaming facilities. When you stream data from one process to another, a process is started and stopped without an easy way for the debugger to jump in between. Thus, to be able to debug and verify if everything works, another strategy is needed. The solution is to use preprocessor directives (discussed in Chapter 6), like the following.

```
#if DEBUG_OUTPUT
            Console.WriteLine("Argument count(" + args.Length + ")");
            foreach( string argument in args) {
                Console.WriteLine( "Argument (" + argument + ")");
            }
#endif
```

The directive code is executed if DEBUG_OUTPUT is defined. In the example, the argument count and arguments are output to the console. To activate the directive, the item DEBUG_OUTPUT is defined at the project level or on the first line of the source code file.

The shell is complete, and all that remains is the implementation of the text processor.

USING TRUTH TABLES

A truth table is a construct that people use to figure out if all combinations and permutations have been processed in the code. For example, say you have two inputs—A and B—and you want to formally describe the previous relationships. Here is a truth table that describes the relationships in terms of truths:

A	B	Result
A = X (T)	B = Y (T)	F
A = X (T)	C = Z (T)	G

The truth table is incomplete because what you have described is whenever something is true, and not when it is false. By missing the false conditions, you are putting your code into an unknown state. Here is a complete truth table:

A	B	Result
A = X (T)	B = Y (T)	F
A = X (T)	C = Z (T)	G
A = X (F)	B = Y (T)	?
A = X (F)	C = Z (T)	?
A = X (T)	B = Y (F)	?
A = X (T)	C = Z (F)	?
A = X (F)	B = Y (F)	?
A = X (F)	C = Z (F)	?

The truth table has gone through all of the permutations of the `if` statement, and you need to determine what action to take when one of the permutation results represented with a question mark occurs.

Whenever you have complicated logic, you should create a truth table. After you gain some experience, you can create the truth table directly in code. For now, you can write it out on a piece of paper, and then implement the code.

The truth table approach incurs redundancies because parts of truth table are identical to other parts of truth table. For example, if you had one test defined as `if A = X and B = Y then do F` and another defined as `if A = X and C = Z then do G`, you could optimize by sharing the test `A = X` between the two states. However, I would advise against that, because then you are breaking the distinctness of each test. I typically leave in the redundancies.

Implementing the TextProcessor Application

In implementing the text processor, the problem that confronts us is how to fix a data stream so that it is consistent. The main reasons for data inconsistencies are human error and carelessness.

Figure 10-3 shows what is displayed when you load the lottery text file in Notepad. It seems very obvious that something is not right with this file.

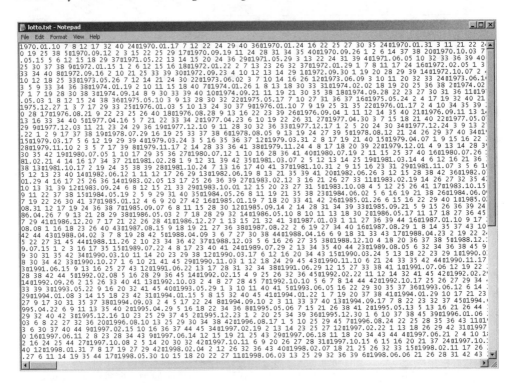

Figure 10-3. *The lottery text file loaded in Notepad*

However, what appears wrong in the Notepad display is not the real problem. When the text file is loaded using another text editor, such as Vim, the text is displayed as shown in Figure 10-4. As you can see, Vim has loaded the text file without any formatting errors.

■**Note** VIM is available from `http://www.vim.org`. It is a vi-derived clone that can be used on Windows systems.

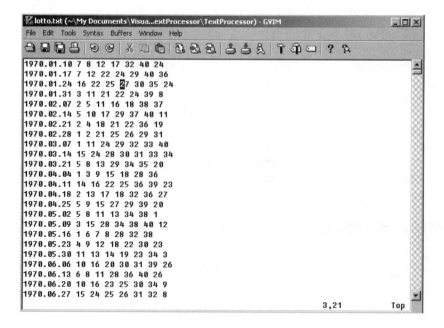

Figure 10-4. *Vim loads the text file in a nicely formatted display.*

The real pressing problem lies in the structure of the data, which is illustrated in Figure 10-5. Here, the data has new formatting, with extra columns, and the first column is not in the proper data format. And to make matters worse, the badly formatted data has repeating information.

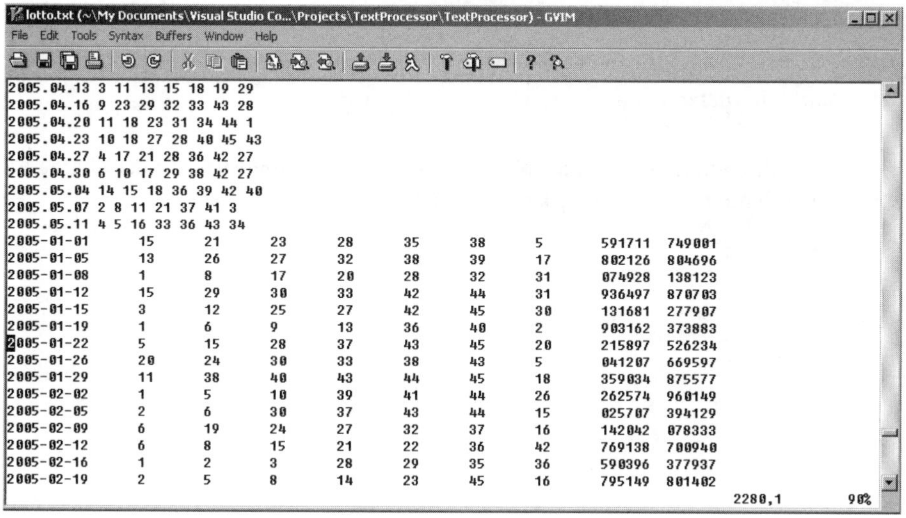

Figure 10-5. *Structural problems of this data stream*

The challenge of the application is to read the stream and fix all of the problems. This requires a thorough understanding of string processing and the different ways that text can be stored, as discussed in Chapter 3. When you are processing data streams, you need to be aware of the format of the data stream. In this example, we are processing ASCII text, and thus will be manipulating bits according to the rules of the ASCII lookup table.

Whitespace characters are special characters in the text lookup table. They are associated with numbers, but their representation is in the form of an action that the user can see. For example, the character between single quotation marks (' ') is a space, the character \t is a tab, and the character \n is a newline. The reason Notepad does not format the lottery text file nicely (Figure 10-3) is because of the whitespace characters used to indicate a newline. In Figure 10-6, the highlighted buffer entry 0A is the hexadecimal character that indicates a line-feed, or newline, in the lottery text file.

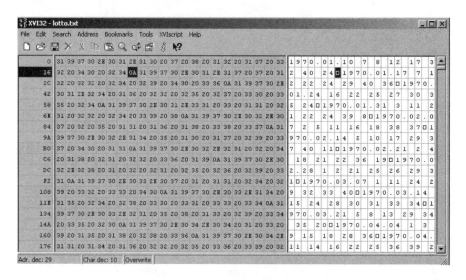

Figure 10-6. *Newline character used in lotto.txt*

Figure 10-7 is a file created by Notepad. Notepad expects not a single whitespace character, but two whitespace characters to indicate a newline: 0D and 0A.

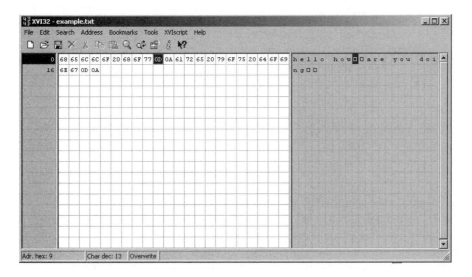

Figure 10-7. *Newline characters used by Notepad*

Deciphering the Format

The echo has served its purpose of providing a way to develop an application in a top-down manner. The next step is to remove the echo code and start writing the code that will fix the data stream.

Fixing the data stream is not a trivial undertaking, because you are yet again faced with a state problem. You don't want to fix one part of the stream, only to end up with a problem in another part of the stream. Thus, you need to incrementally fix the stream and make sure at each step that there are no ramifications.

The first step is to break the data stream into individual fields (each value in a column is a field in this case). In Figure 10-5, the data stream had two parts, where the upper part seemed to have a single space between the numbers and the lower part had the amount of space necessary to align the numbers. The difference between the upper and lower parts is the whitespace characters used. So, the first step will be to clean up the whitespace.

The following is the code that reads the buffer, splits it up, and reassembles the content into a new buffer. The code is intermediate code that adds special bracket markers to indicate what the text contains.

```
...
using System.IO;

namespace TextProcessor {
    // TODO: Fix up this class
    class LottoTicketProcessor : IProcessor {
        public string Process(string input) {
            TextReader reader = new StringReader(input);
            StringBuilder retval = new StringBuilder();
            while (reader.Peek() != -1) {
                string lineOfText = reader.ReadLine();
```

```
            string[] splitUpText =
                lineOfText.Split(new char[] { ' ', '\t' });
            foreach (string item in splitUpText) {
                retval.Append("(" + item + ")");
            }
            retval.Append("\n");
        }
        return retval.ToString();
    }
}
}
```

In the implementation of Process(), the text will be parsed line by line. Then each line is split into the individual fields. You could write the parsing routines yourself, but to parse a buffer line by line, it is more efficient to use StringReader. StringReader accepts the string to parse and is then assigned to a TextReader interface instance.

As each line of text is parsed, the most efficient approach to building a buffer is to use StringBuilder. You could use the += operation available with each string, but if you use that operation too often, the application's performance will suffer. This is because keeping track of memory becomes a bottleneck, and also because of the large number of object reference identifiers.

The string type is an immutable type, which means once an object is initialized, you cannot change the state of the object. The advantage of immutable types is that they increase the speed of your application, because code can assume once an object has been assigned, it will never change. The downside is that once an object is assigned, to modify the object state even slightly, you must instantiate a new object, which would be the case if we used the += operator. The StringBuilder type is like string, except the referenced text can be modified.

In the Process() implementation, the while loop calls the method Peek(), which reads, but does not remove, a character value from the stream. If there is nothing more to read, a -1 value is returned. Otherwise, data is available, and the method ReadLine() can be called. ReadLine() will read a buffer of characters until a newline or return character is encountered (\n or \r, respectively). Having read a line of text, it is assigned to lineOfText. Then using the Split() method, the line of text is split into the individual fields. The split characters are the space and tab character (\t).

When the Split() method returns, the individual fields are assigned to the array splitUpText. Those array elements are iterated and appended to the StringBuilder variable retval, but each element is surrounded by a set of brackets. The brackets provide a set of boundaries that you can inspect to see what data has been found. I include the brackets purely for debugging purposes. Because I am trying to reformat the stream, I append a newline character (\n) to the variable retval.

When all of the lines of text and fields within the lines of text are iterated, a string representation of the StringBuilder instance is returned using the ToString() method. Running the code shows how many fields each line of text has and how you should format the text file. This gives you an understanding of how the file is structured.

The following is sample output from the lotto.txt file.

```
(2000.01.15)(6)(10)(25)(26)(38)(42)(20)
(2000.01.19)(2)(16)(18)(23)(32)(43)(26)
(2000.01.22)(4)(5)(6)(24)(34)(38)(9)
(2000.01.26)(3)(20)(22)(24)(34)(39)(9)
(2000.01.29)(7)(12)(13)(34)(38)(39)(28)
(2000.02.02)(1)(18)(22)(28)(35)(43)(32)
(2000.02.05)(4)(13)(15)(31)(32)(45)(37)
(2000.02.09)(1)(29)(31)(34)(39)(41)(25)
...
(2006-12-27)(11)(13)(17)(21)(24)(26)(38)(578199)(735993)()()
(2006-12-30)(3)(13)(22)(30)(35)(41)(34)(142968)(472679)()
()
()
()
(2007-01-03)(5)(24)(37)(39)(41)(44)(9)(049802)(133875)()()
(2007-01-06)(3)(7)(23)(27)(30)(32)(38)(687442)(874814)()()
(2007-01-10)(7)(9)(13)(23)(35)(37)(25)(039498)(648301)()()
(2007-01-13)(3)(17)(22)(37)(39)(43)(34)(968842)(162860)()()
(2007-01-17)(12)(16)(27)(33)(37)(41)(24)(663824)(765917)()()
```

The sample output shows that we have the following items to fix:

- There are empty lines of text where no data has been defined.

- Some lines of text have empty fields at the end.

- Some fields have an incorrect date format.

- Some dates have duplicates, which need to be removed.

- Some lines of text have too many fields. We need to figure out which fields we want to keep and which we can discard.

■**Note** When processing streams and cleaning them up, it is important to take the stream apart first and see what you are up against. Do not make assumptions until you have looked at the individual pieces of data. Then you will be able to determine the steps you need to undertake to fix the stream.

Fixing the Stream

The final solution uses the same code used to parse the lines of text and individual fields, as follows:

```
IList<string> _dates = new List<string>();
...
public string Process(string input) {
    TextReader reader = new StringReader(input);
```

```
        StringBuilder retval = new StringBuilder();
        while (reader.Peek() != -1) {
            string lineOfText = reader.ReadLine();
            string[] splitUpText = lineOfText.Split(new char[] {' ', '\t' });
            if(_dates.Contains(splitUpText[0])) {
                continue;
            }
            if (splitUpText[0].Length == 0) {
                continue;
            }
            if (splitUpText[0].Contains("-")) {
                string[] dateSplit = splitUpText[0].Split('-');
                string newDate =
                    dateSplit[0] + "." + dateSplit[1] + "." + dateSplit[2];
                if (_dates.Contains(newDate)) {
                    continue;
                }
                _dates.Add(newDate);
                retval.Append(newDate);
                for (int c1 = 1; c1 < 8; c1++) {
                    retval.Append(" " + splitUpText[c1]);
                }
            }
            else {
                _dates.Add(splitUpText[0]);
                retval.Append(lineOfText);
            }
            retval.Append("\n");
        }
        return retval.ToString();
    }
}
```

■**Note** In the downloadable source code, the individual steps taken to clean up the data stream are demonstrated. For reference, the intermediate development steps in the source code are called Process01() through
Process05().

Let's review how this code fixes the five problems we discovered.

Empty Lines of Text

The following code removes the empty lines of text.

```
        if (splitUpText[0].Length == 0) {
            continue;
        }
```

When `lotto.txt` was processed, the output data stream generated a single field array for an empty line. So, we know that if the first field element has a length of zero, the line of text should be ignored.

Empty Fields and Too Many Fields

The next problem in our list is that some lines have empty text fields at the end. Solving this problem would probably entail a solution similar to the previous one, but you should think of the big picture and understand that solving one problem might also solve another problem. In this case, solving the problem of the empty fields also helps solve the problem of having too many fields.

Both of these problems are solved by knowing the data that is being manipulated. The data stream assumes the following format: date, then lottery numbers 1 to 6, and then the bonus number. The parts of the data stream that are not correct have the same format, with some extra information like replay number and empty fields. Thus, the fix is to copy the date and append the remaining fields, as follows:

```
retval.Append(newDate);
for (int c1 = 1; c1 < 8; c1++) {
    retval.Append(" " + splitUpText[c1]);
}
```

The first line of code appends the date to the `StringBuilder` buffer (`retval`). Then in the `for` loop that follows, a space and the fields 1 to 7 are copied to the `StringBuilder` buffer.

Incorrect Data Format

In some of the fields, the date has a period separator; in others, it has a hyphen. The correct format is a period, and the code that fixes the date format is as follows:

```
if (splitUpText[0].Contains("-")) {
    string[] dateSplit = splitUpText[0].Split('-');
    string newDate =
        dateSplit[0] + "." + dateSplit[1] + "." + dateSplit[2];
```

A fix is needed if the first field contains a hyphen. The `if` statement tests for this using the `Contains()` method. If a fix is needed, the first field is separated again into three subfields, where each subfield represents a part of the date (month, year, day). Then those three subfields are recombined and separated using the period and assigned to the variable `newDate`.

Duplicate Dates

The last problem that needs to be solved is having duplicate dates in the data stream. The following code fixes this problem (the duplicate date code is bolded).

```
if(_dates.Contains(splitUpText[0])) {
    continue;
}
if (splitUpText[0].Length == 0) {
    continue;
}
```

```
        if (splitUpText[0].Contains("-")) {
            string[] dateSplit = splitUpText[0].Split('-');
            string newDate =
                dateSplit[0] + "." + dateSplit[1] + "." + dateSplit[2];
            if (_dates.Contains(newDate)) {
                continue;
            }
            _dates.Add(newDate);
            retval.Append(newDate);
            for (int c1 = 1; c1 < 8; c1++) {
                retval.Append(" " + splitUpText[c1]);
            }
        }
        else {
            _dates.Add(splitUpText[0]);
            retval.Append(lineOfText);
        }
```

Of all the problems we needed to solve, this is the trickiest, because it required multiple pieces of code in multiple places. The code processes the data stream and keeps a list of dates. A date is added to the list only if the date does not exist in the list, which is checked using the Contains() method. The .NET lists expose this method to verify if the object being passed to it equals one of the list members. The way that most lists implement the method is to iterate each method and call the Equals() method. The catch is that if you declare a custom type, the Equals() method defaults to verifying if one reference value equals another. You would need to implement a custom Equals() method.

■**Note** When you encounter situations where you need to write multiple pieces of code in multiple places, that is a sign that you are about to create code that is hard to maintain. You should take a close look at the code, and If possible, rewrite it. Of course, this depends on a lot of factors. So sometimes, you will need to just write the code, test it, and hope that it works.

With the final solution, the console application TextProcessor is complete. You could process lotto.txt and get a correctly formatted data stream.

Piping Binary Data

When working with the console, for the most part, you will be transferring text data from one process to another or from one file to another file. However, when developing in .NET, working with text is not always the best choice. A more efficient approach might be to store the data in a binary format.

The easiest way to understand the difference between text data and binary data is to open a binary file using a text editor, as shown in Figure 10-8.

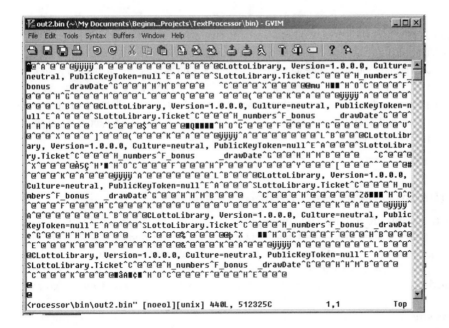

Figure 10-8. *A binary file in a text editor*

In Figure 10-8, you see just a bunch of funny characters with some text scattered throughout. A binary file is different from a text file in that the format of a binary file is whatever the program that reads and writes the binary data decides. The advantage of using a binary file is that you can create complex structures. The disadvantage is that only the developer of the reader/writer program knows what the file contains.

Binary files are not always smaller, but they are more efficient because you do not need to parse and process the data. For example, in the text-based lottery data stream reader, we needed to parse every single line and then split the line of text into individual fields, which were then parsed as integers and assigned to a variable. Using a binary file, you only need to create a binary type, and read or write that type.

In this section, we will continue with the example of the lottery-prediction application, but this time, create it as a console application that converts a text data stream into a binary data stream and then back to a text stream. You'll see how you can pipe the data from one stream to another by sending it from one application to another application. When we are finished building this application, the following command line will be valid.

```
type lotto.txt | TextProcessor.exe | Text2Binary.exe | Binary2Text.exe
```

The command line starts with generating a text data stream using the type command. The command TextProcessor.exe generates a clean data stream that is then piped into Text2Binary.exe, which generates a binary data stream. Finally, the binary data stream is converted back into a text stream using Binary2Text.exe, which displays the data on the console.

The architecture of TextProcessor with its implementation of the IProcessor interface and a general architecture of grabbing a file or console input/output stream worked. However, IProcessor is not usable for binary streams, so we need to implement a new interface and architecture.

> **Note** The examples that follow illustrate a very common situation where an architecture worked and the ideas of the architecture could be applied in the new context. What does not work is the actual implementation of the original architecture. You may be tempted to modify the working architecture so that it will work with the new context. As much as you would like to do that, don't. Often, the abstractions you create will complicate the architecture and make the resulting code more complex. Your challenge is to know when to generalize an architecture and when to keep the ideas of an architecture but create a new implementation, and you'll learn this with experience.

Defining the Interfaces and Implementing the Shell

In .NET, the data streams are split into two types of streams: binary and text. The TextWriter and TextReader types are used to read text-based data streams. As was demonstrated with the StringReader type, when dealing with text-based streams, certain assumptions can be made, such as being able to find new lines in the stream. With binary data streams, no such assumptions can be made. Binary streams have their own format, which is known by only the program doing the reading or writing.

The binary stream-based types can be used to process text data streams, but doing so would require knowing the details of the data stream. Remember that .NET gives you a text-handling system that understands the different Unicode code pages. A Unicode code page is a specific translation map. If you decide to manipulate the text streams using binary stream types, you are telling .NET that you will manage the details of the Unicode code pages. Of course, you don't want to do that, and thus should never mix data streams. So, for our sample application, we need to design two different interfaces: one to stream from text to binary and one to stream from binary to text.

> **Note** For more information about Unicode and other text-related issues, see the MSDN International Text Display section (http://msdn2.microsoft.com/en-us/library/ms776131.aspx).

The following is the binary-to-text data stream interface, IBinary2TextProcessor.

```
...
using System.IO;

namespace Binary2Text
{
    public interface IBinary2TextProcessor {
        void Process(Stream input, TextWriter output);
    }
}
```

The IBinary2TextProcessor interface has a single method, Process(), which has two parameters: the binary stream and the text stream. The implementation of

IBinary2TextProcessor would be responsible for reading the data from the binary stream and saving data to the text stream.

The text-to-binary interface, IText2BinaryProcessor, follows a similar interface design, except that the input and output stream types are reversed.

```
...
using System.IO;

namespace Text2Binary
{
    public interface IText2BinaryProcessor {
        void Process(TextReader input, Stream output);
    }
}
```

The idea of both interface declarations is to focus on transferring data from one stream to another.

The shell for both data stream interfaces is very similar to the shell of the text-processing stream, except that binary and text streams are involved. The TextProcessor shell was responsible for knowing if the data stream was from the console or from a file. When manipulating binary streams, the source still needs to be ascertained, but instead of creating text streams, binary streams are created. If you understand the mechanics of using a text stream, you will understand the mechanics of using a binary stream.

The following is the complete implementation of the text-to-binary bootstrap class (you need to add a reference to the Text2Binary project in the ReaderWriter project).

```
...
using System.IO;

using Text2Binary;

namespace ReaderWriter {
    public static class Text2BinaryBootstrap {
        public static void DisplayHelp() {
            Console.WriteLine("You need help? Right now?");
        }

        public static void Process(string[] args,
                                   IText2BinaryProcessor processor) {
            TextReader reader = null;
            Stream writer = null;
            if (args.Length == 0) {
                reader = Console.In;
                writer = Console.OpenStandardOutput();
            }
            else if (args.Length == 1) {
                if (args[0] == "-help") {
                    DisplayHelp();
                    return;
```

```
            }
            else {
                reader = File.OpenText(args[0]);
                writer = Console.OpenStandardOutput();
            }
        }
        else if (args.Length == 2) {
            if (args[0] == "-out") {
                reader = Console.In;
                writer = File.Open(args[1], FileMode.Create);
            }
            else {
                DisplayHelp();
                return;
            }
        }
        else if (args.Length == 3) {
            if (args[0] == "-out") {
                reader = File.OpenText(args[2]);
                writer = File.Open(args[1], FileMode.Create);
            }
            else {
                DisplayHelp();
                return;
            }
        }
        else {
            DisplayHelp();
            return;
        }
        processor.Process(reader, writer);
        writer.Close();
#if DEBUG_OUTPUT
        Console.WriteLine("Argument count(" + args.Length + ")");
        foreach( string argument in args) {
            Console.WriteLine("Argument (" + argument + ")");
        }
#endif
    }
  }
}
```

The implementation is nearly identical to the Bootstrap class; the differences are bolded. Notice that instead of using the predefined Console.Out data member, the OpenStandardOutput() method is called, and instead of File.CreateText(), the File.Open() method is called.

The implementation of the binary-to-text stream shell is nearly identical to the one for the text-to-binary stream shell. You can find it in this book's downloadable source code.

Defining the Type

The central piece when converting from a text stream to a binary stream or vice versa is the definition of a type. The type might be a class or a struct, and it is identified as being a type that can be read and written. Identifying a type to be read and written is necessary so that when .NET reads or writes the type, the underlying infrastructure knows what to do. Remember that a binary data stream is a data stream where only the program knows what it means. To help .NET read and write those types, you add identifiers that tell .NET what to do. Fortunately, you don't need to know the inner details of binary serialization, but just give .NET an indication of how to manage it.

For the lottery-prediction example, we will define a type that represents a lottery ticket. The lottery ticket will contain the draw date, numbers, and bonus number. Following is the complete declaration.

```
namespace LottoLibrary {
    [Serializable]
    public class Ticket {
        int[] _numbers;
        int _bonus;
        DateTime _drawDate;

        public Ticket() { }
        public Ticket(DateTime drawDate, int[] numbers, int bonus) {
            _drawDate = drawDate;
            _numbers = numbers;
            _bonus = bonus;
        }
        public DateTime DrawDate {
            get {
                return _drawDate;
            }
            set {
                _drawDate = value;
            }
        }
        public int[] Numbers {
            get {
                return _numbers;
            }
            set {
                _numbers = value;
            }
        }
        public int Bonus {
            get {
                return _bonus;
            }
            set {
```

```
                    _bonus = value;
                }
            }
        }
}
```

Ticket is plain-vanilla data class. However, the bolded parts deserve an explanation. The first bolded part is a set of square brackets surrounding the identifier Serializable, which represents a .NET *attribute*. In .NET, you have the ability to describe types, methods, and so on. Attributes are descriptions that are used in a particular context. As opposed to the identifiers public and abstract, which are descriptions that fundamentally describe how a type will behave, the Serializable attribute describes the behavior of a type in a specific context—when the object is to be converted from memory to a data stream and vice versa. Fundamental descriptions are important to the .NET runtime, whereas .NET attributes are generally not important to the runtime, but important to libraries that the runtime will execute.

The Serializable attribute describes the ability to serialize the type as it is declared. When Ticket is converted into a binary stream, the programmer does not need to do anything other than pass an instance to the data stream. The data stream libraries handle all of the other details.

In the declaration of Ticket, the parameterless constructor has been bolded to emphasize that this type of constructor is necessary when converting a data stream into an object instance. When binary streams restore types, they instantiate an empty object and then assign the data members. Thus, when an object is created, a parameterless constructor is needed.

Converting a Text Stream into a Binary Stream

To convert the stream from text to binary involves breaking apart the text stream, instantiating a Ticket instance, assigning the data members, and saving the instance to the binary stream. All of these steps are performed in the following source code (you'll need a reference to LottoLibrary in Text2Binary).

```
...
using System.IO;
using System.Runtime.Serialization.Formatters.Binary;

namespace Text2Binary {
    class LottoTicketProcessor : IText2BinaryProcessor {
        public void Process(TextReader reader, Stream writer) {
            StringBuilder retval = new StringBuilder();
            while (reader.Peek() != -1) {
                string lineOfText = reader.ReadLine();
                string[] splitUpText = lineOfText.Split(new char[] { ' ' });
                string[] dateSplit = splitUpText[0].Split('.');

                LottoLibrary.Ticket ticket =
                    new LottoLibrary.Ticket(
                        new DateTime(
                            int.Parse(dateSplit[0]),
                            int.Parse(dateSplit[1]),
```

```
                                int.Parse(dateSplit[2])),
                    new int[] {
                                int.Parse(splitUpText[1]),
                                int.Parse(splitUpText[2]),
                                int.Parse(splitUpText[3]),
                                int.Parse(splitUpText[4]),
                                int.Parse(splitUpText[5]),
                                int.Parse(splitUpText[6]) },
                                int.Parse(splitUpText[7]));

            BinaryFormatter formatter = new BinaryFormatter();

            formatter.Serialize(writer, ticket);
        }
      }
    }
}
```

The code splits the text stream by reading a line of text and then splitting apart the fields. The split-apart fields are then converted into numbers by using the int.Parse() method. This process of splitting and conversion is called *marshaling* data. Marshaling is a technical term that means to convert a type from one medium to another.

We manage the text marshaling, but .NET manages the binary marshaling, which is still there behind the scenes. The System.Runtime.Serialization.Formatters.Binary.BinaryFormatter type manages marshaling of the Ticket instance to the binary stream. The Serializable attribute is used by the BinaryFormatter as an indicator of what to marshal to the binary stream. In essence, converting from a text stream to a binary stream means to marshal a text-defined ticket into a .NET-defined ticket, and that is then marshaled into a binary-defined ticket. In each of the three media, a ticket representation is managed.

Converting a Binary Stream into a Text Stream

Converting a binary stream into a text stream involves using the .NET-provided formatter to create a Ticket instance that is then converted into text. The following is the complete source code (you'll need a reference to LottoLibrary in Binary2Text).

```
...
using System.IO;
using System.Runtime.Serialization.Formatters.Binary;

namespace Binary2Text {
    class LottoTicketProcessor : IBinary2TextProcessor {
        public void Process(Stream input, TextWriter output) {
            StringBuilder builder = new StringBuilder();
            try {
                while (true) {
                    BinaryFormatter formatter = new BinaryFormatter();
```

```
            LottoLibrary.Ticket ticket =
                (LottoLibrary.Ticket)formatter.Deserialize(input);

            builder.AppendFormat(
                "{0}.{1}.{2} {3} {4} {5} {6} {7} {8} {9}\n",
                ticket.DrawDate.Year,
                ticket.DrawDate.Month,
                ticket.DrawDate.Day,
                ticket.Numbers[0],
                ticket.Numbers[1],
                ticket.Numbers[2],
                ticket.Numbers[3],
                ticket.Numbers[4],
                ticket.Numbers[5],
                ticket.Bonus);
        }
    }
    catch (Exception e) {
    }
    output.Write(builder.ToString());
        }
    }
}
```

In the code, a binary stream is read using the BinaryFormatter class, which reads a type from the data stream. Notice how the method Deserialize() does not ask for which type to read. This is because all of that information is saved in the stream. Deserialize() will read an object, associate the object with a type, instantiate it, and populate the data members.

The bolded code in the preceding listing points out where deserialization becomes tricky, which centers around when to read what type. A binary stream when processed by the BinaryFormatter will read and write objects. BinaryFormatter will instantiate whatever it encounters and assumes that the caller of BinaryFormatter knows which type is being manipulated. If the caller does not know this, an exception will occur because the type cast to the specific type will fail.

The exception block is necessary because you don't know how many Ticket objects have been saved, as the count has not been saved to the stream. .NET provides the Position and Length properties to determine if any instances are left to be read, but those properties work only with files. If the binary stream being read is a console data stream, there is no length or position. Thus, the only real solution is to keep reading until you can't do so anymore and assume processing is complete.

INTENTION AND IMPLEMENTATION

The fact that `Position` and `Length` have different behaviors depending on the implementation might seem to break the contract of being able to separate intention from implementation. It seems to break the component software paradigm because, as a developer, you do need to know about the stream implementation. The rule has not been broken, but been put on hold, because sometimes you are left with no other option. A file stream and console stream share many characteristics, but knowing the length is not one of them. A programmer could force the console stream to give back some value, but that would be incorrect. The smarter approach, and the one chosen by the .NET implementers, is to generate an exception.

The binary stream formatter can become even pickier. Look at Figure 10-8 again and notice how the type information with version identifiers is stored in the stream. Imagine the situation where you create an assembly that saves some objects. Then *x* years and *n* versions of the program later, you try to load the file. You can't, because the version of the type does not exist. It is smart for the binary formatter to not instantiate a version of a type that does not exist, because otherwise there could be serialization failures.

Tweaking Serialization

When dealing with serialization, you may come across a particular text or binary format that will require some extra work. Also, you may have some objects that you want to exclude from serialization.

Performing Custom Serialization

Sometimes I think there are as many file formats as there are grains of sand on a beach. As just two examples, specializations of text formats are XML and JSON (for JavaScript Object Notation, used in JavaScript for your web browser). In most cases, the default serializations will work. However, you may need to tweak a particular serialization.

Many serialization techniques allow custom serializations of a particular object. The default serialization implies a certain marshaling. For example, it might mean an integer will be marshaled as an integer in another representation. Sometimes, however, you might want different representations in different streams. In that case, you need to implement the marshaling of the data member yourself. With most serialization platforms, it means implementing a particular interface.

Following is an example that performs a custom serialization for a .NET binary stream.

```
[Serializable]
class MyObject : ISerializable {
    int value;

    public MyObject() { }
    public MyObject(SerializationInfo info, StreamingContext context) {
        size = int.Parse(info.GetValue("value", typeof(string)));
    }
    public void GetObjectData(SerializationInfo info,
                             StreamingContext context) {
        info.AddValue("value", value.ToString());
    }
}
```

In the example, the interface System.Runtime.Serialization.ISerializable is implemented. This means when BinaryFormatter serializes or deserializes, MyObject BinaryFormatter will not manipulate the binary stream, but delegate the manipulation to MyObject. With many serialization platforms, there is an explicit method, property, or flag to indicate whether MyObject is being written to the stream or read from the stream. In the case of binary serialization, when an object is written to the stream, the GetObjectData() method is called, and when the object is being read from the stream, the constructor MyObject() is called.

Serialization involves two directions, and a developer must implement both, in the same way. In the example, the AddValue() method is called, indicating that the data member is written as a string, and when reading, the value data member must be read as a string.

■Note One of the biggest challenges with serialization is that each and every serialization platform seems to have its own way of doing things. Sometimes there will be common methods and attributes, but other times they will not exist. A universal approach to serialization won't work. You should avoid performing custom serialization whenever possible. Most serialization platforms are smart enough to know what to do with each data member. So the best approach is to let the platform figure things out.

Declaring a Data Member as Nonserializable

In the example of the Ticket type, all of the data members were serialized. However, sometimes that is not desired. Suppose an object that you want to serialize has a network connection. When the object is serialized, the network connection will also be serialized, which is not appropriate. It is not appropriate to serialize a network connection because that object is transient and applies only to the context of the object instance.

To mark an object as nonserializable, attributes are often used, as in the following example.

```
[Serializable]
class MyObject2 {
    [NonSerialized]
    private int _networkIdentifier;
}
```

In the example, _networkIdentifier will not be written or read from the data stream.

Separating Data Objects from Action Objects

Another solution to the serialization problem is to develop a number of data objects whose only role is to be used in serialization and data referencing. Such an approach is useful when using binary serialization, because you are then able to more effectively manage the version problem. The following is an example of how such an architecture would be realized.

```
[Serializable]
class MyObject2 {
}

class Doer {
```

```
    private MyObject2 _object;
    private int _networkIdentifier;
}
```

The class Doer has no serialization attribute and will not be serialized, but it references MyObject2. The network identifier data member has been moved from MyObject2 to Doer. The result is that MyObject2 contains nothing that is transient and implies the least interaction from the programmer.

■**Note** To keep things simple, my preferred approach to serialization is to separate the data objects from the action objects using a data member reference. It is not as object-oriented as other programming techniques, but when dealing with multiple data stream types, it is the simplest and least problematic to create a consistent and maintainable data stream.

Completing Custom Types

When writing custom types, two methods should always be implemented: Equals() and GetHashCode(). These two methods are used by the .NET library API when comparing and manipulating instances in a list or a collection. It just happened in this chapter's example that a list of string types did the right thing. If TextProcessor had used the Ticket type, then the Equals() method of the list used to find date duplicates would not have worked. The default implementations of Equals() and GetHashCode() are not implemented properly. This is no fault of the .NET API. Rather, it is a recognition that Microsoft cannot know the structure of an object and what is considered as making a type unique.

Implementing GetHashCode()

The MSDN documentation for Object.GetHashCode defines the GetHashCode() method as follows (http://msdn2.microsoft.com/en-us/library/system.object.gethashcode(vs.71).aspx):

> *This method can be overridden by a derived class. Value classes must override this method to provide a hash function that is appropriate for the class and that ensures a better distribution in the hash table. Classes that might be used as a key in a hash table must also override this method, because objects that are used as keys in a hash table are required to generate their own hash code through this method. However, if the objects that are used as keys do not provide a useful implementation of GetHashCode, you can provide a different hash code provider, that is based on the System.Collections.IHashCodeProvider interface, when the Hashtable is constructed.*

But what does this actually mean? The purpose of GetHashCode() is to uniquely (most of the time) identify the type in a collection of other types using a unique hashcode. Imagine creating a table of same-type instances. The situation occurs when you create a collection and store a bunch of instances in the collection. With the GetHashCode() method, you can generally separate each instance from each other. I say "generally" because GetHashCode() is an approximation. To verify if one object instance equals another, the Equals() method needs to be implemented.

Implementing a hashcode is best delegated to a helper class that does the heavy lifting. The book *Effective Java Programming Language Guide* by Joshua Bloch (Prentice-Hall, 2001) outlines a robust technique. Basically, you store some constant nonzero value, such as 17, in a variable. Then, for each data member of the type, perform a mathematical operation that results in int values that are successively multiplied and added, where the operation is specific to the type and defined as follows:

- *Bool*: If true return 0; otherwise return 1.

- *Byte, char, short, or int*: Return the value of the type.

- *Long*: Return (int)(f ^ (f >>> 32).

- *Float*: Return Convert.ToInt32 of the value.

- *Object*: Return the value generated by calling object.GetHashCode().

- *Array*: Iterate and treat each element individually.

The rules are implementing in a class called HashCodeAutomater. The following source code is an implementation in an abbreviated form:

```
public class HashCodeAutomater{
    private readonly int _constant;
    private int _runningTotal;

    public HashCodeAutomater() {
        _constant = 37;
        _runningTotal = 17;
    }

    public HashCodeAutomater AppendSuper(int superHashCode) {
        _runningTotal = _runningTotal * _runningTotal +
            superHashCode;
        return this;
    }

    public HashCodeAutomater Append(Object obj) {
        if (obj == null) {
            _runningTotal = _runningTotal * _constant;

        } else {
            if (obj.GetType().IsArray == false) {
                _runningTotal = _runningTotal * _runningTotal +
                    obj.GetHashCode();

            } else {
                if (obj is long[]) {
```

```
                    Append((long[]) obj);
                }
                // Other tests have been removed for clarity purposes
                else {
                    // Not an array of primitives
                    Append((Object[]) obj);
                }
            }
        }
        return this;
    }


    public HashCodeAutomater Append(long value) {
        _runningTotal = _runningTotal * _constant +
            ((int) (value ^ (value >> 32)));
        return this;
    }
    public HashCodeAutomater Append(long[] array) {
        if (array == null) {
            _runningTotal = _runningTotal * _constant;
        }
        else {
            for (int i = 0; i < array.Length; i++) {
                Append(array[i]);
            }
        }
        return this;
    }
    public HashCodeAutomater Append(Object[] array) {
        if (array == null) {
            _runningTotal = _runningTotal * _constant;
        }
        else {
            for (int i = 0; i < array.Length; i++) {
                Append(array[i]);
            }
        }
        return this;
    }
    public int toHashCode() {
        return _runningTotal;
    }
}
```

The different implementations of the Append() method belong to a single grouping for a single data type, long. For example, there is an Append() method that accepts a long and a long array. The full implementation of HashCodeAutomater would have an Append() method for short and short array, and all of the other data types. There is no specific group implementation for the string type, because it is treated like an object that has its own hashcode calculation implementation.

Notice in the implementations of the Append() methods how a calculation is performed and then added to the data member _runningTotal. The return value is a this reference, so that the methods can be chained together. This allows a client to use the HashCodeAutomater class, as the following GetHashCode() implementation demonstrates:

```
class HashcodeExample {
    public int value;
    public string buffer;

    public HashcodeExample(int val, string buf) {
        value = val;
        buffer = buf;
    }
    public override int GetHashCode() {
        return new HashCodeAutomater()
            .Append(value)
            .Append(buffer).toHashCode();
    }
}
```

The implementation of HashcodeExample has two data members: value and buffer. The two data members make up the class's state. Not all data members are used when calculating a class instance's hashcode value. For example, if HashcodeExample had a data member that referenced a database connection, it should not be used when calculating the hashcode, because the database connection is the type used to get the state and does not influence the state—it is a means to an end.

Implementing Equals()

Once the GetHashCode() method has been implemented, the Equals() method can be implemented:

```
public override bool Equals(object obj) {
    if (obj is HashCodeExample) {
        return obj.GetHashCode() == this.GetHashCode();
    }
    else {
        return false;
    }
}
```

Because the rule for GetHashCode() is that two object instances with identical hashcode values must return the same value, it makes sense to implement Equals() using GetHashCode(). However, what started out as a good idea turns out to be a bad idea, as the following illustrates:

```
String s1 = "Hello";
String s2 = "World";
```

```
int x1 = 17 * 17 + s1.GetHashCode();
int x2 = 17 * 17 + s2.GetHashCode();

HashCodeExample h1 = new HashCodeExample (x2 * 37, s1);
HashCodeExample h2 = new HashCodeExample (x1  * 37, s2);

Hashtable ht = new Hashtable();
ht.Add(h1, null);
ht.Add(h2, null);
```

This shows that having two objects with completely different states results in the same hash-code value and generates an exception because Equals() has been implemented incorrectly. In the implementation of Hashtable, when an added object collides with another already existing object, an equality test is made. If the equality test returns true, then the exception is generated because Hashtable does not allow you to add an object with the same state as another object.

The solution is not to fix the GetHashCode() method, but rather to modify the Equals() method:

```
public override bool Equals(object obj) {
    if (obj is HashCodeExampleWorking) {
        if (obj.GetHashCode() != this.GetHashCode())
            return false;

        // todo
        // 1. comparing element by element
        // hard work, not universal
        HashCodeExampleWorking toTest = obj as HashCodeExampleWorking;
        if (toTest.val == this.val) {
            if( toTest.buf == this.buf) {
                return true;
            }
        }
        // or
        // 2. comparing with reflection
        // or
        // 3. comparing the results of ToString()
        // what if not overridden or should this standard practice
        // like GetHashCode and Equals
    }
    return false;
}
```

The logic of the modified Equals() method is to first test if both types are identical. If not, then false is returned. Next, test if GetHashCode() returns unequal values. GetHashCode() will always return different values for objects that have different data members. If the hashcode values are equal, then comes the hard work of individually testing each data member for equality. The hard work is delegated as the last step, because any object that reaches that point will probably be identical, but you need to be 100% certain.

The Important Stuff to Remember

In this chapter, you learned how to process a stream of data using the console. Here are the main items to remember:

- When data is moved from one medium to another, it is streamed.

- There are two major types of streams: text and binary.

- Text streams are universal and can be read by all computers.

- Binary streams are specific to the program and sometimes to the processor. Imagine the situation of having to decipher a C++ data stream generated by a PowerPC chip. Most likely, the numbers that you read will be wrong because of the way that Intel or AMD chips store their numbers. Generally speaking, with binary streams, you will be conversing with two .NET implementations. If not, use text streams.

- When streaming data, it is best to customize as little as possible. Doing so will complicate your program, and potentially introduce errors where none should exist.

- It is important that you understand the concept of marshaling and the fact that each medium will have a different representation of the type. A large part of your programming day will involve moving data from one stream to another.

Some Things for You to Do

Here are some exercises to apply what you learned in this chapter:

1. In the implementation of `TextProcessor`, the display help routine was not very helpful. Fix the implementation.

2. There were no testing routines for `TextProcessor`. Devise some realistic tests. By realistic tests, I mean tests that don't just focus on the class library and consider the application tested. Focus on complete application tests.

3. Having implemented the display help routine, think about whether or not the implementation is correct. The class `Bootstrap` is a general class that uses an `IProcessor` instance, which means that different console applications will process different data. Thus, writing a general help output might work, but it will not help in resolving problems. Fix the console application `TextProcessor` and `ReaderWriter` assembly so that the help message is both specific and general.

4. In the `Bootstrap` class, when the output was redirected to a file (as indicated by the `-output` argument), there was no check on whether or not the file exists. Extend the `Bootstrap` class to include an additional command-line argument that verifies if it is fine to overwrite the output file if it exists. If an output file does exist and there is no explicit overwriting, generate an error and stop processing.

5. The code in the final solution for `IProcessor.Process()` has been identified as being hard to maintain because the code to check for duplicate dates is scattered throughout the method. Rewrite the method implementation so that the code is logical and maintainable.

CHAPTER 11

■■■

Learning About .NET Generics

Chapter 9 explained how to use lists, delegates, and lambda expressions. In that chapter, you also saw an example of .NET generics when using lists to manage a collection of object instances.

The main focus of the chapter is .NET generics and how to use them in a black box context (the code doesn't know the specifics of the .NET generics parameter types). The secondary focus is a more detailed implementation of lambda expressions. To demonstrate these concepts, we'll expand on the spreadsheet example introduced in Chapter 9. The idea is to get you well versed in .NET generics and lambda expressions, which you will likely use in your own production code, so that that there will be no surprises in your projects.

Why Use .NET Generics?

Here's a surprise for you: there is no imperative need for .NET generics, so you could skip this chapter and read the next one, right? Wrong. I could just as easily have said there is no need for C# properties, nor any other C# construct that enriches your programming abilities. The reasons we have C# properties and .NET generics are programming elegance and expressiveness.

To understand what I am trying to get at, consider this sentence:

Ducks walk flat feet quack loud

Reading the sentence, you get an idea of what is being said, but you are not completely sure. C# without .NET generics is like this sentence, in that you express your ideas in code, but some things are not as clear as you would like.

C# with .NET generics is like this sentence:

Ducks walk in a funny manner due to their flat feet, and when they quack, it is very loud.

The sentence is clearer and uses more words to describe the same thing. The reason we talk using a more sophisticated language is that we want to explain concepts and be understood. If you accept that, then you can accept why there is a need and context for .NET generics. And if not, feel free to skip this chapter and read the next one.

An example that illustrates how using .NET generics makes your code clearer, as well as more concise, than code that does not use .NET generics is a container. A container is a type that is used to manage other types; lists and collections are examples of containers. To keep things simple, let's look at a container that manages a single reference. The following is the less concise version that uses the object type.

```
public class Container {
    object _managed;

    public Container(object toManage) {
        _managed = toManage;
    }

    public object Managed {
        get {
            return _managed;
        }
    }
}
```

In the code, the class Container has a constructor with a parameter and a single property, Managed, which references the variable _managed. The idea behind this class is to assign an object in the constructor that can be referenced using the property. The class Container does not know what the variable _managed does or its capabilities. Container does not care, because Container is acting like a basket that holds an instance of whatever is given to it.

The Container class could be used as follows:

```
Container container = new Container(new MyType());

(container.Managed as MyType).Method();
```

When Container is instantiated, the _managed data member is assigned an instance of MyType. MyType is a type that is used for illustrative purposes and has a single method, Method(). To retrieve and use the managed type, the property Managed is referenced. However, the method Method() cannot be called directly because the property Managed is of type object, and thus you need to type cast the property to type MyType so that the call to Method() is legal.

The type cast using the as operator will result in a valid instance of MyType or a null value, resulting in a null object reference exception. Here's a safe way of using the Managed property:

```
Container container = new Container(new MyType());

if (container.Managed is MyType) {
    (container.Managed as MyType).Method();
}
```

The bolded code is the addition of the if block to test whether the container references the type MyType. Not shown is what the code should do if the property Managed is not MyType. The fact that you need to verify that the container references the correct type, and you also need to think of an alternative plan if the type is incorrect, adds quite a bit of code. It's like that sentence about the duck—sure, you get the general idea of what is being said, but are you 100% sure of the meaning?

Now look at the following code, which implements a container using .NET generics.

```
public class GenericsContainer<ManagedType> {
    ManagedType _managed;

    public GenericsContainer(ManagedType toManage) {
        _managed = toManage;
    }

    public ManagedType Managed {
        get {
            return _managed;
        }
    }
}
```

You can write code that uses .NET generics and code that provides types based on .NET generics. The definition of GenericsContainer demonstrates code that provides types based on .NET generics. You'll see the code that uses .NET generics next.

.NET generics parameters are associated with types, such as classes and interfaces, or with methods. In the case of GenericsContainer, the .NET generics parameter ManagedType is a type.

■**Note** Commonly, developers use the notation of a single letter when defining a .NET generics parameter. I am not a fan of that notation, because it tells me nothing, especially when there are multiple parameters. I recommend using an identifier that describes what the parameter does, appended with the word Type, to indicate a .NET generics parameter is being defined.

With GenericsContainer, ManagedType is used as an identifier in the place of the identifier object in the type Container. This is a rule of thumb. Whenever you find yourself using an object generically to define a type, you probably could use .NET generics. Think of .NET generics types as general things.

The following code demonstrates how to use GenericsContainer with MyType.

```
GenericsContainer<MyType> container =
    new GenericsContainer<MyType>(new MyType());
container.Managed.Method();
```

When instantiating GenericsContainer, notice how the identifier ManagedType must be replaced with an identifier that represents an already existing type. This identifier replacement is called *concretizing* the .NET generics type, and results in a new and unique type. The advantage of .NET generics is that when you provide a concrete type, you don't need to check to make sure that everything is correct.

The .NET runtime will generate a type that has an intent similar to the following code.

```
public class GenericsContainerMyType {
    MyType _managed;
```

```
public GenericsContainer(MyType toManage) {
    _managed = toManage;
}

public MyType Managed {
    get {
        return _managed;
    }
}
}
```

C# compiles a .NET generics type as an incomplete type. When the incomplete type is concretized, .NET creates a brand-new type, and does this without requiring the developer to do anything in particular. This means that if you use GenericsContainer with 15 different types, .NET will generate 15 definitions of GenericsContainer while the program is executing.

ABSTRACTION AND .NET GENERICS

With .NET generics, you can verify and ensure that everything is being said properly, with the cost being complexity. Consider the sentence that clearly described the duck. To produce it, you need to have learned additional rules regarding grammar. When using .NET generics, you need to master creating abstractions.

.NET generics are an abstraction. Just as interfaces are an abstraction of classes, .NET generics are an abstraction above interfaces. Interfaces define an intention, and .NET generics define an abstract implementation of an intention.

What is challenging with .NET generics is getting your thoughts together into an abstract intention implementation. It is like writing a document—you write it once, read it over, rewrite it, read it over, and rewrite it again. With .NET generics, you are gathering thoughts together into a general plan of action. This is why some people are completely confused and don't understand .NET generics. Writing your own .NET generics code requires some forethought.

The Theory of a Server-Side Spreadsheet

The example in this chapter is a spreadsheet for security traders. When you trade securities—whether they are equities, bonds, options, or futures—you will be confronted with information overload. You might have seen pictures of traders with desks full of desktop monitors. A trader might have seven to eight monitors displaying various bits of information. A trader is a very specialized type of domain that requires its own ways of processing information. One aspect that makes writing applications for traders difficult is that the nature of the data constantly changes, and types get more in the way than they help. As a result, traders adore spreadsheets.

Spreadsheets are useful because they can process large amounts of information in a relatively ad hoc manner. However, one downside to spreadsheets is that the processing time can dramatically increase due to the constant pushing and pulling of the data to and from the spreadsheet. To speed up processing, we will define and implement a spreadsheet that has the advantages of a traditional client-side spreadsheet.

■**Note** The theory and solution presented here are specific to the domain of trading, where the cost of hardware is well worth the ability to trade properly. Therefore, specific design aspects assume that you have the latest and greatest hardware.

In Chapter 9, we made an initial attempt at a spreadsheet, like this:

```
class Spreadsheet {
    public Func<object>[,] Cells;
    public object[,] State;
    public Spreadsheet() {
        Cells = new Func<object>[10, 10];
        State = new object[10, 10];
    }
    public void Execute() {
        for (int col = 0; col < Cells.GetLength(1); col++) {
            for (int row = 0; row < Cells.GetLength(0); row++) {
                if (Cells[col, row] != null) {
                    State[col, row] = Cells[col, row]();
                }
            }
        }
    }
}
```

The sample spreadsheet is defined using the data members Cells and State. Both data members are arrays with two dimensions. The first dimension represents the rows, and the second dimension represents the columns. You could define as many dimensions as you wish, but for the scope of the server spreadsheet, we take a two-dimensional approach.

The Execute() method goes through the individual rows and columns of the Cells data member, calculates the state of the cell, and assigns the state to the State data member. The data member Cells represents a function that is executed to generate the result of a particular cell that is assigned to the data member State. Both data members store and manipulate objects, which makes the spreadsheet flexible. However, a gain in one aspect means a reduction in another aspect; in this case, the loss is in performance. But performance is what algorithmic trading software cannot sacrifice, and native types would be best.

To make the spreadsheet perform as fast as it can, we need to use fixed-dimension arrays. However, with fixed-dimension arrays, we are moving away from a traditional object-oriented approach. You could argue that spreadsheets are not object-oriented at all and are a problem with respect to programmability. I would agree with that comment, but spreadsheets solve one class of problems very elegantly. In the case of financial trading software, they solve the problem of managing very large amounts of data efficiently.

■**Note** Object-oriented code is maintainable and extendable. However, object-oriented code can be slow. I have done tests where I found fixed-dimension arrays perform two to three times faster than the equivalent object-oriented application. However, performance is not always the primary consideration. Also, fixed-dimension arrays will not always give you the desired performance boost, because other parts of your code might be much slower. Therefore, generally, you should not use fixed-dimension arrays.

The `Cells` data member is a delegate, or lambda expression, that is defined using code similar to this:

```
static class CellFactories {
    public static Func<object> DoAdd(Func<object> cell1, Func<object> cell2) {
        return () => (double)cell1() + (double)cell2();
    }
    public static Func<object> DoMultiply(Func<object> cell1,
                                          Func<object> cell2) {
        return () => (double)cell1() * (double)cell2();
    }
    public static Func<object> Static(object value) {
        return () => value;
    }
}
```

As you saw in Chapter 9, `DoAdd()` has a lambda expression that employs two other lambda expressions to retrieve the values used to generate an additive result. This setup results in a chain of execution.

The sample spreadsheet implementation from Chapter 9 would be as follows:

```
Spreadsheet spreadsheet = new Spreadsheet();

spreadsheet.Cells[1, 0] = CellFactories.Static(10.0);
spreadsheet.Cells[0, 1] = CellFactories.Static(10.0);
spreadsheet.Cells[1, 2] =
    CellFactories.DoAdd(spreadsheet.Cells[1, 0], spreadsheet.Cells[0, 1]);
spreadsheet.Cells[2, 2] = CellFactories.DoMultiply(spreadsheet.Cells[1, 2],
    CellFactories.Static(2.0));
spreadsheet.Execute();
```

The code from Chapter 9 illustrates a rudimentary example of a spreadsheet and how lambda expressions can be used effectively. In this chapter, the focus will be on how to create a spreadsheet implementation that is effective, mostly object-oriented, and maintainable.

Architecting a Server-Side Spreadsheet

To architect a server spreadsheet, the following requirements must be met:

- *Performance*: Wherever possible, the design should not sacrifice performance.

- *Usability*: The server-side spreadsheet must be easy to program from a C# perspective. If the server-side spreadsheet is too complex or difficult to understand, then it will not be used properly, potentially incurring errors.

- *Maintainability*: The server-side spreadsheet implementation should be somewhat maintainable. Otherwise, bugs could creep into the code, impeding the spreadsheet's effective use.

Not listed is the requirement for extensibility. A spreadsheet by itself is not extensible because it implements a certain paradigm, which is a two-dimensional document of numbers and calculations.

And if you are wondering where the spreadsheet code comes from, it is a subset of the actual code that I use in my own security trading system.

■**Note** To code the spreadsheet to do more than it is originally designed for might be an interesting goal, but not one that is worth pursuing. Sometimes it is best to solve a problem, and leave paradigm thinking for another time. I have seen developers think about paradigms, not finish their code, and then have the code made obsolete by a paradigm that they did not consider.

Three projects are defined for this example:

- `Devspace.Trader.Common`: A class library that is a distilled form of my trading library. I decided to include such a library to give you a taste of how a production class library looks and feels.

- `ServerSideSpreadsheet`: A class library that represents the implementation of a server-side spreadsheet.

- `TestServerSideSpreadsheet`: A console application that tests the `ServerSideSpreadsheet` assembly.

Designing the Architecture

The original implementation of the spreadsheet code provides a great starting point. Using lambda expressions to calculate the state of a cell makes it easy to create a worksheet of numbers. What is not so great is the fact that the class `SpreadSheet` is a single worksheet. Most spreadsheets applications (like Microsoft Excel) offer the ability to create multiple spreadsheets.

The server-side spreadsheet that we will create will consist of two concepts: workbook and worksheet, as illustrated in Figure 11-1.

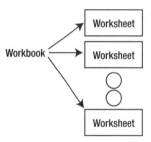

Figure 11-1. *Spreadsheet designed based on workbook and worksheet types*

The workbook is a type that acts like a collection class of the worksheet type. The worksheet type is an individual spreadsheet of fixed dimension that is responsible for storing the state, and the cell calculations reference the individual lambda expressions.

The workbook and worksheet could be defined as interfaces or as classes. Which would be better? Let's assume that the workbook will be defined as an interface and then implemented by a class. The approach is a commitment to a component architecture, allowing you to implement multiple types of workbooks. However, the likelihood of implementing multiple workbook types is rather remote, so why use interfaces? Because interfaces fit better into a bigger context.

Let's say that you have completed your super-duper server-side application and want to programmatically share the code with multiple machines. Having one computer call .NET functionality on another machine is almost trivial, but to attain the best performance and resource usage, you should use interfaces.

Defining the Server Spreadsheet Interfaces

Defining the interfaces for the server spreadsheets is actually rather complicated because of the requirements. The requirements state performance and usability are important, which in this case is asking quite a bit, as you will see as we work through the example. Let's start with a bottom-up development approach and outline the interfaces.

Defining the Debug Interface

Because the spreadsheet is from a production coding example, included in the discussion will be pieces of code that demonstrate good programming practices. The following is the base interface for all of my interfaces, which is defined in the Devspace.Trader.Common assembly.

```
public interface IDebug {
    bool Debug { get; set; }
}
```

The IDebug interface has a single bool property called Debug, which can be assigned and retrieved. The idea behind the IDebug interface is to enable a component to generate debug output. One of the major headaches with debugging applications that process large amounts of data is finding where the problem is. Imagine processing several million records, and the bug happens in record 900,001. You don't want to debug 900,000 records before hitting the bug. Thus, the challenge is figuring what went wrong without using the debugger. This is where IDebug comes into play. It provides a mechanism to let the implementation say what is going on, so if a bug needs to be deciphered, you do so by looking at the output.

The following example demonstrates how to use the Debug flag.

```
string[] baseType = typeToIstantiate.Split(new string[] { "[[", "]]" },
                                    StringSplitOptions.None);
if (baseType.Length == 0) {
    throw new Exception("There is no base type which cannot be");
}
if (Debug) {
    foreach (string str in baseType) {
        GenerateOutput.Write("Workbook.Load", "basetype(" + str + ")");
    }
}
```

The first line of code is used to split up a buffer into individual pieces, where double square brackets delimit the buffers. The Debug property is used to output the split-up buffer using the command GenerateOutput.Write().

■**Tip** Although I have defined my own debugging infrastructure, there is another infrastructure that you can use, called log4net (http://logging.apache.org/log4net/). This is a comprehensive infrastructure that you may want to investigate.

A Debug flag was used to output some text; otherwise, that information is not usually visible. Without a Debug flag, the only way to get that information is by setting a breakpoint after the Split() statement, and then individually investigating the resulting buffers. If you had to do that for 900,000 records, you would become bored very quickly, and let's not even talk about how much time you would waste.

The Debug flag serves two purposes. The first is to generate output to allow you to do a postmortem analysis when trying to figure out a bug. The second is to generate output when a bug occurs in a production context. By giving the user the ability to define a Debug flag, you are no longer reliant on having the user explain to you step by step how to reproduce the bug. All you need to do is tell the user to activate the Debug flag (your program would probably have a menu item for this), run the program until the bug occurs, and then send you the debug log file output for analysis.

Defining the IWorksheetBase and IWorksheet Interfaces

The worksheet is implemented using worksheet and workbook interfaces. Remember that one of the requirements is to have a spreadsheet implementation that is very fast. This would mean if a spreadsheet contained numbers, the best implementation would be a spreadsheet of double types. However, if the spreadsheet contained string buffers, the best implementation would be a spreadsheet of string types. Figure 11-2 shows a spreadsheet of double and string types.

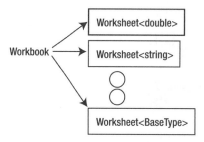

Figure 11-2. *Spreadsheet of strings and doubles*

In Figure 11-2, the workbook references a worksheet of type Worksheet<double> and Worksheet<string>, and in the general case, Worksheet<BaseType>. You can see how an interface using .NET generics for a worksheet could be potentially defined: define a general worksheet and define the actual type using .NET generics. The problem with this solution is that a workbook would define a collection of mixed types.

You might be tempted to believe that Worksheet<double> and Worksheet<string> are of the type Worksheet<BaseType>, and thus are all a single type. This is not the case, because with .NET generics, a type that hasn't been concretized is not a type at all. Think of it as being an "almost type," and to make the program work, you need to concretize everything. Figure 11-2 shows two concretized types: Worksheet<double> and Worksheet<string>. These are two different types. The two different types make it complicated for the workbook, because the workbook wants to maintain a single collection of worksheets. If we assume for the moment that the worksheet interface is defined as follows:

```
interface IWorksheet<BaseType> { }
```

the workbook could reference the worksheet as this collection:

```
List<IWorksheet<BaseType>> _worksheets;
```

However, that reference is incomplete, and the compiler would want to know what BaseType references. To keep your options open, one solution is to not complete the BaseType, but let the user of workbook figure things out, thus defining workbook as follows:

```
class Workbook<BaseType> {
    List<IWorksheet<BaseType>> _worksheets;
}
```

This solution seems to be a good one, but, in fact, it's passing the buck. The solution does not address the problem of Figure 11-2 and forces the end user to solve it. The core problem is that Figure 11-2 uses .NET generics to define worksheets of specific types, which means mixed types that need to be addressed by the workbook. In other words, a workbook can contain only spreadsheets of a certain type, as in this example:

```
Workbook<string> workbook1;
Workbook<double> workbook2;
```

It would seem that .NET generics make everything more complicated. However, there's more to this than first appears.

.NET generics have not made things more complicated, but rather have required us to be more explicit about what we actually want to do. We want to be able to define specific worksheet types, which means we have a mixed list of types that the workbook must manage. As explained in Chapter 9, non-.NET generics list types cannot control whether or not a list contains mixed types.

To solve the worksheet problem, we need to put on our object-oriented thinking caps. First, what is a worksheet? It's a spreadsheet that fulfills the role of a two-dimensional thing, and it applies to all worksheets regardless of types. Therefore, the first interface to define is a base worksheet, as follows:

```
...
using Devspace.Trader.Common;

public interface IWorksheetBase : IDebug {
    void Dimension(int rows, int cols);
    int MaxRows { get; }
    int MaxCols { get; }
}
```

The interface definition of `IWorksheetBase` has one method and two properties. The method `Dimension()` is used to assign the maximum rows and columns of the individual spreadsheet. The properties `MaxRows` and `MaxCols` return the maximum rows and columns. The properties and method have nothing to do with the specific type managed by the worksheet, but the interface manages to uniquely identify the instance as being a type of spreadsheet.

In the workbook code, the list of worksheets would be defined as follows:

```
List<IWorksheetBase> _worksheets;
```

Now the workbook knows it has a series of worksheets, but the workbook does not know or care about the types of the worksheets. When users of the workbook want to manipulate an individual worksheet, they can retrieve the worksheet from the workbook, but the users need to know the worksheet's type.

The spreadsheet is typically addressed using rows and columns, but to simplify declarations, there is also the ability to define something called the `SheetCoordinate`, which is a type that has a row and column. The `SheetCoordinate` is defined as follows:

```
public struct SheetCoordinate {
    public int Row;
    public int Column;
    public SheetCoordinate(int row, int column) {
        if (row < 0) {
            throw new ArgumentOutOfRangeException("Row is below zero");
        }
        if (column < 0) {
            throw new ArgumentOutOfRangeException("Column is below zero");
        }
        Row = row;
        Column = column;
    }
```

```
        public SheetCoordinate OneUp {
            get {
                return new SheetCoordinate(Row - 1, Column);
            }
        }
        public SheetCoordinate OneDown {
            get {
                return new SheetCoordinate(Row + 1, Column);
            }
        }
        public SheetCoordinate OneLeft {
            get {
                return new SheetCoordinate(Row, Column - 1);
            }
        }
        public SheetCoordinate OneRight {
            get {
                return new SheetCoordinate(Row, Column + 1);
            }
        }
    }
```

In the declaration of SheetCoordinate, notice that struct is used rather than class. We could have used a class, but SheetCoordinate serves the purpose of being a piece of data. SheetCoordinate is a type where you store information that is used by another type. A data type might do some processing, but only to make it easier to manipulate the data. For example, notice how SheetCoordinate has methods to generate a new instance of SheetCoordinate that might be one row higher or a column to the right.

The next step is to extend the worksheet definition and use .NET generics to define the type of worksheet. The following is the complete definition of the IWorksheet.

```
public interface IWorksheet<BaseType> : IWorksheetBase {
    void AssignColCalculation(int col,
        Func<IWorksheet<BaseType>, int, int, BaseType > cb);
    void AssignCellCalculation(int row, int col,
        Func<IWorksheet<BaseType>, int, int, BaseType > cb);
    BaseType GetCellState(int row, int col);
    void SetCellState(int row, int col, BaseType val);
    void AssignCellCalculation(SheetCoordinate coords,
        Func<IWorksheet<BaseType>, int, int, BaseType > cb);
    BaseType GetCellState(SheetCoordinate coords);
    void SetCellState(SheetCoordinate coords, BaseType val);
    void Calculate();
    void CalculateCol(int col);
    void CalculateRow(int row);
    BaseType Calculate(int row, int col);
    BaseType Calculate(SheetCoordinate coords);
    BaseType [,] Data { get; }
}
```

The declaration of IWorksheet is as a .NET generics type, where BaseType is a .NET generics parameter that represents the type of the spreadsheet. Since IWorksheet is a type of spreadsheet, it subclasses the IWorksheetBase interface, allowing IWorksheet to be part of a mixed collection of IWorksheet instances. The IWorksheet interface is fairly complex and contains many methods. However, here we are focusing on the interface concept, rather than the individual methods.

Look at the bolded parts and notice how the interface is specific about the operations, but vague about the type used in the operations. This is what you want to achieve when using .NET generics. You want to take a high-level approach and indicate which operations are available, but leave out the types being manipulated in the operations. The types will be specified later by another programmer.

■**Note** The technique of having a .NET generics type (such as IWorksheet) subclass a non-.NET generics type (such as IWorksheetBase) allows you to identify the general type that you are trying to describe with some specialization in the .NET generics type declaration. From an object-oriented perspective, the non-.NET generics base type (IWorksheetBase) acts as a placeholder to indicate that the type of a collection fulfills a certain criterion.

Defining the IWorkbook Interface

Now that we've completed the IWorksheet<> and IWorksheetBase interfaces, we can define the workbook interface. The workbook interface will not be a .NET generics type, since a workbook will contain multiple worksheet types. However, as you will see, we can optimize this interface to make it easier to use the workbook.

For the moment, let's consider the plain-vanilla IWorkbook interface with no .NET generics types, which is defined as follows:

```
...
using Devspace.Trader.Common;

public interface IWorkbook : IDebug {
    IWorksheetBase this[string identifier] { get; set; }
    string Identifier { get; }
}
```

The IWorkbook interface defines one property, Identifier, and an indexer, this. Any class that implements IWorkbook is expected to contain multiple references to IWorksheet<> instances. How those references are managed is not the responsibility of the IWorkbook interface, but of the IWorkbook interface implementation.

■**Note** The IWorkbook interface does not provide a Clear() method to reset the workbook and delete all of the referenced worksheets. It would seem logical to have a Clear() method, but in a garbage-collected environment, that's completely unnecessary. If you don't want to use a workbook anymore, just don't reference it, and the garbage collector will take care of the rest. Think of it as having the option of serving dinner to your guests on real plates or paper plates. Real plates might seem better, but they break and you need to wash them. Paper plates are used once and thrown away. Of course, with paper plates you have recycling issues that you don't have in .NET, because the memory is recycled for you.

The property Identifier is used as a way to identify the workbook to which the instance is referring. The identifier might be a path or filename and is completely dependent on the implementation of IWorkbook.

The indexer is the primary way of getting and retrieving worksheets, where each worksheet is referenced using a string identifier. The identifier does not need to be a string—it could have been a custom type, enumeration, or interface that is implemented. Using a string keeps things simple, but there are maintenance issues.

Let's say all workbooks have a configuration worksheet. So for most of the code, the string identifier "configuration" is used. However, a new programmer decides to use "Configuration" (with a capital C). This slight change will cause problems because "configuration" is meant to have a lowercase c. Here's the example:

```
IWorkbook workbook;
IWorksheetBase worksheet1 = workbook["configuration"];
IWorksheetBase worksheet2 = workbook["Configuration"];
```

The bolded code indicates a buffer that is typed in by hand and is considered hard-coded. The preferred alternative is to hard-code a structure that is then referenced throughout the source code, like this:

```
public static class WorksheetIdentifiers  {
    public const string Configuration = "configuration";
}
```

```
IWorkbook workbook;
IWorksheetBase worksheet1 = workbook[WorksheetIdentifiers.Configuration];
IWorksheetBase worksheet2 = workbook[WorksheetIdentifiers.Configuration];
```

The class WorksheetIdentifiers still contains a hard-coded string buffer, but it has been centralized to a single location. The workbook indexer references the identifier within the class WorksheetIdentifiers. Thus, if you change the class WorksheetIdentifiers, you also change the identifiers used by the indexer. That way, the chances of having a typo break an application are reduced.

Let's get back to the IWorkbook interface and in particular the indexer. The indexer is of the type IWorksheetBase, which is correct, but a bit tedious because the IWorksheetBase interface is a rudimentary interface and most likely not the interface that you will use. The interface you actually want to use is IWorksheet<>, and therein lies the problem. To get an IWorksheet instance, you would need a type cast, as follows:

```
IWorkbook workbook;
IWorksheet<string> worksheet =
    workbook[WorksheetIdentifiers.Configuration] as IWorksheet<string>;
```

The bolded code is the type cast you need each and every time you want to reference an
IWorksheet instance. The type cast is not a big deal, but it is tedious. I personally would prefer
being able to call a property, method, or indexer that returns the type I want.

Therein lies the problem, because the way I want to use an indexer, property, or method is
as a mixed type, and you can't define an indexer with mixed types. You can define an indexer
that is a fixed type. To understand this problem, look at the following declaration of a workbook that compiles.

```
...
using Devspace.Trader.Common;

public interface IWorkbook<BaseType> : IDebug {
    IWorksheet<BaseType> this[string identifier] { get; set; }
    string Identifier { get; }
}
```

In this declaration of IWorkbook, a .NET generics type is used, but then the problem is that
the indexer can return only IWorksheet instances of a single type, such as double or string.
Remember that there are multiple worksheet types (as illustrated in Figure 11-2).

What we want to do is use method-level .NET generics declarations, like this:

```
public interface IMixedType {
    Func<Datatype> this<Datatype>[string identifier] { get; set; }
}
```

The problem with the method-level declaration is that it does compile. There are two ways
to declare a .NET generics parameter. The first is what you have seen the most often, and that
is at the type level:

```
class MyType< GenericType> { }
```

Declaring at the type level means that whenever you use the type and specify a type for
the .NET generics parameter, MyType becomes fixed to a certain type. So say you declared
MyType as follows:

```
MyType<int> cls = new MyType<int>();
```

Now MyType is of type MyType and int. And any references to GenericType within MyType
will become int. This form of .NET generics solves many problems, as illustrated in Chapter 9.

But in the case of the IWorkbook, we don't want a fixed type. We want the ability to have
a collection type contain mixed types of IWorksheet. The way to achieve that is to use .NET
generics methods, like this:

```
class MyType {  GenericType Method< GenericType>() { ... }}
```

Now the .NET generics parameter is associated with the method, rather than the type. And
that means MyType can mix types. So we could have different IWorksheet types. And wouldn't it
be great if there was an indexer with mixed types? But you can't have .NET generics indexers

and properties that are not declared at the type level. Thus, the use of a .NET generics parameter with an indexer or property will not work. In my opinion, that is a real C# language design flaw, because it means we need to write code like this:

```
...
using Devspace.Trader.Common;

public interface IWorkbook : IDebug {
    IWorksheet<BaseType> GetSheet<BaseType>(string identifier);
    IWorksheetBase this[string identifier] { get; set; }
    string Identifier { get; }
}
```

In this modified declaration, the method GetSheet() acts like the get part of the indexer, but notice where the .NET generics parameter BaseType is declared. The declaration is after the method identifier and before the first bracket. In the case of IWorkbook, we use the method-level .NET generics parameter to allow the caller to determine the type of the worksheet instances. The implementation of IWorkbook has to do nothing other than perform the appropriate type cast. Method-level .NET generics parameters are great when you are dealing with mixed types, as in the case of IWorkbook.

The code to retrieve a worksheet that previously needed a type cast is rewritten as follows:

```
IWorkbook workbook;
IWorksheet<string> worksheet =
    workbook.GetSheet<string>(WorksheetIdentifiers.Configuration);
```

The type cast has not disappeared completely. It is done for us in the implementation of the GetSheet<>() method, as demonstrated by the following code.

```
public IWorksheet<MethodBaseType>
    GetSheet<MethodBaseType>(string identifier) {
    lock (_worksheets) {
        IWorksheet<MethodBaseType> retval = null;
        if (_worksheets.ContainsKey(identifier)) {
            retval =
                _worksheets[identifier] as IWorksheet<MethodBaseType >;
        }
        else {
            retval = new Worksheet<MethodBaseType>(identifier);
            _worksheets.Add(identifier, retval);
        }
        return retval;
    }
}
```

The bolded code shows that there is still a type cast, but the type cast is in the method, and it uses the .NET generics parameter declared at the method level.

Implementing the Server Spreadsheet

Now let's look at how the workbook and worksheet are implemented. The following is the complete code for the IWorksheet interface implementation.

```
class Worksheet<BaseType> : TraderBaseClass, IWorksheet<BaseType>,
                            IWorksheetSerialize {
    BaseType[,] CellState;
    Func<IWorksheet<BaseType>, int, int, BaseType>[,] Cells;
    Func<IWorksheet<BaseType>, int, int, BaseType>[] ColCells;
    int[,] CalculationVersion;
    int CurrVersion;
    int _maxRows;
    int _maxCols;

    string _identifier;
    public Worksheet() {
    }

    public Worksheet(string identifier) {
        _identifier = identifier;
    }

    public void Dimension(int rows, int cols) {
        CellState = new BaseType[rows, cols];
        Cells = new Func<IWorksheet<BaseType>, int, int, BaseType>[rows, cols];
        CalculationVersion = new int[rows, cols];
        ColCells = new Func<IWorksheet<BaseType>, int, int, BaseType>[cols];
        CurrVersion = 0;
        _maxRows = rows;
        _maxCols = cols;
    }

    public int MaxRows {
        get {
            return _maxRows;
        }
    }

    public int MaxCols {
        get {
            return _maxCols;
        }
    }
```

```csharp
    public BaseType[,] Data {
        get {
            return CellState;
        }
    }

    public void AssignCellState(int row, int col, object value) {
        CellState[row, col] = (BaseType)value;
    }

    public void AssignCellCalculation(int row, int col,
                                      Func<IWorksheet<BaseType>, int, int,
                                      BaseType> cb) {
        Cells[row, col] = cb;
    }

    public BaseType GetCellState(int row, int col) {
        return CellState[row, col];
    }

    public void SetCellState(int row, int col, BaseType val) {
        CellState[row, col] = val;
        Cells[row, col] = null;
    }

    public void AssignCellCalculation(SheetCoordinate coords,
                                      Func<IWorksheet<BaseType>, int, int,
                                      BaseType> cb) {
        AssignCellCalculation(coords.Row, coords.Column, cb);
    }

    public void AssignColCalculation(int col, Func<IWorksheet<BaseType>, int,
                                     int, BaseType> cb) {
        ColCells[col] = cb;
    }

    public BaseType GetCellState(SheetCoordinate coords) {
        return GetCellState(coords.Row, coords.Column);
    }

    public void SetCellState(SheetCoordinate coords, BaseType val) {
        SetCellState(coords.Row, coords.Column, val);
    }

    public BaseType Calculate(int row, int col) {
        if (CurrVersion > CalculationVersion[row, col]) {
            CellState[row, col] = Cells[row, col](this, row, col);
```

```
            CalculationVersion[row, col] = CurrVersion;
        }
        return CellState[row, col];
    }

    public BaseType Calculate(SheetCoordinate coords) {
        return Calculate(coords.Row, coords.Column);
    }

    public void Calculate() {
        CurrVersion++;
        for (int row = 0; row < Cells.GetLength(0); row++) {
            for (int col = 0; col < Cells.GetLength(1); col++) {
                if (Cells[row, col] != null) {
                    Calculate(row, col);
                }
            }
        }
    }

    public void CalculateRow(int row) {
        CurrVersion++;
        for (int col = 0; col < Cells.GetLength(1); col++) {
            if (Cells[row, col] != null) {
                Calculate(row, col);
            }
        }
    }

    public void CalculateCol(int col) {
        CurrVersion++;
        if (ColCells[col] == null) {
            return;
        }
        for (int row = 0; row < Cells.GetLength(0); row++) {
            CellState[row, col] = ColCells[col](this, row, col);
        }
    }

    bool _generateRowCounter;
    public bool GenerateRowCounter {
        get {
            return _generateRowCounter;
        }
        set {
            _generateRowCounter = value;
        }
    }
```

```
    public override string ToString() {
        StringBuilder builder = new StringBuilder();

        for (int row = 0; row < Cells.GetLength(0); row++) {
            bool needComma = false;
            if (_generateRowCounter) {
                needComma = true;
                builder.Append(row);
            }
            for (int col = 0; col < Cells.GetLength(1); col++) {
                if (needComma) {
                    builder.Append(",");
                }
                else {
                    needComma = true;
                }
                if (CellState[row, col] != null) {
                    builder.Append(CellState[row, col].ToString());
                }
            }
            builder.Append("\n");
        }
        return builder.ToString();
    }
}
```

The class Worksheet<> implements the interface IWorksheet, but does not specify on which type the worksheet should be based. Because the implementation of Worksheet<> is as a container type, it is not necessary for it to specify a particular type.

The complete code for the IWorkbook interface implementation is as follows:

```
class Workbook : TraderBaseClass, IWorkbook, IEnumerable<string> {
    IDictionary<string, IWorksheetBase> _worksheets =
        new Dictionary<string, IWorksheetBase>();

    string _identifier;
    public string Identifier {
        get {
            return _identifier;
        }
    }

    bool _generateRowCounter;
    public bool GenerateRowCounter {
        get {
            return _generateRowCounter;
        }
        set {
```

```
            _generateRowCounter = value;
        }
    }

    public Workbook(string identifier) {
        _identifier = identifier;
    }

    public void Clear() {
        _worksheets.Clear();
    }

    public IWorksheet<StateType> GetSheet<StateType>(string identifier) {
        lock (_worksheets) {
            IWorksheet<StateType> retval = null;
            if (_worksheets.ContainsKey(identifier)) {
                retval = _worksheets[identifier] as IWorksheet<StateType>;
            }
            else {
                retval = new Worksheet<StateType>(identifier);
                _worksheets.Add(identifier, retval);
            }
            return retval;
        }
    }

    public IWorksheetBase this[string identifier] {
        get {
            IWorksheetBase retval = null;
            lock (_worksheets) {
                if (_worksheets.ContainsKey(identifier)) {
                    retval = _worksheets[identifier];
                }
            }
            return retval;
        }
        set {
            lock (_worksheets) {
                if (_worksheets.ContainsKey(identifier)) {
                    _worksheets.Remove(identifier);
                }
                _worksheets.Add(identifier, value);
            }
        }
    }

    IEnumerator<string> IEnumerable<string>.GetEnumerator() {
```

```
        foreach (string identifier in _worksheets.Keys) {
            yield return identifier;
        }
    }

    IEnumerator IEnumerable.GetEnumerator() {
        return (((IEnumerable<string>)this) as IEnumerable).GetEnumerator();
    }

    public override string ToString() {
        string buffer = "";
        foreach (string identifier in this) {
            buffer += "Workbook (" + identifier + ")";
        }
        return buffer;
    }
}
```

The class `TraderBaseClass` is the general `Object` for the algorithmic trading environment. By default, all types subclass `Object`, and that is implied. In most applications, there is some functionality that most classes will need. That common functionality is what I call a domain-specific base class. In the case of `TraderBaseClass`, that is the implementation of the `IDebug` interface.

The explanation of `IWorksheetSerialize` is more complicated and relates to the problem of loading an `IWorksheet` without knowing the type. Say that you are saving a `IWorkbook` with multiple `IWorksheet` instances. Each `IWorksheet` instance is a specific type. When you want to load an `IWorkbook`, how does the loader know what types there are? The answer is that the loader does not, and thus must first load a general type, and then make a specific type cast. Take a look at the serialization sources in the project `Devspace.Trader.Common` and the namespace `Devspace.Trader.Common.ServerSpreadsheet.SerializerImpls`.

Using Lambda Expressions in the Spreadsheet

The data members of `Worksheet<>` are very similar to the previously defined spreadsheet class, except the declarations are lambda-ready. *Lambda-ready* means that I use the `Func<>` type whenever I want to declare a variable that references a lambda expression. The following three data members are used to store the state of the cell, cell calculations that will calculate the state of a cell, and cell calculations that calculate the state of cells for an entire column.

```
BaseType[,] CellState;
Func<IWorksheet<BaseType>, int, int, BaseType>[,] Cells;
Func<IWorksheet<BaseType>, int, int, BaseType>[] ColCells;
```

The data member `CellState` contains the state of the worksheet cell and its type is `BaseType`, meaning that the type of the worksheet cell is whatever `BaseType` is declared as. The data members `Cells` and `ColCells` are declared as lambda expression references, where there are three parameters and a return value.

Before I continue with the lambda expression explanation, I want to shift focus to illustrate a problem: how anonymous methods give you one thing, but act another way. Consider the following delegate (I am using delegates, because that is what lambda expressions are, albeit without the nice syntax).

```
delegate string WhatAmI();
```

We are going to play a game of what animal am I, where we'll use anonymous method implementations to display the animal type. Using an anonymous method, the caller does not need to be concerned with the type of animal, just that when the delegate is called, the correct animal name is displayed.

```
WhatAmI[] animals = new WhatAmI[2];
string animal;

animal = "cow";
animals[0] = delegate() {
    return animal;
};
animal = "horse";
animals[1] = delegate() {
    animal = "(" + animal + ")";
    return animal;
};

Console.WriteLine("Animal 1(" + animals[0]() + ") 2(" + animals[1]() + ")");
```

The example contains an array of WhatAmI delegates, and each of the delegates will be assigned an anonymous method. In the first case, it is a method that returns the value of the variable animal. In the second, it is a buffer where the value of the variable animal is surrounded by brackets. In each of the assignments, we are assigning a new instance of an anonymous method.

Let's say you run the code and Console.WriteLine() generates its output. What do you think animal 1 and 2 will be? Do you expect cow and horse, respectively? Here's the output:

```
Animal 1(horse) 2((horse))
```

The generated output is not what we expected. This demonstrates that anonymous methods or lambda expression are *stateless*. This is a desired behavior, because when array items animals[0] and animals[1] are executed, they will reference the last version of the variable animal.

Things get really tricky if one anonymous method happens to modify a variable not declared in its scope. To demonstrate that the delegate is truly stateless, let's modify the Console.WriteLine() to execute animals[1] first, which happens to modify the state of animal, and look at the generated output:

```
Animal 2((horse)) 1((horse))
```

The output shows that because animal is manipulated, the first anonymous method implementation sees the manipulated version.

To say that anonymous delegates and lambda expressions are totally stateless is not completely true, because there is a way to create a stateful anonymous delegate or lambda expression. Consider the following implementation of the WhatAmI anonymous delegate, which is encapsulated within the context of a factory.

```
static class Builder {
    public static WhatAmI BuildWhatAmI(string animal) {
        return delegate() {
            return animal;
        };
    }
}
```

This time, the anonymous delegate is created in the context of the method BuildWhatAmI(), where the animal type is passed in as a parameter. Modifying the array code to use the factory results in this code:

```
WhatAmI[] animals = new WhatAmI[2];
string animal;

animal = "cow";
animals[0] = Builder.BuildWhatAmI(animal);
animal = "horse";
animals[1] = Builder.BuildWhatAmI(animal);

Console.WriteLine("Animal 2(" + animals[1]() + ") 1(" + animals[0]() + ")");
```

The code is the same as the previous version, with the exception of calling the Builder class. So as to not leave you in too much suspense, here's the output:

```
Animal 2(horse) 1(cow)
```

You can see that when an anonymous delegate or lambda expression is used in the context of another method and returned to the caller, the anonymous delegate or lambda expression becomes stateful. Two different behaviors are created, even though the calling code is similar.

While you might think that this behavior is wrong, it is correct from a functional programming perspective. In Chapter 16, you will see how this behavior is put to good use.

Getting back to the spreadsheet example, some source code will not work because of the just-described behavior. This source code would not work:

```
for (int row = 0; row < items.Length; row++) {
    AssignCellCalculation(row, 1,
        (worksheet, cellRow, cellCol) => {
            return worksheet.GetCellState(row, 0) -
                worksheet.Calculate(items.Length, 0);
        }
    );
}
```

Whereas this code would work:

```
static class Builder {
    static Func<IWorksheet<double>, int, int, double>
               BuildSubtractFromAverage(int row, double[] items) {
        return (worksheet, cellRow, cellCol) => {
            return worksheet.GetCellState(row, 0) -
                worksheet.Calculate(items.Length, 0);
        };
    }
}
for (int row = 0; row < items.Length; row++) {
    AssignCellCalculation(row, 1,
                         Builder.BuildSubtractFromAverage(row, items));
}
```

The difference between the two pieces of code is that one has the lambda expression declared in the context of the method and the other does not. The real difference, however, is in the implementation of a lambda expression or an anonymous delegate. As you learned in Chapter 9, in the early days of C#, you needed a class method. Well, that requirement has not been removed. In this case, C# has created a class for you that happens to contain the delegate methods. In the case of the WhatAmI anonymous method example, the following code is actually generated.

```
[CompilerGenerated]
private sealed class <>c__DisplayClass2
{
    // Fields
    public string animal;

    // Methods
    public <>c__DisplayClass2();
    public string <Variation1>b__0();
    public string <Variation1>b__1();
}
```

The generated class has a data member animal, which actually is the variable declared in the context of the method. And there are two methods, b__0() and b__1(), which happen to be the anonymous methods.

Underneath it all, the code assigns the methods of the class <>c__DisplayClass2 to the array animals. Thus, when each method implementation manipulates animal, it sees the same variable or data member.

So why does one version of the anonymous method keep state while the other does not maintain state? The answer relates to how the anonymous method is implemented. Whenever an anonymous method is declared, a class is created and instantiated in the context of the method. Thus, if you use multiple anonymous methods in the context of a method, they all share the same instantiated class. When you call a method that creates an anonymous method, a class instance is created each and every time the method is called. Therefore, the method Builder.BuildWhatAmI() instantiates an anonymous method class that is returned to the caller. What is misleading about all of this is that an anonymous method is a class instantiation, although the new identifier has not been used.

> ■**Note** Other than the introduction of .NET generics, the .NET virtual machine has not changed that much, but C# programming has changed quite a bit. Many of the changes in the C# programming language are to simplify techniques that programmers commonly employ. This means that the generated code will behave like the code that you would have needed to write yourself if the language features did not exist.

Assigning State Without Knowing the Type

When using .NET generics types, one of the most common problems occurs when you need to work with proper types. In the implementation of the IWorksheet interface, it is necessary to implement the AssignCellState() method defined in the interface IWorksheetSerialize.

The problem is that the function passes in as a parameter of one type and is assigned to CellState, which is another undefined .NET generics type. The implementation of the Assign-CellState() method is as follows:

```
public void AssignCellState(int row, int col, object value) {
    CellState[row, col] = (BaseType)value;
}
```

The code looks so simple and innocent, but is actually masking many potential problems. Here, the value of the parameter value is of type object. Then to convert the value to type BaseType—because that is what CellState is defined to be—you use a type cast. For the most part, this code will work, if value is the correct type.

Consider the following code, which would generate an exception.

```
IWorksheet<double> worksheet = new Worksheet<double>();
worksheet.Dimension(10, 10);
string buffer = "hello world";
worksheet.AssignCellState(1, 2, buffer);
```

The variable worksheet is declared to be of type double. When the method AssignCellState() is called, the cell 1, 2 is assigned to be type string. Calling AssignCellState() is not a problem, but in the implementation, the assignment will fail. You can't willy-nilly assign a string to a double. Of course, this begs the question, "Why have a function of type object?" Sometimes you can't get around it, and you need to write a general object method. The proper way to call the method would be as follows:

```
IWorksheet<double> worksheet = new Worksheet<double>();
worksheet.Dimension(10, 10);
string buffer = "hello world";
worksheet.AssignCellState( 1, 2, Double.Parse(buffer));
```

The bolded code shows that the string buffer is parsed by the Double.Parse() method converting a string buffer into a double value. Of course, the conversion will fail, since the string buffer represents a number, but that is another problem.

Another way of solving the problem is to avoid the object altogether and declare the method as being a .NET generics method. The advantage of the .NET generics method is that you could execute in a type-safe manner without explicitly forcing the user to implement parsing routines. Consider the following modified .NET generics method declaration of AssignCellState().

```
public void AssignCellState<ValueType>(int row, int col, ValueType value) {
    if (typeof(BaseType).IsAssignableFrom(typeof(ValueType))) {
        CellState[row, col] = (BaseType)(object)value;
    }
    else if (value is string &&
            typeof(double).IsAssignableFrom(typeof(BaseType))) {
        CellState[row, col] =
            (BaseType)(object)double.Parse((string)(object)value);
    }
    else {
        throw new InvalidCastException("Could not perform conversion");
    }
}
```

The cell state to be assigned is a .NET generics parameter and defined to be the type ValueType. We can only guess what ValueType is; it is determined when the method AssignCellState<>() is called. For example, suppose this method call is made:

```
string buffer = "hello world";
worksheet.AssignCellState(1, 2, buffer);
```

The type for ValueType will be string, even though we have not explicitly specified it. One of the things that is possible with .NET generics methods is that types can be deduced implicitly. The following would be an explicit usage of AssignCellState<>().

```
string buffer = "hello world";
worksheet.AssignCellState<string>(1, 2, buffer);
```

Knowing that ValueType is string, AssignCellState<>() will then first check if ValueType can be assigned to BaseType:

```
if (typeof(BaseType).IsAssignableFrom(typeof(ValueType))) {
```

This code is rather clever, because it uses what is known as *reflection* to determine if one type can be assigned to another type. Essentially, it asks if it is OK via a type cast to assign value to CellState. You could try to do this without the if statement, but then you risk an unnecessary exception. If it is permissible to assign, then the assignment is done via a two-step casting:

```
CellState[row, col] = (BaseType)(object)value;
```

Here, we first convert the type to an object, and then convert the type to BaseType, which happens to be the type that the spreadsheet is declared as. It is absolutely imperative that the cast to the object is added; otherwise, the C# compiler will complain that the cast is not possible.

But suppose that the type cannot be directly assigned. Let's say that value references a string that contains a number. Then, using reflection, you can verify what ValueType and BaseType are and perform the conversion yourself:

```
else if (value is string && typeof(double).IsAssignableFrom(typeof(BaseType)))
```

The first part of the `if` statement asks if `value` is of type `string`. The second part asks if `double` can be assigned to `BaseType`. If both are valid, it means the input is a `string` and that the spreadsheet type is a `double`, so to convert, you only need to call `Double.Parse()`.

The automatic conversion functionality does not save code, but it centralizes it and makes it general. The caller will not generally need to worry about the most common conversions, as they will happen automatically. Of course, this assumes that you have implemented the most common conversions. For those conversions that cannot be done, a cast exception is thrown, just as the original object-based `AssignCellState()` would have thrown an exception.

Overall, the `AssignCellState<>()` with .NET generics parameters provides the ability to cleanly assign a value to the spreadsheet, and a clean and maintainable method to perform a conversion. This goes back to the original requirement of being able to mix types safely.

Overriding the ToString() Functionality

Debugging a data structure like a spreadsheet is a fairly complex task, because there is too much data. The `Worksheet<>` class implements the `ToString()` method and generates a string. The string can be retrieved and then displayed using a method like `Console.WriteLine()`. But there is another reason you should, as a rule, always implement `ToString()`: the Visual Studio IDE uses it.

Let's say that you are writing the following code that uses an `IWorksheet<>` instance.

```
IWorksheetBase sheet = SpreadsheetManager.CreateEmpytWorksheet<double>("");
sheet.Dimension(10, 10);
sheet.AssignCellState(0, 0, "10.0");
```

You would like to check if the first cell row and column item have been assigned a value of 10. To check the state, you would compile the source and set a breakpoint immediately after the `AssignCellState()` call. Then in the IDE, look in the Locals window and inspect the state of `sheet`, as shown in Figure 11-3.

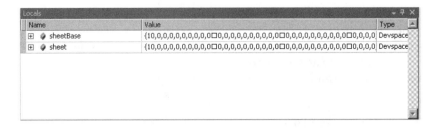

Figure 11-3. *Locals window that uses ToString() functionality*

In the Locals window, the first number beside `sheet` is 10, followed by a series of zeros. This value is the buffer generated by `ToString()` and provides a user-friendly way to investigate the contents of the variable.

■**Note** The ToString() method is useful only when debugging or trying to perform analysis of the state of an object without actually debugging the program. Thus, for improved debugging or runtime analysis, always implement ToString().

Iterating Data Using Enumerators

In Chapter 9's example, the keyword yield was used with an enumerator that had no generic parameters. You can also use yield with the IEnumerable interface that uses .NET generics, but you need to implement two separate interfaces.

The problem lies in how the IEnumerable<> and IEnumerable interfaces are declared. Following is the declaration for both interfaces.

```
public interface IEnumerable {
    IEnumerator GetEnumerator();
}
public interface IEnumerable<T> : IEnumerable {
    IEnumerator<T> GetEnumerator();
}
```

To implement the IEnumerable<> interface, you need to implement the IEnumerable interface. Both interfaces have a single method, with the only difference between the two being the return type, which is where the problems begin.

Programming languages like C# do not allow you to overload a method where the only difference is the return type. For example, the following class declaration is illegal.

```
class Example {
    public int Count() { return 0; }
    public string Count() { return "0"; }
}
```

This class has two implementations of Count(), where only the return type differs. This code is illegal because the compiler cannot distinguish which method will be called. The following code illustrates the decision problem.

```
new Example().Count();
```

When implementing the interface IEnumerable<>, it is necessary to distinguish which interface method is implemented. Adding to the complication is that both methods do the same thing. So you need to implement one variation of GetEnumerator(), and then have the other implementation call the actual implementation. The following is a complete IEnumerable<>() implementation.

```
IEnumerator<string> IEnumerable<string>.GetEnumerator() {
    foreach (string identifier in _worksheets.Keys) {
        yield return identifier;
    }
}
IEnumerator IEnumerable.GetEnumerator() {
    return (((IEnumerable<string>)this) as IEnumerable).GetEnumerator();
}
```

Each of the implementation methods is preceded with the interface identifier, which is necessary to identify which interface method is being referenced. The IEnumerable<>.GetEnumerator() method is implemented because IEnumerable<> subclasses IEnumerator, and thus a downcast to IEnumerator is possible. The type cast is a bit complicated because the IEnumerable<>() method is available only by a type cast, and then you need to downcast to IEnumerable before calling the GetEnumerator() method.

All of this looks a bit complicated, but it illustrates the types of problems that you can run into when using .NET generics-based code that needs to integrate code that does not use .NET generics.

Using the Spreadsheet

With the interfaces and implementations complete, it is possible to use the spreadsheet. The sample application is a spreadsheet that calculates the average of a set of numbers and then calculates how far each number is from the average.

Calculating an Average

The spreadsheet calculates the average of a set of numbers, and then subtracts the average from each number. The example demonstrates reading a complete spreadsheet to get a number and reading individual elements to perform a calculation.

Let's use the following numbers to calculate the average.

```
double[] items = new double[] { 1.0, 2.0, 3.0 };
```

The average number is 2.0, and if you subtract the average from each number, you will get the series –1, 0, and 1.

To make this work for a spreadsheet, the first step is to declare and then populate a IWorksheet<> instance. To instantiate an IWorksheet<> instance, we use a factory that will instantiate the Worksheet<> class. The code looks like this:

```
IWorksheet<double> sheetAverage =
    SpreadsheetManager.CreateEmpytWorksheet<double>("");
double[] items = new double[] { 1.0, 2.0, 3.0 };
sheetAverage.Dimension(items.Length + 10, 3);
for (int row = 0; row < items.Length; row++) {
    sheetAverage.SetCellState(row, 0, items[row]);
}
```

The worksheet is declared as being of type double (IWorksheet<double>), allowing you to manage a double value. To populate sheetAverage, the numbers are iterated in a for loop and assigned to the worksheet using the SetCellState() method. The method Dimension() is needed to create a fixed-length worksheet.

With the worksheet populated, to make sure everything looks right, you could call the method ToString() and see if all is as expected.

The next step is to assign the lambda expressions that will be used to calculate the average and then the individual differences from the average. When you assign a calculation to the worksheet, you need to know whether the lambda expression will be stateful or stateless. Remember that lambda expressions have some state. It is just a question of whether you want a shared-state lambda expression or an individual-state lambda expression. In the case of the lambda expressions for the average calculations, a shared state is acceptable.

To calculate the average, you use a technique where the average calculation is the last element in the series of the array calculations. Thus, when the average calculation is called, it knows how many elements there are because of the row in which the average calculation is stored.

```
sheetAverage.AssignCellCalculation(items.Length, 0,
    (IWorksheet<double> worksheet, int cellRow, int cellCol) => {
        double runningTotal = 0.0;
        for (int row = 0; row < cellRow; row++) {
            runningTotal += worksheet.GetCellState(row, 0);
        }
        return runningTotal / cellRow;
    });
```

In the example, the average is calculated by using the variable cellRow as a maximum row. Every cell (GetCellState()) before cellRow is added to a running total (runningTotal), and then finally an average is returned by dividing runningTotal by cellRow.

With the average calculated, the next step is to calculate the difference between the average and the individual items. The result will be stored in a column to the right of the item cell state. This is done by subtracting the average calculation cell state from the item value, as follows:

```
for (int row = 0; row < items.Length; row++) {
    sheetAverage.AssignCellCalculation(row, 1,
        (worksheet, cellRow, cellCol) => {
            return worksheet.GetCellState(cellRow, 0) -
                worksheet.Calculate(items.Length, 0);
        }
    );
}
```

The number of cell-state calculations depends on the count of numbers in items. Each cell calculation is assigned a locally declared lambda expression, meaning that the lambda expressions of all cell states will be identical and share the same state. The only shared variable is items.Length. All the lambda expressions expect the same length, and so it is acceptable to share this variable. The average difference is calculated by calculating the average and then subtracting it from the worksheet cell item value that is in the zeroth column.

Finally, when everything is assigned, you can call the `worksheet.Calculate()` method to calculate the average and difference from the average.

```
sheetAverage.Calculate();
Console.WriteLine(sheetAverage.ToString());
```

Understanding Why the Calculation Worked

The cell calculations work because the spreadsheet has the ability to track what has been calculated and what has not been calculated. In a typical spreadsheet, you can change one cell in a sheet and have everything magically recalculate. There is no such feature for this spreadsheet. However, this simpler spreadsheet version can make sure that when there are dependencies, they are not calculated multiple times.

Look back at the source code to calculate the difference between the average and a number. The only reason the calculation worked is that the cell that contained the average was called using the `Calculate()` method. Had the `GetCellState()` method been used, the average might not have been calculated, and thus the difference calculation would have been corrupted.

But having each and every cell calculate the average whenever a small change is made is a waste of resources, since the change might not affect a cell that is recalculated. To avoid this, built into the spreadsheet is a version-control mechanism that calculates a cell to the latest version. Then, if another calculation is called with the same version number, the value is retrieved from the cell state. The following is the code from `Worksheet<>` that manages the version number.

```
public BaseType Calculate(int row, int col) {
    if (CurrVersion > CalculationVersion[row, col]) {
        CellState[row, col] = Cells[row, col](this, row, col);
        CalculationVersion[row, col] = CurrVersion;
    }
    return CellState[row, col];
}
public void Calculate() {
    CurrVersion++;
    for (int row = 0; row < Cells.GetLength(0); row++) {
        for (int col = 0; col < Cells.GetLength(1); col++) {
            if (Cells[row, col] != null) {
                Calculate(row, col);
            }
        }
    }
}
```

Calling the method `Calculate()` without parameters indicates a desire to recalculate the entire spreadsheet. In the implementation of `Calculate()`, the variable `CurrVersion`, which represents the version number of the current calculation, is incremented. Then each cell is iterated, and if it exists, the individual cell form of `Calculate()` (`Calculate()` with the parameters `row` and `col`) is called. In the individual cell form of `Calculate()`, a check is made to see if the calculation version number of the cell is the latest of the spreadsheet; if not, the cell's lambda expression is called. After the new `CellState` has been assigned, the cell-state version number is incremented, and the cell state is returned.

■**Note** The calculation of the spreadsheet is nothing earth-shattering, and you might be tempted to argue it is irrelevant to the scope of the book. In fact, the calculation and its side effects are of major relevance. With lambda expressions, you have a form of asynchronous processing, very much like a spreadsheet. The cell calculations of the spreadsheet do not know when they will be called, and they cannot make assumptions about the state. Thus, when a lambda expression is created, the state at the time of the lambda expression may not be the same as when the lambda expression is executed. If you are not acutely aware of this potential pitfall, you could have some major bugs in your code.

The Important Stuff to Remember

In this chapter, you learned how to use .NET generics and also expanded your knowledge of lambda expressions. The main items to remember are as follows:

- .NET generics code can use .NET generics, or it can be code that provides types based on .NET generics. This chapter's example demonstrated using code, where the .NET generics code treated the .NET generics parameter type as a black box.

- Writing .NET generics code requires some forethought because you are creating an abstract intention implementation.

- Performance and type-safe characteristics are primary reasons for using .NET generics.

- You can use .NET generics at the type level or at the method level. Using .NET generics at the type level implies concretizing the type when the type is instantiated. Using .NET generics at the method level implies concretizing the type when the method is called.

- Lambda expressions, because of the way they are implemented, are shared state or individual state, depending on how they are declared and manipulated.

- For complex types, you should always implement `ToString()` as a way of figuring out the state of a type.

- Lambda expressions act asynchronously. When you use them, remember to not make assumptions of a particular state.

Some Things for You to Do

Here are some exercises that allow you to apply what you've learned so far:

1. The Worksheet<> class always requires you to dimension the fixed-cell array ahead of time. Change this code so that the rows and columns can change dynamically. Remember that the focus is on performance, and the fastest approach is a fixed-dimension array.

2. The average calculation knows how many items there are by the row number. Rewrite the average calculation code so that the user of the average code does not need to deal with the complexities of adding more elements, moving the cell calculation, and so on.

3. The methods Calculate() and GetCellState() seem to do the same thing. So, is there a need to have separate methods? Answer the question, and then make any necessary changes to the source code based on your answer.

■ ■ ■

CHAPTER 12

Learning About Application Configuration and Dynamic Loading

All of the examples in the preceding chapters have demonstrated how to use an application with a specific component. You knew which type to instantiate, which interface to use, and which assembly to reference. In these cases, you, as the developer, are in complete control, and when your application is built, all of the assemblies pop out as a nice, neat package.

But what works for the developer might not necessarily work for others. Let's go back to the lighting system presented in Chapter 8. We created a kernel that was responsible for turning on and off the lights. The implementations of the individual rooms were in a predetermined assembly with a specific name. This architecture would not work with a third-party library, because the kernel expected an assembly of a certain name. You might be thinking, "Heck, that's easy to solve—I just delete the old assembly and rename my assembly to match the old name." That technique would work, but it would also be an administrator's nightmare. The solution is to tell the program, "For lighting room implementations, look at this assembly and these types." And to give the program this information, you define some text in a file. A file that tells a program to do some task is called a runtime *configuration file*.

This chapter focuses on two areas: using application configuration files and dynamically executing code. A related topic is how much dynamically executed code should be configuration and how much should be convention.

Convention over Configuration

The question of how to reference and instantiate classes is both philosophical and pragmatic. Consider the architecture shown in Figure 12-1, which is a modular interface and implementation that was presented as an alternative architecture for the lighting system example in Chapter 8. In this figure, each of the boxes represents a single assembly: an assembly that contains the interface definitions, an assembly that contains the implementations, and an assembly that contains the kernel. The idea of all of these assemblies is to make it possible to update a single assembly without needing to update all of them. However, what is not indicated in the picture is the fact that your application must be able to *reference* all three assemblies. If one of those assemblies is missing, you have a problem, because your program cannot function.

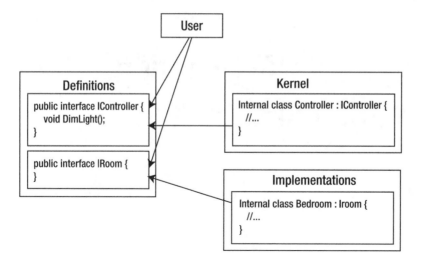

Figure 12-1. *How components can be defined*

The referencing of individual assemblies is not an issue. The issue is how each assembly learns about the others. In previous chapters, I said that you should use a factory, because a factory takes away the decision of what implementation to use.

Let's look at this from the perspective of code. Suppose the following interface definition is in an assembly that contains all interface definitions.

```
public interface IMyInterface { }
```

A class that implements the interface is defined in an assembly called `implementations`.

```
class MyImplementation : IMyInterface { }
```

If a class in another assembly wants to use the functionality of `MyImplementation`, then this factory is created:

```
public static Factory {
    public static IMyInterface Instantiate() {
        return new MyImplementation();
    }
}
```

Because `MyImplementation` is not declared as `public`, the class `Factory` must be defined in the assembly `implementations`. This implies that the assembly that uses the functionality has a reference to `implementations`.

Using a factory is acceptable and solves the problem of decoupling so that the user of the implementation does not need to know about the implementation. The user does not have to know the name of the implementation, but does need to know in which assembly the implementation resides. This means when you develop the code, you need to reference the appropriate assembly while coding. This is called source code component architecture in that you decouple the interface from the implementation, but you couple the assemblies.

You want to decouple the components at runtime (when the application runs) to solve the problem illustrated in Chapter 8, where we created a lighting kernel, but did not know the lighting implementations ahead of time. Using configuration, you could have an end user "plug in" lighting implementations that are controlled by the kernel. Developers like to call runtime decoupling a *plug-in* architecture (http://en.wikipedia.org/wiki/Plugin). And this is where configuration and convention come into play. "Convention over configuration" is a Ruby on Rails philosophy. The idea is that developers define only the nonconventional parts of their applications.

Decoupling Using a Configuration Architecture

In a runtime configuration scenario, the architecture of Figure 12-1 is not altered; it still has the definitions, implementations, kernel, and user assemblies. What is altered is how the references to each of the pieces are created.

Let's start with a simple situation. You have a question, and you happen to know who would know the answer. You know the person and you know she has a telephone. What you don't know is her telephone number. Translated to programming terms, the telephone acts as an interface to an implementation. The challenge is connecting to the implementation. In the case of the telephone, you can discover the telephone number by using the telephone book.

The telephone book contains the names of individuals at specific addresses and their telephone numbers. Names and addresses are easy to remember; telephone numbers are a bit more complicated. Thus, the telephone book serves the purpose of cross-referencing an easy piece of information with a more complicated piece of information. In programming terms, the cross-referencing is a configuration file that is associated with the .NET application. Once you have cross-referenced the information, you have the location of the assembly and can then instantiate the cross-referenced type. In programming terms, the configuration file gives you the location and name of the type.

Decoupling Using a Convention Architecture

Configuration files are useful, but they can become too complicated. Some projects have such complicated configuration files that bugs arise due to an improperly configured application.

Convention architecture attempts to simplify complexity by instituting a familiar pattern to the referencing of the type. Consider a telephone number like 1-800-BIG-CARS. The 1 and 800 are easy to remember, as is BIG CARS. This works because of the convention where a digit on the telephone keypad corresponds to three or four letters. So in the case of BIG-CARS, the number is 244-2277.

Conventions are good things as long as you know what they are. For example, if you were not familiar with the telephone system, you would wonder how BIG CARS represents a telephone number. The missing piece of information is the convention of how to convert the letter into the number.

What is useful with convention architecture is that you are not limited to what is defined in the configuration file, as there is a general logic. When implementing a convention architecture, you are not discarding configuration, but you are making assumptions for the user and implementation of the code. You will still probably have a configuration file, but the configuration is for specific functionality.

Regardless of whether you use a configuration architecture or a convention architecture, you will dynamically load assemblies, as demonstrated in this chapter.

Setting Up the Dynamic Loading Projects

For this chapter's examples, four projects are defined:

- Definitions: A class library that contains the definition for the interface IDefinition and the class ConfigurationLoader. The class ConfigurationLoader will contain the functionality to dynamically load the assemblies Implementations1 and Implementations2.

- Implementations1: A class library that contains the class Implementation and implements the interface IDefinition. The class Implementation is defined in the namespace Implementations1 and is not declared public.

- Implementations2: A class library that contains the class Implementation and implements the interface IDefinition. The class Implementation is defined in the namespace Implementations2 and is not declared public.

- CallRuntimeImplementation: A console application that will be referenced throughout the chapter as the user application.

Figure 12-2 shows the Definitions project in the Solution Explorer. In the Definitions project, the references are to the standard .NET libraries (System, System.Core, and so on). The unique reference that you need to add is to System.configuration. The System.configuration reference contains the types that you need to read the application configuration file.

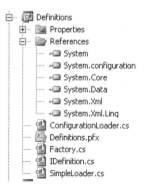

Figure 12-2. *The Definitions project*

The Implementations1 project is shown in Figure 12-3. This project contains the file Implementation.cs, which is the type Implementation and implements the interface IDefinitions. The implementation of Implementation is as follows:

```
namespace Implementations1 {
    class Implementation : IDefinition {
        public string TranslateWord( string word) { return ""; }
    }
}
```

Figure 12-3. *The Implementations1 project*

The class Implementation has a hard reference to IDefinition, so under the References node in the project is a reference to the Definitions assembly. Because there is a hard reference to IDefinition, the interface IDefinition is declared as public, but Implementation is not.

The Implementations2 project has the same implementation and reference to Definitions as Implementations1. What is special about Implementations2 is its use of a strong name. Thus far, all of your assemblies are not unique. To make them unique, you need to enable signing. You must also enable signing in the Definitions assembly. The next section describes how to enable signing.

The CallRuntimeImplementation project is the user application and is shown in Figure 12-4. The user application is responsible for calling the functionality in Implementations1 and Implementations2.

Figure 12-4. *The CallRuntimeImplementation project*

What you need to consider very carefully in the CallRuntimeImplementation project structure is that in the References node, only the Definitions assembly is present. There is no reference to Implementations1 or Implementations2.

It is important to understand that when a project does not have a reference to another project, it does not imply that the functionality cannot be used. To use the functionality of an assembly that is not referenced, you need to write code that will load the assembly dynamically. With a dynamically loaded assembly, you can do whatever is possible with a hard-linked reference.

Signing an Assembly

Signing an assembly is giving the assembly a strong name, which is a unique name. Think of it as follows. My name is Christian Gross, and on this planet we call Earth, there are probably a few dozen people with the name Christian Gross. Our governments distinguish between the various people with my name by way of a passport. A passport is a unique identifier that converts my common name into a strong name. This is exactly what happens when you use strong names with an assembly. A strong name is required when you want to add the assembly to the global assembly cache (GAC). You'll learn more about the GAC in the "Loading a Strongly Named Assembly" section later in this chapter.

By default, signing is disabled. To enable signing, you need to alter the properties of the project. Follow these steps to enable signing for the Implementations1 project and the Definitions project:

1. Right-click the project in the Solution Explorer and select Properties.

2. Click the Signing tab.

3. Check the Sign the Assembly check box, as shown in Figure 12-5.

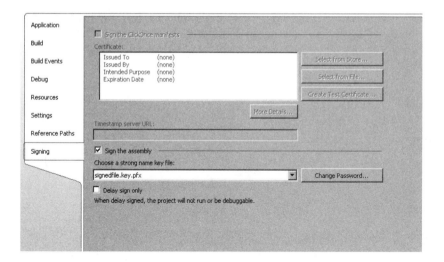

Figure 12-5. *Enabling signing*

4. Select <New...> from the combo box, which pops up a dialog box allowing you to specify the filename.

5. Type in a name and a password, and then click OK.

6. Save your project.

Setting the Output Path

The aim of the chapter is to demonstrate two things: configuration files and the dynamic abilities of .NET. Explaining, debugging, and running the configuration source code is simple, because everything is laid out for you in the Visual C# Express IDE. You will not run into any problems running the configuration code. However, for the dynamic loading, there is a complication.

As you've seen in Figure 12-4, the `CallRuntimeImplementation` project does not have explicit references to `Implementations1` and `Implementations2`. This means that if the code from `Implementations1` or `Implementations2` is referenced from `CallRuntimeImplementations` using dynamic techniques, Visual C# Express will have no clue as to what you are doing. You might argue that there is one Visual C# Express solution, and `Implementations1` and `Implementations2` are part of the overall project, but unless an explicit reference is made, Visual C# Express does not know about this.

However, you can overcome this problem fairly easily by changing where the projects place their compiled output. As a habit, I often make all projects build to a central directory. You can set the output directory in the Build tab of a project's Properties window, as shown in Figure 12-6.

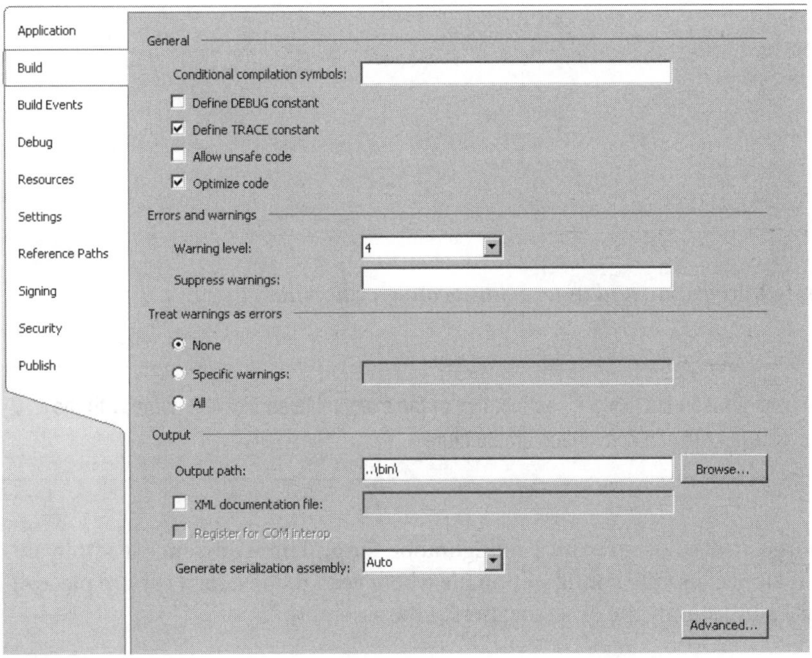

Figure 12-6. *Setting the Output path to a common path (..\bin\)*

You need to set the Output Path field to a common location for all projects. When you do that, a build will result in a directory structure like that shown in Figure 12-7 (in the next section). With all of the files in a common directory, running the dynamic-loading routines becomes trivial.

Defining and Processing a Configuration File

A configuration file is a file that contains information about how a program should behave. Configuration files by themselves do not control how a program behaves. For a configuration file to influence the behavior of a program, the program needs to read and act on the information in the configuration file.

Using a configuration file is not as easy as you may think it is. Yes, it is easy to define a configuration file and read the configuration file. What is difficult is how to define where the configuration file is located.

Suppose you have an application that is installed on the hard disk, and the application must make an assumption about where the configuration file is stored. One assumption could be the root directory of the C: drive. Yet that could be incorrect, because some computers don't have C: as the root drive.

.NET solves this problem in an interesting way: whatever the executing application is called, the configuration file has the same name with a `.config` extension. Figure 12-7 shows an example, in which the console application is `CallRuntimeImplementation.exe`. The configuration file is `CallRuntimeImplementation.exe.config`. A configuration file and executable are located in the same directory.

Figure 12-7. *A console application and its associated configuration file*

■**Note** Naming the configuration file using a combination of the executable application name with the `.config` extension is an example of a convention architecture.

In this section, you'll see how to write a configuration file and then reference it within an application. This setup will use the configuration file whenever a request for a certain piece of functionality is made and supply the exact location of the assembly.

Creating an XML-Based Configuration File

The configuration file contains Extensible Markup Language (XML). XML is a way of structuring a text file.

Consider the following text structure using spaces.

```
First Element
    Second Element
    Third Element
```

First Element is a parent, and Second Element and Third Element are subelements of the parent. The structuring of the parent and child elements is fragile, to say the least. We need a more robust way of structuring the data, which is where XML comes in. Think of XML as having the ability to define folders and folders within folders.

Let's define the XML that makes up a .NET application configuration file. All .NET application configuration files can be created using Visual C# Express, as follows:

1. Right-click the CallRuntimeImplementation project and select Add ➤ New Item.

2. Select Application Configuration file.

3. Leave the name as it is and click Add. The App.config file is created.

It is fine to leave the name as is, because when your .NET application is compiled, the .NET application configuration file will be renamed and placed beside the .NET application.

■Note .NET application configuration files apply to executable .NET applications. Thus, if an assembly uses the configuration API, the configuration file applied will be the one associated with the calling application. By default, a class library assembly is not associated with a configuration file. There are ways to read configuration information associated with a class library assembly. For more information about associating a configuration file with a class library, see Suzanne Cook's blog entry on App.config files (http://blogs.msdn.com/suzcook/archive/2003/06/02/57160.aspx).

Open the new App.config file, and you will see the following XML:

```
<?xml version="1.0" encoding="utf-8" ?>
<configuration>
</configuration>
```

The first line is a declaration of the XML file and the encoding that will be used. The second and third lines define a root XML node (also called an XML element). Think of a root XML node as analogous to a root folder where all of the other folders will be stored.

The root node is started with the identifier configuration surrounded by angle brackets. The node is terminated by the same identifier and angle brackets, with the addition of a slash prefix to the identifier. The only place where another XML node can be placed is between the beginning and ending XML nodes. For example, this XML is invalid:

```
<configuration>
<item>
</configuration>
</item>
```

In the example, <item> is started inside the declaration of <configuration>, but its termination, </item>, is outside the declaration of <configuration>.

Adding the Dynamic Loading Configuration Items

After you've added a configuration file, the next step is to add the elements that will be used by the dynamic loader. The idea will be to define some abstract identifier that will be cross-referenced to a type and assembly. Thus, to load `Implementations1.Implementation`, we'll use the identifier `Impl1`, type `Implementations1.Implementation`, and assembly `Implementations1.dll`. Similarly, `Impl2` will cross-reference to the type `Implementations2.Implementation` and the assembly `Implementations2.dll`.

Modify the configuration file as follows:

```xml
<?xml version="1.0" encoding="utf-8" ?>
<configuration>
  <appSettings>
    <add key="Assemblies"
        value="Impl1,Implementations1.Implementation,Implementations1.dll,
               Impl2,Implementations2.Implementation,Implementations2.dll" />
  </appSettings>
</configuration>
```

The XML node `<appSettings>`, which you could think of as adding the folder `appSettings`, contains XML nodes with the identifier `<add>`. This node defines a section in the configuration file that contains application settings expressed as key/value pairs. Each key/value pair is defined in the XML node using the XML attributes `key` and `value`.

Notice that the XML node `<add>` has a starting element, but not an ending element. This is because the `<add>` node is terminated with an angle bracket prefixed with a slash. This means that the ending element is not necessary.

The configuration file also defines a key `Assemblies` and a value that contains a buffer of comma-separated identifiers. The identifiers represent the identifier, type, and assembly of supported dynamically loaded assemblies.

The configuration file is complete, but will not influence the behavior of the application, because source code must be added to the application that reads the configuration file settings, as described in the next section.

■**Note** For the examples in this chapter, use the XML shown in the listings. XML is not difficult to learn, but for now, you'll get by with what I show you here. For more information about XML, visit the MSDN XML Developer Center at http://msdn2.microsoft.com/en-us/xml/default.aspx.

Reading a Configuration File

Reading a configuration file is very simple because the .NET Framework comes with an easy-to-use configuration API. For example, to read the value for the key `Assemblies`, use the following code, which would be added to your application when the application first starts, such as in the `Main()` method of a console program.

```
string value = System.Configuration.ConfigurationManager.AppSettings["assemblies"];
```

The class `ConfigurationManager` is a static class that provides the entry point to reading items from a configuration file.

In this example, a couple assumptions have been made. The first assumption is that you want to read the configuration settings from the application that is currently executing. The second assumption is that you want to read the configuration items stored within the XML node `<appSettings>`. Based on those two assumptions, the settings are stored in a static property named `AppSettings`, which returns an instance of type `NameValueCollection`. (The way that `AppSettings` is referenced makes it appear as if `AppSettings` were an indexer, which it is not.)

When retrieving the buffer of comma-separated identifiers using `ConfigurationManager`, you need to parse the buffer and then make sense of the information, as described in the next section.

Dynamically Loading an Assembly

In .NET terms, to use the configuration file with a dynamically loaded application, you need to load the assembly, and from the assembly, instantiate the type. You can reference assemblies locally and also reference them from the GAC.

Dynamically Instantiating a Type

The code to dynamically instantiate a type requires parsing the comma-separated buffer into its respective identifiers. To keep things organized, the three pieces of information are stored in a class. This can be called a *data class* because it has only data members.

The data class is a placeholder, needed only by the code used to dynamically load the type. This makes it possible to define the data class as a private class, because a private class implies only the parent class can instantiate it.

With the `ConfigurationLoader` class defined as the class used to dynamically instantiate other types, the private class is declared as follows (added to the `Definitions` assembly):

```
namespace Definitions
{
    public class ConfigurationLoader {
        private class ConfigurationInfo {
            public string AssemblyName;
            public string TypeName;
            public string EasyName;
        }
        Dictionary<string, ConfigurationInfo> _availableTypes;
    }
}
```

`ConfigurationInfo` contains three data members: `AssemblyName`, `TypeName`, and `EasyName`. The class is prefixed with `private`, indicating that nothing external to the `ConfigurationLoader` class could instantiate the configuration. Had `ConfigurationInfo` been declared with the `public` keyword, the following code would have been legal.

```
ConfigurationLoader.ConfigurationInfo cls =
    new ConfigurationLoader.ConfigurationInfo();
```

ConfigurationInfo is used to store the information from the configuration file. The configuration information is cross-referenced using a Dictionary, where the key is the EasyName data member.

To parse the configuration information and create the individual instances of ConfigurationInfo, the following code (part of ConfigurationLoader) is used.

```
public void Load() {
    string value = ConfigurationManager.AppSettings["assemblies"];
    string[] values = value.Split(',');
    for (int c1 = 0; c1 < values.Length; c1 += 3) {
        _availableTypes.Add( values[ c1],
            new ConfigurationInfo {
                EasyName = values[c1],
                TypeName = values[c1 + 1],
                AssemblyName = values[c1 + 2]
            });
    }
}
```

The configuration is read using AppSettings, and then split into an array of string element values. Processing three array elements at a time iterates the array. With every iteration, an instance of ConfigurationInfo is created. Once the buffer has been processed, it is possible to dynamically instantiate a type using the following ConfigurationLoader method.

using System.Reflection;
. . .

```
public RequestedType Instantiate<RequestedType>(string identifier) {
    if ( _availableTypes.ContainsKey(identifier)) {
        ConfigurationInfo info = _availableTypes[identifier];
        AssemblyName assemblyName =
            AssemblyName.GetAssemblyName(info.AssemblyName);
        Assembly assembly = Assembly.Load(assemblyName);

        object obj = assembly.CreateInstance(info.TypeName);
        return (RequestedType)obj;
    }
    else {
        throw new ArgumentException("identifier (" +
                                    identifier + ") is not a listed type");
    }
}
```

Look at the declaration of the method Instantiate(), and you will see that it is a .NET generics method (discussed in Chapter 11). The idea is to instantiate a type and perform an automatic cast to the request type. It avoids needing to define Instantiate() using the object type. The parameter identifier is a string that is used to search the Dictionary data member _availableTypes. If the identifier exists in _availableTypes, the ConfigurationInfo instance is retrieved and used to instantiate the type. If the identifier does not exist, an exception is thrown.

The bolded code is the special code because it is unlike what you have encountered thus far in the book. Built into .NET is the ability to dynamically execute code, as illustrated by these three very powerful lines of code. The first bolded line makes the reflection ability available, and the second is used to load the assembly. So, for example, if the parameter identifier equaled Impl1, the first bolded line would reference and dynamically load the assembly Implementations1.dll. However, and here is the catch, the assembly can be loaded dynamically only if Implementations1.dll exists in the local directory or the GAC. As an alternative, you could specify the entire path in the definition of the assembly. The downside to this strategy is that your assembly must always be located at the same place on different machines.

When the second bolded line assigns the variable assembly, it is to a reference of a loaded .NET assembly. The assembly will be parsed, and from there, it is possible to instantiate a type. The third bolded line calls the method CreateInstance(), with the name of the type that you want to instantiate, including the namespace. So, for example, if Implementations1.dll has been loaded, you could instantiate the type Implementations1.Implementation. The instantiation will work even though Implementations1.Implementation is a private class, because you are using dynamic programming principles.

However, being able to instantiate the type does not imply being able to use the type. To be able to use the instantiated type, you need to be able to type cast to a type that has been declared publicly.

We will continue the Implementations1.Implementation example and figure out how to instantiate and manipulate the instantiated object. But before we get to that code, we need to talk about an additional programming feature: singletons.

Using Singletons

The class ConfigurationManager is a static class, which means that you cannot instantiate the class. A static class and static methods, and static data members, result in a single-purpose class. Another way to get the same effect is to create a *singleton*. A singleton behaves like a static class, except that the class is instantiated. An advantage of using the singleton approach is that you can have multiple singletons of the same type, whereas with the static class, there can be only a single static class.

Consider that locks have keys, and sometimes a lock has a single key. Think of the single key as a static class. If that key is to open a vault, you will most likely want only one person to have a key. But what if the key is to your house door? You would probably want multiple copies, but you will want to control who has those keys. So, maybe you will have a single house key, or maybe you will have multiple house keys, but you will always be in control. The house key example is analogous to the use of a singleton. You could argue that a singleton could just as well be used to open a vault, since you can create a single key. But the problem with a singleton is that using properly written source code, you could instantiate a second or third instance of the singleton. If you use a static class, then source code cannot instantiate a second instance, thus enforcing a certain programming style.

Let's define the class ConfigurationLoader as a singleton, which implies two things:

- The creation of a property called `Instance` that references a single instance of `ConfigurationLoader`.

- The definition of the `ConfigurationLoader` as private, implying that only `ConfigurationLoader` can instantiate an instance of `ConfigurationLoader`. This ensures that `ConfigurationLoader` has similar behavior to a static class in that the consumer cannot instantiate an instance of the type.

The following is the singleton code for `ConfigurationLoader` (placed in the `Definitions` assembly).

```
static ConfigurationLoader _instance;
static ConfigurationLoader() {
    _instance = new ConfigurationLoader();
}

ConfigurationLoader() {
    _availableTypes = new Dictionary<string, ConfigurationInfo>();
}

public static ConfigurationLoader Instance {
    get {
        return _instance;
    }
}
```

The singleton property instance is declared as `static`, allowing a reference of `ConfigurationLoader.Instance`. The implementation of the static property must reference a static data member, which is the data member `_instance` in this example. The data member `_instance` is instantiated by the static constructor `static ConfigurationLoader()`. The instance constructor will instantiate the `Dictionary _availableTypes`. Notice the lack of `public` scope declaration, implying a `private` declaration.

Using the Instantiated Type

Now that we've covered the singleton aspect, we need to get back to the original problem of writing the code to instantiate a type dynamically. The following code is used to instantiate `Impl1`.

```
ConfigurationLoader.Instance.Load();
IDefinition definition =
    ConfigurationLoader.Instance.Instantiate<IDefinition>("Impl1");
Console.WriteLine(definition.TranslateWord("hello"));
```

■**Note** You might get errors running the code. If you do, it is because the assemblies are not in the same path and the dynamic loading methods cannot find the assemblies. Solve this by copying all of the assemblies into a single directory and running the code.

The first line is used to retrieve the assembly and type information from the configuration file. The second line is used to instantiate Impl1 and then typecast Implementations1. Implementation to type IDefinition. The cast will work because the IDefinition interface has been implemented by Implementations1.Implementation. The assigned variable definition will reference a valid object instance that implements IDefinition and the method TranslateWord().

At this point, we need to step back and reflect on what has occurred. We have defined within a configuration file the location of a type. Some source code in the application read the configuration file at runtime and stored the available types. The calling code knew about only the abstract type Impl1 and knew it implemented the interface IDefinition. Then, using some .NET magic involving dynamic techniques, the type's assembly is loaded and instantiated. This process is unique because an administrator has the ability to update where and what type should be instantiated and called, without needing to recompile or update the infrastructure. That flexibility makes it much simpler for you to update functionality without having to update the caller of the functionality.

■**Note** The ability to dynamically update the functionality is of benefit to the administrator of the application. There is minimal benefit to the developer, because the developer has already converted the architecture to use components. In general, developers consider this approach to components as building a plug-in architecture.

Enhancing the Configuration File

The configuration file is a bit of a clumsy definition because all of the available types are stored in a single key/value pair. It would be preferable to be able to define custom items in the configuration file, as follows:

```
<loader easyname="Impl1"
        typename="Implementations1.Implementation"
        assemblyname="Implementations1.dll" />
```

This approach is preferable because it is easier to read and understand, thus reducing the chances that you will have an error. Additionally, because the various identifiers are broken up, you don't need to build a lengthy single-line string.

■**Note** For simplicity, we will have only a single dynamic type, represented by the <loader> XML element. In a complete solution, you would use the same approach with different interfaces and types.

If you were to add the sample XML into the configuration file and run the .NET application, you would get a configuration initialization failure. That's because the XML node <loader> is not a standard configuration item and thus needs custom parsing. And when you want custom parsing, you need to tell the .NET configuration infrastructure what code to execute. The following is the complete .NET configuration file with custom processing tags.

```xml
<?xml version="1.0" encoding="utf-8" ?>
<configuration>
  <configSections>
    <section name="loader" type="Definitions.LoaderSection,Definitions" />
  </configSections>
  <appSettings>
    <add key="Assemblies"
         value="Impl1,Implementations1.Implementation,Implementations1.dll,
                Impl2,Implementations2.Implementation,Implementations2.dll" />
  </appSettings>
  <loader easyname="Impl1"
          typename="Implementations1.Implementation"
          assemblyname="Implementations1.dll" />
</configuration>
```

The bolded section represents a new part of the configuration file that could be called "configuring the configuration." Any XML node that is within the <configSections> section is used to customize the configuration-parsing infrastructure. In the example, the XML node <section> has two attributes that refer to what the configuration infrastructure should do when it encounters a specific XML node. The attribute name specifies the name of the XML node, and the attribute type references a type (Definitions.LoaderSection) and assembly (Definitions) that will process the XML node.

Step back and think about what is happening here. The XML node <section> is used to configure the configuration processor using dynamically loaded types. This demonstrates that the process of dynamically loading and executing pieces of code is not rocket science, but a daily part of developing components in .NET.

Since configuring the configuration infrastructure uses the same techniques as our infrastructure, implementing functionality for the configuration infrastructure implies implementing standard types. In our code, the type Implementations1.Implementation implemented an interface, whereas in the configuration infrastructure, we need to subclass a predefined class. Either approach is acceptable, and as you will see, subclassing a predefined type offers a particular advantage.

Marshaling the Configuration File Data

When you want to use a custom node in a configuration file, you need to implement a class that subclasses System.Configuration.ConfigurationSection. The purpose of the custom class is to process and structure the data in the configuration file into something that the user can manipulate. In other words, we are marshaling the data from the configuration file to the .NET environment.

The .NET infrastructure helps you implement the marshaling routines by providing class types that allow you explicitly associate an XML attribute or keyword with some variable. For example, suppose you want to cross-reference the XML attribute easyname with a .NET type. To do so, first define the nature and type of the property using the type ConfigurationProperty:

```
_propEasyName = new ConfigurationProperty(
                        "easyname", typeof(string),
                    null, ConfigurationPropertyOptions.IsRequired);
```

This example uses the ConfigurationProperty constructor that has four parameters:

- "easyname": Identifies the XML attribute identifier that will be cross-referenced.

- typeof(string): Identifies the type of the attribute, which could also include double and int to indicate a number.

- null: Identifies the default value of the attribute if the attribute does not exist.

- ConfigurationPropertyOptions.IsRequired: Identifies some characteristics of the attribute; in the case of this example, the attribute is required.

■**Note** There are multiple constructors for ConfigurationProperty. For more information, check out the MSDN documentation (http://msdn2.microsoft.com/en-us/library/system.configuration. configurationproperty.configurationproperty.aspx).

Once you have defined a property, you need to cross-reference it with a property and the base class ConfigurationSection:

```
[ConfigurationProperty("easyname", IsRequired = true)]
public string EasyName {
    get {
        return (string)base[_propEasyName];
    }
}
```

Whenever you reference the property EasyName, the attributes associated with the property provide a cross-reference with the configuration file. Whenever the property is called, the base indexer with data member that references ConfigurationProperty is called and marshals the data from the configuration file to the .NET type.

The complete implementation used to process the XML node <loader> is as follows (added to the Definitions assembly):

```
...
using System.Configuration;

namespace Definitions
{

    public class LoaderSection : ConfigurationSection {
        static ConfigurationProperty _propEasyName;
        static ConfigurationProperty _propTypeName;
        static ConfigurationProperty _propAssemblyName;
        static ConfigurationPropertyCollection _properties;

        static LoaderSection() {
            _propEasyName = new ConfigurationProperty(
```

```
                                    "easyname", typeof(string),
                            null, ConfigurationPropertyOptions.IsRequired);
            _propTypeName = new ConfigurationProperty(
                                    "typename", typeof(string),
                            null, ConfigurationPropertyOptions.IsRequired);
            _propAssemblyName = new ConfigurationProperty(
                                    "assemblyname", typeof(string),
                            null, ConfigurationPropertyOptions.IsRequired);
            _properties = new ConfigurationPropertyCollection();
            _properties.Add(_propEasyName);
            _properties.Add(_propTypeName);
            _properties.Add(_propAssemblyName);
        }
        [ConfigurationProperty("easyname", IsRequired = true)]
        public string EasyName {
            get {
                return (string)base[_propEasyName];
            }
        }
        [ConfigurationProperty("typename", IsRequired = true)]
        public string TypeName {
            get {
                return (string)base[_propTypeName];
            }
        }
        [ConfigurationProperty("assemblyname", IsRequired = true)]
        public string AssemblyName {
            get {
                return (string)base[_propAssemblyName];
            }
        }
    }
}
```

The LoaderSection class does two jobs: it tells the underlying configuration infrastructure what LoaderSection is interested in, and it provides an easy-to-use API to the configuration data. The first job is nice to have done, but the second is absolutely essential.

Many parts of the data structure are declared as static because we are using those data members as reference data members to make it easier when retrieving values for data members. To understand what happens, let's see an example of retrieving the values from a configuration file.

Reading the Enhanced Configuration File

As you've seen, the <configSections> element declares a custom XML node that, when encountered, instantiates a specific type—LoaderSection is instantiated in this example.

The values are retrieved from the custom configuration as follows:

- The configuration infrastructure reads the various attributes, such as [ConfigurationProperty("easyname", IsRequired=true)]).

- The configuration infrastructure does a cross-reference of which attributes exist and if they are required. Think of this step as the bookkeeping of the custom configuration information.

- The configuration infrastructure waits for the application code to call the properties EasyName, TypeName, or AssemblyName. In the implementation of the individual properties, the base indexer (such as base[_propTypeName] from LoaderSection.TypeName) is referenced, and the value of the configuration item is retrieved using the property descriptors declared as static members.

We can use the following code to read the custom configuration item (added to the Definitions assembly). This code is an example of replacing the previously declared Load() functionality.

```
public void Load() {
    LoaderSection loader =
      ConfigurationManager.GetSection("loader") as LoaderSection;
    if (loader != null) {
       _availableTypes.Add(loader.EasyName,
           new ConfigurationInfo {
               EasyName = loader.EasyName,
               TypeName = loader.TypeName,
               AssemblyName = loader.AssemblyName
           });
    }
}
```

The only major difference between this code and the previous Load() code is the ConfigurationManager reference. In the previous Load() implementation, it was assumed that all configuration settings were stored in the <appSettings> section. This time, we retrieve the <loader> section, which is defined to be the type LoaderSection. We still create all available types using the _availableTypes dictionary collection, but the parsing and breaking apart of the various buffers are not necessary.

■**Note** Writing your own configuration section is not that difficult, but it is tedious. It is tedious because you need to explicitly tell the configuration infrastructure what every item means and how you will use it. There is no simple way to get around this, because the configuration infrastructure needs to know which configuration items should be processed and how they should be processed. Thus, to implement a configuration section with multiple items, you will need to use more pieces of the predefined configuration infrastructure in the same manner as illustrated by this simple example. See the .NET configuration infrastructure documentation, at http://support.microsoft.com/kb/815786/, for more information.

Loading a Strongly Named Assembly

In the previous section, the example demonstrated the dynamic loading technique in which you explicitly define where the assembly is and then instantiate a type in that assembly. Another approach to instantiating an assembly involves using the formal declaration of a type.

In .NET, there is an easy way to reference an assembly and a more difficult way to reference an assembly. This is analogous to the easy way to identify a person and the more complicated way. The easy way to identify me is to use my name, Christian Gross, and that works to a degree. The problem is that I'm not the only Christian Gross on this planet. The precise way to find me is to look at my passport. The passport approach works, but it has a long, ugly number that is hard to remember.

The assembly `Implementations2.dll` is a generic assembly identifier like Christian Gross. The following is the precise .NET identifier of the assembly.

```
Implementations2, Version=1.0.0.0, Culture=neutral, PublicKeyToken=6bc4c8c27c08ba48
```

The identifier is quite a mouthful, but it says everything you need to know. This specifies the name as `Implementations2`, the version number, the culture (combination of language and country), and a fixed-signed identifier. When culture is defined as `neutral`, it means that only the language is taken into account and not the country-specific bit. For example, if the culture is `en-CA`, with `neutral`, the `CA` bit will be ignored.

Using all of these attributes, you can uniquely identify an assembly. This lets you load a specific version of the assembly, allowing multiple similar assemblies to be loaded simultaneously. This specific referencing allows you to use components according to version and language.

The extra information is specified in the source code file `AssemblyInfo.cs`, which is created by default. The following is an extract from `Implementations2.dll`. To view `AssemblyInfo.cs`, expand the Properties node of a project and double-click the filename.

```
[assembly: AssemblyTitle("Implementations2")]
[assembly: AssemblyDescription("")]
[assembly: AssemblyConfiguration("")]
[assembly: AssemblyCompany("devspace.com")]
[assembly: AssemblyProduct("Implementations2")]
[assembly: AssemblyCopyright("Copyright (c) devspace.com 2007")]
[assembly: AssemblyTrademark("")]
[assembly: AssemblyCulture("")]

[assembly: Guid("9b0a35bc-7170-4104-815b-b97b07a7d2ee")]
```

```
// Version information for an assembly consists of the following four values:
//
//      Major Version
//      Minor Version
//      Build Number
//      Revision
//
// You can specify all the values or you can default the Build and Revision Numbers
// by using the '*' as shown below:
// [assembly: AssemblyVersion("1.0.*")]
[assembly: AssemblyVersion("1.0.0.0")]
[assembly: AssemblyFileVersion("1.0.0.0")]
```

Notice that all of the assembly descriptors are declared as .NET attributes. The bolded attributes reference the version and culture of the assembly. By adjusting these attributes, you can tweak which assembly is loaded, as explained in more detail in the upcoming "Versioning Assemblies" section.

To load a specific assembly, you need to create an assembly name, like this:

```
AssemblyName assemblyName = new AssemblyName(value);
Assembly assembly = Assembly.Load(assemblyName);
object obj = assembly.CreateInstance(info.TypeName);
```

The variable `value` contains the precise .NET identifier of the assembly and is passed as a constructor parameter to `AssemblyName`. The resulting instance is passed to the method `Assembly.Load()`, which loads the assembly. The instantiation of the type follows the same sequence as previously outlined.

Note that there is no indication of where the assembly is located. The default locations that are probed are the local working directory of the executing process and the GAC.

■**Note** For more details about assembly loading, see *Essential .NET Volume 1: The Common Language Runtime* by Don Box with Chris Sells (Addison Wesley, 2002).

Relocating a Strongly Named Assembly to the GAC

Besides having the ability to tweak which assembly is loaded, another reason to use the precise assembly name is to have the ability to load an assembly from the GAC. The GAC is a place where assemblies can be placed to have global shared access. Think of the GAC as the `Windows\System32` directory of the .NET environment. The precise location for the default configuration is `c:\windows\assembly`, as shown in Figure 12-8.

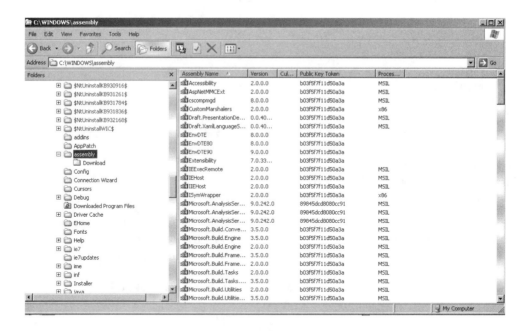

Figure 12-8. *The GAC directory*

Even though the GAC is just another directory, you should not just delete and add assemblies there, as you would with any other directory. To delete a file from the GAC, use the context-sensitive Uninstall menu item, as shown in Figure 12-9.

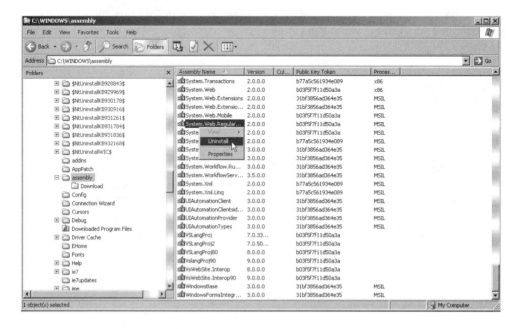

Figure 12-9. *Deleting an assembly from the GAC*

To add an assembly to the GAC, use the utility `gacutil`, which is distributed with the .NET SDK (not with Visual C# Express).

The following command lines demonstrate how to add the `Definitions` and `Implementations2` assemblies to the GAC (assuming the files `implementations.dll` and `definitions.dll` reside in the current directory).

```
gacutil /I definitions.dll
gacutil /I implementations2.dll
```

Remember to add `Definitions`, because `Implementations2` depends on `Definitions`. Failing to add `Definitions` will generate `gacutil` errors.

ORGANIZING DYNAMIC CODE

If you are going to place files in the GAC, don't use the techniques demonstrated in this book when doing a production release. The techniques discussed in this book are meant for developers, and only developers. The techniques are shortcuts that assume you know what the dependencies are and are aware of what you are doing. For distribution purposes, use the Microsoft Windows Installer application to install files into the GAC.

It's possible to write dynamic code in Visual C# Express, but that IDE leaves quite a bit to be desired. The higher levels of Visual Studio are geared toward dynamic coding. Everything needs to be kept properly organized. In Visual C# Express, that organization is dependent on you doing everything properly. In the higher levels of Visual Studio, most of that work is automated.

When writing dynamic code, the idea is to separate and completely compartmentalize the development of the component and the caller of the component. Thus, you should not develop both pieces in the same project. Create separate projects and have them working with test routines. Then, at runtime, combine the functionalities, and everything should work (that is, if you properly tested your code).

Using Version Numbers

Version numbers are a way of being able to control the features and robustness of an application. In the packaged software market, the concept of the version number has nearly disappeared. For example, consider Microsoft's operating system versions: Windows 95, Window 98, Windows XP, Windows 2000, Windows Vista, and so on.

In open source software, version numbers are used extensively and are considered very important. Yes, the version numbers resemble a lottery ticket, but they do follow a convention. Understanding the convention makes it easier to select open source packages. And more important, applying this versioning strategy makes it simpler to understand your assemblies.

Understanding Version Numbers

Let's say you want to download the open source program Capivara (a Java file manager and synchronization program). You see the version number 0.8.2. The version number contains three parts:

Major number: The major number is 0 in the example. If the software has not reached the number 1, the version is considered a beta. But often, a beta identifier does not mean the version is unusable. Changing the major version number indicates a major change of functionality. This means what worked in version 1 may not work with version 2. An example is the Apache HTTPD server project, where the 1.*x* and 2.*x* series are two different implementations.

Minor number: The minor number is 8 in the example. It is used to define minor functionality changes in a piece of software. Changing the minor number (such as 7 to 8) indicates new features, but old functionality is supported. A change may include bug fixes or patches.

Patch number: The path number is 2 in the example. It is used to define a patched version of the software that has bug fixes or other changes. The changes do not include features, and the functionality does not change.

When you attempt to download an open source package, you are typically confronted with multiple versions. For example, you might see the version numbers 4.23 and 4.29 (beta). Because most people want the latest and greatest, they might be tempted to download 4.29. But remember that open source projects make multiple versions available. In the example, you should download version 4.23, because 4.29 is a beta that may or may not work. Version 4.23 is considered stable and therefore usable.

The open source community will often use the following terminology when releasing software.

- *Stable*: A version that can be used in a production environment and should not crash.

- *Unstable*: A version that should not be used in production, but will probably work with some crashes.

- *Nightly*: A version with all bets off, meaning that the version may or may not work. The reason for using a nightly build is to monitor progress and check specific issues. Such a version is not intended for consumer consumption; it is intended solely for developers.

- *Alpha*: A version that demonstrates the concepts that will make up a future version of the software. However, in alpha versions, what was available one day might be gone the next day.

Versioning Assemblies

.NET assembly version numbers are different from those used for open source packages. The following is an example of versioning an assembly.

```
[assembly: AssemblyVersion("1.1.0.0")]
[assembly: AssemblyFileVersion("1.1.0.0")]
```

The attributes `AssemblyVersion` and `AssemblyFileVersion` can be added anywhere in the assembly or application. If you're using Visual C# Express, most likely the attributes are added to the file `AssemblyInfo.cs`.

The versions of the file have four significant parts. From left to right, these are major version, minor version, build number, and revision. The build number can represent a daily build number, but this is not required. The revision identifier can represent a random number, but this is not required either. For my assemblies, I use a revision number of 0, and consider the build number as a patch number.

Visual C# Express has a built-in mechanism that automatically updates the build and revision numbers. Alternatively, you can use a versioning tool, or you can increment the numbers manually. The gacutil tool can be executed multiple times with multiple versions, as shown in Figure 12-10.

■**Note** For more information about using versioning tools, see these two blog entries about auto-incrementing assembly versions: http://weblogs.asp.net/bradleyb/archive/2005/12/02/432150.aspx and http://www.biasecurities.com/blogs/jim/archive/2003/10/08/166.aspx.

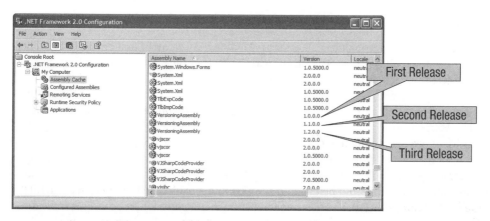

Figure 12-10. *An assembly added three times to the GAC with three different versions*

In the Figure 12-10, the assembly VersionAssembly has been added three times to the GAC with three different versions (1.0.0.0, 1.1.0.0, and 1.2.0.0). With the GAC in this state, an application or another assembly has the option to reference three different versions of the same assembly.

For an application or assembly to use another assembly, you create a reference. When the application or assembly is compiled, a specific version number of the assembly is referenced. For example, if a reference to the version 1.1.0.0 of VersionAssembly is defined, then version 1.1.0.0 of the assembly is executed.

Adding an Assembly Redirection to a Configuration File

Let's say an application or assembly needs to use a new version of the VersionAssembly assembly. To make the application or assembly aware of the new assembly, you update the application or assembly configuration file that references the old assembly. The configuration file update includes an assembly redirection. Essentially, what the redirection says is that if a certain version of an assembly is requested, the new version should be loaded. The following is an example of an assembly redirection.

```xml
<?xml version="1.0"?>
<configuration>
  <runtime>
    <assemblyBinding
        xmlns="urn:schemas-microsoft-com:asm.v1">
      <dependentAssembly>
        <assemblyIdentity name="VersioningAssembly"
         publicKeyToken="bd42f9cb12b40d1b"
         culture="neutral" />
        <bindingRedirect oldVersion="1.1.0.0"
         newVersion="1.2.0.0"/>
      </dependentAssembly>
    </assemblyBinding>
  </runtime>
</configuration>
```

This configuration file includes an `assemblyBinding` XML element that defines a collection of assemblies that will be affected. The collection of assemblies are embedded within the `dependentAssembly` element. Within the `dependentAssembly` element are two child elements: `assemblyIdentity` and `bindingRedirect`. The `assemblyIdentity` element is used to identity the assembly for which a reference will be redirected, and it contains the child element `dependentAssembly`.

The `bindingRedirect` element contains two attributes; `oldVersion` and `newVersion`. The `oldVersion` attribute identifies a reference to the old assembly in the calling assembly or application. If the reference to the old assembly is found, the `newVersion` attribute is used to identify which assembly version should be used. In the example, the old version reference is 1.1.0.0, and the new version is 1.2.0.0. The new version has an incremented minor number, indicating a new version of an assembly. However, the binding redirection does not care whether the `newVersion` attribute references a new version or an old version. The version identifiers identified by the attributes `newVersion` and `oldVersion` are just that: identifiers.

Implementing a Convention-Based Architecture

There has been quite a bit of talk in the software community about convention over configuration. Most of this talk began in earnest with the development of Ruby on Rails (http://www.rubyonrails.org/). Ruby on Rails (Rails for short) is an amazing tool that allows people to very quickly create effective web sites that provide useful functionality. Most developers would love to get their jobs done more quickly, and Rails offers a way to do just that.

Many attribute the success of Rails to its use of convention over configuration. Some say it is the Ruby language. Others say it is because Rails is a professional product. I believe it's a combination of factors, but the convention over configuration angle does play an important role.

Let's go back to the problem of loading code dynamically, or for that matter, executing code dynamically. How much do you expect the programmer to know, and how much do you expect the programmer to guess? Consider this code:

```
interface IDefinition  { }
void DoIt(IDefinition def) {
   // Do Something with def
}
```

In the code, you can see an interface IDefinition and a method DoIt(), with a parameter of type IDefinition. This creates a contract where to call DoIt(), you need to pass an instance of type IDefinition.

Is it correct to assume that the dynamic loading of a type can fulfill the contract of DoIt()? Can you assume that the type even supports IDefinition?

What convention over configuration attempts to do is create pockets of self-contained functionality that can take care of itself. That self-contained functionality may require configuration file settings, and it may require other assemblies. But what it does not require is a directive that includes source code that explicitly states what to do when.

Consider a workplace scenario. Instead of having a manager tell the workers what to do at every step, a certain amount of peer-to-peer intelligence and self-reliance are assumed. The self-reliance is both good and bad. It is good in that there are fewer moving parts, but bad in that the peers might be doing something that they should not.

The following code shows an example of convention.

```
interface ICommand {
    void Run();
}
...
ConfigurationLoader.Instance.Load();
IDefinition definition =
    ConfigurationLoader.Instance.Instantiate<ICommand>("Impl1");
definition.Run();
```

The code runs some other code via the Run() method and does not have any return values or parameters. The code doing the executing is hoping that everything will work out. And that is the gist of convention over configuration—the calling code hopes everything will work out. Again, this is the peer-to-peer analogy.

For the most part, convention works out quite nicely because it is easier to extend and maintain a convention-based system, since there are fewer moving parts. For any complex system, the fewer moving parts the better. The downside is that the administrator needs to understand what the moving parts are.

People have a tendency to make everything configurable and leave nothing to the computer program. Whether or not something works depends on how the configuration is written. In a convention architecture, the called functionality will make decisions about what it deems appropriate.

Here is an example of configuration:

```
[ConfigurationProperty("typename", IsRequired = true)]
public string TypeName {
    get {
        return (string)base[_propTypeName];
    }
}
```

The code should look familiar, as it reassembles the configuration code you saw earlier. But this code is overconstrained and requires too many moving parts. You could simplify it to the following code (which does not compile because you can't change the code base of the .NET library).

```
[ConfigurationProperty()]
public string TypeName {
    get {
        return (string)base[_propTypeName];
    }
}
```

The difference between the two code pieces is the missing parameters in the .NET attributes. The parameters are not necessary because they are already defined by the data member propTypeName, and you can use the identifier of the property as that extra piece of information. So the property identifier TypeName could be used as an identifier for an XML attribute.

Some may argue that by having a cross-reference between the property identifier and configuration identifier, you are creating a hard-coded dependency. That's a valid argument. But is the code's assumption a common-sense assumption? Is it an extreme proposition to say that your property identifier is the name of your XML attribute? The answer is that it is not an extreme proposition, and the Ruby on Rails creators said the same when creating their own architecture.

Let's now consider the ability to indicate whether a configuration item is required. By specifying whether or not an attribute is required, you can avoid an exception at a later point. However, think about the bigger context. The .NET IsRequired attribute is processed when the program is started. The validity of the configuration file is not processed at compile time, and thus the only thing that IsRequired does is generate an exception earlier. Maybe you want to avoid any runtime errors that could bring down a program during processing. I don't think it is a big advantage, but I am sure others will think it is, and thus using the IsRequired property is a judgment call.

■Note The aim of convention-based architecture is to make as many assumptions as possible, without sacrificing the bigger goal of the application. A good convention-based architecture is not easy to create because it requires completely understanding the needs of the developers and those who run the application. My personal rule of thumb is to solve the problem first, and then decide what should be configured and what should be a convention.

Dynamically Loading Base Class or Interface Types

This chapter demonstrated two categories of code that were dynamically loaded. The first category was a type that implemented an interface (Implementation and IDefinition). The second type was a class that subclassed another class (LoaderSection, ConfigurationSection). Each approach has its advantages and disadvantages, but there is a single rule that you can use.

Whether to use an interface or class depends on how much responsibility you want to delegate to the implementation. In the configuration processing example, the .NET infrastructure specifically indicated that the only responsibility of the dynamically loaded class is to indicate which identifiers should be processed. How the value of the identifiers are extracted and converted into .NET types is the responsibility of the base class.

When you instantiate a type and use an interface, you are delegating complete control to the dynamically instantiated type. The calling code is explicitly saying, "Here is your contract. How you deal with it is your responsibility. Just make sure to implement the contract properly." By delegating all the responsibility, you are, in a sense, asking for trouble, because developers might implement a contract incorrectly.

Other factors come into play, such as performance and resources, but I think that they are not as important as understanding the single rule of responsibility.

The Important Stuff to Remember

In this chapter, you learned about configuring an application and dynamically loading code that is executed. The main items to remember are as follows:

- A .NET application configuration file works only because there is code in the application that uses the specified items in the configuration file.

- Applications have .NET application configuration files where the name of the file is the name of the executing application appended with a `.config`.

- A .NET application configuration file is a specially formatted XML file.

- A .NET application configuration file applies to assemblies loaded by the application.

- The default scenario for a .NET application configuration file is to store the settings as key/value pairs in the `<appSettings>` section.

- You can enhance the .NET application configuration file, but that implies implementing types that specifically outline what XML nodes and attributes are to be present in the XML.

- When processing data, you sometimes need a type (such as `ConfigurationInfo`) that is used to store information in a structured manner for a specific reason. By declaring a private class within a class, you fulfill the need for a structure to the data, but do not expose the class for inappropriate use.

- .NET has plenty of functionality that allows a developer to dynamically execute code.

- One way of dynamically executing code is to load an assembly, instantiate a type, and then typecast the instance to a specific known type.

- You can instantiate private types declared in an assembly.

- Dynamically loading assemblies requires using assemblies that are referenced by their path or by their precise name.

- You can use the GAC to store assemblies that will be shared by multiple applications.

- Only use the GAC if you must. If you do use the GAC, you need to create strongly named assemblies using signing.

- Regardless of how an assembly is versioned, a version number should exist and be used.

- In convention-based coding, your code makes assumptions about its behavior. Convention-based coding is more compact, but because assumptions are made, the code is less flexible. However, do not confuse flexibility with being the best way to do something. You should have flexible code when you need it, not just because it can be written that way.

Some Things for You to Do

Here are some exercises for you to do to apply what you've learned in this chapter:

1. Rewrite the configuration code so that the configuration file specifies a directory where all assemblies in that directory are loaded.

2. Having read all of the assemblies with the rewritten configuration, call a predefined type that will tell the caller which types are available and their appropriate types.

3. Modify ConfigurationLoader so that it uses the new configuration architecture to instantiate types.

CHAPTER 13

■ ■ ■

Learning About Multithreading

Your brain allows you to multitask—you can prepare dinner while talking on the telephone. This multitasking has limits, and you can do only two or three things simultaneously. But suppose you could put down the work, start another piece of work, then put that down, and then switch to the original work. How many tasks could you handle at the same time? Probably a few hundred, because what you are doing is *serializing* the multitasking.

Now suppose you and another person are preparing dinner in the kitchen, but you are not communicating with each other. What is the likelihood that you will run into the other person? Probably pretty high. What I am trying to get across here is the difference between multitasking with a single brain and multitasking with multiple brains. Multitasking always has a cost, which is orchestration. And sometimes doing more multitasking is not going to speed things up. There is a limit to how many brains are required to run an efficient kitchen.

The focus of this chapter is how to write code that is capable of multitasking. The operating system multitasks, by default, but whether or not your program multitasks depends on how you write your code. For example, suppose the lighting controller introduced in Chapter 8 had to control 3,000 rooms? To be able to process such a large number of rooms, you would use the same code, except run it in parallel. And therein lies the problem of code that needs to multitask. It's more difficult to make code run efficiently in parallel. A common problem in multitasking applications is the dreaded deadlock. A deadlock occurs when two tasks need data from each other to continue, which means neither can continue.

Running code in parallel requires coding discipline, as you will learn in this chapter. We will use only a single project, named `JugglingTasks`, which is a console application that implements the techniques demonstrated in this chapter.

Understanding Multitasking

One of the biggest jumps in computing history was when the computer went from a machine that carried out a single task to a multitasking machine. The old Commodore 64 and Vic20 were single-tasking machines. You started the computer, and then the computer waited for you to do something. If you decided to make the computer run a loop saying "hello" millions of times, that is all the computer would do. The computer could not do one thing, and then do something else while waiting for an answer from the executing task. How could anyone get anything done? (On the other hand, you could argue that people might be more productive if they could only work in a single program, and not also check their e-mail, look at the latest blog entry from their favorite author, and so on.)

Things changed quite dramatically when computers could multitask. Server computers running operating systems like Unix were multitasking from day one. Operating systems like Windows were not 100% preemptive multitasking until Windows NT and Windows 95. Notice that I used the term *preemptive*, which makes a big difference.

Plain-vanilla multitasking is multitasking where individual tasks cooperate and allocate resources as a collective. It is essentially a dead-end idea, and the best example of how it worked is Windows 3.0 and Windows 3.1 (but these were full of hacks). Now let's see what preemptive multitasking means.

Preemptive Multitasking

Preemptive multitasking is when the operating system controls which application does what and when. Realize that an operating system is an application, and you can run an application because applications are treated as components. You don't believe me? Create a console application and rename the method Main() to Mains(). See what happens. The reality is that the Main() method as it is declared is an API used by the operating system to run your component, which masquerades as a program.

So we have this program called the operating system that runs components called programs. The next question is how can multiple programs run at the same time? The answer is that the operating system program is no ordinary program. It is the foundation upon which applications can be launched and managed. The operating system hooks into special features of the microprocessor that allow the operating system to time slice the individual programs. Because your .NET programs are components, they will never need to access the microprocessor directly. The operating system will not let you access the microprocessor, because that could make the operating system unstable.

Time Slicing

Time slicing is when an operating system can dictate for how much time a program is allowed to execute. Between the times of execution, the program is in a state of deep freeze and does nothing. You, as a user, are not aware of the time slices, because a time slice operates on the order of microseconds. Because time slicing is so fast, you think your program is running continuously. To see the time slicing in action, open the Windows Task Manager.

Look closely at the Task Manager window shown in Figure 13-1, and you'll see that explorer.exe has 6% of the CPU. You can say that the explorer application is using the appropriate amount of time slices that equals 6% of the CPU time. How the CPU slices the 6% is a detail of the operating system.

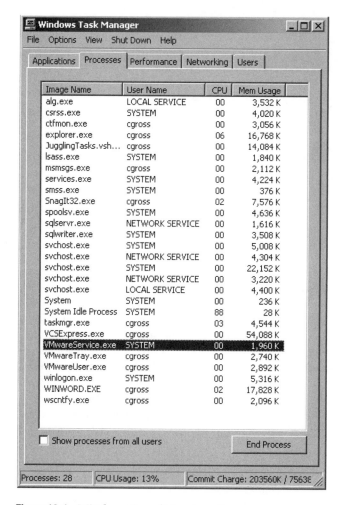

Figure 13-1. *Windows time slicing in action*

This time-slicing concept and its ramifications are not a big issue on single-core CPUs. However, on multiple-core CPUs, time slicing does become an issue.

Say you have a program that runs two tasks: task 1 and task 2. The microprocessor is a single core, and thus when running two separate tasks, there will be two time slices, as illustrated in Figure 13-2. In the figure, the entire processing cycle is represented as a pie, and each time slice is a slice of the pie.

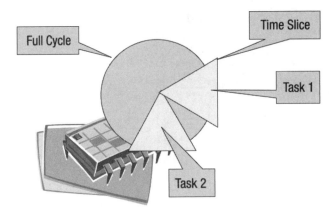

Figure 13-2. *Single-core microprocessor running two tasks*

Notice how task 1 and task 2 run in a serial manner, rather than concurrently. This is because the microprocessor is a single-task device made to look like a multitask device. Splitting a program task into smaller subtasks on a single-core CPU does not provide any real advantage. You would run multiple tasks on a single-core microprocessor when you want to have application background tasks that should not affect the foreground task of the application. For example, when running a word processor, you don't want the spell checker slowing down your typing.

Figure 13-3 illustrates how the same application executes on a multiple-core microprocessor. Did you notice what happened? The operating system, in a bid to make more efficient use of the microprocessor, has put one task on one core and another task on the other core. Now both tasks are running in parallel. And now it's possible that both tasks would want to manipulate the same piece of data at the same time. In a single-core microprocessor, that is not physically possible.

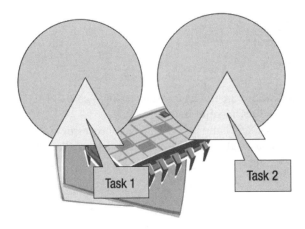

Figure 13-3. *Multiple-core microprocessor running two tasks*

With multiple-core microprocessors, you must pay close attention to how global state is manipulated in a multitasking application. If you are not careful, you could corrupt the state of your program. Corruption might not be as apparent on a single-core microprocessor, because you can't truly run two tasks in parallel.

> ■**Note** As companies like Intel and AMD introduce microprocessors with more and more cores, it is your job as a software developer to write software that can make use of those cores. This is not always easy and requires some forethought, since you need to work out the logic. For example, if you are processing data that is sent to a file, you can't read the file before the data has been processed.

Using Threads

Tasks can run in two ways on the Windows operating system: via threads and via processes. A *process* is when you click a program, causing the operating system to instantiate resources and time slices for the program. A *thread* is a lightweight process that executes in the context of a process.

All processes will start a thread. The thread that is executed as part of the process is the main thread, and when it exits, so does your application. If the main thread creates other threads, when the main thread exits, so do the created threads. From an architectural perspective, when multitasking, the main thread will execute and coordinate the threads that run your code. Two processes cannot reference each other. This is so that if one process crashes, it does not cause the other process to crash. Threads executing in the context of a process have the ability to bring down an entire process.

> ■**Note** You could run multiple processes and then use interprocess communication mechanisms to communicate. However, I can't recommend that solution, since you can get the same effect of a process by using a .NET application domain (AppDomain). For the most part, you don't need to concern yourself with AppDomains. You will use threads, since they are lightweight (compared to a process), easy to manage, and easy to program.

Creating a New Thread

You can create a new thread that will run independently of its originating thread. In the following example, the main thread creates two other threads. Each of the threads outputs some text to the console. Note that the type Thread and other related types used in this chapter's examples are in the System.Threading namespace.

```
Thread thread1 = new Thread(
                 delegate() {
                      Console.WriteLine("hello there");
                 }
);
Thread thread2 = new Thread(
                 () => { Console.WriteLine("Well then goodbye"); });
thread1.Start();
thread2.Start();
```

To create a thread, you instantiate the Thread type and call the Start() method. The Thread type is a class that contains all of the functionality necessary to start and control a multitasking task.

When running a thread, the Thread type needs code to execute. The solution used by Thread is a delegate, which is passed to Thread via the constructor. The name of the delegate is ThreadStart. The example here does not use the ThreadStart type, because both threads use programming constructs that do not need a delegate declaration. The first thread (thread1) uses an anonymous method, and the second thread (thread2) uses a lambda expression. Calling the Start() method starts a thread executing the functionality of the anonymous method or lambda expression.

Running the thread example, you may see this output:

```
well then goodbye
hello there
```

Notice how hello there is after well then goodbye. The output implies that the second thread (thread2) starts before the first thread (thread1). However, your output might be the opposite, which demonstrates the true nature of threading, concurrency, and why threading is so difficult.

Imagine for a moment that the sample thread code were not threaded, but executed in a serial manner. Calling thread1.Start() and then thread2.Start() results in the text hello there being first. The serial behavior is easy to understand for humans. Things become complicated when you need to think of multiple tasks at the same time. While the computer has no problem with threads, a human who is thinking in a serial manner codes the logic, and thus the logic could be wrong.

Writing a good threading application should remind you of herding cats or dogs. If you are not careful with your threads and synchronization, then it is like herding ten cats into a single corner—a nearly impossible task, since cats do not respond well to commands. But if you are careful and conscientious, then it is like herding ten dogs into a corner—fairly easy if the dogs are trained.

Waiting for the Thread to End

Calling Start() will start a thread, causing a task to be executed. The caller of the thread does not wait for the created thread to end, because the created thread is independent of the caller. So if you were running a batch process, you would need to wait until all threads have completed. You start off a number of threads using the caller logic. The caller logic only needs to start the processes, and thus its work requires a fraction of the time that the threads require. If the caller thread were to exit, all threads would be forcibly exited, and potentially, data could be corrupted.

There is a way for the caller thread to know when a created thread has exited. This technique involves using the Join() method, like this:

```
Thread thread = new Thread(
                delegate() {
                    Console.WriteLine("hello there");
                    Thread.Sleep(2000);
                }
```

```
);
thread.Start();
thread.Join();
```

The last line of code calls the Join() method, which means that the thread calling Join() is blocked until the thread referenced by the instance ends. A Thread.Sleep() call is used to put the thread to sleep for the time specified by the parameter—2000 milliseconds, or 2 seconds, in this example.

This code solves the problem of the premature exit of the calling thread, but if the calling thread is going to wait until the created thread exits, what's the benefit? In this simple example, using Join() adds no benefit. However, when the caller thread executes many threads, the caller wants to continue only when all threads have finished executing. So in a multithreading situation, you would want to call Join() on each and every thread.

Another variation of Join() is where a parameter specifies a timeout. Imagine starting a thread, and in the worst-case scenario, you predict a processing time of 5 minutes. If the processing time is exceeded, the logic is to forcibly exit the thread. Here's the code to implement that logic:

```
if(!thread.Join(300000)) {
    thread.Abort();
}
```

In the example, calling Join() will cause the executing thread to wait 300,000 milliseconds (5 minutes) before continuing. If the timeout occurred, a false is returned, and the code forcibly exits the thread using the Abort() method.

Creating a Thread with State

In the threading example, the threads did not manage any state. In most cases, your threads will reference some state. Using state in the context of anonymous methods and lambda expressions poses a challenge. (See Chapter 11 for details on how state is managed with lambda expressions.)

Implementing a ThreadStart Delegate

One way to run a thread with state is to define a type that implements a delegate of the type ThreadStart. The following example defines a class with a method that will be called by a thread. The technique used is where a classic .NET 1.x type delegate is passed to the Thread type.

```
class ThreadedTask {
    string _whatToSay;
    public ThreadedTask(string whatosay) {
        _whatToSay = whatosay;
    }
    public void MethodToRun() {
        Console.WriteLine("I am babbling (" + _whatToSay + ")");
    }
}
```

To use the method, the threading code is changed as follows:

```
ThreadedTask task = new ThreadedTask("hello");

Thread thread = new Thread(new ThreadStart(task.MethodToRun));
thread.Start();
```

In the example, the ThreadedTask type is instantiated with a state, and then Thread is instantiated with the stateful task.MethodToRun() method. When the thread starts, the data member _whatToSay will have some associated state. The code is logical and has no surprises. But what if you were to use the stateful method twice, like this:

```
ThreadedTask task = new ThreadedTask("hello");

Thread thread1 = new Thread(new ThreadStart(task.MethodToRun));
Thread thread2 = new Thread(new ThreadStart(task.MethodToRun));
thread1.Start();
thread2.Start();
```

Here, there are two Thread instances, but a single task instance. There will be two threads doing the same thing, and even worse, two threads sharing the same state. It is not wrong to share state, but sharing state requires special treatment to ensure that state remains consistent. You need to instantiate a single ThreadedTask and associate it with a single Thread instance, like this:

```
ThreadedTask task1 = new ThreadedTask("hello");
ThreadedTask task2 = new ThreadedTask("goodbye");

Thread thread1 = new Thread(new ThreadStart(task1.MethodToRun));
Thread thread2 = new Thread(new ThreadStart(task2.MethodToRun));
thread1.Start();
thread2.Start();
```

If you are running a stateful method, you need to associate a task instance with a thread instance. Having to associate a single task instance with a single thread instance means you can't use in-line anonymous methods that reference state. Instead, you need to use the solution demonstrated in the "Using Lambda Expressions in the Spreadsheet" section of Chapter 11.

Using a Thread Parameter

Suppose that you want to use an in-line anonymous method or lambda expression, and want a stateful thread. You can do this by using a thread parameter. A thread parameter is like a method parameter, except the data is passed to the instantiated thread and could be considered as a thread constructor. Here's an example of using a thread parameter:

```
Thread thread = new Thread(
  (buffer) => { Console.WriteLine("You said (" + buffer.ToString() + ")"); });
thread.Start("my text");
```

The lambda expression now has a parameter. The parameter is the state, which you can manipulate as you would any other variable. Of course, you should not pass the same variable instance to multiple threads. Doing so would cause a concurrency problem, and thus a corruption of state.

Two restrictions apply to using a thread parameter: you can send only a single parameter, and that parameter must be an object.

■**Note** Being allowed only a single thread parameter is an inconvenience, but acceptable. The fact that the single parameter is an object is not understandable, since we have .NET generics. Nonetheless, we need to respect those two restrictions on using thread parameters.

Synchronizing Between Threads

When you have two threads and both share state (such as a variable), a concurrency situation may arise. Sharing state between two independent threads is not a problem if both threads consider the data as read-only. In a multiple-core multiprocessor machine (as illustrated in Figure 13-3), what would happen if one thread on one core read the state of an object, and another thread on the other core modified the state of the object? What does the reading thread read? Is the state consistent? It is probably not consistent, and that is why you need to synchronize access to state.

Let's consider a simple .NET collection class example. The following source code executes in the calling thread, instantiates a list collection, and then adds two numbers to the collection.

```
List<int> elements = new List<int>();
elements.Add(10);
elements.Add(20);
```

In the next step, we define the source code for a thread that iterates the elements collection.

```
Thread thread1 = new Thread(
                 () => {
                     Thread.Sleep(1000);
                     foreach (int item in elements) {
                         Console.WriteLine("Item (" + item + ")");
                         Thread.Sleep(1000);
                     }
                 });
```

This thread iterates the data, and the two Thread.Sleep() calls put the threads to sleep for 1000 milliseconds, or 1 second. By putting the thread to sleep, we can artificially construct a situation where another thread adds to the collection while the collection is being iterated.

The thread that adds an element to the collection is defined as follows:

```
Thread thread2 = new Thread(
                 () => {
                     Thread.Sleep(1500);
                     elements.Add(30);
                 });
```

Both threads are started as follows:

```
thread1.Start();
thread2.Start();
```

Running the threaded code will generate an exception, but not immediately. First, the caller thread creates and starts thread1 and thread2. thread1 goes to sleep for 1 second, and thread2 goes to sleep for 1.5 seconds. After thread1 awakens, one item in the collection is iterated, and thread1 goes to sleep for another second. But before thread1 reawakens, thread2 awakens and adds an element to the collection. When thread1 reawakens and attempts to iterate another element in the collection, an exception is generated, as shown in Figure 13-4.

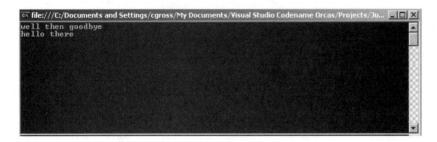

Figure 13-4. *Exception thrown after adding element to the collection, as shown in Visual C# Express*

The InvalidOperationException is thrown to indicate that you can't add elements to a collection while iterating a collection. The collection classes think it is a bad idea to modify and iterate a collection at the same time. I agree with the collection classes, because doing so could give unpredictable results.

The problem in the source code is how to use the collection classes in a multithreaded context. In the example, items are added to the collection while the collection is being iterated. A solution would be to take a snapshot of the collection, and then iterate the snapshot, freeing the main collection for the addition of items. A commonly suggested approach is to use the type System.Collections.ObjectModel.ReadOnlyCollection, as in the following example.

```
...
using System.Collections.ObjectModel;
...

List<int> elements = new List<int>();
elements.Add(10);
elements.Add(20);

Thread thread1 =
    new Thread(
        () => {
            Thread.Sleep(1000);
            foreach (int item in new ReadOnlyCollection<int>(elements)) {
                Console.WriteLine("Item (" + item + ")");
```

```
            Thread.Sleep(1000);
        }
    });

Thread thread2 =
    new Thread(
        () => {
            Thread.Sleep(1500);
            elements.Add(30);
        });

thread1.Start();
thread2.Start();
```

The change is the bolded code, which instantiates the type `System.Collections.`
`ReadOnlyCollection`, to which we pass the `elements` list. The `ReadOnlyCollection` provides the
base class for a generic read-only collection. The `foreach` iterator then iterates a collection
that is read-only, but based on the original collection. However, running the code will result in
the same exception. This demonstrates that `ReadOnlyCollection` does not take a snapshot, but
masks the collection. The mask disables the addition of items to the collection, but because
the other thread is taking a shortcut and editing the original collection, the read-only collection is modified as well.

Let's say that converting the collection into a read-only collection had worked. It would
not have solved anything! A read-only collection means that the second thread would generate an exception because you can't add elements to a collection that is read-only. The point is
that when writing multithreaded code that shares variables, you don't have an easy solution,
because you are trying to solve the problem of how to keep multiple cooks productive in a single kitchen.

We are trying to solve a classic reader/writer problem, where some threads are interested
only in reading the data, and other threads are interested only in modifying the data. One way
to synchronize the readers and writers is to use an exclusive lock, so that only one thread may
read or write.

Using Exclusive Locks

When using exclusive locks in .NET, you are saying, "Only one thread may execute this piece
of code." If two threads want to execute a particular piece of code, one will be granted access,
while the other thread waits until the granted thread has exited the code block. It is important
to understand that an exclusive lock grants access to code, not data, but that code could access
data. And because only one thread is accessing the code, it is implied that only one thread can
access the data.

The following is an example of code that uses exclusive locks.

```
List<int> elements = new List<int>();
elements.Add(10);
elements.Add(20);
```

```
Thread thread1 = new Thread(
                 () => {
                     Thread.Sleep(1000);
                     lock (elements) {
                         foreach (int item in elements) {
                             Console.WriteLine("Item (" + item + ")");
                             Thread.Sleep(1000);
                         }
                     }
                 });
Thread thread2 = new Thread(
                 () => {
                     Thread.Sleep(1500);
                     lock (elements) {
                         elements.Add(30);
                     }
                 });
thread1.Start();
thread2.Start();
```

The bolded lines use the lock keyword, which represents a code block of exclusive access. The thread is granted access to only a single code block in each instance. Looking at the code within the block, you can see that the collection is accessed in two locations. Using the exclusive lock argument where a single thread can access only a single code block, one thread will write to the collection, and another thread will read from the collection.

The lock statement has a parameter that is a reference to lock against. In both threads, the reference is elements. The common reference synchronizes access to code. At any given point in time, the code contained within the lock block will have only a single thread executing. This implements the desired feature, where only one thread is accessing code that reads or writes to the collection. The flow of the program is as follows:

1. Both threads wait.

2. After 1 second, thread 1 acquires a lock because no other thread has done so.

3. Thread 1 executes its code.

4. Once thread 1 executes the synchronized code, no other code can acquire the lock that is associated with the variable elements.

5. When thread 2 wakes up after a sleep of 1.5 seconds, it will attempt to acquire the lock, but it can't because thread 1 is still holding the lock. So the second thread must wait.

6. Once another 1.5 seconds has passed, thread 1 gives up the lock as it exits the synchronized code, allowing the second thread to add an element to the collection. This time, no exception is thrown.

The reference to lock against does not need to be the reference that is manipulated within the code block. The reference is just that: an arbitrary reference. You could use a different object instance, and even instantiate an object called syncRoot, like this:

```
object _syncRoot = new Object();
...
lock( _syncRoot) {
    ...
}
```

When using exclusive blocks, you need to use them when reading or writing the object. Don't think that you need an exclusive lock only when modifying the data, because a reader might be reading a state that is being modified. As the example of the collection demonstrated, modifying a collection while it is being read causes an inconsistency and an exception. The following code does not have a lock for the reading of the collection, and it results in an exception being thrown.

```
List<int> elements = new List<int>();
elements.Add(10);
elements.Add(20);

Thread thread1 = new Thread(
                    () => {
                        Thread.Sleep(1000);
                        foreach (int item in elements) {
                            Console.WriteLine("Item (" + item + ")");
                            Thread.Sleep(1000);
                        }
                    });
Thread thread2 = new Thread(
                    () => {
                        Thread.Sleep(1500);
                        lock (elements) {
                            elements.Add(30);
                        }
                    });
thread1.Start();
thread2.Start();
```

Getting back to the code that worked, it would seem that all is OK. From a code-execution perspective, everything is OK. But from an execution-efficiency perspective, everything is not OK, because the reading of the collection is causing the writer to wait unnecessarily.

Again, this collection example illustrates the difficulty with writing multithreaded code. You want to be able to add elements to a collection without having to wait for other threads to iterate a collection. You want to be efficient, as well as being logically correct.

Synchronizing with Cloning

One way of making a lock more efficient is to clone the object so that the local copy that you read from does not lock and hinder another thread. The two-thread example could be rewritten as follows:

```
List<int> elements = new List<int>();
elements.Add(10);
elements.Add(20);

Thread thread1 = new Thread(
                () => {
                    Thread.Sleep(1000);
                    int[] items;
                    lock (elements) {
                        items = elements.ToArray();
                    }
                    foreach (int item in items) {
                        Console.WriteLine("Item (" + item + ")");
                        Thread.Sleep(1000);
                    }
                });
Thread thread2 = new Thread(
                () => {
                    Thread.Sleep(1500);
                    lock (elements) {
                        elements.Add(30);
                    }
                });
thread1.Start();
thread2.Start();
```

The code still uses a lock, but only in the places where it is necessary. When the collection is being iterated, the lock is applied to the operation of copying the collection to an array (ToArray()). For the array iteration itself, there is no lock. When writing to the collection, there is a lock.

So, how can it be more efficient to take a snapshot of the collection, since taking a snapshot takes time? The answer is that normally it is not more efficient, but it is more time slice-effective.

Consider a word processor that loads some text. When Microsoft Word loads text, it immediately displays the first page, allowing you to edit right away. In the background, you see the other pages being loaded and prepared for editing. Using the snapshot approach, you get the same effect. The snapshot becomes even more effective and efficient when dealing with multiple-core microprocessors.

As a general threading rule, use locks as sparingly as possible, but use them whenever necessary. If you do use them, use them for as little code as possible. Locks synchronize access to resources, and thus only a single thread can be executing for a locked piece of code. The less time code is locked, the faster your code will be.

How Not to Deadlock Your Code (Mostly)

A *deadlock* makes code stop executing. A deadlock occurs when one piece of code has a lock and waits for some information to become available. However, the information does not become available, because another thread that could provide that information is waiting for a lock to become free.

I've said that if you are using locked code, you should use it as sparingly as possible. That's because using locks can lead to deadlocks. Deadlocks are a royal pain in the butt.

Consider the following two-thread collection example.

```
List<int> elements = new List<int>();
elements.Add(10);
elements.Add(20);

Thread thread1 = new Thread(
                  () => {
                      Thread.Sleep(1000);
                      int[] items;
                      lock (elements) {
                          while(elements.Count < 3) {
                              Thread.Sleep(1000);
                          }
                          items = elements.ToArray();
                      }
                      foreach (int item in items) {
                          Console.WriteLine("Item (" + item + ")");
                          Thread.Sleep(1000);
                      }
                  });
Thread thread2 = new Thread(
                  () => {
                      Thread.Sleep(1500);
                      lock (elements) {
                          elements.Add(30);
                      }
                  });
thread1.Start();
thread2.Start();
```

The iteration code waits until the collection count is 3. However, this never happens, because the thread that could make the collection count 3 is waiting for the lock to become free. The bolded code is the waiting code that queries whether the collection count is 3. If it is not, the thread waits for 1 second and asks again. But throughout all of this waiting, the lock is never given up, and thus the second thread that could add an element is waiting. The code will deadlock.

Without modifying the locks, here is a tweak that will avoid the deadlock:

```
List<int> elements = new List<int>();
elements.Add(10);
elements.Add(20);

Thread thread1 = new Thread(
                  () => {
                      Thread.Sleep(1000);
                      int[] items;
```

```
                    lock (elements) {
                        while(elements.Count < 3) {
                            Thread.Sleep(1000);
                        }
                        items = elements.ToArray();
                    }
                    foreach (int item in items) {
                        Console.WriteLine("Item (" + item + ")");
                        Thread.Sleep(1000);
                    }
                });
Thread thread2 = new Thread(
                () => {
                    Thread.Sleep(500);
                    lock (elements) {
                        elements.Add(30);
                    }
                });
thread1.Start();
thread2.Start();
```

The single change (shown in bold) makes the code work. In the first version, the timing of the code was such that the reading thread went first. In this version, the writing thread goes first. This shows that deadlocks are often timing-related.

The annoying part of deadlocks is that your code's behavior is not deterministic. Deterministic behavior is when an action will result in a single result, as in the case with most source code. Typically, when you have a bug, you didn't think far enough ahead and can work through the error systematically. However, with threading, your code ceases to be deterministic, because timing can change the behavior. Timing can be an influence in many ways: resource swapping, debuggers, microprocessor speed, and a host of other features.

To make the code deterministic, you need to fix the part of the code that hung onto the lock when it should not have. Remember the cardinal rule: keep a lock for as short a time as possible.

You need to use a more advanced lock construct that allows you to wait for data to become available. .NET has quite a few constructs related to threading and synchronization, and each construct is specific to the type of problem you are trying to solve. In the case of a deadlock, you want to use the Monitor type. The Monitor type is an advanced synchronization type that allows locking and pulsing of trigger signals for those threads that are waiting.

Let's return to our multiple cooks in the kitchen analogy. Say one cook needs a particular fish pan, which is already being used by another cook. Does the waiting cook tap her foot beside the cook doing the cooking? Or does the waiting cook do something else and ask the cook using the pan to inform her when the pan is free? Most likely, the cook will do something else and wait to be informed that the pan is free.

This concept of working together and being able to notify other lock users is a powerful feature programmed into the Monitor type. Monitor has the ability to take a lock, give it up so others can get the lock, and then take it back again.

When using the `Monitor` type, you do not declare a block of code that is protected, because `Monitor` is much more flexible than that. For example, you could define a class that has an instance-level lock mechanism, like this:

```
class DoSomething {
    public void GetLock() {
        Monitor.Enter(elements);
    }
    public void ReleaseLock() {
        Monitor.Exit(this);
    }
}
```

Any code that uses a `Monitor` is not restricted to where it's placed in the code, but a `Monitor` is bound to a thread. So if a thread grabs a `Monitor`, it has control until the thread dies or the thread gives up control. This has the added benefit that, once having acquired a lock, a `Monitor` can get it over and over again. However, if the same thread locked the `Monitor` five times, the same thread needs to release it five times before another thread can be granted access to the lock.

The following is the rewritten two-thread source code that uses a `Monitor`.

```
List<int> elements = new List<int>();
elements.Add(10);
elements.Add(20);

Thread thread1 = new Thread(
                    () => {
                        Thread.Sleep(1000);
                        int[] items;
                        Monitor.Enter(elements);
                        while (elements.Count < 3) {
                            Monitor.Wait(elements, 1000);
                        }
                        items = elements.ToArray();
                        Monitor.Exit(elements);
                        foreach (int item in items) {
                            Console.WriteLine("Item (" + item + ")");
                            Thread.Sleep(1000);
                        }
                    });
Thread thread2 = new Thread(
                    () => {
                        Thread.Sleep(1500);
                        Monitor.Enter(elements);
                        elements.Add(30);
                        Monitor.Pulse(elements);
                        Monitor.Exit(elements);
                    });
thread1.Start();
thread2.Start();
```

The bolded code lines are the new pieces that use the `Monitor` type. In the definition of the first thread to get the lock, the `Monitor.Enter()` method is called with the parameter `elements`, which, as in the earlier `lock` example, defines the lock reference handle. Once the lock has been acquired, the thread checks to see if the list count is greater or equal to 3. If the counter is less than 3, the `Monitor.Wait()` method is called. The behavior of `Monitor.Wait()` is similar to `Thread.Sleep()`, except that the `Monitor` lock is given up.

Releasing the lock is a unique feature of a `Monitor`. The lock is given up only during the time that the caller is in `Monitor.Wait()`. When the `Monitor.Wait()` method returns, the lock is acquired again. The code says that the thread is reawakened after 1 second. After that second, the thread does not have the lock and needs to wait before it can acquire the lock. If another thread is holding onto the lock for a long time, it could take a while to get the lock back again.

Another way for the `Monitor.Wait()` method to awaken is if a signal is sent by another thread. The code for the second thread uses `Enter()` and `Exit()`, but also `Pulse()`. The `Monitor.Pulse()` method triggers a signal that awakens the first thread, but the first thread will execute only after the second thread has released control of the lock.

The big advantages of a `Monitor` in comparison to `lock` are that the `Monitor` can be used anywhere in the code and that the `Monitor` will release a lock while waiting for an answer. You would use `lock` when you want to control access to a block of code. If the access goes beyond method boundaries, then it is preferable to use `Monitor`. It is not that you could not use a `lock` that spanned boundaries, but if you need to add code that could produce a deadlock, it is easier to control that code using a `Monitor`.

Now that we've covered the fundamentals of multithreading, the next sections focus on more advanced threading architectures. In particular the focus will be on three programming techniques: reader/writer, producer/consumer, and asynchronous calls.

Implementing a Reader/Writer Threaded Architecture

The reader/writer threaded architecture is based on the idea that if one thread is reading and another thread would like to read as well, why not let it? However, if one thread wants to write, then only that thread can write. In other words, multiple threads are allowed to read data simultaneously, but to write, a thread must have an exclusive lock.

.NET implements a `System.Threading.ReaderWriterLock` class, which contains the reader/writer functionality. However, this class is like a `Monitor` in that it gives you the control to manage how data is accessed, but does not determine what you are accessing. The type `ReaderWriterLock` has a number of methods and properties. The most important ones are listed in Table 13-1.

Table 13-1. *Important ReaderWriterLock Methods*

Method	Description
`AcquireReaderLock()`	Acquires a reader lock. Multiple threads can acquire a reader lock.
`AcquireWriterLock()`	Acquires a writer lock. Only a single thread can acquire a writer lock.
`DowngradeFromWriterLock()`	Converts a writer lock into a reader lock. Using this method avoids the need to call `ReleaseWriterLock()` and `AcquireReaderLock()`.
`UpgradeToWriterLock()`	Converts a reader lock into a writer lock. Using this method avoids the need to call `ReleaseReaderLock()` and `AcquireWriterLock()`.

Method	Description
ReleaseLock()	Releases all locks, regardless how many times you have called to acquire the reader or writer locks.
ReleaseReaderLock()	Decrements the reader lock a single count. To completely release a reader lock, you need to make sure the number of times you called ReleaseReaderLock() is equal to the number of times you called AcquireReaderLock().
ReleaseWriterLock()	Decrements the writer lock a single count. To completely release a reader lock, you need to make sure the number of times you called ReleaseWriterLock() is equal to the number of times you called AcquireWriterLock().

Let's look at a collection example that has four threads: three readers and one writer. The example uses Thread.Sleep() strategically, so that you can see how a reader and writer thread interact with each other.

```
...
using System.Threading;
...

ReaderWriterLock rwlock = new ReaderWriterLock();

List<int> elements = new List<int>();
elements.Add(10);
elements.Add(20);

Thread thread1 = new Thread(
                () => {
                    Thread.Sleep(1000);
                    Console.WriteLine("Thread 1 waiting for read lock");
                    rwlock.AcquireReaderLock(-1);
                    Console.WriteLine("Thread 1 has read lock");
                    foreach (int item in elements) {
                        Console.WriteLine("Thread 1 Item (" + item + ")");
                        Thread.Sleep(1000);
                    }
                    Console.WriteLine("Thread 1 releasing read lock");
                    rwlock.ReleaseLock();
                });
Thread thread2 = new Thread(
                () => {
                    Thread.Sleep(1250);
                    Console.WriteLine("Thread 2 waiting for read lock");
                    rwlock.AcquireReaderLock(-1);
                    Console.WriteLine("Thread 2 has read lock");
```

```
                    foreach (int item in elements) {
                        Console.WriteLine("Thread 2 Item (" + item + ")");
                        Thread.Sleep(1000);
                    }
                    Console.WriteLine("Thread 2 releasing read lock");
                    rwlock.ReleaseLock();
                });
Thread thread3 = new Thread(
                    () => {
                        Thread.Sleep(1750);
                        Console.WriteLine("Thread 3 waiting for read lock");
                        rwlock.AcquireReaderLock(-1);
                        Console.WriteLine("Thread 3 has read lock");
                        foreach (int item in elements) {
                            Console.WriteLine("Thread 3 Item (" + item + ")");
                            Thread.Sleep(1000);
                        }
                        Console.WriteLine("Thread 3 releasing read lock");
                        rwlock.ReleaseLock();
                });
Thread thread4 = new Thread(
                    () => {
                        Thread.Sleep(1500);
                        Console.WriteLine("Thread 4 waiting for write lock");
                        rwlock.AcquireWriterLock(-1);
                        Console.WriteLine("Thread 4 has write Lock");
                        elements.Add(30);
                        Console.WriteLine("Thread 4 releasing write lock");
                        rwlock.ReleaseLock();
                });
thread1.Start();
thread2.Start();
thread3.Start();
thread4.Start();
```

The bolded code contains all of the references to the reader/writer .NET class implementation. Unlike the keyword lock or the type Monitor, the ReaderWriterLock type is instantiated and the instance is shared between threads.

The code to acquire a reader or writer lock has a parameter of value -1, which means to wait until the lock is acquired. A positive value means to wait for a number of milliseconds, and if the lock has not been acquired, then return the method call. If you do use a timeout, before you attempt to manipulate shared code, you need to reference the property IsReaderLockHeld or IsWriterLockHeld to ensure that you have acquired the lock. In the reader threads, after having acquired the reader locks, the items are iterated.

■**Note** The example seems to break the rule regarding keeping locks for as short a time as possible, since it holds onto the lock while iterating. In the case of a reader/writer implementation, you have a unique situation in that you should be manipulating data that is mostly to be read, which implies that most of the time, you will be treating the shared data as read-only. For those moments where you are writing to the shared data, it is fine if the thread must wait a moment or two. A reader/writer lock does not make sense if you do not have data that is essentially read-only. In other situations, you should use the `Monitor` approach, as described in the previous section.

The example demonstrates handling data that is mostly to be read, since it has three threads reading and one thread writing. It is important to make sure that you don't end up writing while holding a read-only lock. The read/writer implementation is a guide, but you are not forced to stick to the guidance.

Running the code results in the following output.

```
Thread 1 waiting for read lock
Thread 1 has read lock
Thread 1 Item (10)
Thread 2 waiting for read lock
Thread 2 has read lock
Thread 2 Item (10)
Thread 4 waiting for write lock
Thread 3 waiting for read lock
Thread 1 Item (20)
Thread 2 Item (20)
Thread 1 releasing read lock
Thread 2 releasing read lock
Thread 4 has write Lock
Thread 4 releasing write lock
Thread 3 has read lock
Thread 3 Item (10)
Thread 3 Item (20)
Thread 3 Item (30)
Thread 3 releasing read lock
```

In the generated output, the sequence of events is as follows:

1. Thread 1 wants and acquires a read-only lock.

2. Thread 1 outputs the first number in the collection.

3. Thread 2 wants and acquires another read-only lock.

4. Thread 2 outputs the first number in the collection.

5. Thread 4 wants a writer lock and is kept on hold.

6. Thread 3 wants a read-only lock, but because thread 4 has asked for a writer lock and is queued, thread 3 is put on hold. At this step, threads 3 and 4 are put on hold and are waiting for the read-only locks of threads 1 and 2 to be released.

7. Threads 1 and 2 output the remaining numbers in the collection.

8. Threads 1 and 2 release the read-only locks.

9. Thread 4 is given a writer lock, and thread 3 is still on hold.

10. Thread 4 writes to the collection and releases the writer lock.

11. Thread 3 acquires a read-only lock and iterates the individual numbers, including the number added by thread 4.

Notice that the reader/writer lock makes the sequence of reading and writing events orderly, so that the shared state is always consistent. The reader/writer lock does not hinder or stop deadlocks, which can occur if you are not careful with how you write your code. The reader/writer lock is concerned about only the code that is used to manage data.

Implementing a Producer/Consumer Architecture

The producer/consumer technique has never been defined as a type, but it is used throughout many multithreaded applications. The idea behind a producer-consumer architecture is to split the problem into two subproblems. One side is the producer of data, information, and tasks. The producer wraps up the information into a task to be executed. The other side is the consumer, and it is responsible for unwrapping the task and doing something with it.

Using a Hidden Producer/Consumer Implementation

In Windows graphical user interfaces (GUIs), multithreaded applications are not allowed to access UI components if they are not the thread that created the UI element. To get around that problem, the `Windows.Forms` library uses the `Invoke()` method. To demonstrate, we'll create a GUI application that uses another thread to periodically increment a counter that is displayed in a text box.

Follow these steps:

1. Create a new Windows Forms application, and set it as the startup project if it isn't already (right-click its name and select Set As StartUp Project).

2. Drag a TextBox control onto Form1 in the design window.

3. Select the TextBox control. If the Properties window isn't visible, right-click the control and select Properties.

4. Change the TextBox's `Name` property to `txtMessage`.

5. Right-click the form and select View Code.

6. Add the following code.

```
public partial class Form1: Form {
    public Form1() {
        InitializeComponent();
    }

    private int _counter;
    private void IncrementCounter() {
        txtMessage.Text = "Counter (" + _counter + ")";
        _counter++;
    }

    delegate void DelegateIncrementCounter();

    private void PeriodicIncrement() {
        while(1 == 1) {
            Invoke(new DelegateIncrementCounter(IncrementCounter));
            Thread.Sleep(1000);
        }
    }
    Thread _thread;
}
```

7. Switch back to the design view and double-click the form, which should take you back to the code view in the Form1_Load() method.

8. Add the following code to the Form1_Load() method.

```
private void Form1_Load(object sender, EventArgs e) {
    _thread = new Thread(new ThreadStart(PeriodicIncrement));
    _thread.Start();
}
```

When Form1 is loaded, the Form1_Load() method is executed, which instantiates a new thread, which then executes the PeriodicIncrement()method. Within the implementation of PeriodicIncrement() is a never-ending loop, which calls the Form.Invoke() method, to which we pass a delegate. The delegate is the method IncrementCounter(), which increments a counter and outputs the result to the text box txtMessage.

From a user perspective, it would seem obvious to call the method IncrementCounter() directly from the other thread (_thread). However, hidden in the implementation of Invoke() is a producer/consumer implementation. The producer is the Invoke() method, which adds a delegate that needs to be called to a queue. The consumer is the Windows.Forms.Form class, which periodically checks its Invoke() queue and executes the delegates contained within.

In a nutshell, a producer/consumer implementation is nothing more than a handoff of information from one thread to another thread. This is effective because the producer and consumer are separate and manage their own concerns. The only common information between the producer and consumer is a queue, or list, which is synchronized and contains information of interest to both the producer and consumer.

Implementing a Generic Producer/Consumer Architecture

The architecture implemented by Windows.Forms is elegant and self-containing. You can implement a generic producer/consumer architecture following the Invoke() model, as shown in the following source code.

```
interface IProducerConsumer {
    void Invoke(Delegate @delegate);
    void Invoke(Delegate @delegate, Object[] arguments);
}

class ThreadPoolProducerConsumer : IProducerConsumer {
    class Executor {
        public readonly Delegate _delegate;
        public readonly Object[] _arguments;

        public Executor(Delegate @delegate, Object[] arguments) {
            _delegate = @delegate;
            _arguments = arguments;
        }
    }

    private Queue< Executor> _queue = new Queue<Executor>();

    private void QueueProcessor(Object obj) {
        Monitor.Enter(_queue);
        while(_queue.Count == 0) {
            Monitor.Wait(_queue, -1);
        }
        Executor exec = _queue.Dequeue();
        Monitor.Exit(_queue);
        ThreadPool.QueueUserWorkItem(new WaitCallback(QueueProcessor));
        exec._delegate.DynamicInvoke(exec._arguments);
    }

    public SingleThreaderProducerConsumer() {
        ThreadPool.QueueUserWorkItem(new WaitCallback(QueueProcessor));
    }

    public void Invoke(Delegate @delegate, Object[] arguments) {
        Monitor.Enter(_queue);
        _queue.Enqueue(new Executor(@delegate, arguments));
        Monitor.Pulse(_queue);
        Monitor.Exit(_queue);
    }
}
```

ThreadPoolProducerConsumer has a single public method Invoke(), which is used in the same fashion as the Windows.Forms Invoke() method. What makes the generic producer/consumer work is its use of the Monitor synchronization class.

To understand how Monitor works in the producer/consumer context, consider the overall producer/consumer implementation. The consumer thread (QueueProcessor()) executes constantly, waiting for items in the queue (_queue). To check the queue, the Monitor.Enter() method is called, which says, "I want exclusive control for a code block that ends with the method call Monitor.Exit()." To check the queue, a while loop is started. The loop waits until there is something in the queue. The thread could execute constantly, waiting for something to be added, but while the thread is looping, it has control of the lock. This means a producer thread cannot add anything to the queue.

The consumer needs to give up the lock, but also needs to check if anything is available in the queue. The solution is to call Monitor.Wait(), which causes the consumer thread to release the lock and say, "Hey I am giving up the lock temporarily until somebody gives me a signal to continue processing." When the consumer thread releases its lock temporarily, it goes to sleep waiting for a pulse.

The producer thread (Invoke()) also enters a protected block using the Monitor.Enter() method. Within the protected block, an item is added to the queue using the Enqueue() method. Because an item has been added to the queue, the producer thread sends a signal using the Monitor.Pulse() method to indicate an item is available. This will cause the thread that gave up the lock temporarily (the consumer thread) to wake up. However, the consumer thread executes when the producer thread calls Monitor.Exit(). Until then, the consumer thread is in ready-to-execute mode.

In the simplest case of this implementation, a single thread would constantly execute QueueProcessor(). An optimization is to create and use a *thread pool*. A thread pool is a collection of ready-to-execute threads. As tasks arrive, threads are taken from the pool and used to execute the tasks. Once the thread has completed executing, it is returned to the thread pool in ready-to-execute mode. In the ThreadPoolProducerConsumer constructor, the method ThreadPool.QueueUserWorkItem() uses thread pooling to execute the method QueueProcessor(). In the implementation of QueueProcessor(), the method ThreadPool.QueueUserWorkItem() is called again before calling the delegate. The result is that one thread is always waiting for an item in the queue, but there may be multiple threads executing concurrently, processing items from the queue.

Using the generic producer/consumer is nearly identical to using the Windows.Forms Invoke() method. The following is a sample implementation.

```
public class TestProducerConsumer {
    delegate void TestMethod();

    void Method() {
        Console.WriteLine("Processed in thread id (" +
            Thread.CurrentThread.ManagedThreadId + ")");
    }
```

```
public void TestSimple() {
    IProducerConsumer producer = new ThreadPoolProducerConsumer();
    Console.WriteLine("Sent in thread id (" +
        Thread.CurrentThread.ManagedThreadId + ")");
    producer.Invoke(new TestMethod(Method));
}
}
```

The `TestSimple()` method instantiates the `ThreadPoolProducerConsumer` type. Then the `Invoke()` method is called using the delegate `TestMethod`, which executes the `Method()` method. With respect to `Windows.Forms`, a different type is instantiated, but the same `Invoke()` method is used. The implementation is also a bit different in that the consumer is not a single thread, but as many threads as necessary.

Using an Asynchronous Approach

Using asynchronous techniques means to perform a task, such as read a file or database result, and then rather than wait for the results, let some other code handle the results. The asynchronous interaction is an example of the producer/consumer architecture, except that the details of the producer are hidden. You, as a developer, are expected to start the producer and provide a consumer.

The asynchronous technique used throughout the .NET API is consistent and is easily demonstrated by reading a file asynchronously. In Chapter 10, you learned how to read a file or console stream using synchronous techniques. You could just as well have read that file or stream asynchronously.

You would use asynchronous techniques when you don't want to wait around for the task to complete. For example, imagine needing to wait 15 seconds for a file to load. That sounds quick, but from a UI perspective, it is quite a bit of time. If the application is frozen during that time, the user experience is a bit awkward.

To read a file asynchronously, the following source code is used.

```
FileStream fs = new FileStream(filename,FileMode.Open);
Byte[] data = new byte[200000];

IAsyncResult asyncResult = fs.BeginRead(data, 0, data.Length,
    (lambdaAsync) => {
        FileStream localFS = (FileStream)lambdaAsync.AsyncState;
        int bytesRead = localFS.EndRead(lambdaAsync);
        string buffer = System.Text.ASCIIEncoding.ASCII.GetString(data);
        Console.WriteLine("Buffer bytes read (" + bytesRead + ")");
        localFS.Close();
    },fs);
asyncResult.AsyncWaitHandle.WaitOne();
```

The first code segment is used to initiate the file reading, and the second code segment is used to process the read information.

The file-reading part is as follows:

```
FileStream fs = new FileStream(filename,FileMode.Open);
Byte[] data = new byte[200000];

IAsyncResult asyncResult = fs.BeginRead(data, 0, data.Length,
    (lambdaAsync) => {
    },fs);
asyncResult.AsyncWaitHandle.WaitOne();
```

To read a file, you need to open a file stream, just as in Chapter 10's examples. However, instead of reading the data directly, the BeginRead() method is called, and it starts a read operation. What distinguishes the asynchronous operation is that BeginRead() returns immediately. Think of it as starting the producer.

When you call BeginRead(), the first three parameters represent the variable that contains the read bytes. The first parameter is the byte array where the data should be written. The second and third parameters are the starting and ending locations of the write operation in the byte array. The fourth parameter to BeginRead() is the delegate that will be called when the data is ready to be processed. The last parameter is like a thread parameter and is assigned to the IAsyncResult.AsyncState data member. IAsyncResult is in the System namespace and is therefore part of the .NET API.

When you call BeginRead(), you are saying, "Please fill up as many bytes as possible in the byte array. When you have read the bytes, call my consumer code, which is defined as a lambda expression." The filling of the array and calling of the consumer code occur in a separate thread.

For illustration purposes, the AsyncWaitHandle.WaitOne() method is called so that the main calling thread continues only after the data has been read and processed. It is a superfluous method call, since doing this would make the file-reading behavior resemble a synchronous operation.

The second part of the code processes the read information:

```
FileStream localFS = (FileStream)lambdaAsync.AsyncState;
int bytesRead = localFS.EndRead(lambdaAsync);
string buffer = System.Text.ASCIIEncoding.ASCII.GetString(data);
Console.WriteLine("Buffer bytes read (" + bytesRead + ")");
localFS.Close();
```

The consumer code is executed on another thread and is responsible for reading all the bytes. The code converts the AsyncState data member into a FileStream and reads the remaining bytes from the stream. The byte stream is then converted into a string buffer. When all the data has been read, the file stream is closed.

When using this asynchronous approach, you are really writing producer/consumer code. The use of IAsyncResult, BeginRead(), and EndRead() is quite common. The purpose of the asynchronous interface is to convert a synchronous operation into an asynchronous operation.

The Important Stuff to Remember

In this chapter, you learned the essentials of using threads and how to write multithreaded code. The main items to remember are as follows:

- With the release of multiple-core microprocessors, it has become extremely important to be able to write applications that can multitask.

- The operating system is a program that treats your applications as components and assigns time slices to your application.

- A time slice is a predefined amount of time in which your program can execute and has full control of the microprocessor.

- To implement tasks, you use threads.

- Each program that is started is a task and has a main thread from which you can start other threads.

- Threading is not difficult and easily implemented. What is more difficult is synchronization between the threads.

- Synchronization is not about the data, but about synchronizing access to code that modifies data that is shared. If your data is not shared, you don't need synchronization.

- In the context of a single application, you will use either the exclusive lock or the Monitor for synchronization.

- Locking code slows down the code. You should keep the locks for the shortest time possible.

- To improve throughput, you can take a snapshot of the data.

- Higher-level synchronization abstractions are the reader/writer and producer/consumer architectures.

- Reader/writer locks are exclusive locks, but they separate code that reads from code that writes. To improve code efficiency, reader/writer locks allow multiple readers, but only a single writer. Reader/writer locks are effective only if, for the most part, you are reading data.

- Producer/consumer locks split the task of producing and consuming data into two separate steps. The .NET API uses the producer/consumer concept extensively; examples are Windows.Forms and IAsyncResult.

- Deadlocks occur because timing changes cause your code to not be deterministic.

- Deadlocks can be partially avoided using Monitors, but the most effective way of avoiding deadlocks is to use the producer/consumer development technique. This is because the producer/consumer architecture takes the approach of handing off data, rather than sharing data.

- Applications that multitask effectively are applications that have been designed using logic, rather than development techniques where you think up the code as you go along.

Some Things for You to Do

Here are some exercises to help you apply what you learned in this chapter:

1. Regardless of how you look at the threading code, it is a bit awkward. It's awkward because you need to create a type if you want stateful threads. If you use a lambda expression/anonymous method, you can pass in only a single parameter. Using your object-oriented skills, design a base class that makes threading less awkward for stateful threads.

2. Write a general architecture that generates a series using multiple threads. For the first series, generate the square of all numbers between 1 and 100. For the second series, generate the Fibonacci series. That is, after two starting values, each number is the sum of the two preceding numbers. The first Fibonacci numbers (sequence A000045 in the On-Line Encyclopedia of Integer Sequences, http://www.research.att.com/~njas/sequences/) are 0, 1, 1, 2, 3, 5, 8, 13, 21, 34, 55, 89, 144, 233, 377, 610, 987, 1597, 2584, 4181, 6765, 10946, 17711, 28657, 46368, 75025, 121393, 196418, and 317811. Outline the limits of multithreading when generating a series.

■■■

CHAPTER 14

Learning About Relational Database Data

Literally hundreds of techniques, tips, tricks, and libraries are associated with relational databases. Covering relational databases would take an entire a book, and in fact, many books are devoted to that subject. This chapter will cover the basics and give you enough knowledge to read and write to a database.

The focus of this chapter is to demonstrate accessing relational databases with ADO.NET and the Visual Studio Dataset Designer. Since we'll need a database to work with, you'll also learn how to create a database with Visual C# Express.

A relational database stores data, such as the lottery numbers in Chapter 10's example. Building on that lottery-prediction example, in this chapter, you'll see how to create a database application that reads and writes the lottery numbers, and associates winners with a particular lottery drawing.

Understanding Relational Databases

As a beginner developer, one of your greatest challenges will be how to manage relational database data. A *relational database* is an old piece of technology. The relational model on which it is based was written in about 1969 (according to the relational model entry at `http://en.wikipedia.org/wiki/Relational_model`). A relational database is defined as follows (`http://en.wikipedia.org/wiki/Relational_database`):

> *Strictly speaking, a relational database is merely a collection of relations (frequently called tables). Other items are frequently considered part of the database, as they help to organize and structure the data, in addition to forcing the database to conform to a set of requirements.*

Relational Database Tables

A relational database is a collection of tables. When you were reading and writing a file in Chapter 10's example, you were actually reading and writing a table of lottery numbers, which looked something like this:

```
2000.05.31 5 6 13 23 25 37 43
2000.06.03 7 10 11 18 32 41 5
2000.06.07 15 23 24 28 38 39 45
2000.06.10 1 3 12 23 29 33 27
2000.06.14 2 4 13 19 39 45 26
2000.06.17 3 8 17 19 21 25 35
```

The data is arranged as a table, and thus could be easily converted into a relational database table. In relational database-speak, each row in the file corresponds to a row of data. But to create a row of data, you need fields, which also create a column. A relational database table is a grid of rows and columns. When working with a relational database, you don't manipulate columns; you manipulate individual rows.

What distinguishes a relational database is that you can combine tables and create more complicated data structures. It is the relationships (called *relations*) between pieces of data that make a relational database so powerful. For the lottery data, a relation could be who won the jackpot on the draw dates. Modifying the table to include the person who won would look this:

```
2000.05.31 nobody 5 6 13 23 25 37 43
2000.06.03 nobody 7 10 11 18 32 41 5
2000.06.07 nobody 15 23 24 28 38 39 45
2000.06.10 jack 1 3 12 23 29 33 27
2000.06.14 nobody 2 4 13 19 39 45 26
2000.06.17 nobody 3 8 17 19 21 25 35
```

For the most part, no one won the jackpot. But on June 10, 2000 (2000.06.10), a person named Jack won the jackpot. You might know a Jack. I might know a Jack. But would he be the same Jack? Probably not. So to distinguish winner Jack from another Jack, you would need his full name, address, and other details. But where do you put this extra information?

Do you put the information about Jack into the lottery data table? Or do you create another table? The answer is that you create another table. But since you are working with files, it will be a file, not a table. The file will be called jack.txt because the winner of the lottery jackpot was Jack. The jack.txt file could contain the following information.

```
Jack Smith
Address
City
Country
```

The information in jack.txt and the information in the lottery data file have a relation. The relation is the winner of the jackpot. This is what a relational database is all about. The reason you use a relational database and not files that cross-reference each other is because a relational database is extremely efficient at managing tables and relations. The techniques demonstrated in Chapter 10 are nowhere near as efficient and effective as using a relational database.

Relational databases are quite capable of handling terabytes of data. Additionally, relational databases are capable of building efficient relations that span terabytes of data.

Database Relations

Relations are very powerful, but they can also make things extremely complicated. When you split tables and create relations between the tables, you are *normalizing* the data. Database normalization is defined as follows (http://en.wikipedia.org/wiki/Database_normalization):

> *Database normalization is a technique for designing relational database tables to min-imize duplication of information and, in so doing, to safeguard the database against certain types of logical inconsistency. When multiple instances of a given piece of infor-mation occur in a table, the possibility exists that these instances will not be kept consistent when the data within the table is updated, leading to a loss of data integrity. A table that is sufficiently normalized is not vulnerable to problems of this kind, as its structure prevents it from holding redundant information in the first place.*

For example, the relation between a lottery ticket in one table and its winner in another table is normalization. The data on the winner and the data on the lottery ticket are kept in separate tables, making the overall data structure more efficient from a maintenance and per-formance point of view.

Creating relations between tables is a form of referencing, where one table says informa-tion here references information in another table. The referencing is carried out using fields of one table that are cross-referenced with fields of another table.

The lottery ticket example is interesting because of the relations between the lottery draws and the winners, which could be of two types:

- *One draw to many winners*: When a lottery ticket is drawn, there can be many winners.

- *One winner to many draws*: Even though it is improbable, one winner could win multiple draws.

In the file example, you saw the one-winner-to-many-draws relation. You probably did not think it was that type of relation, and more likely thought it was a one-draw-to-one-winner relation. But consider the following text file, where jack is referenced twice.

```
2000.05.31 nobody 5 6 13 23 25 37 43
2000.06.03 jack 7 10 11 18 32 41 5
2000.06.07 nobody 15 23 24 28 38 39 45
2000.06.10 jack 1 3 12 23 29 33 27
2000.06.14 nobody 2 4 13 19 39 45 26
2000.06.17 nobody 3 8 17 19 21 25 35
```

The table of draws has the ability to reference the same winner twice, which means the relation of one winner to many draws is possible. To add the relation of one draw to many winners, the table would need to be modified like this:

```
2000.05.31 nobody 5 6 13 23 25 37 43
2000.06.03 jack jill 7 10 11 18 32 41 5
2000.06.07 nobody 15 23 24 28 38 39 45
2000.06.10 jack 1 3 12 23 29 33 27
2000.06.14 nobody 2 4 13 19 39 45 26
2000.06.17 nobody 3 8 17 19 21 25 35
```

Here, another field indicates Jill as the second winner of the draw. Adding another field throws a monkey wrench into the entire table structure and makes processing much more complicated, because the parsing routines will need to verify if another field is present. This breaks the nice grid structure and is plain wrong.

Another approach using the text file would be to create a third file that cross-references the winners with the dates. So the lottery file would go back to the original version:

```
2000.05.31 5 6 13 23 25 37 43
2000.06.03 7 10 11 18 32 41 5
2000.06.07 15 23 24 28 38 39 45
2000.06.10 1 3 12 23 29 33 27
2000.06.14 2 4 13 19 39 45 26
2000.06.17 3 8 17 19 21 25 35
```

And a winners table would be created:

```
2000.06.03 jack
2000.06.03 jill
2000.06.10 jack
```

The winners table is a grid of draw dates and winners on those dates. Notice how there is no entry for nobody, so only draw dates with winners are included.

Note These three tables are an example of correctly normalized data. When the data is well normalized, each table contains unique data. In this example, one table contains all of the lottery drawings, but who the winners are is stored in another table. Using database relations, the winners and lottery data are related, yet neither table needs to know about the other table.

Now what happens if two different people named Jack are lottery winners? The data might look like this:

```
2000.05.31 nobody 5 6 13 23 25 37 43
2000.06.03 nobody 7 10 11 18 32 41 5
2000.06.07 nobody 15 23 24 28 38 39 45
2000.06.10 jack 1 3 12 23 29 33 27
2000.06.14 jack 2 4 13 19 39 45 26
2000.06.17 nobody 3 8 17 19 21 25 35
```

We know the two jack entries are not for the same Jack. So now we have an additional problem of uniqueness. Uniqueness is not unusual when dealing with relational databases, and the common technique is to identify each Jack with a unique key. For example, a unique key could be jack_1 or jack_2. The problem with using jack_1 and jack_2 is that you need to search the database to see if there is a jack entry, and then find out the last jack entry. Those steps are resource-intensive and typically avoided. Another solution is to use a database-provided field that generates a unique key, which could be a row number or globally unique identifier (GUID). If the unique identifier were to be computer-generated, the table would look as follows:

```
2000.05.31 1877_ds 5 6 13 23 25 37 43
2000.06.03 1877_ds 7 10 11 18 32 41 5
2000.06.07 1877_ds 15 23 24 28 38 39 45
2000.06.10 1023_ad 1 3 12 23 29 33 27
2000.06.14 1022_xy 4 13 19 39 45 26
2000.06.17 1877_ds 3 8 17 19 21 25 35
```

In the modified table, you would have no idea who the identifiers represent. The way to find out is to take a key and open its associated field—say 1877_ds and the file 1877_ds.txt. Upon opening the file, you would know that the winner is nobody. The process of finding out who the winner is involves more steps, but a relational database knows how to manage these types of relations quite effectively.

WHY THE THOUSANDS OF APIS, LIBRARIES, AND TECHNIQUES?

In the space of 12 years, the following technologies have emerged: Open Database Connectivity (ODBC), Remote Data Objects (RDO), the Jet Database Engine, Data Access Object (DAO), ActiveX Data Object (ADO), Object Linking and Embedding, Database (OLE DB), ADO.NET, and Language Integrated Query (LINQ). This means that every 2 years, a new database technology is introduced. Each database technology has libraries to make it easier to write code. The result is an amazing number of ways to access a piece of technology that is nearly 40 years old.

So why do we have so many ways to access and manipulate the database? Wouldn't we, as developers, get our act together and work toward a common approach to manipulating a relational database? I can't give a logical and accepted answer as to why there are so many database-access technologies. But I can tell you what I think.

Database programming is boring. Database programming is extremely important, yet writing database code is one of the most tedious programming tasks because of the complexity and sheer size of database tables. For any real production application, it is not uncommon to have tables that have 30 fields. When writing code to add, delete, and modify a row in a table that has 30 fields, you are, for the most part, trying to figure out which field goes to which piece of data. Thus, people try to automate the job. After all, it is more interesting to work through a threading bug than an incorrect-field-placement bug.

Another issue is a technology mismatch between a programming language and a relational database. A relational database treats data as a set. There are no individual pieces of data in a relational database. Programming languages treat data as individuals. Even in a collection class, you have an individual class managing a set of individual references. This causes a mismatch, and trying to bind to the two technologies is difficult.

So when you are writing database code, you are trying to automate the fitting of a square peg into a round hole. You get many extremely creative ideas and results, but at the end of the day, you are still fitting a square peg into a round hole.

The essence of the problem when dealing with sets of data in a programming language is how to integrate the two. There is light at the end of the tunnel, in the form of programming language alterations such as LINQ and anonymous methods. LINQ will be discussed in the next chapter.

Accessing Relational Databases

Regardless of the database implementation that you use, a common architecture is employed, as illustrated in Figure 14-1.

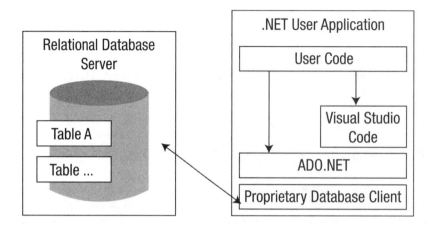

Figure 14-1. *Common database architecture*

Most relational database servers are separate applications that run on their own. To interact with a running relational database, the database vendor provides a database driver. In .NET, a database driver is a piece of proprietary code that talks to the relational database server, but exposes its functionality using the ADO.NET layer.

The ADO.NET layer is a technology that abstracts the database client into a neutral set of interfaces. By itself, ADO.NET does not implement any technologies, but it defines the interfaces that a database needs to have implemented. ADO.NET is similar to the lighting manager application introduced in Chapter 8, where specific lighting implementations need to implement interfaces.

The ADO.NET code can be accessed directly in your application by your code. However, doing that means accessing the individual rows, columns, and database tables. It is not a difficult undertaking, but it means you need to do everything manually. With respect to the lottery example, it means manipulating the lottery winners and the lottery draws table.

Visual C# Express and other Visual Studio editions have a number of tools that will generate code that automatically binds to tables and rows, reducing the amount of work that you need to do. In Figure 14-1, the user code has arrows pointing to both the Visual Studio-generated code and the ADO.NET code. These arrows indicate that your code does not have to use the Visual Studio-generated code; it is optional. But the advantage of using the Visual Studio code is that it reduces the amount of grunt work that your code needs to do. The Visual Studio-generated code is a thin functional layer on top of the ADO.NET code that maps directly to the tables that you are manipulating.

When you are developing an application that accesses a relational database, you need to consider the following issues:

Access to the relational database server: Can the relational database server be easily accessed by your code in a development context? When you are developing, you will have literally thousands of write code/test code cycles, resulting in plenty of connections and broken connections to the database. The database server must be able to cope with such stress. In general, this is an issue that a database administrator needs to think about, since it could place extra load on a strained database server.

A username and password strategy: The requirement for a good username and password strategy is not to be underestimated. I recommend that you talk to a security professional (not just someone who knows a bit about security).

■**Note** For more information about security strategies, see the "Resolving the ASP.NET Database Security Dilemma" article (http://www.eggheadcafe.com/articles/20021211.asp). For an idea of what I mean by "security professional," visit Dominick Baier's web site (http://www.leastprivilege.com/).

ADO.NET drivers: When you write ADO.NET code, you will need an ADO.NET driver for each database. Thus, if you use Microsoft SQL Server and wish to use MySQL, you will need a MySQL driver. However, for the most part, the code will remain identical.

Abstraction: There will always be differences in the code used to access different relational databases. Be prepared to abstract your database code if you access the database directly using ADO.NET.

With Visual Studio, you can integrate any relational database that supports the ADO.NET interfaces. To discover whether a database supports ADO.NET, you need to ask the database vendor. It is not an automatic given that all database vendors support ADO.NET.

Designing a Database Using Visual C# Express

Visual C# Express is very helpful when designing and building database applications. It provides interface-based tools for designing the database, managing connections, and managing data access.

With Visual C# Express, you can directly integrate the ADO.NET drivers for only the Microsoft relational databases. (This does not mean you cannot use a different ADO.NET driver using code.) If you want to use the GUI tools for a database driver other than Microsoft, you will need to upgrade your Visual Studio edition. For this chapter's examples, we'll use the Microsoft SQL Server Compact Edition driver.

You can add the GUI tool-based database support to any C# project type. For this chapter, we'll use a console project called DatabaseConsoleEx.

After you have created the DatabaseConsoleEx console project in Visual C# Express (using the procedure outlined in Chapter 1), you can set up the database, and then add tables to your new database.

Configuring the Data Source

Using the Visual C# Express Data Source Configuration Wizard, you can add a database as your data source, set up the database connection, and select database objects to include in the project. Follow these steps to use the wizard:

1. Select Data ➤ Add New Data Source to start the Data Source Configuration Wizard.

2. Choose Database as the data source and click Next.

3. You're asked to choose a data connection. When choosing the data connection, you are defining the connection settings to your relational database. Since we are creating a new database in this example, click the New Connection button.

4. In the Add Connection dialog box, fill in the database filename and define a password. For this example, enter the name `lottery` for the database and `lotto.12` for the password. Visual C# Express will automatically add an `.sdf` extension to the filename to indicate that it is a SQL Server file, as shown in Figure 14-2. Click OK to add the connection.

Note If you choose a password that has fewer than six characters, doesn't contain a number, and doesn't contain a punctuation mark, you will get a warning. Visual C# Express does not stop you from continuing, but it is advising you to use strong passwords. A strong password is a password that is not easily guessed. For example, if your pet's name is butch, and your favorite car is Nova, then a strong password could be butch.nova.

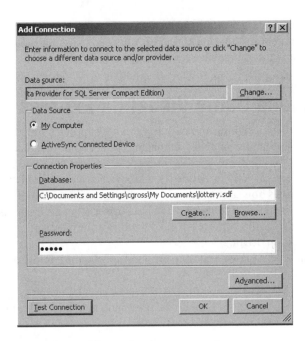

Figure 14-2. *Adding a database connection*

5. To verify that everything worked, click the Test Connection button. You should see a success message. (If the test fails, create a new database, with a new filename and new password, and test it again.) Click the OK button.

6. The Choose Your Data Connection screen reappears with your data connection filled in, but the Next button is disabled, as shown in Figure 14-3. The password used to access the database is the issue. You have two options: embed the password in the connection string or write code to pass the password to the connection. In a production setting, you would choose the first option, to exclude the password. However, for this simple example, click "Yes, include sensitive data in the connection string." Then click Next.

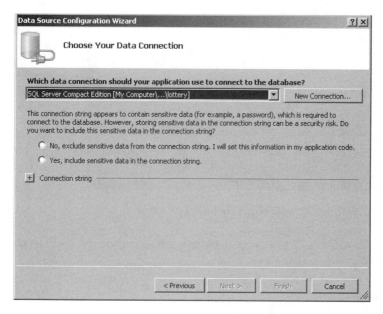

Figure 14-3. *Dealing with password information in a connection string*

7. Since we're using a SQL Server Compact Edition driver for this example, the dialog box shown in Figure 14-4 appears. It asks if the database file can be copied into the project. Click Yes.

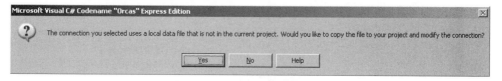

Figure 14-4. *Adding the SQL Server Compact Edition file to the local project*

8. You are asked if you want the application configuration information added to the project. Click Next to add the information.

9. The Choose Your Database Object screen appears. Since this is a SQL Server Compact Edition file that has no tables, only a single Tables object is listed, as shown in Figure 14-5. If the database connection referenced a relational database that already existed, more database objects would be available. Select the Tables object, and then click Finish.

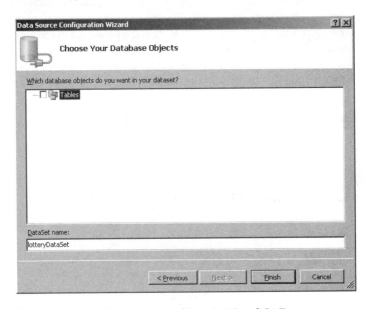

Figure 14-5. *Enabling database objects in Visual C# Express*

Visual C# Express will rebuild your project. When it is finished, the result will be similar to the project structure shown in Figure 14-6.

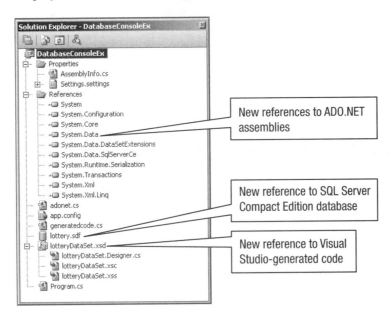

Figure 14-6. *Modifications made to the Visual C# Express project*

The Visual C# Express project contains a reference to a file that is provided by Microsoft SQL Server Compact Edition. The diagram shown earlier in Figure 14-1 indicates that a database server is another process that you access using a client library. In about 80% of the cases, this is true, but a class of database servers are file-based. These types of databases are used in simpler single-user database applications. In our example, the database is file-based. From a programming perspective, nothing changes, and the source code should not even be aware of whether the database is a file or server process.

Adding the Tables

In Visual C# Express, you can add tables to your database using the Database Explorer. Through the Database Explorer, you can modify all of the data objects available within the database. Here are the general steps for adding a table:

1. Right-click the `lottery.sdf` file in the Solution Explorer and select Open to open the Database Explorer. The Data Explorer displays information about the database, as shown in Figure 14-7.

Figure 14-7. *Viewing the database structure in the Database Explorer*

2. Right-click the Tables node and select Create Table to open the New Table dialog box, as shown in Figure 14-8.

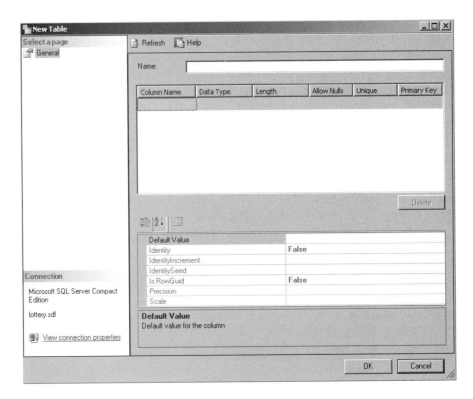

Figure 14-8. *Creating a new table*

3. Enter a name for the table. Then specify the column name and type. You can also specify other details about each column, such as its length and whether it must be unique.

Each column of a table must have a name and type. Just as C# has types, so does a database. What is frustrating about database types is that they are similar but not identical to C# types. To make things even more frustrating, not all databases have the exact same types. Fortunately, If you use the Visual Studio tools, the wizard will map a specific database type to a C# type.

For this example, we will add three tables: draws, persons, and winners. The following sections describe the columns and types for these tables. We will use the Microsoft SQL Server data types.

■Tip The Microsoft Visual Studio documentation has an excellent reference on the various data types and their accuracy. See the "Data Types" section of the Microsoft SQL Server Books Online documentation (http://msdn2.microsoft.com/en-us/library/ms130214.aspx).

Draws Table

The draws table contains all of the drawn lottery numbers. Table 14-1 shows the column names and types for this table.

Table 14-1. *Draws Table Columns*

Name	Type
draw_date	datetime
first_number	int
second_number	int
third_number	int
fourth_number	int
fifth_number	int
sixth_number	int
bonus	int

The draw_date column holds the date of the draw. The declared type is datetime, which is like the datetime type in .NET. However, you will need to be careful in mapping types, as explained in Chapter 3.

The rest of the columns represent a number in the winning draw, including the bonus number. As in C#, SQL Server includes various numeric types. The number columns in the draws table are declared as the int type.

■**Note** The one SQL Server numeric type that does not exist in .NET is numeric. This type behaves like the decimal type in .NET, except for the precision. With numeric, you can specify the number of digits before and after the decimal point.

Persons Table

The persons table lists all of the people who have won a lottery drawing. Table 14-2 shows the column names and types for the persons table.

Table 14-2. *Persons Table Columns*

Name	Type
id	uniqueidentifier
first_name	nvarchar(100)
last_name	nvarchar(100)

The persons table is a collection of people with their first names, last names, addresses, and so on. The challenge in a relational database is uniquely identifying a user. Think of it as trying to define a unique hashcode. The solution most databases use is a number. When you have millions of records, a number might not be adequate as a unique identifier. In that case, you can use the SQL Server uniqueidentifier type, as we're doing for the id column of the persons table.

The first_name and last_name columns both have the type nvarchar(100). A string in a database behaves like a number type, in that strings have length limits. In the example, we use the nvarchar type, for a variable-length string with a maximum length of 100 characters. In contrast, specifying char(100) would give you a string 100 characters long, regardless of how many bytes contain letters. If the entry in a char column has fewer characters than specified, the remainder of the char string is filled with space characters, by default.

Winners Table

The winners table matches the winning people to their lottery drawing. Table 14-3 shows the column names and types for the winners table.

Table 14-3. *Winners Table Columns*

Name	Type
id	uniqueidentifier
draw_date	datetime

Both columns are the types of the tables being referenced. The idea is to use the winners table in conjunction with the persons table, and the draws table to create the list that shows who won which lottery drawing and their numbers.

After you've created the three tables, your Database Explorer will resemble Figure 14-9.

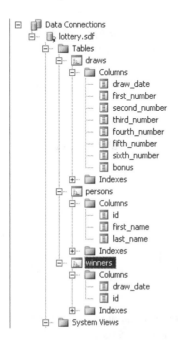

Figure 14-9. *Modified database structure with the added tables*

Now that we have a database with some tables, let's see how to access that database directly, using ADO.NET.

Accessing the Database Using ADO.NET

Accessing the database directly using ADO.NET involves using the ADO.NET interfaces. The first step is to define a connection. Once the connection has been established, you can manipulate the tables in the database—to add, remove, and update records in a table.

Now we will continue with the sample `lottery` database created in the previous section, using the SQL Server Compact Edition ADO.NET driver. We'll write code to add, select, and delete records.

■**Note** Writing the ADO.NET code can be easy, or it can be tedious, because not all ADO.NET drivers are built the same way. In this section, the focus will be on the essentials of ADO.NET, and not the idiosyncrasies of SQL Server Compact Edition. If you will be writing code strictly for the SQL Server Compact Edition, check out `http://arcanecode.wordpress.com/tag/sql-server-compact-edition/`.

Connecting to a Database

Define a database connection with the following code, which illustrates a general approach (added to the `DatabaseConsoleEx` application).

```
IDbConnection connection =
  new SqlCeConnection(
    DatabaseConsoleEx.Properties.Settings.Default.lotteryConnectionString);
```

The variable `connection` is an instance of the database client. Think of it as picking up the telephone and hearing the dial tone. The connection requires a username, password, and the name of the database to which you want to connect. That information is stored in `lotteryConnectionString`, which was defined when you configured the data source in Visual C# Express (Figure 14-3).

Once you have a connection instance, you can create a live connection, which is akin to dialing a telephone number and hearing that telephone ring. Here is the code for opening the connection:

```
connection.Open();
```

Now you can work with the tables in the database.

Adding Table Data

The `draws` database table you created early is empty. Now we will add some content. To add data to a database using SQL, use the SQL `INSERT` command, as follows:

```
IDbCommand cmd =
  new SqlCeCommand(@"INSERT INTO draws (draw_date, first_number, second_number,
                    third_number, fourth_number, " +
                    @"fifth_number, sixth_number, bonus)
                    VALUES (?, ?, ?, ?, ?, ?, ?, ?)");
cmd.Connection = connection;

IDbDataParameter paramDate = new SqlCeParameter();
paramDate.ParameterName = "@pDrawDate";
paramDate.DbType = System.Data.DbType.DateTime;
paramDate.Size = 8;
paramDate.SourceColumn = "draw_date";
paramDate.Value = DateTime.Now;
cmd.Parameters.Add(paramDate);

IDbDataParameter param = new SqlCeParameter();
param.ParameterName = "@pFirstNumber";
param.DbType = System.Data.DbType.Int32;
param.Size = 4;
param.SourceColumn = "first_number";
param.Value = 1;
cmd.Parameters.Add(param);

...

param = new SqlCeParameter();
param.ParameterName = "@pBonus";
param.DbType = System.Data.DbType.Int32;
param.Size = 4;
param.SourceColumn = "bonus";
param.Value = 1;
cmd.Parameters.Add(param);

cmd.ExecuteNonQuery();
connection.Close();
```

To execute a command, you need to instantiate an IDbCommand instance, where the constructor parameter is the SQL statement that you want to execute. The SQL statement is a bit strange in that it contains question marks. The question marks are placeholders that are considered SQL parameters. How a SQL parameter is defined often depends on the ADO.NET implementation, but a generally accepted approach is to use question marks. The command is associated with the database connection using the cmd.Connection property.

Each parameter, regardless of the database driver used, is of type IDbDataParameter or IDataParameter. The type associated with IDbDataParameter is SqlCeParameter, which is specific to the SQL Server Compact Edition. If you were to use another database, the type that implements the IDataParameter or IDbDataParameter interface would be identified differently, yet still implement the same interface.

The properties of `IDbDataParameter` are as follows:

- `ParameterName`: Specifies the name of the parameter and must be prefixed with an at sign (@) character.

- `DbType`: Specifies the type of the parameter.

- `Size`: Specifies the size of the parameter.

- `SourceColumn`: Specifies in which column the parameter will be stored. Since the `INSERT` statement does not have named parameters, this property will be used to figure out where to place the value.

- `Value`: Specifies the value that will be stored in the table.

■**Note** As a general rule of thumb, stick to using and manipulating the standard ADO.NET interfaces, rather than the type specific to the ADO.NET driver.

The example shows code that you would write when you want to explicitly define the attributes of every parameter. This was to allow you to see what is happening when parameters are converted and stored in a table. A simpler notation is as follows:

```
IDbConnection connection = new SqlCeConnection(
DatabaseConsoleEx.Properties.Settings.Default.lotteryConnectionString);
connection.Open();

IDbCommand cmd = new SqlCeCommand(
                @"INSERT INTO draws (draw_date, first_number,
                  second_number, third_number, fourth_number, " +
                @"fifth_number, sixth_number, bonus) VALUES (@draw_date,
                  @first_number, @second_number, @third_number," +
                @"@fourth_number,@fifth_number,@sixth_number,@bonus)");
cmd.Connection = connection;

cmd.Parameters.Add(new SqlCeParameter("@pDrawDate", DateTime.Now));
cmd.Parameters.Add(new SqlCeParameter("@pFirstNumber", 1));
cmd.Parameters.Add(new SqlCeParameter("@pSecondNumber", 1));
cmd.Parameters.Add(new SqlCeParameter("@pThirdNumber", 1));
cmd.Parameters.Add(new SqlCeParameter("@pFourthNumber", 1));
cmd.Parameters.Add(new SqlCeParameter("@pFifthNumber", 1));
cmd.Parameters.Add(new SqlCeParameter("@pSixthNumber", 1));
cmd.Parameters.Add(new SqlCeParameter("@pBonus", 1));
```

Once you have defined the parameters, and assigned them with a value, the SQL query can be executed. In the case of a SQL `INSERT` statement, no data will be returned, because you are sending data from the application to the database. Thus, you will need to execute the method that does not expect any return data, which is `ExecuteNonQuery()`, like this:

```
int retval = cmd.ExecuteNonQuery();
Console.WriteLine("retval (" + retval + ")");
```

Selecting Data from a Table

After your tables have some data, you probably will want to retrieve it. To do that, you use the SELECT statement. Here is the code for viewing data in the draws table:

```
IDbConnection connection =
  new SqlCeConnection(
    DatabaseConsoleEx.Properties.Settings.Default.lotteryConnectionString);
connection.Open();

IDbCommand cmd = new SqlCeCommand(@"SELECT * FROM draws");
cmd.Connection = connection;
IDataReader reader = cmd.ExecuteReader();
while (reader.Read()) {
    Console.WriteLine("(" + reader.GetDateTime(0) + ") " +
        reader.GetInt32(1) + "");
}
reader.Close();
connection.Close();
```

To select data, the steps are to open a connection, create a command, and execute the command. In the example, the SELECT statement did not have any parameters. SELECT * means to select all columns. Alternatively, you could define identifiers to select specific columns.

When you are using a SELECT statement, the server will return data. To read the returned data, you call the method ExecuteReader(). This is different from the ExecuteNonQuery() method you use to insert data, mainly in that ExecuteReader() returns an instance of IDataReader. IDataReader is an interface used to iterate individual records, which gives you the chance to retrieve the individual fields of the records.

To access the fields, use the appropriate GetNNN() method, with the index of the field. Knowing which index to use is a bit perplexing. The index of the appropriate field is related to the position of the column in the table. For example, the following code retrieves the fourth column from a result set that is at least four columns wide.

```
reader.GetDouble(3)
```

Deleting Data from the Database

Of course, you may need to delete data from table. The SQL statement for removing data from a table is DELETE. The following example deletes a particular lottery drawing entry from the draws table.

```
IDbCommand cmd = null;
cmd = new SqlCeCommand (
    @"DELETE FROM draws WHERE draw_date=? ",
     connection);
```

```
IDbDataParameter paramDate = new SqlCeParameter();
paramDate.ParameterName = "@pDrawDate";
paramDate.DbType = System.Data.DbType.DateTime;
paramDate.Size = 8;
paramDate.SourceColumn = "draw_date";
paramDate.Value = DateTime.Now;
cmd.Parameters.Add(paramDate);

cmd.ExecuteNonQuery();
connection.Close();
```

As with the INSERT statement, you use ExecuteNonQuery() with DELETE, which does not return any results.

Closing a Database Connection

After having processed your SQL statements, you should close the connection to indicate that you are finished using the database. Here's how:

```
connection.Close();
```

Recapping ADO.NET Usage

Looking at all of the code presented in this section, you should notice the following points about using ADO.NET directly:

- There are general interfaces, implemented by a specific library.

- The IDbConnection and IDbCommand interfaces are implemented by all ADO.NET drivers.

- SqlCeConnection, SqlCeCommand, and SqlCeParameter are specific classes from the database driver.

- ADO.NET does not require you to use predefined factories. You can access a default factory, but the factory is optional. You may want to write your own factory. Programmers tweak the ADO.NET initialization code to suit their settings, and thus want full control. But once the code is initialized, developers want to keep things general and use interfaces.

- The database code involves opening a connection; defining a SQL command such as INSERT, SELECT, and so on; assigning the SQL parameters; executing the SQL command; and then closing the connection.

■**Note** For more details on SQL, see Wikipedia's SQL entry (http://en.wikipedia.org/wiki/SQL) and W3School's SQL tutorial (http://www.w3schools.com/sql/default.asp). These provide a good explanation of the basics of SQL. The MSDN documentation is fairly good as well.

Next, let's take a look at another Visual Studio tool for working with database applications.

Using the Dataset Designer

The Dataset Designer is a helper application provided by Visual Studio to help you write database applications. MSDN provides a detailed tutorial on how to create client data applications (http://msdn2.microsoft.com/en-us/library/h0y4a0f6(VS.80).aspx). The tutorial describes how to click options and use the wizards, but it does not explain some of the underlying details. Here, we'll use the Dataset Designer to set up the relations between the lottery database tables, and take a look at the code that is generated automatically to create those relations.

Building Relations Between Tables

The first step in using the Dataset Designer is to convert the tables in the Database Explorer to something that the Dataset Designer can use. To do this, from the Solution Explorer, double-click the file that has the extension .xsd—lotteryDataSet.xsd in our example. The .xsd file is the XML Schema Definition file, which translates the database's datasets into XML files.

The lotteryDataSet.xsd file has a number of child files, which you can open and inspect. These files are part of a collection that is used by the Dataset Designer. The only file that you can modify is lotteryDataSet.cs. The other files are managed by the Dataset Designer.

We want to build relations between the three tables. Relations are important because they allow you to maintain database consistency. For example, imagine adding a winner to the winners table for a lottery drawing date that does not exist. Using relations, you can enforce a consistency check, so that the drawing date must exist in the database before you can add a winner for that date. We will define two relations: winners with draws and winners with persons. Remember that the winners table is a cross-reference between the persons and draws table.

Follow these steps to define the relations:

1. Double-click lotteryDataSet.xsd in the Solution Explorer. You will see a message similar to the one shown in Figure 14-10, which indicates that the Dataset Designer has no data.

Use the Dataset Designer to visually create and edit typed datasets.
Drag database items from <u>Database Explorer</u> or the DataSet <u>Toolbox</u> onto the design surface, or right-click here to add new items.

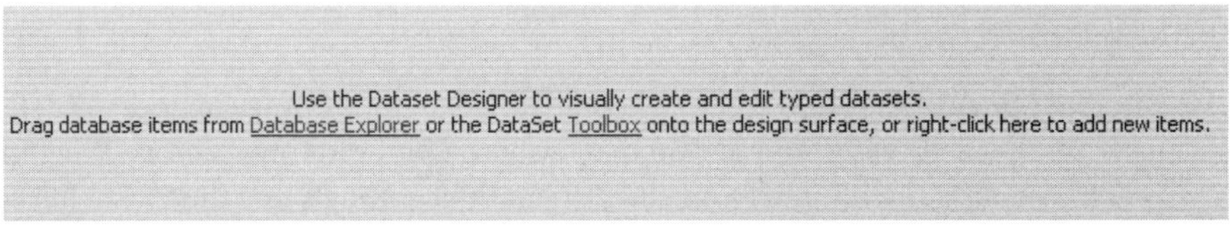

Figure 14-10. *The Dataset Designer has no data to display.*

2. Drag and drop each of the three tables you created earlier from the Database Explorer onto the surface of the Dataset Designer, as shown in Figure 14-11. This automatically adds default support for the three tables.

Figure 14-11. *Dataset Designer with the three tables*

3. To build a relation, right-click the data generator surface and choose Add ➤ Relation. The Relation dialog box appears. This dialog box allows you to associate two tables via a specific field.

4. As shown in Figure 14-12, specify `winners` as the parent table and `persons` as the child. The key column is `id`. Click OK to create the relation.

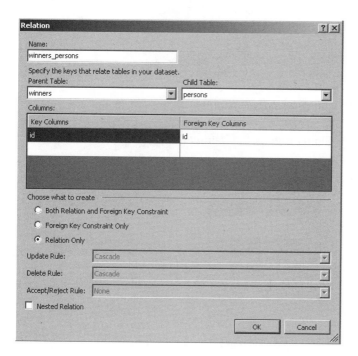

Figure 14-12. *Creating the winners and persons relation*

The winners and draws relation is created in the same way as the winners and persons relation, except that the columns linked are draw_date, as shown in Figure 14-13.

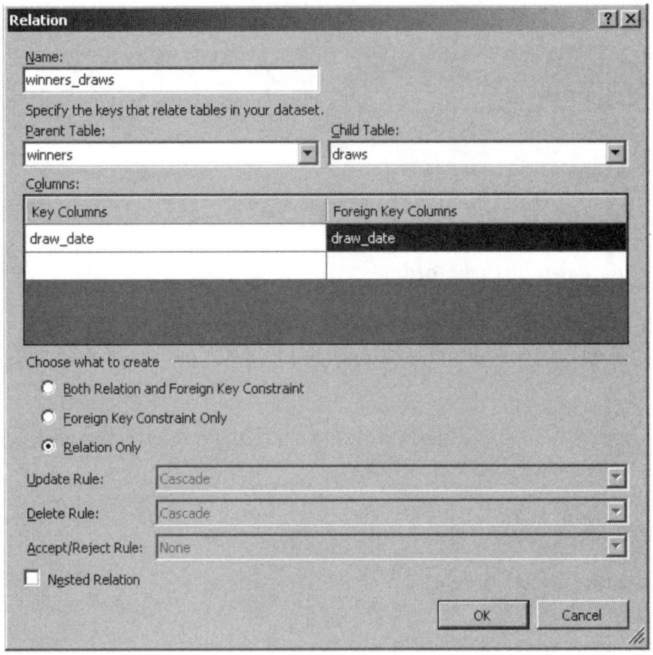

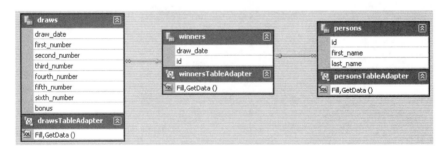

Figure 14-13. *Creating the winners and draws relation*

After you have created both relations, the Dataset Designer surface should look like Figure 14-14.

Figure 14-14. *Dataset Designer surface with all tables and relations*

Figure 14-14 illustrates a well-defined database structure that includes relations. The structure is very important for the Dataset Designer, because it defines how the generated code will appear. Look closely at Figure 14-14 and notice how each table representation shows Fill, GetData() at the bottom. The Fill() and GetData() methods are used to retrieve the data from the database and convert it into data that C# can process.

If you were to click on the text Fill() or GetData(), the Dataset Designer would display the properties, similar to Figure 14-15.

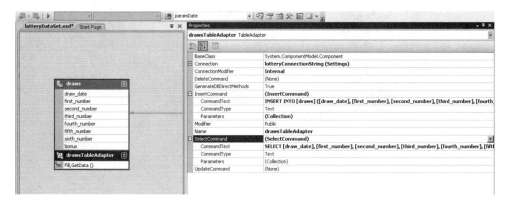

Figure 14-15. *Properties of Dataset Designer table structure*

The properties show the exact syntax of the SQL INSERT and SELECT commands. Remember, these two statements are used to add and select data from database tables. This illustrates that the Dataset Designer code is no different than the ADO.NET code.

Now consider the following code, generated by the Dataset Designer, to bind the columns of the draws table to the generated data structure.

```
private void InitAdapter() {
    this._adapter = new global::System.Data.SqlServerCe.SqlCeDataAdapter();
    global::System.Data.Common.DataTableMapping tableMapping =
        new global::System.Data.Common.DataTableMapping();
    tableMapping.SourceTable = "Table";
    tableMapping.DataSetTable = "draws";
    tableMapping.ColumnMappings.Add("draw_date", "draw_date");
    tableMapping.ColumnMappings.Add("first_number", "first_number");
    tableMapping.ColumnMappings.Add("second_number", "second_number");
    tableMapping.ColumnMappings.Add("third_number", "third_number");
    tableMapping.ColumnMappings.Add("fourth_number", "fourth_number");
    tableMapping.ColumnMappings.Add("fifth_number", "fifth_number");
    tableMapping.ColumnMappings.Add("sixth_number", "sixth_number");
    tableMapping.ColumnMappings.Add("bonus", "bonus");
    this._adapter.TableMappings.Add(tableMapping);
    this._adapter.InsertCommand =
        new global::System.Data.SqlServerCe.SqlCeCommand();
    this._adapter.InsertCommand.Connection = this.Connection;
    this._adapter.InsertCommand.CommandText =
        "INSERT INTO [draws] ([draw_date], [first_number], [second_number],
        [third_number]" +
        ", [fourth_number], [fifth_number], [sixth_number], [bonus]) VALUES
        (@p1, @p2, @p" +
        "3, @p4, @p5, @p6, @p7, @p8)";
```

```
this._adapter.InsertCommand.CommandType =
    global::System.Data.CommandType.Text;
global::System.Data.SqlServerCe.SqlCeParameter param =
    new global::System.Data.SqlServerCe.SqlCeParameter();
param.ParameterName = "@p1";
param.DbType = global::System.Data.DbType.DateTime;
param.IsNullable = true;
param.SourceColumn = "draw_date";
this._adapter.InsertCommand.Parameters.Add(param);
param = new global::System.Data.SqlServerCe.SqlCeParameter();
param.ParameterName = "@p2";
param.DbType = global::System.Data.DbType.Int32;
param.IsNullable = true;
param.SourceColumn = "first_number";
this._adapter.InsertCommand.Parameters.Add(param);
param = new global::System.Data.SqlServerCe.SqlCeParameter();
param.ParameterName = "@p3";
param.DbType = global::System.Data.DbType.Int32;
param.IsNullable = true;
param.SourceColumn = "second_number";
```

The bolded code shows how close the generated code is to a variation of the code used to insert data in the ADO.NET section. The generated code is more explicit and verbose than the previous code, but that does not matter, since you are not supposed to edit the generated code. You are supposed to use the Dataset Designer.

■**Note** The Dataset Designer gives you the advantage of not having to provide bindings between C# and a database, and an easy binding between a user interface and the database. The Dataset Designer generates the same ADO code that you would write manually. By providing a GUI where you can drag, drop, and so on, the Dataset Designer just makes it much simpler to write that code.

Using the Generated Code

Using the code generated by the Dataset Designer is easy, as long as you know what is going on. The Dataset Designer generates two major pieces of code: a table adapter and a dataset. The table adapter is code used to interact with the table directly. If you wanted to add, select, or delete items, use the table adapter. When you select data, the data will fill a dataset.

The following is the code to insert a record into the draws table (in the DatabaseConsoleEx application).

```
DatabaseConsoleEx.lotteryDataSetTableAdapters.drawsTableAdapter table =
    new DatabaseConsoleEx.lotteryDataSetTableAdapters.drawsTableAdapter();
table.Insert(DateTime.Now, 2, 2, 2, 2, 2, 2, 2);
```

The code is a trivial two-liner. It instantiates the `drawsTableAdapter`, and then calls the `Insert()` method to add a record. Connecting to the database, executing the command, and assigning the parameters are done automatically.

Note Generated code is both a blessing and a curse. Generated code hides complexity and makes it simpler for you to get your job done. But as you saw in the code excerpts, there is quite a bit going on behind the scenes, and if you don't understand ADO.NET, you will not know what to do when things go wrong. For example, when is a connection to the database made? The only way to know that is to look at the generated source code and follow the ADO.NET calls. A connection to a database is made the first time you call one of the SQL methods (for example, `Insert()`), not when the adapter is initialized.

To retrieve and iterate the data in the table, use the following code.

```
DatabaseConsoleEx.lotteryDataSet dataset =
    new DatabaseConsoleEx.lotteryDataSet();
DatabaseConsoleEx.lotteryDataSetTableAdapters.drawsTableAdapter table =
    new DatabaseConsoleEx.lotteryDataSetTableAdapters.drawsTableAdapter();

int count = table.Fill(dataset.draws);
Console.WriteLine("Record count is (" + dataset.draws.Count +
    ")(" + count + ")");
foreach (DatabaseConsoleEx.lotteryDataSet.drawsRow row in dataset.draws) {
    Console.WriteLine("Date (" + row.draw_date +
        ") (" + row.first_number + ")");
}
```

The variable `table` is initialized to an adapter that connects to the `draws` table. The variable `dataset` is an empty collection to the `draws` table.

To fill the collection, the method `table.Fill()` is called, and the destination is the `dataset.draws` data member. After having called `Fill()`, the number of records read is returned and assigned to `count`.

To iterate the individual rows, a `foreach` loop is used. It references the type `drawsRow`, and each instance of `drawsRow` has data members that represent the `draw_date`, `first_number`, and other columns. The iteration of the individual rows resembles the iteration of a collection. The ADO.NET example used a `while` loop and required you to know which column was associated with which SELECT field.

The Important Stuff to Remember

In this chapter, you learned about the basics of ADO.NET and the Dataset Designer. Here are the main points to remember:

- The real problem when using a relational database and a programming language like C# is the mismatch of set-based operations and individual object operations.

- To access a relational database, you can use ADO.NET. Each relational database has its own ADO.NET database driver. If your particular flavor of database has no ADO.NET driver, it becomes more difficult to access the relational database.

- The Dataset Designer code is based on ADO.NET, and thus if you understand ADO.NET, you will be able to understand how the Dataset Designer works and how it can be optimized.

- When using ADO.NET, the steps are typically to connect to a database, create a command, populate the parameters, execute the command, retrieve the data (if necessary), close the command, and close the connection.

- SQL is a language used to manipulate the tables of a relational database. You need to learn SQL on top of learning how to use ADO.NET.

Some Things for You to Do

The following are two exercises for applying what you've learned in this chapter.

1. The basis of the lottery application is defined in terms of a database, tables, and data. Write a console application that populates the draws table using a lottery file. Write a console application that dumps the contents of the draws table as a lottery file.

2. Create a console application that accepts as command-line arguments a winner and the date of the draw. Your console application must account for doubles and populate both the persons and winners tables.

■■■

CHAPTER 15

Learning About LINQ

In the previous chapter, you learned about how to access a database using the traditional ADO.NET technologies. When you make ADO.NET requests, you are making SQL calls and organizing the result set data using SQL.

Language Integrated Query (LINQ) is a technology that lets you organize your results in a consistent manner, regardless of the underlying source of the data. Why yet another technology to query information? The answer is related to XML.

XML is a technology used to represent information in a hierarchical manner. You saw an example of XML in Chapter 12. XML has solved many problems in an elegant and understandable manner. One of the solutions proposed by XML is the ability to reference information in an XML structure with XPath, which is a way of referencing an object structure using a set of filters. Using XPath, you can find any element, and the filters can include the presence of dependent elements, which is not easily possible in other technologies. Put simply, XPath and XML are very powerful techniques used to find information.

You can consider XML and XPath as inspiration for LINQ. Where LINQ and XML XPath deviate is that LINQ can be used to query C# objects, XML documents, and relational databases. Think of LINQ as a general mechanism used to search a hierarchy of information. The focus of this chapter will be to explain the mechanics of LINQ, and demonstrate how to write queries and use the methods associated with the LINQ library.

Finding the Frequency of Winning Numbers

The lottery application we've been working with in previous chapters collects information about lottery drawings to predict the next set of winning lottery numbers. The idea is to find patterns. Again, the reality is that lottery drawings are random, so even if you could identify patterns, that wouldn't mean you could predict winning numbers. However, what is interesting about this problem is that you can use LINQ to slice and dice the data. LINQ lets you keep the data as objects, and to perform SQL- and XPath-like operations, as you'll see in this chapter.

In Chapter 10, you saw a streaming architecture, where a console application read in text data and spat out text data. You also saw examples of text-to-binary and binary-to-text conversions. The application in this chapter (in the FrequencyProcessor project) will read in text, process the data, and then generate text. Thus, we need to use the text-to-text interface, which was defined in Chapter 10 as follows:

```
public interface IProcessor {
    string Process(string input);
}
```

The input is a text stream that looks like this:

```
2006.03.11 3 7 15 28 30 38 44
2006.03.15 10 18 30 34 41 43 5
2006.03.18 3 11 12 16 20 40 9
2006.03.22 2 3 7 13 42 43 41
2006.03.25 3 10 36 40 43 44 35
2006.03.29 3 4 8 16 34 39 45
```

If you want to find the frequency of the individual numbers, you could parse each individual number, and then increment the count of the individual number as an array, like this:

```
string[] splitUpText = lineOfText.Split(new char[] { ' ' });
frequency[int.Parse(splitUpText[ 0])] ++;
frequency[int.Parse(splitUpText[ 1])] ++;
...
```

The split line of text contains the individual numbers in text form, which is then converted to a number and used as an index for the frequency. The solution is fast and works, but it has a big problem: it is not extendable. The solution solves a single problem and only a single problem.

For example, let's say that you want to figure out other statistical information, such as which numeric combinations occur most often. Using the previous solution, that would require reparsing the text stream again. That is an expensive and tedious solution. The better solution would be to convert the stream into a series of objects that could be processed.

However, the problem at hand is calculating the frequency of individual numbers. So why exert the extra effort if the solution that solves the single problem works? Writing good code means solving problems using a generic but specific approach. You want to write specific code to not get bogged down in thinking about details in the future, and you want to write generic code so that any future requirement does not cause you to completely rewrite the old application. Knowing when to write specific code and when to write generic code is really a matter of experience—the only way to learn is to write code.

Extending the Lottery-Prediction System

In Chapter 10, the IProcessor interface was a good first step because it solved the problem at hand. The problem was to convert each line of text into another line of text. However, in this chapter's example, that interface is not enough. We need to add two other methods: Initialize() and Finalize().

We want to find the frequencies of an individual number in the drawn lotteries. The original interface method IProcessor.Process() is used to process an individual line of text, and the frequencies can be calculated only after all of the draws have been processed. Thus, we add Finalize(), which is called after all of the lines of text have been read. Common coding convention says that if you have a Finalize() method, you should have an Initialize() method that is called before the lines of text are processed.

Having extra requirements is not a problem and is fairly common. But you want to add the extra requirements without disrupting existing functionality. After all, if some code works, you don't want to break it because of additional requirements. Thus, you don't want to add the methods to the IProcessor interface like this:

```
public interface IProcessor {
    string Initialize();
    string Finalize();
    string Process(string input);
}
```

This code is a no-no because you are breaking existing functionality. Any class that implements IProcessor must now implement the methods Initialize() and Finalize(), even though those classes don't need those methods.

Thus, when adding requirements, you should not change existing interfaces. You create new interfaces and subclass the existing interfaces, like this:

```
public interface IExtendedProcessor : IProcessor {
    string Initialize();
    string Finalize();
}
```

The new interface IExtendedProcessor has the new methods Initialize() and Finalize(), but inherits the method Process(). The old functionality still has only a single method, and the new functionality is free to implement either interface.

Adding new interfaces and new methods does not mean everything will work as is. If you go back and look at the source code, you'll see that the IProcessor interface was used by the Bootstrap class. So, if you want the IExtendedProcessor interface to be recognized, then you must update Bootstrap. Updating Bootstrap is fine, because it does not mean that IProcessor implementations must be updated (or, at least, Bootstrap should not require that IProcessor implementations be updated).

The original abbreviated implementation of Bootstrap is as follows:

```
public static class Bootstrap {
    public static void DisplayHelp() {
        Console.WriteLine("You need help? Right now?");
    }

    public static void Process(string[] args, IProcessor processor) {
        TextReader reader = null;
        TextWriter writer = null;
        if (args.Length == 0) {
            reader = Console.In;
            writer = Console.Out;
        }
        // Removed for clarity

        writer.Write(processor.Process(reader.ReadToEnd()));
#if DEBUG_OUTPUT
```

```
            Console.WriteLine("Argument count(" + args.Length + ")");
            foreach(string argument in args) {
                Console.WriteLine( "Argument (" + argument + ")");
            }
#endif
        }
}
```

In the original implementation, the method `Process()` is called to read an input and write an output stream. Since `Initialize()` and `Finalize()` should be called before and after the string is processed, the most logical location of each method would be before and after the `processor.Process()` method, like this:

```
public static class Bootstrap {
    public static void DisplayHelp() {
        Console.WriteLine("You need help? Right now?");
    }

    public static void Process(string[] args, IProcessor processor) {
        TextReader reader = null;
        TextWriter writer = null;
        if (args.Length == 0) {
            reader = Console.In;
            writer = Console.Out;
        }
        // Removed for clarity

        if (processor is IExtendedProcessor) {
            writer.Write(((IExtendedProcessor)processor).Initialize());
        }
        writer.Write(processor.Process( reader.ReadToEnd()));
        if (processor is IExtendedProcessor) {
            writer.Write(((IExtendedProcessor)processor).Finalize());
        }
#if DEBUG_OUTPUT
        Console.WriteLine("Argument count(" + args.Length + ")");
        foreach( string argument in args) {
            Console.WriteLine( "Argument (" + argument + ")");
        }
#endif
    }
}
```

In the solution, the `processor` interface is tested to see if the interface is an instance of `IExtendedProcessor`. If so, then the `Initialize()` and `Finalize()` methods can be called.

Extending interfaces and extending those classes that consume the old and new interfaces at the same time is keeping *backward-compatibility*. Backward-compatibility is an important concept, because it implies you can gradually introduce new functionality into a working application without breaking old functionality.

Keeping backward-compatibility without breaking working functionality is difficult, and there is a point where adding new functionality becomes too complicated. Once you reach this stage, you need to break backward-compatibility by doing the following:

```
public interface IExtendedProcessor {
    string Initialize();
    string Finalize();
    string Process(string input);
}

[Obsolete("IProcessor is obsolete, plus used IExtendedProcessor ", true)]
public interface IProcessor {
    string Process(string input);
}
```

The example will break backward-compatibility due to the Obsolete attribute being associated with the IProcessor interface. Thus, when any class or interface references the IProcessor interface, a compile error results. The second parameter of Obsolete is true, which forces the compiler error. If you left out that parameter, when the interface is referenced, a compiler warning is generated, rather than a warning.

The IExtendedProcessor interface does not reference IProcessor and includes the method Process(). Thus, there are no more dependencies, and all functionality must use IProcessor.

■**Note** Breaking backward-compatibility is a major step, because your code cries that some code is broken and requires alteration. Depending on what you break, it could be dramatic or simple. However, sometimes you will need to break code, and when you do, make sure that the code cries "broken!" very loud. Otherwise, you might get unexpected errors.

Now that we've updated the Bootstrap class and added the IExtended interface, all of the samples in Chapter 10 will continue to function, and we can implement the frequency solution.

Implementing a Frequency Solution

The solution that we want to use is to read in the text, convert the text into binary objects, calculate some statistics, and finally write out the text. The interesting part of this solution is that pieces of it have already been written. If you remember in Chapter 10, there was a requirement to convert the lottery draws into binary form. That code will be borrowed to implement the statistics functionality.

The statistics console application (FrequencyProcessor) requires an IExtendedProcessor implementation. The following is the complete implementation.

```
...
using System.IO;

using ReaderWriter;
using LottoLibrary;
```

```
namespace FrequencyProcessor
{
    class LottoTicketProcessor : IExtendedProcessor {
        List<Ticket> _tickets = new List<Ticket>();

        public string Process(string input) {
            TextReader reader = new StringReader(input);

            while (reader.Peek() != -1) {
                string lineOfText = reader.ReadLine();
                string[] splitUpText = lineOfText.Split(new char[] { ' ' });
                string[] dateSplit = splitUpText[0].Split('.');

                Ticket ticket =
                    new Ticket(
                        new DateTime(
                            int.Parse(dateSplit[0]),
                            int.Parse(dateSplit[1]),
                            int.Parse(dateSplit[2])),
                        new int[] {
                                    int.Parse(splitUpText[1]),
                                    int.Parse(splitUpText[2]),
                                    int.Parse(splitUpText[3]),
                                    int.Parse(splitUpText[4]),
                                    int.Parse(splitUpText[5]),
                                    int.Parse(splitUpText[6]) },
                                    int.Parse(splitUpText[7]));
                _tickets.Add(ticket);
            }
            return "";
        }


        #region IExtendedProcessor Members

        public string Initialize() {
            return "";
        }

        int FrequencyOfANumber(int numberToSearch) {
            var query = from ticket in _tickets
                        where lst.Numbers[0] == numberToSearch
                        || lst.Numbers[1] == numberToSearch
                        || lst.Numbers[2] == numberToSearch
                        || lst.Numbers[3] == numberToSearch
                        || lst.Numbers[4] == numberToSearch
                        || lst.Numbers[5] == numberToSearch
```

```
                    select lst.Numbers;
            return query.Count();
        }

        public string Finalize() {
            StringBuilder builder = new StringBuilder();
            for (int c1 = 1; c1 < 46; c1++) {
                builder.Append("Number (" + c1 + ") Found (");
                int foundCount = 0;
                foundCount += FrequencyOfANumber(c1);
                builder.Append("" + foundCount + ")\n");
            }
            return builder.ToString();
        }


        #endregion
    }
}
```

Let's examine how the implementation works.

Borrowing Code to Solve Another Problem

The borrowed code is the implementation of the Process() method, shown here in abbreviated form:

```
public string Process(string input) {
    TextReader reader = new StringReader(input);

    while (reader.Peek() != -1) {
        string lineOfText = reader.ReadLine();
        string[] splitUpText = lineOfText.Split(new char[] { ' ' });
        string[] dateSplit = splitUpText[0].Split('.');

        Ticket ticket =
            new Ticket(
                new DateTime(
                    int.Parse(dateSplit[0]),
                // ... abbreviated
                new int[] {
                            int.Parse(splitUpText[1]),
                            // ... abbreviated
                            int.Parse(splitUpText[6]) },
                            int.Parse(splitUpText[7])));
        _tickets.Add(ticket);
    }
    return "";
}
```

Other than the new `tickets.Add(ticket);` line, the code is identical to the `Text2Binary`. `Process()` implementation. The bolded code adds the lottery draw to the list of drawn numbers. Once the tickets have been instantiated, they can be added to the list of tickets that will be queried and searched.

CODE REUSE

The borrowed code demonstrates code reuse through copy and paste. Realize that code that was used to process binary objects is now being used in a completely new context.

The copied and pasted code reuses classes and functionality from another problem context. You copied and pasted the functionality to parse and instantiate the `Ticket` type, but reused the `Ticket` type itself.

When we worked on the code for the `Ticket` type, you probably had no idea that we would reuse the same code. In fact, even *I* had no idea that we would reuse the code. I find this happens a lot in my projects.

So how does this work? I write code to fulfill two criteria: minimal to solve the task and general enough to not restrict further usage. So I don't actually design for code reuse, and I don't have code reuse on my mind. What I have on my mind is to design code in such a way that it could potentially be reused.

Let's look at that code that could have solved the frequency problem previously.

```
string[] splitUpText = lineOfText.Split(new char[] { ' ' });
frequency[int.Parse(splitUpText[0])] ++;
frequency[int.Parse(splitUpText[1])] ++;
...
```

Is this code minimal? No, even though the lines of code are minimal, the code itself is not minimal. If I wanted to use the same code to perform another frequency analysis, which could happen, I would need to copy and paste yet again, and thus the code is not minimal.

Is this code general enough to be used in another context? Absolutely not, because to reuse the code, you would need to copy and paste it, and do some slight alterations.

This is an excellent example of code that can be written very quickly and is very effectively used by copying and pasting it everywhere. You are productive and can solve a problem quickly, but it cannot be easily extended or maintained. Imagine finding a bug and having copied and pasted the code ten times. That would mean you would need to find the ten different locations and see if the bug exists in those different locations.

Using LINQ

To find the frequency of a specific number, you don't need to use LINQ. In fact, LINQ can always be avoided by using C# code. So then why use LINQ? It makes it easier for you to write complicated search queries that are agnostic of the source. An example is two versions of the code used to solve the frequency problem: one that is not reusable and one that is reusable. The code that is not reusable is the query without LINQ, and the reusable code is the query with LINQ.

So let's look at the frequency code that is not reusable.

```
int FrequencyOfANumberNotReusable(int numberToSearch) {
    int runningTotal = 0;
    foreach (Ticket ticket in _tickets) {
        if (ticket.Numbers[0] == numberToSearch ||
```

```
            ticket.Numbers[1] == numberToSearch ||
            ticket.Numbers[2] == numberToSearch ||
            ticket.Numbers[3] == numberToSearch ||
            ticket.Numbers[4] == numberToSearch ||
            ticket.Numbers[5] == numberToSearch) {
            runningTotal++;
        }
    }
    return runningTotal;
}
```

Notice the similarity of the code to code presented in Chapter 9. The problem with this code is that you are iterating and solving a particular problem. The code cannot be easily adapted to solving another problem.

The reusable code is in the form of a LINQ expression:

```
int FrequencyOfANumber(int numberToSearch) {
    var query = from ticket in _tickets
                where ticket.Numbers[0] == numberToSearch
                || ticket.Numbers[1] == numberToSearch
                || ticket.Numbers[2] == numberToSearch
                || ticket.Numbers[3] == numberToSearch
                || ticket.Numbers[4] == numberToSearch
                || ticket.Numbers[5] == numberToSearch
                select ticket.Numbers;
    return query.Count();
}
```

The LINQ expression uses many constructs similar to a SQL SELECT statement. Here are the basic rules of LINQ:

- All LINQ queries must have a data source (from).

- All LINQ queries must have a filter (where); however, if the filter does not exist, an automatic include-everything filter is implied.

- All LINQ queries must have a resulting dataset creator (select).

To execute a LINQ expression, you need a data source. The data source could be an object list, an XML document, or even a relational database table. In the example, the data source is an object list and is defined using the from statement:

```
from ticket in _tickets
```

Looking at the from statement, you could get the idea that it is a foreach statement without the types. Indeed, that is what is happening. The from statement is saying to iterate the data source and assign each element (a Ticket) to the variable ticket. Note, however, that there is no type information, which is one of the strengths of LINQ—you have the ability to easily slice and dice data to suit your needs.

As you retrieve each item, you want to verify whether the item matches your needs. If you go look to the code that isn't reusable, you'll see that it checks this with an if statement. In

LINQ, you use the where statement, which is identical to its SQL equivalent. With the where statement, you test to see if the item matches your criteria. In our case, we check each number in the Ticket instance to see if it matches the number we're currently seeking.

If the where returns true, we have a match and we will want to do something. In the code that isn't reusable, that means incrementing the runningTotal integer. In LINQ, the aim is to filter the dataset (_tickets in our case), and thus the select statement is used to create a new dataset of drawn numbers. This dataset contains all of the draws with the number we're looking for (numberToSearch), and if the draws are counted, we can get the frequency of that number, which we then return.

Here is a C# version of the code that is not reusable:

```
List<int[]> FrequencyOfANumberNotReusable(int numberToSearch) {
    List<int[]> retval = new List<int[]>();
    foreach (Ticket ticket in _tickets) {
        if (ticket.Numbers[0] == numberToSearch ||
            ticket.Numbers[1] == numberToSearch ||
            ticket.Numbers[2] == numberToSearch ||
            ticket.Numbers[3] == numberToSearch ||
            ticket.Numbers[4] == numberToSearch ||
            ticket.Numbers[5] == numberToSearch) {
            retval.Add(ticket.Numbers);
        }
    }
    return retval;
}
```

As I said previously, whatever you can do in LINQ, you can write out in longhand in C#. However, the longhand is not reusable, nor minimal, whereas the LINQ code is. Because filtering has occurred, there is no reason why you could not use the dataset for further filtering purposes, such as the frequency of two numbers in a draw. Had you used the original frequency code of iterating and incrementing the runningTotal variable, you would need to use copy-and-paste techniques to figure out the new frequency.

Let's look at the LINQ that could be used to find the frequency of two numbers being drawn.

```
int FrequencyOfTwoNumbers(int number1ToSearch, int number2ToSearch) {
    var query = from ticket2in
                from ticket in _tickets
                where ticket.Numbers[0] == number1ToSearch
                || ticket.Numbers[1] == number1ToSearch
                || ticket.Numbers[2] == number1ToSearch
                || ticket.Numbers[3] == number1ToSearch
                || ticket.Numbers[4] == number1ToSearch
                || ticket.Numbers[5] == number1ToSearch
                select ticket
            where ticket2.Numbers[0] == number2ToSearch
            || ticket2.Numbers[1] == number2ToSearch
            || ticket2.Numbers[2] == number2ToSearch
            || ticket2.Numbers[3] == number2ToSearch
```

```
                || ticket2.Numbers[4] == number2ToSearch
                || ticket2.Numbers[5] == number2ToSearch
                select ticket2.Numbers;
        return query.Count();
}
```

The LINQ statement is a concatenation of two LINQ queries, where one LINQ query is bolded. When the query is executed, the embedded query is executed and generates a result set. The result set is a data source on which the outer and second query operate, which then generates another result set.

You do not need to embed LINQ queries as in the preceding code. You could write functions and embed the result of a LINQ query as the data source of another LINQ query. The power of LINQ is that you can, in theory, arbitrarily embed many queries within other queries, since you are creating a filtering mechanism where one result set is the data source of another query.

■**Note** LINQ's strength is in its ability to slice and dice data to find the information that you want. LINQ requires more resources than similar C# code in longhand format. But the benefit you get with LINQ is reusable code that you can maintain.

In the preceding section, we used LINQ to solve the frequency problem in a manner that promoted reusability. For example, if you wanted to find out more statistics of the lottery draws, you could focus on the statistics and not the infrastructure supporting the statistics. All you would need to do is write more LINQ statements that sliced and diced the existing list of lottery draws. It would require adding only the method calls to the IExtendedProcessor.Finalize() method. However, let's consider the problem solved and think about what else can be done with LINQ.

Learning More LINQ Tricks

LINQ is not the only way to filter data. Associated with LINQ are a number of extension methods that can be applied to lists. For example, to filter for the frequency of a particular number, the following code could also have been used.

```
int FrequencyOfANumberList(int numberToSearch) {
    var query = _tickets.Where(
        (ticket, index) =>
            ticket.Numbers[0] == numberToSearch
            || ticket.Numbers[1] == numberToSearch
            || ticket.Numbers[2] == numberToSearch
            || ticket.Numbers[3] == numberToSearch
            || ticket.Numbers[4] == numberToSearch
            || ticket.Numbers[5] == numberToSearch);
    return query.Count();
}
```

The ideas of LINQ that include from, where, and select are not lost; they just have not been used. The from part is the _tickets variable itself. The where part is the method Where(), and the select part is a default selection of the currently selected node.

To specify an action with Where(), you use a lambda expression, which has two parameters: the object and the index of the object. The lambda expression expects that you return a Boolean value indicating whether the ticket item should be added to a returned list.

When you use the list methods associated with the type, you are using a different functionality than LINQ in the abstract sense. LINQ is a syntax that wraps SQL-like text. LINQ is much easier to understand and program. Using the methods gives you more flexibility, but they also are more complicated to write.

For example, if you wanted to find the frequency of two numbers in a list, you could use this code:

```
int FrequencyOfTwoNumbersList(int number1ToSearch, int number2ToSearch) {
    var query = _tickets.Where(
        (ticket, index) =>
            ticket.Numbers[0] == number1ToSearch
            || ticket.Numbers[1] == number1ToSearch
            || ticket.Numbers[2] == number1ToSearch
            || ticket.Numbers[3] == number1ToSearch
            || ticket.Numbers[4] == number1ToSearch
            || ticket.Numbers[5] == number1ToSearch
        ).Where(
        (ticket, index) =>
            ticket.Numbers[0] == number2ToSearch
            || ticket.Numbers[1] == number2ToSearch
            || ticket.Numbers[2] == number2ToSearch
            || ticket.Numbers[3] == number2ToSearch
            || ticket.Numbers[4] == number2ToSearch
            || ticket.Numbers[5] == number2ToSearch);

    return query.Count();
}
```

In the code, the bolded line demonstrates how the output of one method can serve as the input for another method. This chaining of methods works because the list method returns other lists. Thus, you could add multiple criteria by concatenating multiple Where() method calls.

The methods are used to filter or manipulate the set where the details of the method are provided by a lambda expression. Table 15-1 briefly describes some of the useful methods that you can use to filter and manipulate a list. The best way to learn about all of the methods is to use Visual C# Express, declare a list, and use IntelliSense to discover the different methods available. Also, see http://msdn2.microsoft.com/en-us/vcsharp/aa336746.aspx for many examples that demonstrate the various list-manipulation methods.

Table 15-1. *Some Methods for Filtering and Manipulating Lists*

Method	Description
Aggregate()	Returns a fact about the list. A fact could be how many even numbers there are or the frequency of a particular number. All of the elements in the list are iterated and returned as a single fact not a list.
All()	Iterates all elements of the list and tests according to a lambda expression, where a true or false is returned. For example, the test could be to find out if all objects have a value greater than 10. The test only needs to return a true or false value for the individual object, where the All() method will correlate the results and return a determination of the question in the form or a true or false.
Any()	Like All(), except that the question is changed to test if any of the objects have a value greater than 10. If so, then a true value is returned; otherwise, a false value is returned.
Average()	Calculates the average of a sequence of values. The average value returned is a numeric double value. This method is a bit odd, because to calculate an average, you need numbers, even though the lambda expression could calculate the average of objects.
Cast()	Returns a list where each item is converted from the list type to another type. This is a good method to use when you need to perform bulk conversions of instance types in a list.
Concat()	Concatenates one list onto the current list.
Contains()	Verifies whether an item is present in the list. The method uses the lambda expression to verify each item and returns true or false to indicate if the data has been found.
ConvertAll()	Returns a list where each item is converted from the list type to another type. This is a good method to use when you need to perform bulk conversions of instance types in a list.
Distinct()	Removes all duplicates from a list. By default, the implementation of Distinct() checks for equality by calling GetHashCode() first, and then calling Equals()if necessary. A variation of the Distinct() method is to supply an IEqualityComparer interface instance that can be used to determine whether two types are equal. However, a better approach would be to implement GetHashCode() and Equals().
Except()	Takes the current list and a passed-in list and performs a difference between the two sets, which is returned to the caller as a new dataset. The equality tests are identical to Distinct().
Find()	Finds an element of a particular list. Note that the lambda expression you use when it has found an element will cause the Find() method to stop processing the list and return what you marked as found.
FindAll()	Like Find(), except you can find multiple elements in a list. This is like the Where() method.
FindLast()	Like Find(), except the search starts at the end of the list.
ForEach()	An iterator that uses a lambda expression to process each element. The ForEach() method is a simplification of the code illustrated in Chapter 9.
GroupBy()	Takes a list and splits it into specific groupings as per the provided lambda expression. For example, you could use it to split the earnings of individuals into brackets.
Intersect()	Takes the current list and a provided list and determines the elements that are common to both lists. Uses the same equality tests as Distinct().
Max()	Finds the maximum value of a list.

(Continued)

Table 15-1. *(Continued)*

Method	Description
Min()	Finds the minimum value of a list.
Reverse()	Reverses the order of the list.
Select()	Selects an individual item from the iteration being executed.
SelectMany()	Selects many items from a list where the selected items form another list.
Sum()	Calculates the sum of a list.
Union()	Takes the list and the passed-in list and calculates the union of the two lists. Uses the equality test as defined in the Distinct() method.

■**Note** With C# 3.0, lists and the manipulation of lists have dramatically changed for the better. The general structure is to define methods that allow a developer to specify a lambda expression that is then chained together with other methods. Take some time to learn about all of the possibilities.

As an example of the power of the various methods, consider the following code, which compacts the frequency code into a couple of lines of source code.

```
int FrequencyOfANumberFunc(int numberToSearch) {
    return _tickets.SelectMany(
        (ticket) => ticket.Numbers
            ).Where((num) => num == numberToSearch).Count();
}
```

Here, each ticket is iterated by calling the SelectMany() method. This returns an array of numbers, which represents the drawn numbers. The purpose of SelectMany() is to combine the individual arrays of numbers into a large array of numbers. The code then calls Where() to filter out only those numbers that equal the number to search for, and finally the Count() method is called to return the number of found values.

The following sections present examples of using the extension methods with LINQ. They are in the LINQExamples project, which is a console application.

■**Note** In all of the examples, I have taken shortcuts for simplicity. So you will see some coding practices that are not recommended, such as creating public data members and not using properties.

Selecting and Altering Data

When running a LINQ query, the data that you filter and manipulate does not need to stay in its original form. Let's say that you have a list of customers, and you have identified a set of customers who deserve more loyalty points. You want to select those customers, increment their points, and then return the list of altered customers. To do that, you can mix LINQ with the extension methods.

Consider the following simplified customer declaration.

```
class Customer {
    public string Identifier;
    public int Points;
    public override string ToString() {
        return "Identifier (" + Identifier + ") Points (" + Points + ")";
    }
}
```

A list will be created with two customers, where one customer has no points and the other one does. Here is the source code to create that list:

```
List<Customer> customers =
        new List<Customer>() {
            new Customer {
                Identifier = "Person 1",
                Points = 0
        },
        new Customer {
            Identifier = "Person 2",
            Points = 10
        }
    };
```

The customers that have enough points are selected and rewarded with extra points. To do that, use the following LINQ statement.

```
var points = (from customer in customers
              where customer.Points > 5
              select customer).Select(
              (pCustomer, index) => {
                  pCustomer.Points += 5;
                  return pCustomer;
              });
```

The LINQ query is combined with a modification operation. The LINQ statement that uses from, where, and select is not new. New are the parentheses enclosing the LINQ statement. By using a set of parentheses, you are identifying the LINQ statement as an object that references a result set.

In the example, the method called on the LINQ statement is Select(). Using the Select() method, each item in the result set is iterated and passed as a parameter to the lambda expression (pCustomer). Passed with the item is the index of the item in the list. The role of the lambda expression is to do something with the item and return what should be used as a basis for another list. In the example, an instance of the type Customer is passed in, and an instance of type Customer is passed out. But before the instance is returned, it is manipulated to get an additional five bonus points.

What might concern you is that there is no test to check if the customer warrants an actual five bonus points. That would be a concern if you were not using the LINQ expression. The LINQ expression is responsible for filtering out only those customers who should get the additional bonus points. Thus, when the method Select() is called, you are 100% sure that only the customers who should get bonus points actually get bonus points. Think of this as building a pipeline of manipulations.

Selecting with Anonymous Types

The Select() method and statement are used to generate a resulting dataset after finding a particular element. As demonstrated in the previous section, a select statement is used to generate a new dataset. For example, what if you want to find all of the customers who fulfill a certain criterion, but do not want to copy all of the associated data? You might want only the customer identifier and accumulated points. To do that, you could modify the Select() part of the LINQ statement to return a new type that you declare dynamically. The following is the previous example rewritten to use an anonymous type.

```
var points = (from customer in customers
              where customer.Points > 5
              select customer).Select(
              (customer, index) => {
                  customer.Points += 5;
                  return new {
                          identifier = customer.Identifier,
                          points = customer.Points
                      };
              });
```

In the example, the return statement uses the keyword new without an identifier, but with the syntax of an object initializer. This is defining an anonymous type. An *anonymous type* is an object instance that has no identifier. The anonymous type has properties, but it does not have methods.

Anonymous types are useful only in the context of the method in which they are declared. For example, the variable var is an untyped type and could be assigned an anonymous type. However, if you tried to pass the untyped type instance of an anonymous type, you wouldn't have any support for the syntax.

This code is illegal:

```
void ExampleFunction(var obj) { }
```

But let's focus on the sample code. Here's how that could be legally written:

```
foreach(var customer in points) {
    Console.WriteLine("Customer (" +
        customer.identifier + ")(" +
        customer.points + ")");
}
```

The compiler that translates the LINQ expression knows that the final result set contains anonymous types with the properties identifier and points. This is all determined when the compiler processes the C# code.

But what if you wanted to manipulate an anonymous type? All anonymous types are objects, and thus if you declare the method parameter or property as type object, you could reference an anonymous type. However, you can't call the properties identifier and points, since there is no type information. You can reference the properties using dynamic invocation, but this approach is complex and tends to be slow. So, in a nutshell, when working with anonymous types, remember that they are to be used only in the context of a method.

Processing Multiple Streams

In all of the LINQ examples so far, a single dataset has been manipulated, processed, and filtered. You can process multiple streams at the same time, but you will get a combinatorial type answer.

For example, suppose you had this LINQ:

```
int[] set1 = { 1, 2, 3, 4, 5 };
int[] set2 = { 1, 2, 3, 4, 5 };
int[] set3 = { 1, 2, 3, 4, 5 };

var triples =
    from a in set1
    from b in set2
    from c in set3
    select new { a, b, c };
```

In pseudo-code, the following would be identical.

```
List<object> items = new List<object>();
foreach (int a in set1) {
    foreach (int b in set2) {
        foreach (int c in set3) {
            items.Add(new {
                        a,
                        b,
                        c
                    });
        }
    }
}
```

When you specify multiple from clauses, you are creating a looping mechanism where each item is iterated against the other elements. This sounds useful, but it can have a disastrous side effect: a seemingly innocent query can take much longer than it should. After having written the individual from statements, you can use where and select as usual.

Sorting the Results

After having selected elements, you will probably want to sort the result set. Using LINQ, you can sort by anything you deem important. The obvious approach is to sort according to a number or letter, but you could also sort according to length of the word.

Regardless of how you sort, the keyword that you use in LINQ is orderby or the method OrderBy(). The following is a LINQ example that does an alphabetic sort.

```
string[] words = { "cherry", "apple", "blueberry" };

var sortedWords =
    from w in words
    orderby w
    select w;
```

The keyword orderby is inserted before select. In this case, it will sort the words in ascending alphabetical order.

The way that the orderby works is that the *value* of the variable is compared, rather than the actual variable. Let's say that you are processing the LINQ statement and there is an orderby word. Because the identifier w is used, it implies to sort by the field w, but in reality, you are not sorting by w. You are sorting by the value of w.

If you want to sort in reverse order, you can use the keyword descending, as follows:

```
var sortedWords =
    from w in words
    orderby w descending
    select w;
```

This approach allows you to perform sorts according to other values. For example, you could sort by the length of word, like this:

```
var sortedWords =
    from w in words
    orderby w.Length
    select w;
```

The orderby queries for the value of w.Length, which returns a number. If that number happens to be longer or shorter than another word, it is placed after or before the other word. Note you could put in random values that have nothing to do with the item from the list, and the items would be sorted according to the random values.

You could also sort according to multiple criteria. For example, you could sort the words alphabetically and then by length:

```
var sortedWords =
    from w in words
    orderby w, w.Length
    select w;
```

To sort by multiple criteria, append them to the orderby keyword, each separated by a comma.

Splitting Results into Groups

In the previous examples, the LINQ queries generated a list of customers who should be rewarded. What if you did not want to reward the customers immediately? What if you just wanted to divide customers into groups of those who should get rewards and those who should not get rewards? You can do this by using LINQ grouping functionality.

The following query groups the customers of the previous examples into those who should get rewards and those who should not get rewards.

```
var groupedCustomers =
    from customer in customers
    group customer by customer.Points > 5 into rewarded
    select new { ShouldReward = rewarded.Key, Customers = rewarded };
```

When using the group keyword, the nature of the select changes. Think of the group keyword as a specific form of the select keyword. Before reaching select, group creates a new list of items that are passed as individual lists to the select statement.

In the example, what this means is that from will select each and every individual customer. The individual customer is passed to the code that performs an operation, which returns a value. The returned value is a Boolean true or false value to indicate whether or not the customer should be rewarded. If the value is true, the customer should be rewarded. Regardless of the state, the customer is added to the grouping that would be temporarily called rewarded.

If you were to translate the from and group keywords into C#, the code would be similar to the following (though not exactly, but close enough to give you a good idea of what is going on).

```
Dictionary<bool, List<Customer>> grouped =
    new Dictionary<bool, List<Customer>>();
grouped.Add( true, new List<Customer>());
grouped.Add( false, new List<Customer>());
foreach (var customer in customers) {
    if (customers.Points > 5) {
        grouped[true].Add(customer);
    }
    else {
        grouped[false].Add(customer);
    }
}
```

The group keyword creates a keyed list where each key references a list of customers. The translated C# code demonstrates that group creates a new list of items that is iterated when select is referenced.

The select code is creating a new set of objects that reference the key or grouping and the list of customers that fulfill the criteria. Translating the select statement into C# pseudo-code looks something like this:

```
List<object> resultSet = new List<object>();
foreach (var key in grouped.Keys) {
    resultSet.Add(new { ShouldReward = key, Customers = grouped[key] });
}
```

The result is a list of objects that contains the various keys and the customers who match the keys. To iterate the list, you need to perform a two-level iteration, assuming that you used the LINQ code shown at the beginning of the section.

```
foreach (var grouping in groupedCustomers) {
    Console.WriteLine("Should be rewarded (" + grouping.ShouldReward + ")");
    foreach (var customer in grouping.Customers) {
        Console.WriteLine("Customer (" + customer.ToString() + ")");
    }
}
```

In the example, first you iterate all of the keys, and then iterate all of the customers who are associated with the key.

Performing Set Operations

The last major topic that you need to know about when using LINQ is the ability to perform set operations on a dataset. The major downside, however, to performing set operations is that you must use the methods, and at the time of this writing, no LINQ command syntax existed for set operations.

Knowing about set operations is useful because they enable you to sort and organize multiple result sets. The examples in this section involve the Customer type again. However, to make sure that the set operations function properly, you need to implement the Equals() and GetHashCode()methods, like this:

```
class Customer {
    public string Identifier;
    public int Points;
    public override string ToString() {
        return "Identifier (" + Identifier + ") Points (" + Points + ")";
    }
    public override bool Equals(object obj) {
        if (obj is Customer) {
            Customer otherObj = obj as Customer;
            if (otherObj.Points == Points &&
                otherObj.Identifier.CompareTo(Identifier) == 0) {
                return true;
            }
        }
        return false;
    }
    public override int GetHashCode() {
        return Points * Identifier.GetHashCode();
    }
}
```

Note The GetHashCode() implementation here is rudimentary. In the source code that comes with this book, you will find a GetHashCode library class, which makes it simpler to implement GetHashCode(). The source code is in the project ServerSideSpreadsheet/Devspace.Trader.Common/Automators.

Implementing Equals() and GetHashCode() for custom types is absolutely imperative, because the set operations use that information to determine whether two objects are identical. If you don't implement either method, the set operations will use the default implementations of Equals() and GetHashCode(), which are incomplete and will give you the wrong results.

The next step is to create two separate lists of customers. In this example, both lists contain the same valued customer. Realize that the identical customer is not the same object instance, but contains the same values.

```
List<Customer> customers1 =
        new List<Customer>() {
    new Customer {
        Identifier = "Person 1",
        Points = 0
    },
    new Customer {
        Identifier = "Person 2",
        Points = 10
    }
};
List<Customer> customers2 =
        new List<Customer>() {
    new Customer {
        Identifier = "Person 3",
        Points = 20
    },
    new Customer {
        Identifier = "Person 2",
        Points = 10
    }
};
```

The bolded code represents the customer that exists in both lists. But what if the lists were like the following ones?

```
List<Customer> customers1 =
        new List<Customer>() {
    new Customer {
        Identifier = "Person 1",
        Points = 0
    },
```

```
    new Customer {
        Identifier = "Person 2",
        Points = 10
    }
};
List<Customer> customers2 =
        new List<Customer>() {
    new Customer {
        Identifier = "Person 3",
        Points = 20
    },
    new Customer {
        Identifier = "Person 2",
        Points = 20
    }
};
```

Now even though Person 2 exists in two places, the values for Points are not identical, and it begs the question, "Should Equals() and GetHashCode() return the state that the objects are not identical?" The answer lies in your application. If your code says that two customers with the same Identifier and different Points represent the same person, then Equals() and GetHashCode() must not take into account the value of Points. You need to consider this, because if you are going to call the method Distinct(), and you take into account the value of the Points property, there will be two instances of the same person.

To get a list of all unique customers, you can use Union(), as follows:

```
var uniqueCustomers = customers1.Union(customers2);
```

Contained within the list represented by the variable uniqueCustomers will be the three customers of the two lists.

Using LINQ in Other Contexts

So far, all of the examples in this chapter involved using LINQ and objects. However, LINQ is not just an object-searching technology. It is also usable with XML and relational databases. Using LINQ with these other data sources is not a problem, since the querying is identical. What is a problem is getting the query to work in the first place.

Consider Figure 15-1, which illustrates the LINQ architecture.

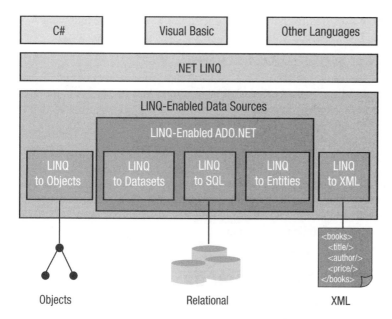

Figure 15-1. *LINQ architecture (based on an image in MSDN Magazine,* http://msdn. microsoft.com/msdnmag/issues/07/06/csharp30/default.aspx)

As you can see in Figure 15-1, all .NET programming languages can access the LINQ library. The data manipulated by the LINQ library comes from what is called a LINQ-enabled data source. The examples that you've seen use the LINQ to objects data source.

However, there is also the possibility to use a LINQ-enabled ADO.NET connection. The good news is that you can use LINQ with a relational database. The bad news is that the relational database's ADO.NET driver must support the special LINQ characteristics. At the time of this writing, only the Microsoft SQL Server driver supports LINQ. Currently, the drivers for Microsoft Access, MySQL, and other relational databases do not support LINQ.

Consider this LINQ query:

```
NorthwindDataContext northwind = new NorthwindDataContext();
var products = from p in northwind.Products
    where p.OrderDetails.Count == 0 && p.UnitPrice > 100
    select p;
```

Notice the bolded code in the from statement. The data source is an object that references the relational database Products table. If a database driver is optimized for LINQ, it will understand the LINQ query and optimize it as if it were a SQL statement.

If your database driver does not support LINQ, then you have a problem because, in theory, you would need to download all the data from the table, and then execute the LINQ query. That would waste resources and is not recommended.

■Note For examples of LINQ using relational databases, see *Beginning C# 2008 Databases* by James Huddleston and Vidya Vrat Agarwal (Apress, 2007).

Let's say that you want to execute LINQ on an XML document. Consider the following XML LINQ code (from `http://www.hookedonlinq.com/LINQtoXML5MinuteOverview.ashx`).

```
XDocument loaded = XDocument.Load(@"C:\contacts.xml");

// Query the data and write out a subset of contacts
var q = from c in loaded.Descendants("contact")
        where (int)c.Attribute("contactId") < 4
        select (string)c.Element("firstName") + " " +
                (string)c.Element("lastName");
```

Notice how the same LINQ syntax that you've seen in the previous examples is used, but the source of the data that is to be manipulated by LINQ is different. Keep in mind that when you are manipulating data using LINQ, you are manipulating objects that may point to XML files, relational databases, or plain-vanilla data objects.

The Important Stuff to Remember

In this chapter, you learned about the basics of LINQ and how to write queries. Here are the key points to remember:

- LINQ is an API that sits on top of other technologies such as C# objects, relational databases, and XML documents.

- LINQ can work effectively only if the underlying data source technology has been optimized for LINQ. Otherwise, you are left with having to load a single record set and then manipulate that record set.

- Regardless of the data source, the techniques used to query and write LINQ are identical.

- When manipulating LINQ objects, the methods and properties associated with the various data sources are different. For example, when searching XML documents, you can use XML Document Object Model (DOM) methods and properties that are not available when manipulating plain-vanilla objects.

- LINQ is not just a syntax, but a series of extension methods associated with datasets. The methods allow for more sophisticated data pipelining and processing of information.

Some Things for You to Do

The following are two exercises to help you apply what you've learned in this chapter.

1. The solution for finding a frequency presented in this chapter went from text to text to calculate the statistics. Can you think of another approach that would require minimal changes in the interface structure? Hint: the way the objects were parsed into objects borrowed code from another application. Could that other application be used somehow?

2. You saw a LINQ query embedding another LINQ query when finding the frequency of two numbers. Rewrite the code to generate the frequency of all combinations of single, pairs, and triples.

CHAPTER 16

■ ■ ■

Writing Functional Code in C#

C# is predominantly an imperative programming language, which means that it deals primarily with changes in state. However, C# 3.0 is starting to show its functional programming side. Functional programming aims to create code that does not produce any side effects. Many of the previous chapters included functional programming aspects, without calling it functional programming. In this chapter, I am going to put the stake in the ground and explain functional programming.

Chapters 9 and 11 covered .NET generics and lambda expressions in the context of C#. You learned how to use those features to solve problems in an object-oriented manner. In this chapter, you'll learn how to use them to solve problems in the context of a functional language. (Review Chapters 9 and 11 if you need a refresher on .NET generics and lambda expressions before continuing here.)

Why Functional Programming?

You might have heard that functional programming is an advanced topic. I don't think functional programming is any more advanced than say threading or designing and implementing components. However, functional programming is a *different style* of programming. The situation is similar to a programmer encountering object-oriented code for the first time. It seems like an advanced topic because it introduces new concepts.

As an introduction to functional programming, I highly recommend listening to a videocast interview of Anders Hejlsberg speaking about LINQ and functional programming (http://blogs.msdn.com/charlie/archive/2007/01/26/anders-hejlsberg-on-linq-and-functional-programming.aspx). Anders is the creator of Delphi and C# (see http://en.wikipedia.org/wiki/Anders_Hejlsberg for more information). Here's the big functional programming message I received from that interview:

> *Writing code that is side-effect-free.*

Side-effect-free code is functional programming.

Programming with side effects is *imperative programming*. C# is an imperative language. Imperative programming means to write code that modifies state. The following is an example of imperative programming.

```
int x = 0;
x = x + 1;
```

This code declares x, which is a state, and then adds a value of 1 to x, which is an example of modifying state using operations. Of course, this seems a bit obvious—after all, if you want to solve a problem, you need to modify state.

Let's see an example of imperative programming creating side effects:

```
class SomeObject {
    public int Value;
}

class AnotherObjectThatEmbedsSomeObject {
    SomeObject _child;

    public AnotherObjectThatEmbedsSomeObject(SomeObject child) {
        _child = child;
    }

    void MyMethod() {
        _child.Value = 10;
    }
}
```

Suppose you have this method:

```
void SomeMethod(AnotherObjectThatEmbedsSomeObject obj) {
    obj.MyMethod();
}
```

Here, calling MyMethod() causes the side effect of SomeObject.Value being changed to 10. In Chapter 6, I demonstrated that this type of code is very good, because it hides information and lets the type AnotherObjectThatEmbedsSomeObject focus on manipulating SomeObject without interference. Yet that goodness is a double-edged sword, in that it causes side effects that the caller of SomeMethod() does not know about. (Of course, one could argue that AnotherObjectThatEmbedsSomeObject should have been made thread-aware, but this example is for illustrative purposes.)

The component-oriented imperative approach, in theory, lets you build an infrastructure that you can use to solve many problems. Let's say that you are going to repaint and repair a house. You could surround the house with scaffolding, and then let the repairmen and painters fix the house. Having scaffolding is safer, but the workers must watch out for other people when walking on the scaffolding. And on top of that, putting up and taking down the scaffolding takes time. The scaffolding is like the imperative language approach, where you need to worry about many things, including concurrency.

Alternatively, you could let the painters and repairmen run around the house with ladders. The ladders are quicker to put up and take down, and allow each individual to work independently. The downside of using ladders is that workers must move the ladders whenever they want to do something and must worry about where to place the ladder, as well as figure out how to fix and paint the house. This is analogous to the functional language approach.

Writing code that has no side effects is possible, but it comes with a direct conflict to imperative programming. Avoiding all side effects would require writing code where everything is stored on the stack, and that simply is not always possible and probably quite confusing. Imperative and object-oriented programming provide the benefit that they modularize and isolate code, letting you write code that is focused on a particular problem.

As a rule of thumb, you use object-oriented programming techniques to create pieces of functionality that process data, and you use functional programming techniques when the data cannot be easily described or solved using object-oriented programming techniques. For example, in the lighting controller introduced in Chapter 8, the individual rooms and the room groupings would remain as components. There still would be a kernel that operates on the individual rooms and groupings. Functional programming would not give you anything extra. On the other hand, the spreadsheet example in Chapter 11 would be a perfect candidate for functional programming. In the spreadsheet example, the idea is to interact with different pieces of information that are connected, which is hard to describe in object-oriented terms. Another situation where functional programming would be suitable is Chapter 4's example of trying to find the shortest route between two cities. There, the problem was recursion and remembering the routes that you had already tried.

So, there is a time to use imperative techniques and a time to use functional techniques. You could say that object-oriented programming is more often than not related to solving data problems and data structures, whereas functional programming is related to creating algorithms that operate on data structures.

In the end, neither functional nor imperative programming is better at everything every time. Functional programming offers benefits, but there are drawbacks, just as imperative programming has drawbacks and benefits. The solution that C# offers is a hybrid that allows you to combine functional and imperative programming techniques.

The Essence of Functional Programming

To completely understand functional programming, you need to understand its four main characteristics (http://en.wikipedia.org/wiki/Functional_programming):

Higher-order functions: Higher-order functions make it possible to define functions as arguments and return them as results. This allows functions to be curried, as explained shortly.

Pure functions: The concept of a pure function relates to side-effect-free programming. Overall, it says a function that is pure and has arguments that are pure will not be prone to variations due to evaluation order. Say you call a function X once and then call function X again with the same arguments. The second call should not be dependent on the first. The answers generated by function X are the same, regardless of how many times X is called.

Recursion: Iteration is accomplished using recursion, where one function performs an evaluation, and then to evaluate the next item, the function calls itself.

Function evaluation: How functions are evaluated matters in a functional programming language, because that helps determine which kind of operations are possible.

Let's look at each of these functional language characteristics in the context of C#.

Higher-Order Functions

As noted, higher-order functions allow for *currying*. Brian Beckman has the following explanation of currying on his blog (http://weblogs.asp.net/brianbec/archive/2006/06/01/ Lambdas_2C00_-Closures_2C00_-Currying_2C00_-and-All-That.aspx):

> *This is called currying. To be a bit more precise about it, currying is a language feature (or just a theoretical construct) that allows you to call a function one argument at a time, left-to-right down the argument list. Each call returns a new function that takes the remainder of the arguments until you're left with a function of one argument. Its utility is not just to pretty up scenarios like this, but also to support a simple theoretical calculus of programming, in which every function is, at heart, just a function of one argument, albeit one that may return other functions. In this calculus, a function of many variables—a multiary function—is modeled as a chain of unary functions. Of course, the calculus is the lambda calculus.*

In truth, regardless of which resource you use, the explanation of currying is downright confusing, and a practical explanation of why you would want to use it is hard to find.

Simply put, currying is about being able to define functions that contain state and are used to help evaluate other functions. To help you understand it, we'll work through two examples: one is academic and explains the details of currying, and the other is a practical example of calculating sales tax.

An Academic Example

Currying functions was possible in earlier versions of C#, but the code to accomplish it was rather complicated. With the introduction of lambda expressions, writing a curried function is rather easy. In a nutshell, a curried function is a function with extra functionality tacked on without the caller actually knowing about it, which is also called *decorating a function*.

Imagine the situation where you want to generate a buffer that is enclosed in other text. The trick is that you don't want the caller to know the details of how to decorate the buffer. You just want it to happen. You could define a lambda expression like this:

```
(surrounding, core) => surrounding + "_" + core + "_" + surrounding
```

The caller of this lambda expression would use code similar to the following, assuming the lambda expression has been assigned to the variable `expression`.

```
expression("+++", "hello");
```

The caller of `expression` does not know what `expression` does to build the string, but does know the individual pieces of the buffer. The problem with the expression is that it is not that convenient, since you need to provide all of the parameters to the lambda expression at all times. The first parameter does not change very often in the course of running the program, and thus would be ideally suited for conversion to a variable.

■**Note** The parameters to the lambda expressions are called *hard-coded*, because they are string buffers rather than variables. Hard-coded parameters can also be numeric or any other value that is compiled into the sources. Hard-coded parameters can be problematic when the same value is used in multiple places. If you want to change the value that is used multiple times, you need to find each and every occurrence, and then change the text.

You could convert the first parameter into a variable that can be referenced at various locations, like this:

```
string surrounding = "+++";
expression(surrounding, "hello");
```

Writing code using parameters is not a problem. However, now you need to drag around a common parameter, and that can become very inconvenient. You want to build a buffer, but you don't want to be bothered with the details of how to do the buffer modifications. This is why object-oriented programming became popular. Object-oriented programming lets you drag around a simple object reference that knows how to manage the details.

In functional programming, the approach that you can use is to curry a function. You create a function that has a state and that will call your desired method properly. To create a curried function, use the following lambda expression.

```
surrounding => core => surrounding + " " + core + " " + surrounding;
```

This lambda expression looks scary, but it is rather simple if you look at the anonymous method version:

```
delegate (string surrounding) {
    return delegate (string core) {
        return surrounding + " " + core + " " + surrounding;
    };
};
```

You are creating an anonymous method within an anonymous method, which creates two levels of calls, or a higher-level function, as is characteristic of functional programming.

When dealing with lambda expressions that return lambda expressions, the definition of the lambda expression can be a bit tricky. The complete declaration of the curried function is as follows:

```
Func<string, Func<string, string>> curry =
    surrounding => core => surrounding + " " + core + " " + surrounding;
```

You pass in a string value and receive a lambda expression that accepts a string value and returns a string value.

You can call the curried function as follows:

```
curry("+++")("hello");
```

This way of calling the `curry` expression is similar to using the lambda expression shown at the beginning of this section, except that a set of parentheses replaces the comma. This is because you are calling a function that returns a function that you can call again.

This approach has the advantage that you can create a lambda expression that can be assigned to a variable and then called at a later time. The arrangement makes it possible to avoid dragging around the first parameter, since it is embedded in the first method call, as follows:

```
Func<string, string> curriedFunction = curry("+++");
curriedFunction("hello");
```

The variable `curriedFunction` contains state. When it is called, the method will generate a buffer, just as was done by the original lambda expression shown at the beginning of this section.

A Practical Example: Calculating Sales Tax

Academic examples help you understand what the feature does at a technical level, but don't help you solve real problems. So, let's look at the practical problem of calculating the sales tax and grand total when buying some items. In a traditional approach, the first thing to design is the idea of the sales tax as an interface, as follows:

```
interface ICalculate {
    double SalesTax { get; }
    double Calculate(double total);
}
```

The interface has a property called `SalesTax`, which represents the current level of sales tax, and a method `Calculate()`, which calculates the grand total that includes sales tax. An implementation of the `ICalculate` interface could be like this:

```
class LocalSalesTax : ICalculate {
    double _salesTax;

    public LocalSalesTax(double amount) {
        _salesTax = amount;
    }
    public double SalesTax {
        get { return _salesTax; }
    }

    public double Calculate(double total) {
        return total + total * SalesTax;
    }
}
```

The implementation of `LocalSalesTax` has a constructor parameter that defines the sales tax levels. Let's calculate the sales tax for a country where the tax happens to be 16.5%.

```
ICalculate country = new LocalSalesTax(0.165);
double amount = 100.0;
Console.WriteLine("I bought (" + amount +
    ") and with tax that is (" + country.Calculate(amount) + ")");
```

This interface, implementation, and usage demonstrate how you would write a sales tax calculator using an imperative programming approach.

Now look at the complete implementation that does the same thing using a functional programming approach.

```
Func<double, Func<double, double>> salesTax =
    localSalesTax => totalBought => totalBought + totalBought * localSalesTax;

Func<double, double> country = salesTax(0.165);
double amount = 100.0;

Console.WriteLine("I bought (" + amount +
    ") and with tax that is (" + country(amount) + ")");
```

First, notice how compact the code has become. We have gone from 21 lines of code to 8 lines of code. The functional code is much more compact because you solve the task and no more. The variable salesTax is a currying function that calculates the sales tax based on an amount that you pass to the embedded function. Then a variable named country represents calculating the country's sales tax.

Pure Functions

A language that supports pure functions will allow you to define a function that is given all of the data necessary, and then returns the answer to the caller. As mentioned earlier, the idea of pure functions relates to side-effect-free programming.

Writing code using object-oriented programming techniques implies producing code that has side effects. This is a given, because with object-oriented programming techniques, you are supposed to hide your implementation and not reveal the state of your object.

The big deal with side effects is that they make your code exhibit stochastic behavior, which means that you are presented with the same situation, but are left with multiple future results. In general, stochastic behavior is bad because it leads to inaccuracies.

Consider the following addition operation.

```
2 + 2 = 4
```

This is not stochastic. Whenever you add a 2 to another 2, you will get 4. There is no way that you will ever get any other answer. This is what mathematics is all about. You put in the data, turn the crank, and you get a predictable answer. Imagine the chaos that would ensue if tomorrow 2 plus 2 resulted in 20. The following code is an example of that chaos, because the caller of GetMeAValue() does not know what to expect.

```
class ClassWithSideEffects {
    public ClassWithSideEffects() {
        _isInitialized = false;
    }

    bool _isInitialized;
    string _value;
```

```
public void Initialize(string value) {
    _isInitialized = true;
    _value = value;
}

public string GetMeAValue() {
    if (_isInitialized) {
        return _value;
    }
    throw new NullReferenceException("Not initialized");
}
}
}
```

The caller of GetMeAValue() has a problem in that it is going to get two different answers, or two different futures. The first future is a valid answer, and the second future is an exception. Which future the caller gets is out of the caller's control, and thus this is stochastic behavior. This is an example of side-effect coding, because to make the code work, the Initialize() method must be called ahead of time. However, the caller of GetMeAValue() does not know to call Initialize(), since there is no directive that enforces that behavior.

Side-effect-free code, simply put, is a function that gets all of its data via a set of parameters and returns the modifications to the caller. The function itself does not store any of the modifications. For example, consider this code:

```
(val1, val2) => val1 + val2
```

The code is side-effect-free and not stochastic because the returned state depends only on the parameters given to it. The result is the same if the parameters are the same.

Now consider this example:

```
(val) => { val.DoSomething(); return val.GetMeAValue(); }
```

This is not a pure function, because it calls DoSomething(), which will probably alter the state of an external function, and thus potentially create the situation where some action has multiple futures. DoSomething() might not exhibit stochastic behavior in the context of the lambda expression, but it might do so indirectly.

Using Immutable Types

To write imperative code that is side-effect-free, you can use *immutable objects*. In fact, you have already used an immutable type throughout this book. Do you know which one it is? It is the string type. A string is immutable in that once assigned, you cannot change it. Having an immutable type solves many problems, including concurrency, consistency, and side effects. However, immutable objects have a downside in that they do require more resources and, depending on the code, might be slow performance.

■**Note** From experience, I can say that using an immutable type is generally on par with a using a type that is not immutable. The exception is when your code is treating the object as a fine-grained object, meaning instantiating and destroying hundreds of thousands at any given point in time.

The following code is a rewritten form of `ClassWithSideEffects` that is immutable.

```
class ClassWithNoSideEffects {
    private readonly string _value;

    public ClassWithNoSideEffects(string value) {
        _value = value;
    }
    public string GetMeAValue() {
        return _value;
    }
}
```

The bolded keyword, `readonly`, is one that you have not encountered previously. Whenever `readonly` is applied to a variable in a class, it means that the variable can be assigned as a variable initializer or in the constructor, but from that point on, it can never be manipulated. The following code would initialize a `readonly` field as a variable initializer.

```
class MyClass {
    readonly int value = 10;
}
```

`ClassWithNoSideEffects` has no side effects, because the answer that `GetMeAValue()` returns is always the same: the value given to the class when the class is constructed. There is no need for an initialization, since instantiating the class initializes it. Combining the initialization with the instantiation means that whenever you need an instance of an object, you initialize it.

This class has no stochastic behavior, and thus could be considered logically correct. But don't confuse logically correct and no side effects with no bugs. The returned value of `GetMeAValue()` might still be wrong, but at least you can pinpoint that the bug does not lie with the class, but with the code that instantiated the class. Writing code using immutable objects takes some getting used to, since it is a different way of programming.

Let's see how to use an immutable type with the previous example of calculating a sales tax. This time, the same idea of calculating sales tax will be explored, but in the context of an immutable object. The example demonstrates how to combine imperative programming techniques with functional programming techniques to get a type that is consistent, side-effect-free, and has no concurrency issues. The implementation of the sales tax type is as follows:

```
class SalesTax {
    private readonly double _percentage;

    public SalesTax(double percentage) {
        _percentage = percentage;
    }
    public double Percentage {
        get {
            return _percentage;
        }
    }
}
```

```
    public double CalculateGrandTotal(double itemTotal) {
        return itemTotal + itemTotal * _percentage;
    }
}
```

The SalesTax class has a single data member _percentage, which is the tax percentage
applied to the grand total of the items to be bought. The data member is declared as readonly,
thus ensuring that it can be assigned only in the constructor and never altered. The percentage is read using the property Percentage.

The grand total, including sales tax, is calculated using CalculateGrandTotal(), which is
a pure function, because there is only one result whenever you call it. Since _percentage is read-
only, it means once you have reached CalculateGrandTotal(), that data member is assigned to
a value that never changes.

Manipulating Immutable Types

But how do you deal with immutable types when you need to make changes? For example, in
many countries, hotel charges include a tourist tax plus a sales tax. Needing to combine two
tax values means to keep the old approach and create a new one. When you have an immutable
object and wish to manipulate it using a pure function approach, you can use three different
techniques: type methods, external expressions, or extension methods. Each of these three techniques has advantages and disadvantages.

Using *a type method* to manipulate an immutable object means writing a method that
instantiates and returns a new instance of a type, where the method is declared in the type
itself. The string type uses this approach. In the case of SalesTax, it would mean redefining
the type as follows:

```
class SalesTaxWithMethod {
    private readonly double _percentage;

    public SalesTaxWithMethod(double percentage) {
        _percentage = percentage;
    }
    public double Percentage {
        get {
            return _percentage;
        }
    }
    public double CalculateGrandTotal(double itemTotal) {
        return itemTotal + itemTotal * _percentage;
    }
    public SalesTaxWithMethod AddPercentage(double percentage) {
        return new SalesTaxWithMethod(percentage + _percentage);
    }
}
```

The bolded code demonstrates how the local value of the percentage is added to the
value for the sales tax percentage specified as an argument of AddPercentage(). The new
value is passed as a constructor parameter to the new instance, which is returned to the

caller of `AddPercentage()`. It is a run-of-the-mill operation, and it is a pure function because nothing is altered and the new state is returned.

Note If you start with a pure function, it is easier to write pure functions that rely on that pure function. Functional programming is easier if you start on the right foot and don't attempt to force it.

Note the following points about manipulating immutable objects using a type method:

- It is easy and does not require learning new C# programming constructs.

- It requires altering the base type, and if you have already released a production version, it means altering the type. However, because the type is immutable, the old logic remains intact.

- It is slightly unsafe because, as you saw in Chapter 8, methods associated with a type can alter private data members of another instance of the same type. In the example of `SalesTax`, that is not a problem, since the `readonly` keyword is used. It can become a problem when you have not used the `readonly` keyword.

To alter and manipulate using *an external expression* means to use a method on another type or a lambda expression. The following lambda expression could be used to add two sales taxes together.

```
(salesTax, percentage) => new SalesTax(percentage + salesTax.Percentage)
```

Using external expressions to manipulate immutable objects is the simplest and most noninvasive approach. You don't need to change the base type. However, it is also the clumsiest approach, because it requires that you know about the external expression. If you don't, then you'll probably reinvent the wheel.

The approach of using *extension methods* to manipulate immutable objects is my favorite, because it combine the benefits of methods defined on the type and the noninvasiveness of the external expressions, and doesn't have any of the drawbacks of the other approaches. In this context, using extension methods, you manipulate an immutable object in a way that results in a new immutable object being created.

Using extension methods, you define an external expression, but because of the extension method declaration, it makes it seem as if the method you declared were on the type. In the case of `SalesTax`, the extension method would be declared as follows:

```
static class ClassExtension {
    public static SalesTax AddPercentage(this SalesTax cls,
                                    double percentage) {
        return new SalesTax(cls.Percentage + percentage);
    }
}
```

The implementation code looks like the lambda expression, but the method signature looks like the type method.

In general, whenever you are creating pure functions with immutable types, it's best to use extension methods.

Function Evaluation

Immutable objects and pure functions are useful, but they require you to program in a certain manner. In some cases, you may not be able to write immutable objects. You might then write code that has side effects and hope for the best. There is another solution, which involves how functions are evaluated.

Without going into the detailed theory of function evaluation, basically, you want a situation where, regardless of how you evaluate an expression, you will always get the same answer. Getting this to work in an imperative language is not easy, unless the imperative language has built-in techniques to help. For example, one thing that an imperative language can build in is function currying.

First, let's look at some code that has side effects.

```
class ClassWithSideEffects {
    public ClassWithSideEffects() {
        _isInitialized = false;
    }
    bool _isInitialized;
    string _value;
    public void Initialize(string value) {
        _isInitialized = true;
        _value = value;
    }
    public string GetMeAValue() {
        if (_isInitialized) {
            return _value;
        }
        throw new NullReferenceException("Not initialized");
    }
}s
```

The bolded code is the code that needs to be fixed. The approach I'll demonstrate is a lazy evaluation using a curried function. A *lazy evaluation* is one where the results are calculated when you need them, and until those results are calculated, the state of the call is stored. Here's the complete solution:

```
delegate void LazyInitialization();

class ClassWithoutSideEffects {
    string _value;
    public ClassWithoutSideEffects(Func<string> remoteInitialize) {
        Initialize = delegate() {
            this._value = remoteInitialize();
            Initialize = delegate() { };
        };
    }

    protected LazyInitialization Initialize;
    public string GetMeAValue() {
```

```
            Initialize();
            return _value;
        }
    }
```

First, notice the declaration of `Initialize`:

```
protected LazyInitialization Initialize;
```

The declaration of `Initialize` is clever in that it looks and feels like the original method `Initialize()`, albeit without a parameter. The declaration of `Initialize` is like a data member. Where the trickery is in that the data member is a declaration of a delegate, and thus behaves like the actual declared method `Initialize()`.

The idea behind the lazy declaration of `Initialize` is to call it when it is needed and no earlier. This means that you don't need to declare what `_value` should be ahead of time, but be able to retrieve that value when it is needed. This is like when people give explanations and say, "Follow the instructions, and if you get into trouble, give me a call." The "give me a call" is a lazy evaluation that allows for further information retrieval when it is needed.

The further information retrieval is a curried function that is called at some later point in time. Initializing state should be done once only and not again later. Thus, the lazy evaluation must be able to update itself at a later time. This is carried out by the anonymous method declaration in the constructor of `ClassWithoutSideEffects`:

```
public ClassWithoutSideEffects(Func<string> remoteInitialize) {
    Initialize = delegate() {
        this._value = remoteInitialize();
        Initialize = delegate() { };
    };
}
```

This passes the curried function `remoteInitialize` to the constructor. The curried function is part of the anonymous method that, when called, will call the curried function and retrieve the initialization state. Once the state has been retrieved, it is assigned to `_value`, and the data member `Initialize` is reassigned to an anonymous method that does nothing.

The clever trickery is the reassigning of `Initialize`. It has the effect that you can call `Initialize` as often as you want, but the state will be initialized only once. Thus, in the method `GetMeAValue()`, the decision is replaced with a call to `Initialize`, as follows:

```
public string GetMeAValue() {
    Initialize();
    return _value;
}
```

In the new implementation of `GetMeAValue()`, `Initialize` is always called and a value is always returned. And since you need to define a lazy initialization function when instantiating the type, you have code that is side-effect-free, to the furthest extent possible.

To complete this solution, the following code uses the newly defined side-effect-free class.

```
Func<string, Func<string>> lazyString = (stringToRetrieve) => () => {
    return stringToRetrieve;
};
```

```
ClassWithoutSideEffects cls = new ClassWithoutSideEffects(lazyString("hello"));
Console.WriteLine("Value (" + cls.GetMeAValue() + ")");
```

The declaration of lazyString is the curried function. The function is used to temporarily store a reference to a string buffer. However, the curried function does not need to be used just for that. The curried function could contain references to database connections that need to be created.

The curried function is passed to the constructor of ClassWithoutSideEffects, and then calling GetMeAValue() will call the lazy instantiation and return the initialized state.

Recursion

You've seen that you can use the foreach keyword to iterate a collection. Functional languages do not iterate, but rather use *recursion* for this purpose. Say you wanted to count from zero to a specific number. A lambda expression to do that would be as follows:

```
delegate void Counter(int iterations);
Counter RecursiveCount = (iterations) => {
    if (iterations > 0) {
        RecursiveCount(iterations - 1);
    }
    Console.WriteLine("Curr count( " + iterations + ")");
};
RecursiveCount(10);
```

In the source code, a delegate is defined that declares the Counter() method, which has a single parameter called iterations. Using the iterations parameter, you count how many more times the recursion must occur. In the implementation of the lambda expression, the variable RecursiveCount, which is the assigned lambda expression, is called to invoke a recursion. However, this recursion solution does not compile nor work. This is the approach that you would expect to work, because it seems to make sense.

To make recursion work using lambda expressions, the code become much more complicated. This approach is discussed in two blog entries: Wesner Moise's entry at http://wesnerm.blogs.com/net_undocumented/2007/03/anonymous_recur.html and the MSDN entry at http://blogs.msdn.com/madst/archive/2007/05/11/recursive-lambda-expressions.aspx. If you spend a moment to read those entries, you will very quickly realize that making recursion work using lambda expressions is incredibly complex. So why do it? The answer is that you should not do it, because it requires too much knowledge of the details of lambda expressions.

The following is an example of a simpler way to implement recursion using anonymous delegates, although it's not an elegant approach.

```
delegate void Counter(Counter counter, int value);
class Program {
static void Main( string[] args) {
Counter counter = delegate(Counter paramCounter, int iterations) {
    if (iterations > 0) {
        paramCounter(paramCounter, iterations - 1);
    }
```

```
        Console.WriteLine("Curr count( " + iterations + ")");
};
counter(counter, 10);
}
}
```

When calling the delegate, you need pass in the delegate that will be called recursively (`counter( counter..)`). This double step can introduce bugs and irregularities.

The Important Stuff to Remember

In this chapter, you learned the essentials of functional programming. Here are the key points to keep in mind:

- Functional programming is not more complicated than learning object-oriented programming for the first time.

- Functional programming solves the problem of writing code that is side-effect-free and can be used efficiently in a multithreaded context.

- Four attributes of a functional language are higher-order functions, pure functions, recursion, and functional evaluation.

- When implementing higher-order functions, one of the things that you can do is curry a function. Currying is the ability for a function to return a function. Using currying, you can define functions that implement a lazy evaluation, as they are holding state that will be evaluated at a later time.

- Pure functions are functions that are careful not to alter state such that side effects are created. Side effects make it possible for stochastic behavior in a method or state and thus will introduce bugs.

- Recursion is the ability to iterate without using `for` loops. For C# 3.0, recursion and lambda expressions are too complicated and should be avoided.

- Function evaluation is the evaluation of a state at a later point in time, for lazy evaluation. Lazy evaluation lets you focus on the logic and not worry about if you have assigned all of the state.

Some Things for You to Do

Here are two exercises for you to try your hand at functional programming:

1. Rewrite the `ClassWithoutSideEffects` class presented in the "Function Evaluation" section to use a canned infrastructure. You should have `ClassWithoutSideEffects` subclass another class that provides the initialization functionality.

2. Write a curried sales tax function that has the ability to add multiple sales tax values.

■ ■ ■

CHAPTER 17

Learning About Other C# Techniques

This last chapter in the book is about tying up loose ends. The techniques discussed in this chapter are those that you will use in specific situations. This chapter covers the following topics:

- How to use arithmetic operators to manipulate numbers

- How to overload operators

- When you might use the `goto` statement

- How to use .NET generics constraints

- How to use nullable types

- How to use partial classes and methods

Operators

You have seen various operators used in examples throughout the book, such as the assignment operator (a = 3;), and the logical operators (if(a == b)). C# has many more arithmetic operators that you can use to process types. You can also define custom operators.

Using Arithmetic Operators

The subtraction (-), multiplication (*), and division (/) operators are typically applicable to only numeric values. These operators are directly comparable to the mathematical operators you learned about in elementary school. Let's look at what the other arithmetic operators do.

Addition

The addition (+) operator is used to indicate the addition of two values, like this:

```
a = c + 1;
```

The addition has a left-hand side and right-hand side, separated by the equal sign (=). On the right side, the variable c is added to 1 and assigned to the variable a.

The notion of a left-hand side and a right-hand side as two separate parts is important when you consider this code:

```
a = a + 1;
```

In the example, the variable a is added with the value 1 and assigned to the variable a. All of these operations do not happen at the same time; they happen sequentially. First, the right-hand side is executed, and then the left-hand side is executed. By executing the left-hand side, the existing value of the variable a is overwritten.

Here's another example that employs the serial behavior:

```
b = a = a + 1;
```

In the example, b is equal to the value of a, which is equal to the value of a added to the value of 1.

The addition sign does not imply addition for all types. In the case of the string type, it performs a string concatenation:

```
string a = b + c;
```

Bitwise Operators

A *bitwise complement* (~) is the inverse of a number. The inverse of a number needs some careful consideration, because the result is not always obvious. Consider this example:

```
a = ~8;
```

The answer is –9. You might think that the algorithm to determine the inverse takes the number, adds 1, and switches the sign. This approach might work, but it is not an accurate explanation of what happened. Actually, the inverse is calculated on the binary bits. The number 8 in binary looks like this:

```
1000
```

If the number 8 were a short value, the accurate representation of 8 would be as follows:

```
0000000000001000
```

Taking the inverse, you get this value:

```
1111111111110111
```

And because the value is a short, the first digit is a sign indicator and the remainder represents the number, which is –9.

Overall, the bitwise complement operator is useful only if you are using the number as a way of storing flags.

Let's look at example of using the bitwise operators. Say that you want to know whether a person is tall, wears hats, and runs slowly. Using Boolean data members, you would write the following code.

```
class PersonWithAttributes {
    public bool IsPersonTall;
    public bool WearsHats;
    public bool RunsSlowly;
}
```

In this definition, each attribute of PersonWithAttributes is its own data member. Another way to achieve the same effect is to consider each attribute as its own binary flag that is encoded into PersonWithAttributes. The class would be rewritten as follows:

```
class PersonWithAttributes {
    public int Attributes;
}
```

In the rewritten example, the Boolean attributes are encoded into the data member Attributes using bitwise operators.

To encode a flag in a number means to tweak the individual binary bits of a number. To access the individual bits, you need to create constant numbers that are a power of 2. We use a power of 2 convention because binary is a counting system based on the power of 2. Thus, the three Boolean data members are converted to constants:

```
const int isTall = 1;
const int wearsHats = 2;
const int runsSlow = 4;
```

Now you could create a person that is tall and runs slowly like this:

```
PersonWithAttributes person = new PersonWithAttributes();
person.Attributes = isTall | runsSlow;
```

The variable person.Attributes is assigned the operations of isTall and runsSlow. So if isTall is 0001, and runsSlow is 0010, taking the bitwise OR (|) of the two values results in 0011.

A bitwise OR is when you compare two values, and if either value is nonzero, then the answer is nonzero. If you were to convert the binary number into a decimal number, you would get the value of 3. But that value is irrelevant, since you are performing bitwise operations.

You could verify that the person isTall like this:

```
if ((person.Attributes & isTall) != 0) {
    Console.WriteLine("Person is tall");
}
else {
    Console.WriteLine("Person is not tall");
}
```

The bolded code is the bitwise AND (&) operation, where the bits of the value isTall are compared to the bits of person. A bitwise AND operation is the comparison of two values, where both must be nonzero for the answer to be nonzero. If there are any matches, the returned value will not equal zero. In this example, there would be a match to isTall, which happens to be the case for person.

Suppose you apply the bitwise complement operator like this:

```
person.Attributes = ~person.Attributes;
```

Then the decision for isTall will equal zero, and wearsHat would be nonzero. This is because of the inverse operation, where whatever was zero is nonzero and whatever was nonzero is zero.

A bitwise shift is the shifting of the bits to the left or to the right by the number of places indicated by the shift. The following code demonstrates shifting the bits two places to the left (<<).

```
int shifted = 8;
shifted = shifted << 2;
```

When the code is executed, the value held in shifted is 32. The value 8 has the binary representation 1000. Shifting two places to the right is 32, which has the binary representation 100000.

Here's an example of shifting to the right (>>):

```
int shifted = 8;
shifted = shifted >> 2;
```

The result is 2, which has the binary value 10.

For the most part, you probably will not use the binary shift operators. Unless you are dealing with hardware-related programming (such as GUI interactions), whatever you can do with flags can be replicated using a combination of Boolean types and structs. However, when you do encounter bitwise operators, you will recognize what they are doing.

Modulus

The modulus operator (%) is very useful when you want to perform division operations and need to know how much is left over. For example, the following calculation yields a value of 2.

```
int a = 12 / 5;
```

Yet because it is an integer division, you don't know if the value is evenly divided by 2. The following calculation lets you figure out the remainder for the division.

```
int remainder = 12 % 5;
```

Increment and Decrement

The increment (++) and decrement (--) operators are useful in place of addition and subtraction operators. However, you do need to understand their priority.

Let's say you execute this code:

```
int a = 2;
a ++;
```

By default, the variable a will have a value of 3.

Now suppose you run this code:

```
class Program
{
    static int Loop( int counter) {
        return (counter ++);
    }
    static void Main(string[] args)
    {
        int count = 0;
        for( int c1 = 0; c1 < 10; c1 ++) {
            count = Loop( count);
            Console.WriteLine( "Value (" + count + ")");
        }
    }
}
```

You might believe that the variable count is incremented, since Loop is incremented in the method. However, the answers you get are as follows:

```
Value (0)
Value (0)
Value (0)
Value (0)
Value (0)
Value (0)
Value (0)
Value (0)
Value (0)
Value (0)
```

The count variable is not incremented. The reason goes back to the original C programming days. The original C language defined operator priority, and what is happening is that the return keyword is executing before the ++ operator.

■**Note** C is a programming language devised in the 1970s. These days, C is typically used to write only device drivers and similar programs. Most developers don't write applications in C.

To make the program work as expected, you need to change the Loop method as follows:

```
static int Loop( int counter) {
    return (++counter);
}
```

The increment operator is prefixed to the variable identifier, and thus it is executed before the return keyword.

Overloading the Operators

As you've seen, the + operator behaves very differently with `string` and `int` types. How did the `string` type manage to change the behavior of the + operator? A way of changing this behavior is to implement the + operator in a custom type.

As an example, let's walk through implementing the + operator for the complex number type. Complex numbers are numbers that have two parts: real and imaginary. For example, a + b is a complex number where a is the real part and b is the imaginary part. To add a complex number, you would add the real parts, and then add the imaginary parts, and that would give you the new number. The following is the complex number declaration.

```
public sealed class ComplexType {
    readonly double _real;
    readonly double _imaginary;

    public ComplexType(double real, double imaginary) {
        _real = real;
        _imaginary = imaginary;
    }
    public double Real {
        get {
            return _real;
        }
    }
    public double Imaginary {
        get {
            return _imaginary;
        }
    }
}
```

`ComplexType` is an immutable type that has two data members representing the real and imaginary number parts.

The goal is to define the + operator so that the following code can be compiled.

```
ComplexType a = new ComplexType(1.0, 10.0);
ComplexType b = new ComplexType(2.0, 20.0);

ComplexType c = a + b;
```

Overloading the + operator means to add a method that has a special notation. The following is the modified `ComplexType` type with the overloaded operator implemented (bolded).

```
public sealed class ComplexType {
    readonly double _real;
    readonly double _imaginary;

    public ComplexType(double real, double imaginary) {
        _real = real;
        _imaginary = imaginary;
```

```
    }
    public double Real {
        get {
            return _real;
        }
    }
    public double Imaginary {
        get {
            return _imaginary;
        }
    }
    public static ComplexType operator +(ComplexType a, ComplexType b) {
        return new ComplexType(a.Real + b.Real, a.Imaginary + b.Imaginary);
    }
}
```

The declaration of the overloaded operator is a specially defined function, which follows these rules:

- The method is always declared as `static` in the context of the type.

- The method has a return type, which should be the type that you want to construct. In most cases, it is the type of the declaration.

- The method identifier starts with the operator, followed by a space, and then the operator being overloaded (+, -, ++, and so on).

- The parameters to the method depend on the operator being overloaded. For example, if you are overloading the ++, it means that there is a single parameter.

Some pitfalls are associated with operator overloading. To understand these, let's look closely at two sample implementations of the increment operator. Assume that `ComplexType` is not immutable.

```
public static ComplexType operator ++(ComplexType a) {
    a.Real++;
    return a;
}
public static ComplexType operator ++(ComplexType a) {
    return new ComplexType( a.Real + 1, a.Imaginary);
}
```

The increment operator is an in-place manipulation operator. So, should you do an in-place manipulation or should you create a new instance? This is not an easy question to answer, because if a new instance of `ComplexType` is instantiated, then the complete state of the parameter a must be transferred to the new instance.

In general, the approach is to create a new instance and copy the contents of the old instance into the new instance. However, this approach has ramifications, which must be considered very carefully. Let's say that you instantiate a new instance and copy the state correctly. In that case, you will have problems of losing data. Consider this code:

```
static void CallMethod(ComplexType val) {
    val++;
    Console.WriteLine("--- " + val.ToString());
}
static void ComplexIncrement() {
    ComplexType a = new ComplexType(1.0, 10.0);

    Console.WriteLine(a.ToString());
    CallMethod(a);
    Console.WriteLine(a.ToString());
}
```

In the example, the ComplexIncrement method instantiates the variable a, and is assigned a value of 1.0 and then 10.0. The value is generated, and the output will be 1 + 10i. Then CallMethod is called, and the variable val is incremented using the ++ operator. The generated output is then 2 + 10i. When the last generated output is created, the value of the complex type should be 2 and 10, but the generated output is 1 + 10i. The reason is that the reference to val has changed to the instantiation of the new type.

The reassignment occurs transparently, and you are not aware of the change. Thus, when CallMethod exits, it still has a reference to the old a, not the new a. Changing the location of the ++ operator does not fix the problem. And in light of this information, it would seem that the proper solution is to do an in-place edit. But that is not the correct solution—you should not do an in-place edit. What you should do is treat the type ComplexType as immutable, thus not allowing the ++ operator and fixing the problem.

The goto Statement

The goto statement allows you to jump from one spot in the code to another. In the past, when we did not have objects, methods, and other advanced programming constructs, developers used the goto statement because they had no other choice. Currently, many in the software industry dislike the goto statement. They think that the goto statement is a sign of poor programming, and that you never need to use it. The Channel 9 forum (http://channel9.msdn.com/ShowPost.aspx?PageIndex=1&PostID=14652) has a good discussion on the use of goto statements. In this discussion, a person who was against the goto statement said this:

> *The only possible exception would be if you are doing some sort of computer graphics app, where I would tolerate a (for y) (for x) nesting, because the inner loop is likely to be quite simple and the structure makes more sense as an entirety.*

So, he would tolerate the goto statement in a specific situation, and that means that one can't argue that goto is all bad.

What I like about how C# implemented goto is that it is designed to solve a particular problem, but not raise the old problems. So if you need to use a goto statement, go ahead; just don't use it excessively.

One example where it is not easily possible to avoid using a goto statement is in the following pseudo-code.

```
while( FirstActionLoop()) {
    while( SecondActionLoop()) {
        if( BreakOutOfLoops()) {
            goto EXIT_ALL;
        }
    }
}
EXIT_ALL:
```

This code has two loops. If the code is executing the second loop and decides to end processing, then exiting the loop becomes very difficult, as you can break execution only one loop at a time using the break statement. Thus, the only real solution is to use the goto statement, as shown.

The goto statement is associated with an identifier that represents a label. The label can be placed almost anywhere in the declared method. An exception is that you can't place a label in a switch case statement. However, you can place the label before or after the goto keyword.

.NET Generics Constraints

.NET generics have been covered in several chapters. An additional aspect of .NET generics is *constraints*, which can be optionally used to optimize programming. .NET generics do not need to be just black boxes. The code can make method and property references, as long as the code uses constraints.

Three types of constraints are class, new, and type. As a general rule, a constraint is added in the form of a where statement, as follows:

```
class Example<DataType> where DataType : new() {
}
```

The bolded code gives you the sense that you are establishing an inheritance, where DataType subclasses new. That is partially true, because the act of subclassing is the definition of a specific functionality. However, in this context, you are not subclassing the .NET generics parameter; rather, you are saying that the .NET generics parameter has this sort of functionality.

Using the type Constraint

Type constraints allow you to associate a type with the .NET generics parameter. For example, suppose this interface is defined:

```
interface IExample {
    void Method();
}
```

Adding an IExample constraint to the .NET generics parameter allows you to define a class as follows:

```
class ExampleMgr<DataType> where DataType : IExample {
    DataType _inst;
```

```
    public ExampleMgr(DataType inst) {
        _inst = inst;
    }
    public void DoSomething() {
        _inst.Method();
    }
}
```

In the example, the constraint of IExample allows a developer to call Method. If the constraint were not there, the reference to Method would generate a compiler error.

But is this ability to reference a method an advantage? After all, you could write the ExampleMgr code without using .NET generics, like this:

```
class ExampleMgr {
    IExample _inst;

    public ExampleMgr(IExample inst) {
        _inst = inst;
    }
    public void DoSomething() {
        _inst.Method();
    }
}
```

The .NET generics code and the interface-based code do the exact same thing, and using .NET generics offers no advantage. But that is not always the case. Consider the following modified example of ExampleMgr.

```
class ExampleMgr<DataType> where DataType : IExample {
    DataType _inst;

    public ExampleMgr(DataType inst) {
        _inst = inst;
    }
    public void DoSomething() {
        _inst.Method();
    }

    public DataType Inst {
        get {
            return _inst;
        }
    }
}
```

With .NET generics, you can write a property that references the base type in the property. Had you used the pure interface-based code, the Inst property would need to be of type IExample, and to get the same effect as the .NET generics example, a type cast would be involved. A type cast is not the end of the world, but it is inconvenient and not type-safe, since you don't know if a type cast will work until you execute the code.

You can add multiple interfaces and classes as constraints, although you are limited. The limitations are identical to the limitations when subclassing a class or interface:

- You can subclass only a single class.

- You can subclass as many interfaces as desired, but they must be declared after the class.

Using the new Constraint

The purpose of the new constraint is to allow you to instantiate a data type, as in this example:

```
class Example<DataType> where DataType : new() {
    DataType _value;

    public Example() {
        _value = new DataType();
    }
}
```

Without the new constraint, the bolded code cannot be compiled. The constructor that is defined with the new constraint does not take parameters, and it would seem that this is a bother. After all, you might want to instantiate the type with some state. What you can do is constrain DataType, and then instantiate the type using object initializers. For example, the following is an interface that has a single property.

```
interface IBase {
    int Value { get; set; }
}
```

Combining the IBase interface and the new keyword as constraints, you could write the following code.

```
class Example<DataType> where DataType : IBase, new() {
    DataType _value;

    public Example() {
        _value = new DataType { Value = 10 };
    }
}
```

In the modified example, the bolded code instantiates DataType, and then using the constraints, the object initializer that defines value is possible.

Using the class Constraint

The main purpose of the class constraint is to indicate whether the .NET generics type is a value type or a reference type. Here is an example of a type that wants to manage only reference types:

```
class AssumeReferenceType<DataType> where DataType : class {
    DataType _value;
```

```
      public AssumeReferenceType(DataType value) {
      }
}
```

If you were to declare the AssumeReferenceType using an int, the code would not compile. The following is an example that demonstrates the noncompilable code.

```
AssumeReferenceType<IExample> cls =
    new AssumeReferenceType<IExample>(null);
```

The reason for using the class constraint is to enforce a coding standard where the type will support only reference types.

Nullable Types

In .NET, a null means no value, and we all understand what it represents, right? For example, the following code shows how to use a null.

```
Object value = null;

if( value == null) {
    Console.WriteLine( "Yup a null");
}
```

The example is obvious and does nothing useful. If you attempted to call the method Object.ToString(), an exception would be generated. So, what the code has created is a variable value that references nothing and is nothing. This works because the example uses a .NET reference type. Let's see what happens when you assign a null value to a value type.

```
int value = 0;

if( value == 0) {
    Console.WriteLine( "Yup a null?");
}
```

This time, value is not of the type Object, but is of the type int. And value is assigned a value of 0 to indicate a null value. Now many of you will be saying, "Hey, wait a minute— 0 != null." Yet, in the programming languages C++ and C, null and 0 have the same contextual meaning.

.NET 2.0, and C# specifically, have a new programming construct called the *nullable type*. The nullable type solves the problem of knowing whether or not a value type has been assigned. This is needed when interacting with relational databases. For example, there is no way to indicate that an integer value is not assigned, since declaring a value type means declaring a stack variable, and it will have a default value.

A nullable type in C# is used to define a variable that has a null state. In the value type example, the integer value was assigned a value of 0, but a value of null would have been more appropriate. However, value types cannot be assigned a value of null; they must be assigned some valid value.

To further demonstrate the restrictions of a value type, the following example uses a struct declaration.

```
struct ExampleStructure {
    int value;
}
ExampleStructure ex = null;
```

The structure ExampleStructure is defined using the struct keyword, which means that ExampleStructure is a value type. The next line, where the variable ex is assigned a value of null, will result in a compilation error. It is not possible to assign a null value to a structure type because it is value type. The inability to assign a null is odd, because structures behave similarly to reference types in many ways. Instantiating a default value of a structure is not always the right answer, since the data members might not have a default value.

The nullable type makes it possible for value types (for example, structures) to behave like reference types. In C#, you define a nullable type by adding a question mark (?) after the type declaration:

```
ExampleStructure? ex = null;
```

Using nullable types, it is possible to assign a null value to a value type. For this to work, the C# compiler converts the C# syntax so that it uses a standard .NET library class called Nullable. Rather than using the nullable type notation, you could use the System.Nullable<> type directly:

```
System.Nullable< ExampleStructure> ex = null;
```

Let's look at another example that doesn't use a nullable type:

```
int unknown1 = 0;
int known1 = 10;
int result1 = unknown1 + known1;

ExampleStructure? unknown2 = new ExampleStructure( 0);
ExampleStructure known2 = new ExampleStructure( 10);
int result2 = unknown2.value + known2.value;
```

In the example, the integer variable unknown1 represents an unknown value, and the ExampleStructure variable unknown2 represents an unknown struct value. The unknown variables imply that the value cannot be determined for these variables. But even though the values are unknown, some known value must be assigned. In the example of the integer variable, this means using a value of 0. In the case of ExampleStructure, it means allocating an instance of ExampleStructure. When a value is assigned, the addition operations can be carried out without any problems. The problem with this approach is that it is wrong. Any operation that involves a known value and an unknown value must result in an unknown value.

The problem of operating on an unknown value is solved using nullable types, as follows:

```
int? unknown1 = null;
int known1 = 10;
int result1 = (int)unknown1 + known1;
```

```
ExampleStructure? unknown2 = null;
ExampleStructure known2 = new ExampleStructure( 10);
int result2 = ((ExampleStructure)unknown2).value +
    known2.value;
```

In this modified example, unknown1, and unknown2 are nullable types and assigned a value of null to indicate an unknown state. To perform the addition operations, a slight modification in the addition is needed: a type cast to the type is made. The code that uses nullable types is functionality identical to the code that uses only value types. The difference is that if the additions are attempted, a System.InvalidOperation exception is generated, indicating that the values are not consistent, and hence the operation cannot be carried out. This is the correct behavior and clearly illustrates the need of nullable types.

■**Note** Nullable types are not intended to be used in conjunction with reference types. Nullable types are designed for use by value types, and there is no other mystical or magical reason to use a nullable type.

Partial Classes and Methods

By default, whenever you create a type, you must declare the complete type in one file and as one entity. For example, the following class would need to be declared in the context of a single file.

```
class Example {
    const int BaseValue = 10;
    public void AddNumbers(int value1, int value2, ref int response) {
        response = BaseValue + value1 + value2;
    }
}
```

The Example class has a single method AddNumbers, and the method implementation adds two numbers to a base value (BaseValue). Everything is in a single file. But suppose you wanted to automatically generate Example, and have it generate the data member BaseValue, but not the method AddNumbers. To do that, you would need to split the class into two separate classes, where one class subclasses the other:

```
class BaseGenerated {
    protected const int BaseValue = 10;
}
class Example : BaseGenerated {
    public void AddNumbers(int value1, int value2, ref int response) {
        response = BaseValue + value1 + value2;
    }
}
```

Having one class subclass the other is OK, and it works. The class BaseGenerated would be stored in one file, and Example would be stored in another file. But that approach can be a bit problematic, as it implies a specific architecture where one class subclasses the other. Another approach would be to use the partial keyword in the context of a class, as follows:

```
partial class BaseGenerated {
    const int BaseValue = 10;
}
partial class Example {
    public void AddNumbers(int value1, int value2, ref int response) {
        response = BaseValue + value1 + value2;
    }
}
```

When you use the partial keyword, you are defining a partial class. The complete class is the sum of multiple source code files. Thus, one part of the class could be autogenerated, and the other piece hand-coded.

A requirement of partial classes is that they must be wholly defined in an assembly. The partial class is of relevance only to the C# compiler, and not to the .NET language.

Another usage of the partial keyword is to have methods that are defined in one place but implemented in another. Think of partial methods as defining an abstract class method and implementing it within the same method. The following is an example of using a partial method.

```
partial class Example {
    partial void AddNumbers( int value1, int value2, ref int response);

    public void Method() {
        int response = 0;

        AddNumbers(1, 2, ref response);
        Console.WriteLine("Added numbers (" + response + ")");
    }
}

partial class Example {
    partial void AddNumbers(int value1, int value2, ref int response) {
        response = value1 + value2;
    }
}
```

Partial methods are defined in the context of a partial class. In one part of your class, you would prefix the identifier partial to the method and define a declaration of the method. In the other part of the class, you would implement the method.

Partial methods, like partial classes, have some restrictions:

- They must be declared to return void.

- They must be declared to be private.

- The methods can be static and use extension methods.

- The methods cannot use the out parameter identifier.

Overall, partial methods and classes should not be used as a general programming practice, because they are intended to be employed in the context of autogenerated code. When used in that context, partial methods and classes are an excellent solution.

The Important Stuff to Remember

In this chapter, you learned about some C# techniques that are useful in specific situations. Here are the points you should keep in mind:

- You will need to use the arithmetic operators. Some are obvious; others are not. Take the time to get used to coding with them.

- Overloading operators makes sense when you need to define custom types and you want them to support basic operators such as add, subtract, and so on. When implementing the operators, be careful to do a logically correct implementation.

- To be able to use methods or properties on .NET generics parameters, they need to be constrained. Constraints are an effective way of indicating functionality possessed by .NET generics types. Even though you could achieve the same results using interfaces, that approach is not as elegant.

- C# has added the goto keyword, even though some consider the use of goto as poor programming. C# has recognized the need for such a statement and ensured that you can't easily shoot yourself in the foot.

- The nullable type is used to indicate whether or not a value type has been assigned. You will use this type when interacting with a database type.

- Partial methods and classes are useful in the context of autogenerated source code. They make it easier to split apart the functionality that is autogenerated and store it in one file, while the hand-coded part is stored in another file.

Some Things for You to Do

The final exercises for this book are as follows:

1. Build a two-dimensional matrix class that supports the + and - operators.

2. Write a question to the author asking him to solve two problems that you have encountered. Send the e-mail to christianhgross@gmail.com.

Index

You Need the Companion eBook

Your purchase of this book entitles you to buy the companion PDF-version eBook for only $10. Take the weightless companion with you anywhere.

We believe this Apress title will prove so indispensable that you'll want to carry it with you everywhere, which is why we are offering the companion eBook (in PDF format) for $10 to customers who purchase this book now. Convenient and fully searchable, the PDF version of any content-rich, page-heavy Apress book makes a valuable addition to your programming library. You can easily find and copy code—or perform examples by quickly toggling between instructions and the application. Even simultaneously tackling a donut, diet soda, and complex code becomes simplified with hands-free eBooks!

Once you purchase your book, getting the $10 companion eBook is simple:

❶ Visit **www.apress.com/promo/tendollars/**.

❷ Complete a basic registration form to receive a randomly generated question about this title.

❸ Answer the question correctly in 60 seconds, and you will receive a promotional code to redeem for the $10.00 eBook.

2855 Telegraph Ave. • Suite 600 • Berkeley, CA 94705

eBookshop

ASP**Today**

Offer valid through 05/08.